WILF O' M

POLITICS & POWER

POLITICS & POWER

BARBARA CASTLE

A biography by Lisa Martineau

ANDRE
DEUTSCH

First published in Great Britain in 2000

This edition published in 2011
by André Deutsch Ltd
a division of Carlton Books Ltd
20 Mortimer Street
London, W1T 3JW

A catalogue record for this book is available from the British Library.

ISBN: 978 0 233 00282 8

Typeset by Derek Doyle & Associates, Liverpool
Printed and bound in the UK by
CPI Mackays, Chatham ME5 8TD

For Dee and for Rascha

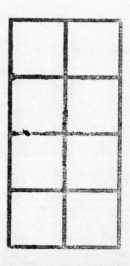

Contents

Acknowledgements

Thanks are due first and foremost to my long-suffering family who have stoically endured my preoccupation over the past two and a half years with all things Barbara Castle; especially my husband Paul who, at the panic-filled end, graciously schlepped to copy-editors and fact-checked things for me.

Thanks, too, to all those people I interviewed and who gave so generously of their time and knowledge - those who are quoted in this book and those who are not.

I wrote much of this book in the much-maligned beautiful new British Library and I should like to thank the staff of the Humanities 2 reading room for making it an even nicer place to work.

Finally thanks are due to my editors: Louise Dixon who enthusiastically bought this biography and Ingrid Connell who got it through the system in impossibly quick time.

Lisa Martineau
London, September 2000

Abbreviations

AAM	Anti-Apartheid Movement
ACAS	Advisory, Conciliation and Arbitration Service
AEU	Amalgamated Engineering Union
ARP	air-raid precautions
BMA	British Medical Association
BOT	Board of Trade
CAP	Common Agricultural Policy
CDS	Campaign for Democratic Socialism
CIM	Commission for Industry and Manpower
CND	Campaign for Nuclear Disarmament
CPGB	Communist Party of Great Britain
DAC	Direct Action Committee
DEA	Department of Economic Affairs
DEP	Department of Employment and Productivity
DHSS	Department of Health and Social Security
DM	dissenting minister
E(E)C	European (Economic) Community
EOKA	Ethniki Organosis KipriakouAgonos (National Organisation for Cypriot Struggle)
GLC	Greater London Council
GMC	General Medical Council
GNP	gross national product
HCF	Hell Corner Farm
ILP	Independent Labour Party
IMF	International Monetary Fund
LCC	London County Council
MCF	Movement for Colonial Freedom
MEP	Member of the European Parliament
MISC 205	inner cabinet committee on monetary policy
MISC 230	special committee on White Paper *In Place of Strife*
MOD	Ministry of Defence

MOT	Ministry of Transport
NALGO	National and Local Government Officers' Association
NEC	National Executive Committee
NUR	National Union of Railwaymen
NUWM	National Unemployed Workers' Movement
ODM	Ministry of Overseas Development
PLP	Parliamentary Labour Party
POUM	Partido Obrero de Unificación Marxista (Workers' Marxist Unification Party)
PPS	Parliamentary Private Secretary
PTA	Passenger Transport Authority
TGWU	Transport & General Workers' Union
TUC	Trades Union Congress

PART I

Forward to Socialism

Chapter One

MINE FOR LIFE

It was Barbara's father who set her going: Frank Betts, 'tall, raw-boned, hawk-nosed, black-haired',[1] demanding, imperious, this 'very powerful . . . slightly eccentric, rather alarming'[2] man was the seminal and profoundest influence of and on her life. Frank, and the childhood he made for her, have never been far away; 'it's eerie how much the associations of my childhood survive',[3] she said some fifty years after his death: Barbara's childhood was Frank.

Barbara Castle was born Barbara Annie (soon shortened to Anne) Betts at 64 Derby Road, Chesterfield, Derbyshire, on 6 October 1910 into a middle-class, nonconformist, devoutly political family. The redhead baby with china-blue eyes was the last of the Bettses' three children and was named by Frank for St Barbara, the apocryphal patron saint of gunners, miners and assorted others, portrayed as a Titian-haired beauty in an Italian triptych hanging in the family's house. Marjorie, the eldest, was accorded the accolade of the most academic of the children; Tristram (Frank was fond of *Tristram and Isolde*), almost always called Jimmie, was the most disappointing; and Barbara, Frank made clear, could do better.

Frank was a tax inspector and as a civil servant had to keep his political activities at least quasi-covert; nevertheless, he was a well-known Independent Labour Party (ILP) personality, which was popularly taken to mean a Bolshevik. The ILP had been born in Bradford in 1893, a year after Frank himself. Its purpose had been to send working men to Parliament. In 1900, it joined with the trade unions (formerly aligned with the Liberals), the Fabians and the Social Democratic Federation to form the Labour Representation Committee, which became the Labour Party six years later. The ILP was the Party's radical reservoir and until 1918 the way individuals joined. Its policy slogan was 'Socialism in our Time', whereas Ramsay MacDonald's Labour Party posited an evolutionary socialism that would (somehow) come about in a couple of generations, a policy 'more of a running buffet than a set meal', as one ILP member remarked.[4]

Frank edited the ILP's newspaper, the *Bradford Pioneer*, writing editorials under the initials FB, although, as Barbara said, 'Everybody knew who the FB was'.[5] The FB kept off the more public platforms, holding political meetings in his living room; but he did lecture for the Fabian Society on town planning, and on socialism in modern literature, and later wrote pamphlets for the Socialist League, which was even more radically left-wing than the ILP.

Frank was a late-Victorian, a product of a chapel-going family of Coventry corn merchants. He was a big rambling man, who incongruously spoke in a high, unmelodic, squeaking voice, sometimes very loudly and just for the hell of it when discussing something risqué on the tram or in the hushed halls of an art gallery. He liked to shock and he could be exuberant and even charming, but he was a jumble of discontents and resentments: a frustrated classical scholar who hated his own father for forbidding him a classical education (insisting instead that he read science); a thwarted politician, he poured his stymied ambitions into his children. The one that set early and hard in Barbara was the desire to be a politician. In his wallet Frank kept a slip of paper on which Barbara, aged 6, had scrawled her first electoral address: 'Vote for me and I will give you houses',[6] written before women had the vote; the chance to be voted for was as yet unthinkable.

Disappointment fermented within Frank, erupting into hot rages; he wasn't who he thought he should be. He was the kind of father who could make or break a child; the kind of parent, at once tyrannical and inspiring, found standing in the shadow of many prodigies.

He was, Barbara said, a very difficult man to live with. There were times when she hated him. He could be foul-tempered and cruel. But, convinced of his greatness, she always sought to please him. She needed to '*show* him that she could do it', one friend thought, because he 'never felt that she did her brains justice'.[7]

Only a certain kind of success would do: intellectual success, political success, certainly not material success, nothing as crude as money-making. Frank rounded on Barbara after she confessed to him once that she had started 'having ambitions like everyone else about going out into the world and making money ... Oh money, he said in a tone of contempt' she never forgot, 'if it's *money* you're interested in ...' If she was, she felt she shouldn't be; his disdain filled her with shame. She felt, she said, 'like a pygmy'.[8]

What Barbara thought of as Frank's strong puritan streak was tempered, she said, by an equally strong, richly Rabelaisian nature. He was a sensualist with a love of Rubens; and he liked the things that money could buy: good wine, good food and foreign holidays. Barbara liked the good things of life, too: all the above plus expensive clothes, beautiful furniture and paintings; but like Frank she was queasy about money. It felt grubby but she thought she never had enough. In the first dozen pages of her autobiography *Fighting All the Way* (1993), she mentions more than half a dozen times how straitened the family's circumstances were. Their home was cramped or modest and they were forever dogged by financial worries.

Relatively speaking the Bettses were quite well off. Barbara's mother may have been reduced to having just one general maid when her children were in full-time education, but most people's mothers were maids, or mill hands, or factory or shop workers, or barefoot and continually pregnant, and only 17 per cent of 14–17-year-olds went to secondary schools in the late 1920s. It's a reflex action, this reaching back for a poor, working-class background that isn't there, one honed by the class antagonisms of the Labour Party Barbara grew up in when 'middle-class' was the nastiest of epithets.

Frank liked a big canvas; he needed, he said, not only 'a cause to die for [but] a woman to love'.[9] More than one. Other than his wife, Annie, there was Nell (whom Barbara doesn't recall meeting), a schoolteacher. They had a long-standing affair. Every year Frank and Nell went to the Continent for a holiday, leaving Annie – who yearned to travel abroad and whom Frank only took once – to cope with the children in, as Barbara put it, the 'cheap boarding houses'[10] of Whitby or Scarborough. Jimmie found out about the affair and, 'because he was a puritan',[11] Barbara said, he told their mother. There were rows aplenty between her parents, and not just over Nell. The Bettses had a tempestuous forty-year marriage, one long duet of high-pitched recrimination.

The life of a tax inspector was a peripatetic one; soon after Barbara was born the family left Derby Road and moved to Hull and then to Pontefract in West Yorkshire, where she spent her early childhood. They lived in Love Lane at first, in the old market town itself. Pontefract still had its rural heart, despite the liquorice factories of Wroe's, Wilkinson's and Hillaby's and the coalmines on the outskirts. The miners lived quite close to Barbara. She used to see them on the tram, coming home from the pits, their faces smeared black, faces formed by another kind of life: edgy, dangerous, dirty; shaped, Barbara thought, by 'all the sorrows and excitements and loyalties and romance' of their lives.[12]

The town's main thoroughfares had old, magical names: Beastfair and Horsefair, where the trams and the soldiers off to the First World War clattered up and down. When war was declared the Betts removed to the nascent suburb of Carleton. Frank, who was thirty-two, was exempt from fighting because tax-collecting was categorised as work of national importance. Nothing much happened that felt like war, except for a Zeppelin raid which left an impressive crater in Pontefract Park. But as the war progressed the soldiers, who had marched off wreathed in flowers and smiles, were replaced by those marching with tight-lipped quiet desperation. Barbara sensed this and listened to Frank ranting against the slaughter caused by competing imperialisms and nauseating jingoism.

Her first school was Love Lane Elementary, a state school with toilets which were only flushed weekly. If Nancy Astor had to send her children there the toilets would be flushed every day, Frank liked to say: 'Separate is unequal.'[13] When she was eight Barbara went on to Pontefract and District Girls' High School, bang next door to the racetrack. On race days the girls were sent home, to prevent encounters with the low life. Barbara's perception of herself at this age was of a little body 'immensely nervous and shy',[14] and yet she was the gang leader, in a *Just William* sense, the naughty girl who led the others astray down over the railway tracks to explore places they shouldn't.

Barbara said that whatever she mastered she had to use publicly; it was no good kept to herself; she had to show it off, to let everyone know what she could do; at Pontefract High she discovered she could act and speak in public. She performed in the school plays and in Frank's amateur dramatic productions. Her first public performance was in John Galsworthy's *Strife*, a play about a strike, put on by Frank in lieu of commentary when the miners were locked out in 1920 for refusing to accept a pay cut. It was not an auspicious debut. Barbara, playing a maid, tripped and fell flat on her face. But her love of the stage remained undiminished and she represented her school in West Riding's inter-school competitions in prose and poetry readings and in French-speaking contests, winning the oral French competition in 1922. She had found she had a gift. She could hold an audience.

All the houses the family lived in over the years were run by Barbara's mother, the tiny but fiercely resolute Annie, for Frank's uttermost convenience, his infidelity and their roaring arguments notwithstanding. Annie, intense, single-minded, channelled her considerable energies into organising her home and everyone in it. Frank's happiness lay in his books, beer and baccy, especially books. The 'house always seemed to be plastered with books, thousands and thousands of books all over the place',[15] delineating the importance of Father's intellect. Annie ensured that there was always a room set aside as Frank's study, where he could retreat to write his *Pioneer* articles or his lectures, work on his translations, his plays or his poetry. A small book of poetry entitled *The Iron Age* was published with help from Gilbert Murray, regius professor of Greek at Oxford, who said of Frank's writing that it was 'full of life and power and sympathy, and curious erudition penetrated by imaginative brooding'.[16]

Frank's intellectual dominance of the family was accepted with awe by Barbara and her mother. He was brilliant at chess and fond of cricket; he did not suffer fools at all and he did not stand on ceremony. If uninteresting people found their way into his living room Frank would get up and go to bed. Absolute silence was required at mealtimes while he read, behaviour described by Barbara as inconvenient, but from which she says she learnt a 'respect for knowledge at whatever social cost'.[17]

There's more than a little of the Victorian paterfamilias about Frank, reclining in his inviolate study, sealed off from the domestic shambles, although he did emerge to spoonfeed his children the classics: the *Iliad* and the *Odyssey*; or the near contemporary fiction of William Morris. Morris, Pre-Raphaelite artist, poet, writer, socialist, romantic revolutionary, co-founder of the first Socialist League, had a profound effect on socialists of both Barbara's parents' generation and her own.

Morris was important to Barbara for his sense of socialism as an ethical philosophy and a spiritual condition. She loved much of his poetry, especially poems such as 'The March of the Workers' and 'The Message of the March Wind', in which love and politics intermingle. When she was about 11, Frank read the children *The Water of the Wondrous Isles*, Morris's penultimate novel, and it remained one of her favourite works of fiction, the one fifty years on she chose to take to her desert island when she appeared on Radio 4's *Desert Island Discs*.

It is a quest story, set in an allegorical landscape, in which the heroine, Birdalone, escapes from the House of Captivity, where she has been kept prisoner by a witch. Birdalone embarks upon her journey (part Voyages of Sinbad, part Labours of Hercules) in search of 'the love of some man whom thou must needs love'[18] and not only her own soulmate but the lost loves of her two friends. Birdalone is a warrior woman, complete with thigh-high deerskin boots and short tunic, a sort of prototype Emma Peel, 'the swash-buckling female of the 1960s sexual revolution'[19] presaged.

There was much here to appeal to a romantic young girl, not least the conquest of fear, necessary for a swashbuckling life. A fear of being afraid eats away at Barbara. She was afraid she would be paralysed by the sort of fear Morris described, that which 'entered into her soul, so that now the flesh crept upon her bones';[20] she was afraid that she would act in a cowardly manner of which she would be permanently ashamed. Birdalone, Morris's New Woman, is nothing if not a vanquisher of fear.

Annie, petite and wispily pretty with her pale blond hair and delicate features, was herself a William Morris socialist. Ugliness must be transformed into beauty; pastoral England conjured up on the slag heap; the maypole erected and adorned with ribbons, with Barbara and her siblings dancing round it. Annie and Frank met in the local Congregational chapel on Vine Street in Coventry when they were in their teens, and married in September 1905 when she was 22 and he 23. As a young girl Annie Rebecca Farrand had been considered daring, paddling in the river, shockingly showing her ankles, and cycling around with her redhead sister, Eleanor, the pair of them in bloomers, suffragettes manquées. But Annie was not seen, by herself or others, as Frank's intellectual equal and her role was attenuated to providing for his needs and acting as a buffer between him and the children, insulating them, as best she could, from what Barbara thought of as his innate temperamental difficulties.

Annie thought all her children geniuses; she was not critical of Barbara, as Frank could be. She did not take the girl's poetry away and subject it (and her) to a pitiless critique, as Frank did. Annie was warm, protective, loving, a devoted mother to Barbara, even a little indulgent, although her youngest child was perhaps not as close to her mother as she was to her father. The mother and daughter relationship was often sartorial. Annie was a milliner by training and made all Barbara's clothes, and made them very well, to her exacting instructions, nourishing Barbara's lifelong passion for, and preoccupation with, her clothes and her appearance.

9

The socialism that Barbara learnt from her parents was a religion, the rock upon which their lives were to be built; a socialism that would create heaven on earth. The ILP had plenty of ex-chapelgoers in its ranks and it formed Labour churches and socialist Sunday Schools to preach the socialist faith. Although Frank had long left Christianity, via High Anglicanism, his socialism retained its Christian moral force. Socialism wasn't just about material progress; it was a holistic aesthetic, the intermingling of Morris and Marx: spiritual beauty, economic justice and the fellowship of man walking hand in hand over the Elysian fields.

This was what Barbara reached for. She never wanted to stoop to what Morris derided as 'gas and water socialism'. To her socialism was 'a rescue operation, not merely in the welfare state sense of the term'; it wasn't ever just about rescuing people from poverty; its purpose was to be vast and fundamental; it sought to rescue people and society 'from spiritual impoverishment'.[21]

Frank and Annie's socialism pervaded everything. To them 'it wasn't enough to think Socialism, feel Socialism and talk Socialism', Barbara said, 'you had to act Socialism too', by, say, setting up a soup kitchen in the house to feed miners' children during the 1920 lockout, or the 1926 General Strike; or later, after the Spanish Civil War, sheltering Republican refugees, all things her parents, or rather Annie, organised (she did the work while Frank did the theory). For Barbara this practical side of socialism wasn't always easy. She felt torn, resenting, as any child might, the intrusions into her home and having to share her things, but she was proud to be a part of that kind of family.

Despite Frank's eccentricities and his barely hidden radical left-wing politics, he was eventually promoted to inspector of taxes, and in 1922 the family moved to Bradford, a place Frank loved. In comparison with the other towns where they had lived it was the big city: cosmopolitan, rich in culture and radical politics. More than ever now, their house was full of people and ideas. Play-readings were held in the living room – Chekhov and Shaw; both Annie and Frank produced plays for the ILP Arts Guild, and Barbara once again acted in them.

Bradford was a mill town, close to the Yorkshire moors, where Barbara, who always regarded herself as a country girl, used to ramble, away from the soot and the grime. It was at the centre of the wool and worsted trade, known 'as a place where riches are quickly made and money is freely spent',[22] where a small pocket of mill-owners was extremely wealthy but 'the great mass ... possess only very limited means',[23] to which the Bettses' ILP had the answer: nationalise the mills (and the railways, mines and banks). It had other answers too: workers' control, a guaranteed living wage which would support husband and wife, and child allowances.

The unions were opposed to the living wage and child allowances because they thought the former would interfere with free collect-ive bargaining and the latter threatened union claims for a family wage. The unions considered the ILP to be interfering with trade-union business, as Ernest Bevin, general secretary of the Transport & General Workers' Union (TGWU), pointedly told the 1927 party conference. Socialism was all right in its place but not if it poked its nose into union affairs, an attitude Barbara was to spend the next forty years trying to change.

Half of Bradford's population was employed in the textile industry; almost 80 per cent of the girls went to the mill at 14, and, as 40 per cent of all Bradford women worked, many stayed on through marriage and babies. The mills stank and walking past them made Barbara retch. If she couldn't stand it, she thought, how could anyone else? Why should anyone else? Many of the houses were back-to-backs slung up to accommodate the mill workers, and equipped only with outdoor privies. Barbara's house, by contrast, was large and airy and located in the leafy outskirts of Toller Lane. Here Frank entertained his adopted local working-class talent, such as the teenage Victor Feather, a future leader of the Trades Union Congress (TUC), and his most famous protégé.

Frank, a natural educator, made a great and lasting impression on Vic, whom he taught an appreciation of art and literature. He taught him how to write as well, letting him loose on the *Pioneer* to report on politics and dig up scandals on the local Tories. Barbara made an impression on Vic too, one that left him with deep envy and resent-

11

ment. He envied not only her wonderful father but her chances, her opportunities, all the privileges this poor boy who had to leave school at 14 and work in the Co-op had not had. More, he felt that her attitude towards him was patronising, that she looked down on him. He fought back, treating her like a kid, even though there were only two years between them; he sneered at this child in a gymslip doing her homework at the kitchen table while he, well versed in hard work and hard knocks, sat with Frank in the parlour discussing the 'world and its books'.[24]

The malignancy of this early encounter lingered, getting topped up throughout the years as their political differences crystallised. One of the things Frank had taught Barbara and Vic was to fight to the death, that the game is never finished; he did not expect any child under his tutelage to give up. It was a mantra that resonated within them and got sung out in their great confrontation in 1969, which brought the Labour government to the brink of destruction.

Frank was odd to look at, 'very wrinkled, with a greyish face, rather saturnine', and he looked odder in Bradford, a bigger town with more pretensions, perhaps; his dress sense was, by local standards, decidedly bohemian. 'His clothes were careless and unusually casual for a civil servant,' Vic Feather noted, 'he always seemed to have a great woollen muffler'[25] around his neck. Frank slumped about in a long, loose coat with his hat punched onto his head atop of his shockingly long hair; he had an annual subscription to the pukka barber used by the wealthy wool merchants but he seldom had either the time or the inclination to go there.

The sight of Frank embarrassed the teenaged Barbara. She dreaded getting on the tram with her friends and finding him there, 'sitting in front with his head buried in his Greek book, his shaggy hair sticking out from under his battered trilby'. He would call her over and she'd be 'absolutely crushed, praying that I could disappear through the floor'. This normal teenage embarrassment about a deeply unconventional parent sat uneasily with what he'd taught her: that her 'first duty in life was to refuse to conform for convention's sake, to expect to be different'.[26]

When she was sixteen, Barbara joined the ILP's Guild of Youth.

The recent general strike had had a rapturous effect on many of her fellow guilders. They had discovered that politics, even if, as in this instance, it ended in tears, was *the* something big outside themselves, something liberating, exhilarating, a higher purpose which gave meaning to their lives: God at ground level. It was that way for Barbara, too, of course, but her political commitment ran deeper and wider. It went back for as long as she could remember and it was more sophisticated, more all-encompassing, separating her from her contemporaries. She wasn't lonely as such: 'lonely's not the word', she said. 'One felt different.'[27] The one apart.

The guild was not all high-purpose or about the greater good; it was also a quasi-youth club, eager and able to provide entertainment for its young recruits. The guild held dances and Barbara learnt to do the Charleston. There were rambles and socials, and, with the exception of the very serious-minded, the girls in the guild were like the girls outside it: would-be flappers with Eton crops and sleeveless, shapeless frocks and even lipstick, quite capable of enjoying the boys in their Oxford bags and pineapple haircuts.

A pretty child, Barbara had grown quite beautiful. Like her mother, she was tiny and never weighed more than seven and a half stone. Her colouring was striking: the red hair, the piercing blue eyes, the English rose complexion. Her features were delicate: a small nose, and a mouth arranged in a pleasantly determined manner. She looked like a much more focused version of Annie; she was much lovelier than the taller Marjorie, who had got the lion's share of Frank's ramshackle features. Barbara had become curious about sex, but her parents were, in this sense, typical of the period: neither could bring themselves to talk to her about it. Although she was allowed to read any book in the house, books on sexuality, basic or otherwise, did not adorn the shelves, and her friends knew even less.

Frank was unhappy with Barbara's teenage experimentation. He sneered at frivolities such as silk stockings, which he said should have been beneath her, as should vulgarities such as dancing. She wanted to be glamorous like the film stars she saw on the silver screen in the new talkies. Sultry, slinky, tinsel-town glamour, all cigarettes and curves and pouting lips. She bobbed her hair and sneaked off with her friend Evelyn Carter to plaster herself with the make-up Frank forbade. He thought it common. He was happy for her to 'wish to be a beautiful Rossetti woman',[28] but not a two-bit vamp. Her brother concurred: 'You look like a tart,' Jimmie was fond of telling her.

When it came to his children's education, separate may have been unequal but it was going to be so at the secondary level. Neither Mrs Astor nor Mr Betts sent their children to a free secondary school. The Betts children went to the fee-paying Bradford grammar schools, where the curriculum for the girls was 'designed to secure ... a thoroughly sound, liberal education which will fit them for home life, or for entering upon any of the careers now open to women'.[29] Taking the Oxbridge entrance exam at 18 was very much part of its culture and this was an expectation on and of Barbara and Marjorie.

Barbara did not admit to having many friends at the grammar school; most of the girls were the daughters of wealthy wool merchants, and their parents were Tory or Liberal; the Liberals and the Tories, having consistently colluded in Bradford's municipal elections to keep Labour out, were one and the same to Barbara. The girls were little toffs, she thought, who looked down on the likes of poor scholarship girls such as Evelyn Carter (a quarter of the places at both the girls' and boys' grammar were reserved for city council scholars). Barbara said she felt ostracised for her political beliefs, but nevertheless she was popular enough with the toffs; she was in the netball team, which perhaps helped; she ended up head girl, politically somewhat of an embarrassment perhaps, as she has always made light of it, claiming that the formidable headmistress, Mildred Hooke, was trying to turn a poacher into a gamekeeper.

Barbara stood as the Labour candidate in the school's mock election in 1929, losing badly; she polled seventeen of the six hundred votes. In politics guts is all, Barbara said over and over again; as perhaps is a love of confrontation. As Clifford Allen, the chairman of the ILP, remarked: 'The revolutionary ... is the man who presents an

14

idea to his fellow human beings which he believes to be right, in a tone of voice that will make them listen, and stands by it in a minority or majority.'[30] Barbara was more than willing to be such a revolutionary. She liked the razor's edge; she liked the adrenalin rush that confrontation brings.

Barbara went door to door in Bradford North campaigning for the Labour candidate, Norman Angell, author of the best-selling *The Great Illusion*, published the year she was born. Angell's thesis was that no country can harm another economically in war without doing almost as much economic damage to itself, which was borne out by the Great War. The Labour government won the real election of 1929, and so did Norman Angell. Labour took all Bradford's four seats and was returned to parliament for the second time, but still without an overall majority.

Barbara was almost always the only girl to speak in her sixth-form class debates, certainly the first to speak. Girls did not speak out publicly, not even to each other; it wasn't ladylike. To Barbara, when they did open their mouths their debates were amateurish. She was used to a much higher, complex debate with her father and his friends; she was accustomed to being taken seriously, to having to account for herself. She was anxious about Frank's judgements, of course, always on edge, but he treated her as he would have done if she had been a boy and therefore of some importance. Frank, Barbara said, 'didn't see why a woman should be treated ... differently from a man';[31] and to this end he started her smoking at 16, one of her lifelong pursuits.

Naturally, it was Barbara who led the girls' team in the annual debate with the boys' grammar, an event which had been going on since 1874, with accompanying warnings that 'bella, horrida bella', the 'Amazons in debate',[32] were en route. The boys' school often turned to the subject of women within their debating society, usually along the lines that 'the influence of women has increased, is increasing, and ought to be diminished', because 'the non-domestic influence of women [was] unnatural',[33] ideas with which, flappery notwithstanding, most of the girls and their families would have concurred.

Barbara, with her love of combat and her conviction of her own worth as an equal of men, was the feared Amazon incarnate. Yet she saw herself in this debate as a poor soul intimidated by masculine self-confidence which almost (but not quite) shut her up as she mumbled and fumbled through. The contrary seems to be true, as the unusually fulsome review of her performance in the boys' school magazine, *The Bradfordian*, suggests: 'At length Barbara Betts proposed that National Temperament is incompatible with International Peace, achieving an admirable proportion of fact and phrase. After denouncing Jingoism and Disarmament Conferences, Barbara expressed her disapproval of Peace Pacts and the sad conviction that International Peace was never more to be realised.'[34]

She had begun as she meant to go on, at length, with plenty of facts and pithy phrases, and the well-aimed verbal Molotov cocktail. She assailed her male opponents as 'people who pronounced Jones as Germans without the m', and were therefore 'doomed to perdition'. Not all the girls approved. Constance Craven lived up to her name and 'shyly but shrewdly supported the opposition', the magazine reported, 'shunning ... the notoriety of association with her auburn-haired companion'. The auburn-haired companion's motion was lost by thirteen votes to seven.

Frank perhaps invested more in his daughters than he would have done if his son had been different. As Frank had 'almost *despised* his father'[35] for what he saw as his Philistine narrowness, Jimmie exhibited signs of the same towards Frank; he switched from classics to 'modern' subjects, an action guaranteed to anger his father. Jimmie stood up to Frank, in short, denying him the classical education Frank had so desired, refusing to let his father live through him. Jimmie got a Bradford City Council scholarship and went up to Edinburgh to study forestry.

Barbara and Frank were too meshed together for her to take him on head to head like that; she has, she says, 'never been able to cast off his standards'.[36] Frank was the scaffolding on which her politics and ambition were draped. He had made her, not quite in his own image – she was too vibrant for that, too singular; but he had made possible what she became, although as her friend and another of

Frank's protégés, Mary Hepworth, noted, she certainly didn't appreciate him when she was twenty.

Barbara followed Marjorie up to Oxford in autumn 1929, in the same breath as the Wall Street crash. Only just over 6 per cent of the tiny secondary-school population went to university in the late 1920s and early 1930s, and no more than a quarter of the annual intake was female; even fewer women went to Oxford. Marjorie Betts's little sister, as she was at first known, was one of only 820 women out of 4353 students admitted, making Barbara a member of the tiniest elite within the favoured few. She had won an exhibition scholarship to read French but switched to politics, philosophy and economics (PPE), a course of study more suited to the life she was planning for herself.

Barbara arrived at St Hugh's with a suitcase full of new clothes Annie had made for her. Her friend and contemporary Olive Shapley found her that first evening, scattering her opinions around the Junior Common Room, sturdy as a little pony. She spent most of the time telling Olive how 'infinitely superior the north was to the south and what poor characters we southerners were'.[37] Olive was amused, but a little alarmed, too, and not for the last time. Barbara's relentless drive for all-round perfection left Olive 'quite scared of her at times'. There she would be, Olive said, 'creaming her face and hands at night and wearing gloves, drinking fruit juice, eating rusks and reading some obscure economics handbook all at the same time'.[38]

Barbara exuded a voluptuous self-confidence that she says she never felt. And she could be blunt to the point of rudeness. Like Frank, she didn't see why she should tolerate foolishness. Olive recalled walking with her and their mutual friend Freda Houlston, when Freda remarked that the bare trees looked like 'the hair of some Botticelli angel'. Barbara stopped and rounded on her. 'My God, what a damnably silly thing to say,' she snapped. 'I hope you are not going to go on like this all the time!'[39]

It was Barbara who went on all the time. 'Nobody else had a chance to open their mouths',[40] one contemporary recalled.

Another thought that 'she used to lecture a bit', and yet another felt 'inadequate' around her certainties. Others found her more than opinionated. She could be strident, even arrogant; 'rather trying'.[41] Marjorie Betts's little sister soon metamorphosed into the fiery redhead. Barbara was single-minded, it was noted, as if it were a sign of depravity. She knew what she wanted, in and of itself an oddity for a girl, and what she wanted was even odder: she was shockingly determined on a political career. There was a woman cabinet minister now, the first, Margaret Bondfield, the minister of labour, Barbara's aspirations made flesh. It was obvious Barbara would be prime minister or at least in the cabinet, Olive thought, as a minister, not a woman minister; Barbara made clear she wanted very much to be a woman in a man's world. And she couldn't and wouldn't disguise her enormous ambition, the desire to make an impact.

Barbara's perception of her time at Oxford is one of almost unbroken unhappiness. Her friends dispute this. 'She'd have her occasional miseries,' said Mary Hepworth, who sometimes spent weekends with Barbara at Oxford, 'but she mostly seemed very gay to me ... She may look back on it now as an unhappy time, but I don't think it was at all.'[42] Olive agreed: Barbara had more fun than she likes to remember, she said. But Oxford was an alien world to Barbara, self-contained and self-regarding; there was much to dislike. St Hugh's was a prudish Church of England establishment, an odd choice for Barbara, who would have known from Marjorie the nature of the beast. It was physically isolated from the other colleges and the subject of put-downs: not only was it too far down the Banbury Road, but it was the place women went if they weren't brainy enough for Somerville or posh enough for Lady Margaret Hall.

Five years earlier, when Barbara Gwyer had taken over as principal, following a malicious academic intrigue of the type familiar to Inspector Morse, the *Oxford Magazine* had editorialised that St Hugh's was 'not a college at all ... It is a girls' school, of which the Principal is Headmistress.'[43] The magazine was alluding to its organisational problems but its atmosphere, too, was that of a girls' boarding school, with the principal 'a magnificent episcopal presence'[44] known as the Gwyer; Barbara found this jolly hockey sticks hee-hawing insufferable.

It was also a women's college, with all that implied: bad food, inadequate conditions, everything second-rate compared to the men's colleges. Male chauvinism at Oxford was de rigueur. 'Absurder Dons ... attempted to keep the atmosphere of their lectures pure by peppering the women with obscenities.'[45] To many of Oxford's professors – overstuffed repositories of grotesque snobbery and the implacable put-down – the presence of women loitering among the dreaming spires was at best a nuisance, at worse an outrage. Women were unwelcome interlopers, at once desirable sirens, distracting male effort and endeavour, and humourless, unattractive bluestockings.

And it wasn't just the professors who held those views. Women were not allowed to be members of the Oxford Union, that 'cadet class of the establishment',[46] as Barbara called it. This was something decided upon by the debating society itself and remained unchanged until 1963. 'Women are not intelligent', the undergraduate magazine *Isis* sighed in 1930, and here at Oxford 'we see women at their very worst'.[47]

Barbara 'smouldered resentfully against ... the entrenched masculinity of the place', the 'institutionalised and restrictive atmosphere in which women felt themselves relegated to the status of second class citizenry',[48] but, with the exception of Olive and Freda, the women weren't much more companionable. Most came out of expensive private schools such as Roedean and Cheltenham Ladies', not from the provincial grammars. The accents and attitudes of these upper-middle-class freshers grated. If they found her over the top, she found them barely conscious. She thought these cosseted young women as immature and unworldly as the girls at the grammar.

The women's colleges had especially strict chaperone and curfew rules, irritating restrictions 'under the excuse that every precaution must be taken that the city should not be littered with illegitimate babies'.[49] A female undergraduate could have tea publicly in a tea shop with a man, but could not walk alone with him in the park, nor take a ride in a punt or a car *à deux*. She could go to tea in a man's room with another woman, and have a man to tea in her room with a friend present – but only, Olive said, if she dragged her bed out into the corridor, rules and regulations that left Gerald Gardiner, who as lord chancellor later sat in the same cabinet as Barbara, to suppose 'Oxford to be the most Victorian and reactionary spot in Europe'.[50]

Such elaborate precautions were as nothing against hungry libido: sexual mores were the main topic of discussion in the women's common room. Should they sleep with their boyfriends and, if so, when? They almost all wanted the experience but were rightly afraid of the consequences. How could they stop getting pregnant? It was Barbara who had a whip round and collected enough money to send away for Michael Fielding's explicit and illustrated guide to sex, *Planned Parenthood*.

Barbara said that ordering Fielding was part of her own quest for sexual enlightenment; but Olive thought it was because Barbara couldn't bear her contemporaries' ignorance. Barbara was grown up, 'emancipated and ... knew quite a lot about sex', Olive said.[51] After they read Fielding, 'Barbara tested us on it which was delightfully typical of her. She wanted to make sure we got it straight.'[52] Not everyone did. By the time they came down, several of St Hugh's class of 1929 had had abortions.

Barbara was a believer in the old adage that plums do not fall into plain girls' laps; she spent much of her life ensuring that they fell into hers, taking meticulous care over her hair and her make-up and her clothes; and at Oxford she began to perfect the art of flirtation. Olive thought Barbara wanted to be a femme fatale, an avocation in which she had considerable lifelong success. Men found Barbara stunningly attractive. She enjoyed the power it gave her, but at first there wasn't much pleasure. Her initial faltering sexual encounters were a disappointment. Boys came and went. Barbara watched others having affairs like women choosing chocolates out of a box, seemingly content. She wasn't. Her romantic, passionate nature yearned for 'the love of some man whom thou must needs love'.

At first Barbara had 'got a measure of protection' against the alien nature of Oxford life from Marjorie. Barbara was very close to her sister, three years her senior and very much an older sister to her: a support, a confidante, a cheerleader. Marjorie was a 'blue-stocking who [later] gave up being a blue-stocking in order to have children'.[53] She had gone on to teacher-training college, where she kept a watch over Barbara. Barbara responded at first, easily getting through her preliminary exams; then something snapped, she said. She'd had enough of working, of being on the academic treadmill; it was in part a rebellion against Frank and the weight of his expectations. She couldn't work, she wouldn't work.

Although perhaps she worked harder than she remembered. Olive and Mary Hepworth certainly thought so. But she was not going to have that glittering academic career; she was going to fail Frank. She was apprehensive about this, Mary said, she 'worried she wasn't doing enough work to please her family, particularly her father',[54] but she didn't do anything about it. Barbara said that she flirted a lot, indulging her frivolous side that Frank so disliked.

With Olive she did all the usual Oxford things, clambering over the locked college gates in long ballgowns, either coming from or going to dances (if caught, they might have been sent down); whizzing about the countryside on men's knees in open-top cars; going to dances in London or Reading, staying up all night drinking champagne. Or, more restfully, floating down the Cherwell in a punt to the accompaniment of 'Ain't She Sweet', or drinking cocoa with friends or cycling through the countryside.

Another distraction came in her second year, when her brother, Jimmie, came up to Oxford after graduating from Edinburgh, to be groomed for the Colonial Service. There were two years between Jimmie and Barbara, and they were the closest brother and sister Olive had ever seen, so much so that they were taken as lovers by a nosy undergraduate who reported them. The mistake was easy to make. Jimmie, good-looking and always fashionably well-dressed, fussed over his sister, taking her to dances and the theatre and plying her with chocolates.

But Barbara's main distraction was politics. Oxford was almost as political as she was; religious too: whom socialism didn't call, God did. Freda found God. Olive found communism and joined the October Club (which resulted in her receiving regular visits from MI5 until she was in her sixties). And Barbara joined the Labour Club.

Although Barbara supported the Bolshevik Revolution, the October Club was too outré, too marginal and rarefied; moreover, she was too imbued with ILP politics to do anything but join the Labour Club, which had the added advantage of being the liveliest and the most important of the political clubs. As the magazine *Isis* declared, the most 'mentally proficient' of the students who bothered about politics at all 'possess distinct Socialist leanings'[55] and tended to fall in the direction of the Labour Club, which, like the Guild of Youth before it, was as much a social as a political club: dances were held, films were shown, party games were played, skits and acts produced, and Sunday rambles were common.

The club was the best place to meet members of the opposite sex; it 'blazed the trail of sex knowledge',[56] as Barbara put it, in theory as well as practice: Norman Haire, a well-known expert in sex, came to talk to them about the bedroom arts. One of the men in the club was 'the young Adonis of the Labour Party',[57] Tony Greenwood, the son of the minister of health. Tony was debonair, a flirt, very attractive to women, but Barbara dismissed him as slick, protesting – perhaps a little too effusively, in view of the rumours that circulated about them in the 1950s – that she did not find him attractive.

She held several offices in the club, eventually becoming treasurer, as Marjorie had been before her, the highest office a woman could obtain; it took another twenty years for the club to be ready for its first woman chairman: Shirley Catlin, as Shirley Williams then was. Barbara was always doing something with and for the club, throwing herself into political activism. The club attracted a slew of charismatic orators such as Nye Bevan, Jimmie Maxton, John Strachey and Bertrand Russell; Jennie Lee also spoke and then came to visit Barbara wearing a big hat, Olive remembered. Jennie, only six years Barbara's senior, had been elected to parliament in 1929, at only 24 the youngest woman MP, and she was already something of an icon in the Labour movement for her soft 'dark smokey beauty'[58] and her hard uncompromising rhetoric.

Another charismatic and familiar speaker on the Labour Club circuit was William Mellor; the first time Barbara may have seen this man, who was to become the love of her life, was when he came and spoke to the club in 1931, although he was often around Oxford for one reason or another. Bill Mellor, like Frank Betts, was a mentor to the young; with G. D. H. Cole, one of Barbara's tutors, he propagated the concept of Guild Socialism,* co-writing several books with Cole and writing several of his own.

Bill, 'a product of Northern Nonconformity . . . added the popular thunder to Cole's more academic lightning, and together they had a tremendous influence over the undergraduates of the Left'.[59] They were known as 'the Mellor and Cole Board' and jointly wrote 'Judex', a column of industrial and trade union notes, for the radically left-wing *Daily Herald*, which was 'read eagerly not only by the middle classes but also by shop stewards and other manual workers'.[60] Bill became a nationally known figure in socialist circles through 'Judex' and his books and speeches. He became editor of the *Herald* in 1926 and was considered 'one of the most effective, though not the least temperamental, of the personalities of the left'.[61]

Bill Mellor was an impressive figure, a man of tremendous presence, and one of nature's orators. His straightforward eloquence was delivered in a magnificently resonant voice. Like Barbara he had a love of good clothes, and he was always immaculately turned out in Savile Row suits. He always wore bone-coloured kid gloves and a tiepin. He was tall and broad-shouldered, with coal-black hair and a generous mouth. His face when he smiled was 'adorned . . . with the most incongruous dimples'.[62] He couldn't be called handsome – Margaret

---

* Control and ownership of production by workers organised in national guilds, except, as their Storrington Document stated, the distaff half, whose involvement in industry would involve a 'lowering of the standard of Guild workmanship to meet the peculiar disabilities of women'.

Cole, G. D. H.'s wife, found him hovering on ugly – but he was alluring, brooding, sensual, with a prepossessing personality and an intellect which not only came through in his books but seared all who met him.

To Barbara, this glamorous, powerful man was irresistible, at once all she wanted to be, and physically all she desired. He was also married. (Beatrice Webb,* who afforded her own marriage, and the importance of marital partnership in general, a cult status, thought the Mellors a model couple.) But it wasn't unusual in Barbara's milieu for women to have affairs with married men. Jennie Lee was having an affair with Frank Wise, a socialist eco-nomist prominent in the ILP; Ellen Wilkinson, MP, called Red Ellen for her hair and politics, was involved with a married man, too. They were Modern Women, sexually emancipated, believing if not quite in free love then love on their own terms, without the bourgeois entrapment of marriage and domesticity.

The Labour government was showing itself less than socialist in dealing with the effects of the Depression. In June 1931 G. D. H. and Margaret Cole set up the Society for Socialist Inquiry and Propaganda, known as Zip, with the aim of trying to encourage the government to behave like a socialist one. Ernest Bevin had been persuaded by Cole to be the chairman and Bill Mellor was on the executive.

Members included Labour stars such as Clement Attlee and Stafford Cripps and Zip actively recruited from the trade unions and the university Labour clubs; Barbara went to some of their meetings, which she found dry and overly intellectual. Certainly this group of loyal grousers, as they called themselves, were singularly unsuccessful in provoking socialism out of Ramsay MacDonald's Labour government. If capitalism was perishing, the government seemed to be doing what it could to prop it up, in the end, and most disastrously, at the expense of the unemployed themselves.

* Writer and socialist theorist, who, with her husband, Sidney, was a stalwart of the Fabian Society, and founder of the LSE and the *New Statesman* magazine.

In summer 1931 the right to the dole was removed for seasonal, part-time and most married women workers; then the May Committee, set up to look into government expenditure, issued a doomsday report forecasting a monumental budget deficit the following year and recommending that the meagre unemployment benefit be cut by 20 per cent and that public sector workers be subject to swinging pay cuts.

The report, 'the most foolish document I have ever had the misfortune to read', as John Maynard Keynes famously observed,[63] provoked the crisis it predicted, causing a run on sterling. The New York bankers would not issue a loan to Britain without severe retrenchment, the government was informed. The cabinet split. Nine ministers refused to accept any further cuts in benefit. MacDonald and Philip Snowden, the 'Iron Chancellor', insisted that the dole had to be cut by at least 10 per cent. The unions, in the persons of Bevin and Walter Citrine of the TUC, both of whom 'understood a great deal more about economics than MacDonald or Snowden',[64] felt that the poor should not be made to save the wealthy from ruin, and refused to accept the cuts, causing the wealthy colonial secretary, Sidney Webb, to explode that they were pigs. MacDonald, his cabinet rent asunder and the Labour movement in rebellion, decided to join the enemy. According to Webb, he intimated that it was the King, George V, who desired a coalition government with MacDonald as prime minister.

The majority of the Labour cabinet listened in disbelief as MacDonald informed them that he was going to lead an all-party, Tory-dominated National Government. Only Snowden and the dominions secretary, Jimmy Thomas, followed MacDonald into the new dawn which ingloriously ended the Labour government, as Beatrice Webb seethed; it was a victory for American and British bankers; they had settled 'the personnel and policy'[65] of the British government after creating the mess in the first place. What had happened was 'an attempt ... to dictate the internal policy of Great Britain', the *Daily Herald* said.[66] The left were particularly incensed at the American intervention; it was a deliberate attempt to undermine the Labour government, the Labour movement, and the very existence of the dole, which the Americans, fearful their own workers might demand the same, regarded as dangerous Bolshevism.

Barbara's awareness of the limitations of the 'special relationship' between Britain and the USA came sharply into focus then, too, but her immediate reaction was fury against the instigator of the great betrayal, MacDonald. Labour's first prime minister, a former ILP member, a man whom she had once regarded as a hero, had picked the pockets of the dispossessed and defected to the enemy in order to prop up capitalism. Barbara and Tony Greenwood saw to it that he was deposed as the Labour Club's honorary president and Cole installed in his stead.

MacDonald's daughter, Sheila, a student at Somerville, was isolated. She wrote plaintively to Tony Greenwood, complaining of the 'evil rumour ... that the MacDonalds are said to consort now solely with Tories and Titles'.[67] Barbara thought it so. MacDonald had been seduced by the duchesses of England, those who, as Beatrice Webb observed, 'lived in great houses and conversed in cultured tones about the unessentials of life'.[68]

MacDonald became a hate figure in the Labour movement and, with Snowden and Thomas, was thrown out of the party.

No Labour supporter who lived through it ever forgot August 1931. The expression 'It's 1931 all over again' went into the lexicon, to be trotted out at times of crisis; the aftershocks were felt for decades. At Oxford it made politics more urgent. Membership of the Labour Club doubled to six hundred and discussions therein became more serious, sincere to the point of earnestness: plummy epigrams were out. Cleverness clearly was not enough. In the party itself, power moved decisively and rapidly away from the Parliamentary Labour Party (PLP) back from whence it had come: the party in the country and the unions. To young socialists like Barbara the lessons of 1931 were clear. A Labour Party with no proper theoretical underpinning had proven itself unable and unwilling to deal with the crisis in capitalism in any way but within the confines of capitalist economic orthodoxy: shrinking public expenditure in the face of a depression instead of adopting socialist expansionary policies.

'The lesson I learned,' Barbara wrote, 'was that Labour governments cannot win power or survive by adopting the economic policies of their political enemies.'[69] It was a lesson she never forgot and a political philosophy from which she never deviated. Nineteen thirty-one did not radicalise Barbara in the way it did many young socialists; she was already on the radical left. What it did was to set her off on a quest for theoretical truth; it showed her the importance of adopting and conforming to hard socialist theory, without which a socialist Labour Party could not exist.

Capitalism seemed indeed to be sinking under the weight of its own contradictions. Industry was at a standstill; bankruptcies multiplied. But the first action of the National Government was to reduce the dole by 10 per cent and to make it means-tested. In London there were riots. The great army of the unemployed, 'humiliated, degraded and intimidated by the Labour Exchanges, the Means Test, the Poor Law and the police', grew.[70] Hunger marchers passed through Oxford on their way south to London, 'a dark singing worm' which Barbara, Tony and Olive helped feed and take care of; this 'vast malleable force which only needed a leader to become a threat'[71] was left by Labour leaders to the ministrations of students and the organisation of the National Unemployed Workers' Movement (NUWM), a communist-led group. Some Labour politicians even went so far as to condemn the hunger marchers as a rabble.

The party itself was in retreat; it turned inwards and yelped blindly; it didn't want any more trouble. Frank let the 21-year-old Barbara cover the post-MacDonald pre-election Labour Party conference for the *Pioneer* in October 1931, an assignment that would have normally gone to Vic Feather. Feather was accustomed to being shoved aside by top names when big stories erupted, but being elbowed out by the neophyte Barbara rankled deeply. He 'was left to report election meetings, and write a post mortem'[72] while Barbara gloried in the front-page story.

Barbara found a conference full of 'cautious determination to preserve a united front at all costs'.[73] There was little attempt to get the ex Labour ministers to account for the past government. The

68-year-old Arthur Henderson, 'Uncle Arthur', was the acting Party leader and the troops were ready and all too willing, Barbara wrote, to 'rally once again round a standard of personal loyalty'. Any 'whither the party?' debate was firmly squashed. Members of the ILP, in a phrase that was to resonate down the years, and be levelled in one form or another at Barbara, were dismissed by Uncle Arthur as part of an 'organised conscience'. The left were warned not to make capital of the crisis; the important thing was to win the forthcoming election.

All the arguments about who controlled party policy, conference or cabinet, and whom the PLP should obey, arguments that Barbara engaged in throughout her political life (if not always from the same side), were all here. Uncle Arthur, Barbara wrote, 'did not seem to believe in too much control by the Conferences'. The job of conference was, he said, to lay down big political principles; the Cabinet was about deciding the details of policy and the PLP must obey the Cabinet. 'This is surely the way in which MacDonald led his colleagues to the brink of the precipice!' Barbara thundered, sure of her stand if not of her metaphors. She let Jimmie Maxton, chairman of the ILP, have the last word from his 'fine and stirring' speech: 'The people are not going to respond to academic resolutions, but to the demand for working-class power, power!'[74] Barbara's sentiments exactly.

By now, Barbara, too, was in crisis. She was coming up to her finals and she knew she should work, but she was totally caught up in the election, vigorously campaigning against MacDonald's National Government. It was returned with 521 seats: Labour got 52 seats and the Liberals 37. She took her written exams, and then went off on holiday with a boy with whom she was having an affair. She was supposed to prepare for her viva (the interview with the examiners) but she didn't. She was immobilised by panic; she couldn't even think about thinking. She should be working. She should be making some attempt to catch up. But she did nothing. It was as if she was trying to fail, or, knowing that she would fail, had decided to do so spectacularly. There was no way back. She didn't prepare for the viva and she arrived late. She knew that what she offered the examiners was 'truculent political generalizations'.[75] She crawled back home to her parents' house to await the results. When they came Frank was devastated. And so was Barbara. She had got a poor third.

Chapter Two

AGITATE, AGITATE, AGITATE

Barbara had found a commanding father figure in Bill Mellor, a man almost twice her age, another late-Victorian, just six years younger than Frank; he was not dissimilar to him, either. He, too, expected much of Barbara and was a fundamental influence on her life. Barbara said that Bill did for her what Frank had done for Mary Hepworth. She became Bill's political protégée, and he clarified and polished her thinking. Emotionally there was a straight line from father to lover. Bill was also a big man, unable to tolerate baseness in any shape or form, and they had the same values and integrity and many of the same faults, too. Bill wasn't an easy man. Like Frank, he had temperamental difficulties. He was, said Michael Foot, who adored him, 'the most irascible man I ever knew', prone to vigorous verbal 'protest against the imbecilities of the world in general and anyone who dared cross him in particular'.[1] Yet, much as it did in Frank, 'a wonderful gentleness and generosity mingled with these ferocities'.[2]

Bill came with baggage: his long marriage, a small son, Ronald, a child who had come after eleven years. His health had been profoundly undermined by his sojourn in gaol during the First World War. He had been a conscientious objector who, instead of keeping quiet, like Cole, had made a revolutionary speech to the military tribunal. Bill served time in Wormwood Scrubs and

30

Dartmoor, revolutionising the cooking in the latter, his son said; Bill, too, was a gourmet, a lover of elegance in all things.

He was often taken for a Yorkshireman, Margaret Cole said, but he was born in Crewe, the son and brother of Unitarian ministers, a grammar schoolboy who, en route to the ministry, found socialism instead at Exeter College. Before the First World War he'd gone to work for the Webbs as secretary of the Fabian Research Department. Beatrice found him honest, shrewd, hard-working and a good judge of character, but she bemoaned his lack of wit and verbal elegance. Bill (and Cole) fell out with her over guild socialism, of which she disapproved.

Politically Bill did what he thought right, not expedient. He was a founder member of the Communist Party of Great Britain (CPGB) in 1920, and one of the first to leave it four years later, after he'd written his revolutionary manifesto, *Direct Action*, which as the title suggests called on workers to take direct industrial action to overthrow capitalism. His communist antecedents dogged him; he contested the Enfield seat for Labour in 1931 and drowned in a tide of black propaganda. To Barbara this was all part of the attraction. Nothing shifted Bill or Frank from what 'they believed to be right, no matter how inconvenient or dangerous it was to them personally', she said.[3]

Theirs was a grand passion of love letters and snatched time; a high romance made more so by the piquancy of absence, his essential unavailability. Bill had something of the Yorkshire Moors about him: the dourness, the remoteness, a harsh and exacting pulchritude. But Barbara could melt him, turn him into mush. It was her warmth, he wrote, that he missed most when they were apart.

> Love mingles with love, and no evil is weighing
> On thy heart or mine

William Morris wrote in 'The Message of the March Wind'. It was Bill who gave Barbara the book of Morris's work with this poem in which the 'hope of the people now buddeth and groweth' along with the love that overtook Barbara and Bill, the 'lover and lover'.

Reading it she made, she said, the 'exciting discovery that sensualists often make the best revolutionaries because they find ugliness spiritually unbearable'.[4]

Bill lived in Battersea Park in London. He would come up to Hyde, just outside Manchester, where the Bettses were now living, to take Barbara to the best restaurants in Manchester, notably the glorious Midland Hotel. He taught her about food and wine (Frank's gourmet proclivities having not reached down to his family) and escorted her around the countryside in a chauffeur-driven car, sitting in the back with his bone-coloured gloves folded in his lap, smoking Churchill cigarettes, talking, always talking. He stole her away on holidays and took photos of her in her bathing suit, shockingly beautiful and radiantly alive, laughing.

It was Barbara who had first taken him to bed – in her parents' house. Afterwards she told her father, who, although unable to discuss sex with his daughter, was apparently unperturbed to find that it had been going on under his roof. Bill, Barbara said, told Frank about his wife, Edna, told him he was in love with Barbara and that he wanted his daughter's hand in marriage, but that both he and Barbara agreed that Edna had to be moved gradually towards the idea of divorce, rather than be forced to endure a sudden rupture.

'Divorce was not the sort of thing that happened to Unitarian Nonconformist families', such as ours, his son, Ronald, remarked;[5] nor to many others. Sudden or otherwise divorce in the 1930s was scandalous; despite the steady increase throughout the decade, it ruined lives, especially women's lives. Barbara, like Jennie Lee and Ellen Wilkinson, 'could risk a discreet affair, even engage in a long-standing relationship, but they could not afford divorce. It was out of the question.'[6] Barbara's political career would be over before it had begun. She could not help but be mindful of this, but nevertheless Bill's divorce lingered throughout the years as a potentiality, a prospect, if increasingly dim, due, Barbara told her parents, to Edna's continual intransigence.

Barbara had been profoundly shaken by her academic failure. She had swotted to get into Oxford, to get the scholarships. She was seen and saw herself as academic. Marjorie hadn't failed. Nor had Jimmie. It was only she who had returned home in ignominy, unemployed and unemployable, she thought, in Hyde of all places, in the midst of the Depression. The town was, like much of the North, Wales and Scotland, a Distressed Area, desolate and dismal, where unemployment ran as high as 80 per cent.

Olive Shapley thought Hyde a wonderful, romantic place with its 'rows of small grey houses, steep cobbled streets, sad little shops [and] clanging trams'.[7] Not so Barbara. She, Olive noted, longed with a violent intensity to get away from its narrowness. So did Frank. Unlike in Bradford, there was nothing that could be called culture and Frank, half suspecting he was being punished for his political activities, found it almost intolerable.

It was Bill more than anyone who pulled Barbara out of her funk. He had failed academically, too, coming down with a fourth, and so what? The important thing was to think, he told her. He gave her economic and political treatises to read. They were comrades as well as lovers. He made her do her best. She read White Papers and Blue Books, and read and re-read Marx. Bill forced her to think, she said, goading her on, saying he knew it would hurt at first.

She joined the Hyde Labour Club and was appointed propaganda secretary, a job which entailed all kinds of public speaking. Barbara, who was to become one of the party's best orators, learnt to hold and entice a sceptical, indifferent or barracking audience the hard way, on the street corners of the North. She was in continual demand, becoming the opening act for party luminaries such as Susan Lawrence,* who, suitably impressed, told the audience that they had just listened to one of the future leaders of the Labour Party.

Barbara's early thespian experience and her prose and poetry recitals, in which diction and projection are all, had provided a solid training. She had, and continued to have in old age, a big voice on stage, a boombox voice, rich, resonant, seemingly coming

---

* A well-known Labour woman and prominent Fabian, Susan Lawrence was MP for East Ham North and held a minor post in the 1929–31 Labour government.

out of all sides of her, much bigger than her diminutive stature might suggest and very different from her ordinary speaking voice, which some people found grating, even shrill. And she had the X factor, star quality, charisma; the sheer force of her personality filled the stage. The words gushed out of her, wave upon wave; 'she sort of rolled while she spoke,' Paul Foot said, 'and watching her you suddenly realised: this is what public speaking is all about. She was a tremendously inspirational speaker.'[8]

Barbara could feel an audience, massage it, manipulate it, cajole it. 'It was never just tub thumping', Gerald Kaufman said. She was 'quite ruthless and cynical in the methods she employed – she had a genius' for putting herself and her message over.[9] And there was nothing off the cuff, ever. As she did all her political life, she boned up on facts and statistics before she spoke, whatever she needed to make and back up her point. She left nothing to chance.

When she was 23 Barbara made her first attempt to get selected for a parliamentary seat at Blackburn. She failed; it was another decade before Blackburn was ready for her. She had had only one job offer since Oxford, as a reporter on a local paper, but the paper folded before she could begin. And now she got another offer through a family friend – which was neither what she imagined nor wanted: a confectionery sales demonstrator, setting up a stall in the large stores and trade shows, for Samuel Hanson and Sons of Eastcheap, London. This was to be the only job outside of journalism or politics Barbara ever held and it was, she said, 'the most miserable year of my life'.[10]

The work was often monotonous and 'after eight or nine hours standing about in draughts, I felt half-dead, fit only to drag myself to bed', Barbara said.[11] It was an experience she never forgot. The boredom, the rules and regulations, the physical discomforts, the dehumanisation of the small cog in a big wheel, the affront to her dignity of being searched for stolen goods as she left a store: she could and did recall it all, forty, fifty, sixty years and more after the event.

Barbara was sent to London by the firm to work in the sales and marketing department at their headquarters in Eastcheap. She was thrilled. She could be near Bill and away from Hyde at last; it was a desk job, no more standing about in draughty stores. It was, she thought, a job she could make something of, but it ended before it had really begun. She quickly fell out with her immediate boss, whose ways she found stuffy and who objected to her going above his head with her ideas: she was fired.

Losing her regular income had its advantages: she could more or less support herself by freelance journalism, some of it for the trade press such as *The Tobacconist*, and more importantly she could pursue her politics full-time. Events crowded in. The Nazis, the second largest party in Europe, inched closer and closer to power in Germany. The unemployed in Britain swelled to three million. The National Government and the Labour Party both seemed para-lysed by the economic crisis.

The political fallout from 1931 continued apace: the Independent Labour Party (ILP), the 'organised conscience', which had been toying on and off with leaving the party since the 1920s, now found itself subject to party discipline which curtailed its right to dissent verbally from the official Labour line. The ILP disaffiliated itself. A few months later Zip and the ILP Affiliation Committee – ILP members who had disagreed with disaffiliation – amalgamated to form the Socialist League – named in remembrance of William Morris's league – another self-described group of loyal grousers affiliated to the Labour Party, which would act 'with a view to giving a more Socialist character to the party's policy and leader-ship'.[12] Bill was on the first executive and Barbara was one of its founder members, as was a future leader of the Labour Party, Michael Foot.

Michael, three years Barbara's junior, was a shy, rather gauche young man, who suffered from both eczema and asthma. He came from a prominent Liberal family and had been chairman of the Liberal Club at Oxford, before becoming a convert to socialism. He soon became a convert to Barbara, finding her 'strikingly attractive, full of self confidence, vehement in manner, endlessly talkative and argumentative'. She 'made a vivid impression' on him as she did 'on everyone who met her'.[13] Barbara and Michael teamed up as a roving propoganda unit, taking the league's Austin 7 and setting up a portable soapbox outside Mornington Crescent Tube station or on Hampstead Heath or as far away as Wales where they would regale the downtrodden crowd with socialist possibilities and copies of the *Socialist Leaguer*, for which Barbara also wrote.

Bill had been ejected from the editor's chair of the *Daily Herald* in 1931, after it came under the joint control of the TUC and Odhams Press, his Marxist views and/or his personality being unacceptable to Ernest Bevin. Bevin had an aversion to 'intellectuals' unless they were housetrained, and had a particular enmity towards Bill, whom he neither liked nor trusted. The dislike was, as Margaret Cole observed, mutual. Bill was now on the editorial board of Odhams Press, where he was being subjected to increasing pressure to drop his political activities. His job, his family and his activism kept him busy, making it difficult for him to spend as much time with Barbara as perhaps both would have wanted. Barbara often saw more of Michael than of Bill; they spent 'many happy hours together, reading from the works of Beatrice Webb or Karl Marx' in her flat, Michael said, 'and engaging in a whole gamut of even more joyous pursuits' such as dinner at Chez Victor and sunbathing on the roof of her building.[14]

'Michael would have been glad if these comradely evenings had turned into a love affair', his biographer wrote,[15] though leaving it to Barbara, rather than Michael, to say that they did not: she says they were never lovers. Most people who know them both are convinced that they were at one time or another, although both deny it, in Barbara's case vehemently, in Michael's case reluctantly. He had a mischievous streak; the suggestive 'more joyous pursuits' implies a little more than sunbathing and gossipy dinners. He loved to tease Barbara with nudges and winks to the audience at party conferences; or to make remarks to interviewers, suggesting a dalliance.

Barbara never took to being teased; she was never very good at laughing at herself and did not like others to do so, not even Michael – perhaps especially not Michael. It struck at her sense of loyalty, all-important to her, and also undermined her ability to control her public image – equally important. Stepping over the line, he would hear the 'waspish note of warning in her voice'[16] that he got to know all too well over the years.

Michael's future wife, the film-maker Jill Craigie, whom he married in 1949, never took to Michael's teasing about Barbara, either, or to Barbara herself, in no small part because she resented their intimacy, which predated her arrival in his life. She also resented Barbara's treatment of her as a 'wife' and therefore a person of no importance. Michael and Barbara were, at the very least, as Barbara said, very close friends and their relationship was indeed like a marriage. It lasted, with one serious breech and much squabbling, the rest of their lives, his barbed public teasing notwith-standing.

At first it looked as if the Socialist League could take the mori-bund Labour Party, bereft of ideas and energy, and shake it into socialism. At the 1932 Labour Party conference, the league's first, it triumphed, getting a commitment that the next Labour government would enact 'definite socialist legislation ... immediately ... on taking office'.[17] As it was a bankers' cabal that had forced the Labour government out of office, it followed that the next one must remove the power of capitalism immediately, which meant, among other things, nationalising the banks and all other 'vital points of power'. The significant union block votes that swung the league's way came from the miners and railway workers, two unions committed to the ideas of workers' control promulgated by Bill and Cole. It was a success the league did not repeat, in part because it had alienated Bevin, who with Walter Citrine wrested considerable control of the party after 1931 through the National Council of Labour, to which the reduced and ineffectual Parliamentary Labour Party (PLP) and Labour's national executive doffed their caps.

Cole had wanted Ernie Bevin, the former Zip chairman, to be chairman of the league. In negotiations with the ILP, he 'argued strongly that there ought to be a working-class chairman', prefera-bly Bevin.[18] The ex-ILP contingent, led by Frank Wise, insisted that Wise chair the new organisation 'in such a way that it became obvious' that if Zip refused 'negotiations were bound to break down'. Wise's group moved before any such mishap could occur, going 'ahead with the organisation of the Socialist League'.[19]

Cole wrote a conciliatory letter to Bevin, asking him to serve on the league's executive, but Bevin took umbrage, declaring the league would have the same 'bias against Trade Unionists'[20] as the ILP had had, no matter who was on the executive. Writing twenty years later, on Bevin's death, Cole said that the ILP's refusal to make Bevin chairman of the league was a calamity. It drove Bevin 'sharply to the Right and confirmed his suspicions of Socialist ideologues and all their works',[21] which perhaps overstated the case. But Bevin was not a man to have as an enemy and from the outset 'there was much suspicion of the Socialist League in "orthodox circles" at Transport House' (where both the TUC and the party had their headquarters),[22] Hugh Dalton, one of the most powerful Labour politicians of the period noted; it was a suspicion he shared.

Bevin flexed his power and led the unions against the league, decisively setting the 'industrial' side of the party against the 'intellectuals', which is to say the educated left wing. The powerful unionists and theorists whom the Coles had tried to bring together in Zip – never particularly compatible – were rent asunder and were to stay in their mutually hostile camps for the next several decades.

The conflict – which began with the ILP – between the unions, who until the sixties backed Labour's right wing, and the left, was in part a straightforward power battle over who controlled the Labour Party; in part a matter of political difference between those, Marxist and non-Marxist, who believed in the old ILP adage of 'Socialism in our Time' and the gradualists at the running buffet, conflicts exacerbated, as is usual in Labour Party schisms, by more than an element of class antagonism.

Radical socialists like the members of the league were, by and large, middle-class by education if not origins. In its five-year existence, two Etonians, two Wykehamists and a Harrovian graced the league's council, with nine council members being Oxbridge graduates and four more from London University. The league – whose membership never exceeded 3000 throughout 100 branches – boasted a glittering array of Labour talent, including, albeit briefly, a future prime minister, Clement Attlee, well-known socialist theorists and writers such as H. N. Brailsford and Frank Horrabin, former ministers such as Charles Trevelyan, and future ministers such as Stafford Cripps, the postwar president of the Board of Trade and subsequently chancellor of the exchequer, and Barbara Castle and Michael Foot.

The league was the only place for people who, like Barbara, wanted to stay within the Labour Party while trying to change it. For Barbara socialism is about fighting 'on the nearest battleground to hand' – an expression she used throughout her life – not about discussion for discussion's sake, something of which she is impatient. Barbara threw herself into the league's work, becoming its representative on the Hunger Marchers London Reception Committee and later on the Spanish People's Front Committee. She ran the league's prolific publications department, which produced dozens of pamphlets and study guides each year; one or two, such as *Socialism for the Small Town*, were by 'FB', who had followed his daughter into the league. The league organised dozens of conferences, study groups, public meetings, lectures and weekend schools; Barbara, Bill and Stafford Cripps especially spoke everywhere and anywhere they could.

Michael had been at Oxford with Cripps's son, John, and he and Barbara became Cripps's favoured protégés. They were often invited for weekends up to Goodfellows, Cripps's vast country pile in Gloucestershire, to play tennis and engage in political badinage with the 'Red Squire', as the *Daily Express* dubbed him. He was Beatrice Webb's nephew and, as she wryly observed, for 'leadership in the labour movement Stafford had a most unfit upbringing. Born and bred in a luxurious Tory household, brilliantly successful as a Winchester scholar, winning a New College scholarship ... he married, at a little over twenty years old, a wealthy girl with a millionaire mother.'[23] He had come late to politics and even later to socialism, and achieved hero status in the the labour movement as the barrister who put the mine-owners in the dock for the 1934 Gresford colliery disaster, in which 262 men died. He won the case, free of charge, for the miners.

If Bill was 'the most dominating figure in the Socialist League',[24] Stafford Cripps's 'was the name which quickly became almost synonymous' with it.[25] He bankrolled it, leaving it open to charges that it was, as Hugh Dalton said, 'little more than a rich man's toy',[26] a plaything for a rather prissy, wealthy, dilettante lawyer. Cripps was more than that; he was many things during his 'dazzling and contradictory political career'.[27] He had become the youngest KC at the bar. In 1929, at the age of forty, he entered parliament for the first time, going onto the front bench the following year as solicitor-general, joining his father, Lord Parmoor, and his uncle by marriage, Lord Passfield, as Sidney Webb had become.

Cripps was one of a handful of MacDonald's ex-ministers who, having declined to join the National Government, kept their seats as Labour MPs in the 1931 election. Another punctilious dresser, he was, Bill's son recalled, 'the only man except the doctor I'd ever seen wearing spats'.[28] Although he could be personally dry, cold and arrogant – 'There but for the grace of God, goes God', as Churchill remarked – he had the charisma to rally 'the whole of the younger generation of socialists to his side' and was 'perhaps, the one man in the party who [had] the ability and the personality to set against Sir Oswald Mosley's unmistakable, if lamentable, glamour'.[29]

Frank Wise died suddenly in 1933 and Cripps became chairman of the league, which assured its activities were kept firmly in the public eye. The press trailed the Red Squire around from meeting to meeting; he did not disappoint. Cripps could have been forgiven for thinking that more column inches were dedicated to his so-called Buckingham Palace speech than to the fact that Hitler had become Germany's chancellor. When the Labour Party came to power, Cripps had declared, not only would the power and influence of the House of Lords and the City have to be dealt with, but opposition from Buckingham Palace would have to be overcome. His speech brought on an outbreak of British indignation. It was one thing to nationalise the banks, quite another to invoke the monarch as a force of wickedness. Cripps backed off, saying he meant the courtiers, not the King, but it didn't help. 'To ring the front door bell of Buckingham Palace and to run away – that is not what we expect of our revolutionaries!' the *Morning Post* jibed.[30]

But Cripps wasn't speaking extemporaneously. Sidney Webb let it be known that King George V had 'intimated' to MacDonald his 'desire' for a coalition government, which had encouraged MacDonald in his wicked ways. And the league's suspicions of potential interference from Buckingham Palace were less than assuaged by assurances from Sir Clive Wigram, the King's private secretary, that the crown would use its prerogative only if it needed to save the country from catastrophe.

What would a real socialist Labour government be to the estab-lishment, if not a 'catastrophe'? It would therefore be necessary, the league concluded, immediately on taking office for the Labour government to enact an Emergency Powers Act to deal with 'finan-cial strikers' who would seek to prevent it carrying out its manifesto. The idea that, between the announcement of the election results and the assumption of power, 'the capitalist parties' would declare a state of emergency and ask the King to refuse to summon parlia-ment was frequently discussed in the House of Commons Group, a think-tank charged with working out a future Labour government's practice and policies. Bill was a member, as were Cripps, Attlee, the Coles and Hugh Dalton. Dalton, a gradualist Fabian, fiercely anti-Marxist, dissented from this view. 'Our candidates are being stabbed in the back and pushed onto the defensive', he complained of Cripps's public utterances.[31] People were unlikely to vote for what they would consider a socialist dictatorship. As Bevin growled: 'I do not like emergency powers, even if they are operated by my friends.'[32]

Unlike Barbara, Bill or Michael, Cripps did not have much grasp of the socialist theory they so valued and showed no inclination to put this to rights by picking up a book. 'His Marxist slogans were undigested', Michael wrote; 'he declared the class war without ever having studied the contours of the battlefield.'[33] It was left to Bill, the league's 'granite-like Socialist conscience',[34] who exercised considerable influence over Cripps, to supply the ballast and direc-tion. The league, he declared, should be no longer 'a mere umbrella for loyal grousers but an instrument for co-ordinating what I would call Marxist opinions and action within the wider Labour Movement'.[35]

The league took on the party at the annual conference, in fine gladiatorial style, throwing itself at the blunt instrument of the union block vote, arriving in 1934 with its own manifesto, *Forward to Socialism*, and seventy-five amendments to the party's election manifesto, *For Socialism and Peace*. The party swiftly reduced the amendments, some several pages long, to twelve, all of which were unceremoniously trounced. Both Cripps and Bill spoke repeatedly. 'Cripps in the end wearied the Conference,' Dalton noted, 'Mellor did better. He seemed more warm blooded.'[36] Barbara was proud of Bill's efforts. 'I had never admired him more than when he went to the rostrum time and again to confront the open hostility of conference', she wrote.[37]

There was an element of courting this hostility, of course, of bear-baiting Ernie Bevin, Walter Citrine and Dalton. At the previous conference, the novelist, journalist and league supporter Storm Jameson had watched as Dalton swayed about on the stage singing 'Auld Lang Syne', 'his large gleaming head tilted back, only the whites of his eyes visible, smiling at once cold and hearty'. Behind her, 'a ragged handful led by Bill Mellor ... [was] trying to start The Red Flag',[38] trying to start Marxist opinions and action in the Labour movement, a technique later called agitprop – agitation and propaganda – street politics using Conference as the market square. It was often the nearest battleground to hand and Barbara would fight on it for much of her political life.

The league's overwhelming defeat at the 1934 conference was as nothing. Bill, writing in the *Socialist Leaguer*, explained it thus: socialism 'cannot be created on a diet of theory or kept alive by telling workers to wait until the General Election comes. It must be created and kept alive by constant agitation within capitalism.' The league was going to lead the agitation: it had decided to become a 'disciplined organisation, which would aim at mass membership',[39] to take the Labour Party from within by the sheer strength of its numbers as well as its ideas.

Bill's own agitation within capitalism eventually cost him his job. He had written to Cripps telling him that his speeches at the league's conferences 'have landed me in another jam at the office. Warnings are floating about once again. I shall be seeing Mr Dunbar* in a minute.'[40] Mr Dunbar wanted to know whether Bill intended to go on rabble-rousing and more whether he intended to stand for parliament again (he stood for Enfield once more in 1935 and once more lost). Mr Dunbar now not only wanted him to cease all political writing and speaking but forbade him to stand for parliament or else face the sack. Bill took the latter course. At nearly 48 he was jobless. Barbara wrote to her mother, telling her that things were grim. Bill was taking it hard, 'having no place in the world and no money'.[41]

But Bill wasn't out of work for long. He put his redundancy money into buying Town & County Council Publications Ltd, and became editor of its main publication, *Town & County Councillor*. Barbara worked with him, commissioning articles from experts in various fields: transport, housing, gas, water, public health, education, sewage and so on, and acting as general dogsbody. The 'Journal for Public Representatives & Local Government Officials', as it styled itself, promised to keep readers, 'au fait with Local Government developments'. Its inside front cover was given over to 'Civic Personalities', the mayor from here and there and anywhere, photographed in finery with an accompanying short, and anodyne, bio. There were parliamentary reports and reviews of weighty tomes such as *A Century of Municipal Progress in the Last 100 Years* (sic). The magazine was attractive to look at and not especially turgid to read. There was a poke or two at the government, and there were left-leaning articles on education and malnutrition, housing and the like, but although it was published from offices adjoining the Socialist League's in Victoria Street, London, the *Councillor*'s socialism was municipal rather than Marxist.

Barbara moved from lodgings in Taviton Street to a flat in Endsleigh Court in St Pancras, to another at 35 Coram Street in

* The managing director of Odhams Press.

Bloomsbury, a neighbourhood which embodied the renaissance radicalism of the 1930s. All around her were writers, poets, playwrights, actors, painters and students, all caught up in the revolutionary zeitgeist, sharing a dream in which everything would be changed utterly.

'Frustrating, hate-filled though they were, the thirties were un-deniably exhilarating',[42] recalled Leah Manning.* The material world of hunger, depression and fascism would be overthrown by the people; and the hearts and minds of these people would undergo a seismic shift in consciousness. But to a great extent Barbara lived to the side of this common dream. Her consciousness was single-minded and assiduously political; she was, as Michael said of them both, absolutely steeped in politics and political action. The first Surrealist exhibition and the first edition of *New Writing*, which published working-class writers and concerned itself with working-class issues, would probably have been seen as something woolly, flabby, a bourgeois distraction, had it been seen at all.

By 1936 the centre no longer held. Hitler ruled Germany, Mussolini Italy. The Spanish Civil War had begun in July. All heads turned towards the peninsula. The spectre of fascism slouched closer. You were either on one side or the other, at the edges, on the extremes. The harsh Spanish wind would tolerate no bystanding. For the right, Franco was a bulwark against Bolshevism. For the left the Republican cause was a people's war against fascism. Spain 'awoke people to political consciousness who had been indifferent to politics before',[43] sent them scurrying into one camp or the other, mostly to the left and mostly outside the mainstream parties, which were seen as irrelevant at best.

What to do about Spain was unequivocal for the leaguers. They wanted the Labour Party to call for a lifting of the arms embargo, which it was refusing to do, actively supporting the National Government. Conference that year was the last straw for Barbara, Bill and Michael. Official Labour, 'sluggish, wary and bureaucratically pedantic',[44] was all fudge: it decided not to decide on

* Labour MP, activist and educator.

rearmament; and reluctantly agreed to support supplying arms to the Spanish government, but only if it could be proven that the Non-intervention Pact was being violated in the fascists' favour. It was, in the phrase of the day, MacDonaldism without MacDonald.

In the autumn came the Jarrow Crusade, actually only one of many hunger marches over some five years, but the one that became synonymous with 1930s unemployment and poverty. It was led by Ellen Wilkinson, who was Jarrow's MP, and was a protest more against the hated family means test than against chronic unemployment and poverty. The means test was a defilement of human dignity; a 'policy of economic prurience',[45] wherein everything considered non-essential – Mother's brooch, Granny's Sunday Best cake plate – was removed by officers prowling around the family home and sold before any relief was forthcoming. Dwellings were 'stripped bare, down to bed, boards, cooker, table and chairs',[46] and unemployed men were forced to live off their children's earnings if such existed, a situation which, as Nye Bevan observed, ate 'like acid into the homes of the poor', reducing them to 'hells of personal acrimony and wounded vanities'.[47]

The hunger marchers were well named. Those in families of the unemployed were in a condition of what 'experts would call malnutrition [and] you and I would call semi-starvation'.[48] As the league's representative on the Hunger Marchers London Reception Committee, Barbara knew the terrible truth of this. She was enraged that the TUC and segments of the Labour hierarchy condemned the marchers, condemned Red Ellen for dragging ill-clad and ill-fed men from one end of the country to the other, and actually instructed local parties and trades councils along the route not to give them assistance – instructions that were mostly ignored.

The men had their dole docked for the time they were out of Jarrow, on the absurd grounds that they weren't available for work should it have arisen. The usual suspects lined up to condemn the dispossessed for taking to the streets: the bishop of Durham denounced the march as revolutionary mob pressure. And many MPs wanted the drawbridges of London raised and the riffraff kept out because they were organised from Moscow, a reference to the

National Unemployed Workers' Movement (NUWM), which continued to do the job the Labour Party and the unions should have been
doing: helping and organising the unemployed. As they had on
previous occasions, people in their tens of thousands swarmed into
Hyde Park to greet the marchers and in turn be greeted by police
on motorbikes who would ride into the crowd, swinging their trun-
cheons in an attempt to break up the rallies (the National Council
for Civil Liberties had been started two years earlier in good part in
reaction to this).

The Socialist League was now set. The only way forward, the only
way to get the working classes supported at home and abroad, was
to form a united front of working-class parties, to wit, the league,
the ILP and the communists, a coalition which, with indivi-dual
Labour MPs, such as Ellen Wilkinson and Nye Bevan, had already
unofficially formed through the various committees on Spain and
the unemployed. A Popular Front government consisting of socialists of various hues and communists already ran France, and the
wish for such a coalition at home was prompted not just by Spain
or the claims of the unemployed but by the growing threat of
fascism, and another impending world war.

To many socialists, 'the rise of Fascism appeared as a staggeringly
accurate fulfilment of the Marxist prophecy', Michael said,[49] in
which capitalism inevitably gives way to fascism. The leaguers
could not support British rearmament because capitalist countries
could not be trusted with arms. But they were not pacifists; indeed
Barbara took a dim view 'of the pacifist-on-principle [who] puts
individual salvation before any communal responsibility'.[50] It was
simply, as Bill proclaimed, that 'War arises out of capitalism itself'[51]
and the only way to stop such a war happening was for the workers
of the world to unite.

Barbara, writing in the *Socialist Leaguer*, spelt it out: 'Our allegiance as workers ... is to our fellow workers. Our battle is with the
exploiters and never in any circumstances with the workers in
other countries ... War is not a moral lapse on the part of some
country's Government. It is a weapon in the economic struggle
which capitalist governments must wage, or, at its best, an incid-

ental result of that conflict. War resistance, therefore, is part of our constructive fight for Socialism ... Socialist Youth should only be asked to die for Socialist ends and Socialist ends are not served by capitalist wars.'[52]

There was no room in this Marxist analysis for the role of nationalistic passions in war, one of the criticisms levelled by Dalton and others against the league. As Bill, speaking with his usual Cromwellian certainty, put it: 'Our enemy is here'.[53] Guns in the wrongs hands would not defeat fascism. Socialism would. The people should resist war by every means in its power, including a general strike. For the leaguers everything followed from its slogan 'Forward to Socialism!' 'Advance, attack, have courage, translate principles into action',[54] or acquiesce in fascism.

The league was unwavering; it said that the Labour Party should not support the League of Nations, nor rearmament, nor conscription, nor sanctions against Italy when it invaded Abyssinia (now Ethiopia). The last gave Barbara pause, not least because Jimmie, who was working in Africa, informed her that the Africans wanted sanctions applied. But the sanctions the British government eventually imposed were meaningless; they exempted oil. The French prime minister, Pierre Laval, and the British foreign secretary, Samuel Hoare, then signed the now infamous Hoare–Laval Pact which would cede two-thirds of Abyssinia to Italy if Mussolini would stop the war. The war was not stopped: Mussolini's conquest went on, with the aid of poison gas. Barbara felt vindicated. The league's argument that capitalist governments could not make collective security work had been proven.

We were, she said, overwhelmed by a 'sense of helplessness as we saw the governing classes appeasing' the fascists, 'we were all terrified by fascism'.[55] The Labour Party was a long way off offering something lucid and rigorous to put up against fascism or Prime Minister Stanley Baldwin's oligarchy – which 'appeared as the willing abettor of the Fascist counter-revolution'.[56] Barbara was also terrified that fascism would take root in Britain, a home-grown variety, sprouting up in aristocratic gardens. The left feared that the 1935 election might have been the last. There was a belief in 'wide circles of British life that we should all have to fight to retain our liberties' at home,[57] Kingsley Martin, the editor of the *New Statesman*, said. 'People of the governing classes think only of their own fortunes,' Harold Nicolson noted in his diary, 'which means hatred of the Reds. This creates a perfectly artificial but at present most effective secret bond between ourselves and Hitler. Our class interests, on both sides, cut across our national interests.'[58]

A significant segment of the aristocracy held fascist sympathies; not just Mosley and some of the Mitfords or even the so-called 'Cliveden Set' – the appeasers, pro-Germans, crypto fascists, assorted royals and myriad lesser mortals, such as Neville Chamberlain, a man with the 'mind and manner of a clothes-brush',[59] and others besotted by Nazi theology who hovered around the Astors and frequented their country estate at Cliveden. John Jacob Astor held the controlling interest in *The Times*, which echoed and reinforced the views of the ruling class. It was the most quoted newspaper in the world, and under the editorship of Geoffrey Dawson it was quoting the appeasement line, culminating in its 1938 leader urging Czechoslovakia to give up its 'fringe of alien population' to the Nazis.

The influence of the Cliveden set was undoubtedly exaggerated. Appeasement attitudes, and pro-fascist sympathies in the ruling classes were so widespread as to need no organisation, encouragement or gathering place. Harold Nicolson, wandering into his club, found 'three young Peers who state that they would prefer to see Hitler in London than a Socialist administration.'[60] Fascism, dictatorship from above, in which they could share, was infinitely preferable to the upper classes than the dictatorship of the proletariat, in which they could not. Tory MPS publicly confessed to 'admiration for the new spirit' abroad in Hitler's Germany.[61] Emerald, Lady Cunard, a woman 'rather éprise with Herr Ribbentrop',[62] the German ambassador, was thought to have convinced Edward VIII of the virtues of fascism; his princely German relatives may have also played a role, keeping him abreast of the delights of the Reich.

Chips Channon, socialite, dilatory Tory MP and diarist, noted that the King was 'going the dictator way, and is pro-German, against Russia and against too much slip-shod democracy'.[63] It wasn't a lonely journey. Channon's own Bertie Woosterish musings – 'It is very difficult to spend less than £200 a morning when one goes out shopping'[64] – were interspersed with appeasement sympathies, pro-Franco opinions and boyish enthusiasms about his and his chums' various trips to Nazi Germany; his glimpses of the Führer, and his attendance at parties, as he put it, chez Goering and chez Goebbels. 'No one ever accused me of being anti-German,' he said.[65] Nor many others in his milieu.

For five years there had been a National Government. The country was run by a small, unvarying clique. The party system had broken down and, as Nye Bevan said, the only thing to replace a national government of the right was a national government of the left. Barbara had been elected to the Socialist League's Executive Council, its youngest member; Bill was now chairman, and in December 1936 they, with Cripps, were appointed by the league to negotiate with the ILP and the communists to form a Unity Campaign for a United Front of working-class parties to resist war and fascism. The league was now operating as a de facto autonomous party, and it also decided to start its own weekly newspaper which would be aimed at a mass audience.

Such a movement of unity had, in theory, a broad-based appeal. Anti-war sentiment was high. The memory of the carnage endured in the First World War – and the essentially imperialistic causes of that war – lived. A generalised pacifist sentiment prevailed throughout the land. The Oxford Union had passed its opprobious resolution that 'This House will in no circumstance fight for its King and Country' three years earlier, a fact broadcast all over the world as a symbol of British decadence and retreat. This was swiftly followed by the East Fulham by-election in which the Tory candidate advocating rearmament was trounced by Labour's John Wilmot, who accused him of being a warmonger.

In summer 1935 in a peace ballot, over 11 million British people voted ten to one in favour of disarmament and collective security.

Prime Minister Baldwin had not rearmed when he had wanted to, in deference to the public's anti-war mood, he told the Commons in 1936; by then the Peace Pledge Union – started two years earlier as an appeal from a curate for postcards renouncing war – had a hundred thousand members, including Bill's wife. A political anti-fascist intelligentsia was forming around the Left Book Club, founded by Victor Gollancz, which soon had 50,000 subscribers, ten times more than the original estimate. If Britain was not ready to adopt an anti-fascist, anti-war government now, it never would be.

The Unity Campaign negotiations were anything but. The communists and the ILP were more natural enemies than collaborators. Some of the negotiations took place in Barbara's flat over plates of the bangers and mash she cooked in her 'pocket-handkerchief kitchenette'.[66] Other meetings were less homey. Many were held at Cripps's spartan chambers in Middle Temple; most were on the edge of breaking down. The ILP were incensed by the 'knowledge of what many good Socialists (and good Communists) had suffered at Communist hands' in the show trials and elsewhere.[67] Many league members felt similar anti-communist sentiments and a suspicion that the communists wanted to destroy the league. (The idea for a United Front had originally come from the CPGB; it had been Comintern policy since 1933.) Harry Pollitt, the CPGB leader, seduced the Red Squire with his working-class ways. But not so Bill. 'Mellor was the most decisive personality to set against Pollitt,' the ILP's Fenner Brockway noted.[68] Bill was as capable of using Pollitt as Pollitt was of using him.

The Labour Party saw the negotiations for a United Front as entryism by the communists, who had been trying to affiliate with the Labour Party nationally since 1920. When turned away they had attempted to infiltrate and take over constituency parties, successfully sometimes: twenty-three local parties were disaffiliated by Labour because of communist entryism. The Labour Party bosses were outraged. Here was the Socialist League trying to bring the communists in through the front door. Association with the CPGB was an electoral liability for Labour – the Moscow show trials had 'caused a deep revulsion' in the populace.[69] The big unions took the same view. Vic Feather, who had gone to work with Walter Citrine at the TUC, watched as Barbara and the other 'intellectuals' allowed the CPGB to make 'capital out of the United Front activities';[70] Feather set himself unambiguously against any and all communist infiltration and became the TUC's most ruthless communist-finder-general over the next twenty years.

But despite the mutual suspicion and dislike of the parties involved – and official Labour opposition – an agreement of aims was arrived at and the Unity Campaign was launched in January 1937. It began in Manchester, at the Free Trade Hall, the Princess Theatre and the Theatre Royal, all on the same night. Thousands of people signed the pledge cards for working-class unity. Nye Bevan, who had not originally joined the league for reasons both personal (Frank Wise was his rival for Jennie Lee's affections) and political (a brief flirtation with pre-fascist Oswald Mosley's New Party had made him temporarily cautious), was a signatory to the campaign, as was Ellen Wilkinson. *Tribune*, the Socialist League's lasting legacy, was launched too, with Cripps and George Strauss's* £20,000, to propagandise for unity and for arms for Spain.

* Left-wing Labour MP for North Lambeth.

Chapter Three

HOPE AND HISTORY

New Year's Day 1937 was a balmy 54 degrees. At the Old Vic Laurence Olivier was playing Hamlet in a four-hour-plus production; the panto season continued at the Palladium with Elsa Lanchester and Charles Laughton in *Peter Pan*. The *Daily Mirror* worried that Russian Amazons engaged in men's work would upset the balance of nature, as 'at heart women are happiest as homemakers'.[1] On the screen Katharine Hepburn starred in *A Woman Rebels* and Errol Flynn led *The Charge of the Light Brigade*. In the *Tribune* offices, Bill Mellor, the editor, had put the first copy of 'Cripps's Chronicle', as the newsboys soon dubbed it, to bed.

The industrial affairs column was called 'Judex', after the 'Mellor and Cole Board' column in the *Herald* twenty years earlier. Bill gave it to Barbara and Michael to write, and they soon fell into a pattern of putting it together in her flat on Monday or Tuesday evenings. Michael also worked in the *Tribune* offices, as a general dogsbody, laying out the paper at some times, acting as courier at others. Barbara wrote feature articles and had her own column, 'Barbara Betts Says', and, like Michael, she reviewed books. (She had also taken over the day-to-day running of the *Councillor* from Bill, who no longer had the time.) Nye Bevan wrote the *Tribune*'s parliamentary sketch, and was on the editorial board with Ellen Wilkinson, Cripps, George Strauss, Harold Laski and H. N. Brailsford.

Cripps was pleased with the first copy of the *Tribune* and sent Bill a letter telling him he had read every line of it, including the ads (Eno's Fruit Salts, arthritis cures, books on married love and enduring passion, and the Co-op Bank). Congratulations were in order; it was a 'very first rate production', Cripps wrote. But. There was always a but with Stafford. His 'main criticism' was of the 'comparative weakness' in the non-political part of the paper. However, 'these things will develop', he assured Bill.[2] The letter is cordial enough, Cripps respected Bill's ability, though they clashed in good measure because Bill was no respecter of persons, not even one as eminent as the Red Squire. The two men were polar opposites. Bill, with his volcanic energy, his loquaciousness, was intense, a man of voracious appetites; he had nothing in common with the teetotal vegetarian, dryly arrogant and parsimonious lawyer.

Their relationship wasn't furthered by Bill's profligate ways. He had always been 'casual in his accounting', tending to leave 'unidentified piles of small change lying about'[3] and he had, as Michael put it, the 'convenient and attractive compromise between Roundhead principles and Cavalier tastes ... and as often as he could afford it, he ate like a gourmet, generously insisting on paying the bill, even if he had to use his last bean for the purpose'.[4] Or Cripps's last bean: Cripps 'laid great stress on financial probity';[5] Bill did not. He 'was capable of spending the huge sum of ten pounds of the *Tribune*'s money – which, of course, was Cripps's money – on lunch', often for Barbara, Michael and himself. One of the trio's favourite hangouts was Simpson's in the Strand, a haunt of the haute bourgeoisie.

Bill and Nye Bevan didn't get on either. Their presence in the same offices at least 'marked one minor victory for unity', Michael said dryly: their ideas meshed – both were Marxists with profound doubts about the Labour leadership – but 'their mental processes jarred'. Nye was one of the few people unafraid of Bill's wrath and was 'always ready to bait the endearing ogre', coming late to meetings, ignoring the agenda, entertaining the troops with his shambolic rhetorical virtuosity, his wild theoretical flights of fancy which would leave Bill, who had 'no patience with these dazzling performances', growling 'his resentment for hours afterwards'.

Bill thought Nye lax, intellectually decadent, and Nye thought Bill too 'fastidious' by far.[6]

Nye, at 40, was almost ten years younger than Bill and thirteen years older than Barbara. He'd been in parliament since 1929 and had become the voice of the unemployed, clear, angry, sometimes splenetic, but always on the side of the downtrodden, those who had sent this miner's son from South Wales to Westminster. He was an extraordinary speaker, probably the best in Labour Party history. Articulate, funny, cutting and fearless, he specialised in the ingenious apposite metaphor. He didn't care whom he offended; he was utterly disenthralled. Brendan Bracken, Tory MP, one-time editor of the *Financial Times*, dubbed him a 'Bollinger Bolshevik' for his love of the high life, sumptuous dinners at the Savoy and parties with West End swells at Lord Beaverbrook's house at Hyde Park; none of which turned his head, changed his mind, or tempered his speech.

Over the years Barbara became very ambivalent about Nye, but he always represented something to her: integrity, a largeness of vision; he had a grip of socialism as a state of grace, as Frank had, as Bill had, as she had. For them, as Bill would have put it, spiritual well-being preceded economic well-being. Nye was 'a political poet', Barbara said. Not that he always lived up to it – he often didn't – but he reached for it. He was someone she could walk beside. He followed Frank and Bill in completing her political education, he was the last of her big three influences, the men who, she said, ran like '*a golden thread through my political life*'.[7]

Nye had married Jennie Lee the year after Frank Wise died and he was in love with her, but she wasn't in love with him. She was fond of Nye, but Wise had been the great love of her life and remained so. Nye was her companion, her friend, a man who would leave her to pursue her own life, who would not try to domesticate her. It was enough, or at least she was willing to settle for it. They lived close to Barbara's Coram Street flat, but they didn't socialise that much, certainly not as a foursome. Nye and Bill were at odds and Barbara and Jennie were competitors, in their careers, their place in the movement, their clothes, their looks. There was not an area left unchallenged.

Throughout their lives, the women were often in political concordance but they did not like each other. Barbara was better looking, more glamorous, six years younger and much cleverer than Jennie; and a much better political operator. Jennie was a great flouncer-out. She did not have Barbara's staying power, her killer instinct, her ambition. Jennie lacked the necessary steel and astuteness. She wouldn't play the game. 'Barbara as well as being dominating could be very good in a committee but Jennie could only be dominating', observed Richard Clements*.[8] Barbara was willing to play on a team when necessary, to do the work and stay the course. And she was much more likely to win her point, or her job, or whatever she wanted, something that Jennie resented.

Perhaps Jennie sensed and resented Nye's attraction to Barbara as well. Despite his love for Jennie, he was fond of what he called 'physical conversations'. He was not subtle. One morning when Barbara went over to their flat to talk to him she found him 'alone and listening, enrapt, to Beethoven's "Eroica" symphony, a bottle of wine half drunk on the table in front of him'. After a few perfunctory minutes he made a lunge at her. She 'disentangled herself with some difficulty and much embarrassment' and fled, to the sounds of Nye bellowing that she 'was a prissy provincial miss'.[9]

The first three weeks of 1937 were intensely exciting for Barbara. As well as putting out the *Tribune*, she, Bill, Michael, Cripps, Nye and others were careering from one end of the country to the other speaking at Unity meetings: Hull, Birmingham, Plymouth, Bristol, Manchester, Wales, Scotland, Norwich, Leeds, Wigan. There was not a big town, city or region left untouched. The line-up of speakers was impressive. Jimmie Maxton or Fenner Brockway, say, for the ILP, Harry Pollitt for the CPGB, with Nye Bevan or Ellen Wilkinson, Cripps and/ or Bill, and the young rising stars Barbara and Michael for the Socialist League.

As an affiliated socialist group within the Labour Party, the league

---

* Editor of the *Tribune* for twenty-two years and Michael Foot's political adviser when Foot was Party leader.

was openly flouting the party's 1936 conference resolution which rejected unity with communist parties. To the league this was irrelevant. They were doing what had to be done. They were operating in a state of emergency. They were trying to unite the working class against war and fascism. Official Labour was wilfully deaf to the 'mighty tide of emotion and anger and exhilaration [that] was swelling in the distressed areas, on the hunger marches, at the United demonstrations, at the universities, in the Left Book Clubs, in literature, in the very spirit of the age', Michael wrote. The league embodied this spirit of the anti-fascist socialist future, which 'seemed to penetrate almost everywhere only to lap in vain against the locked doors of Transport House'.[10]

Transport House now affixed a deadbolt and bars. The party moved abruptly. The league was disaffiliated on 27 January, an event accompanied by blizzards. In March, the party decreed membership of the league incompatible with membership of the party and gave league members until June to quit one or the other. At their Whitsun conference the league argued about what to do. Cripps wanted to fold up the tent. Bill argued strongly that it was important a coherent socialist group remain within the party. Coherent it might be but it could not be called the Socialist League and remain within the party, as Barbara pointed out: among 'those who supported the League's suicide was Miss Barbara Betts who declared that the dissolution was "not a funeral but a conscious political tactic" '.[11] After all, she argued, they could, as individuals, still continue the campaign for Unity. The Socialist League dissolved itself and, at a conference in Hull the following month, the Labour Unity Committee was formed, consisting of many ex-members of the league and their pro-Unity Labour Party friends.

For official Labour, the league and all its works had been, in Dalton's words, 'a piece of clotted nonsense . . . a most exasperating diversion of the Party's mind and energies'.[12] But the league had succeeded in its own terms in one important respect: it got the 1932 party conference to accept its resolution that the next Labour government, whether a majority government or otherwise, must immediately enact legislation committing the party to 'full and rapid Socialist economic planning, under central direction',[13] a commitment that survived through manifesto after manifesto to be enacted in good part by the postwar Labour government.

There were other successes, too: the Constituency Party Association, which was backed by the league, and of which Cripps was a member, had succeeded in getting the party to accept that seven members of the National Executive Council (NEC) would be voted in by the constituency parties alone; hitherto the whole of the NEC had been appointed by union block votes. Individual membership in the party had doubled since 1928 and Dalton had hoped that extension of their franchise would satisfy the constituencies' left-wing tendency to 'side with bodies like the ILP or the Socialist League'.[14] He couldn't have been more wrong. Cripps, Harold Laski and D. N. Pritt, three pro-Unity left-wingers, were immediately elected, an omen of what was to come. The party in the country is always to the left of the party at Westminster. The seven-seat constituency section became the focus of left-wing dissent; most notably, the power base of the Bevanites in the 1950s, of which Barbara was a leading member.

The urgency of bringing about a unity of working-class parties was made more so by the noises emanating from Gollancz's Left Book Club; Gollancz and his supporters were trying to drum up enthusiasm for a Popular Front, which would include progressive Tories, Liberals, Labourites, communists, socialists – anyone who wanted to bring about an anti-fascist, capitalism-with-a-human-face government. This was anathema to Barbara. Socialists could not make common cause with capitalists. The campaign for Unity continued its frantic pace. Barbara addressed a communist women's conference on Unity in Manchester in June and became part of the Great Open Air Campaign in July. One 'excellent meeting addressed by Barbara Betts' in Brighton managed to collect 28 shillings.[15] Bill in Ammanford, Michael in Abertillery and Cripps in Oldham also managed to raise a few shillings and more hackles.

The party now forbade its members to speak on any platform with a communist or else face expulsion; as a punishment for his Unity activities, Bill was blocked by the NEC from standing as the

Labour candidate for Stockport. At the 1937 party conference the concept of a United Front was once again rejected. The 'word of Ernest Bevin ... mistaken ofttimes for the word of God' had prevailed, Bill wrote.[16] The Labour Unity Committee would have to go the same way as the Socialist League.

But by the summer the fizz was hissing out of the Unity bottle; such public interest in Unity as there had been dribbled away on news of yet more of Stalin's show trials. News from Spain, too, was less than unifying. The communists were attacking the Partido Obrero de Unificación Marxista (the Workers' Marxist Unification Party), which the ILP supported, as Marxist critics of Stalin; POUM were called anarchists or Trotskyists, depending on who was doing the calling. Not that it mattered. One way or another they were done for: the 'cleaning up of Trotskyists and Anarchists has begun' in Spain, *Pravda* reported, 'and it will be carried out with the same energy as in the USSR'.[17]

Jennie Lee and George Orwell were both in Spain and witnessed some of this cleaning up. Orwell, an ILP member who fought in the Spanish Civil War, ended up fighting to defend the POUM offices against their communist brethren. The *New Statesman* refused his report on the violence, and the Left Book Club refused to publish *Homage to Catalonia*, his book on the subject. Orwell had unveiled what Michael Foot called 'the inconvenient horror' that communists and the communist state could indulge in acts of murder and grotesque inhumanity.

With very few exceptions, the left in Britain had taken a collective decision to ignore or explain away the inconvenient horror of the show trials. The Russian revolution, and the promise of that revolution, had to be protected at almost all costs. And, moreover, the Soviet state was seen by the left as *the* bulwark against fascism. This was very much *Tribune*'s line. All papers have their 'Achilles' heels, their blind spots', Michael wrote twenty-one years later. 'Ours was the Russian trials. We said nothing or next to nothing on the subject ... lamentably failing to assist H. N. Brailsford in *Reynolds News* as he stripped aside the curtain of lies and saved the honour of Socialist journalism in face of the inconvenient horror.'[18] Saying nothing or next to nothing would have been preferable. The *Tribune* actively engaged in 'praising Stalin [and] denouncing Trotsky'.[19] As Bill wrote, in a signed editorial in November 1937, his attitude to the Russian trials and towards Trotsky was the same as the Webbs' in the postscript to the second edition of their book *Soviet Communism: A New Civilisation*, published by the Left Book Club, minus the question mark the first edition had borne.

The Webbs' long tortuous apologia for the show trials made comparisons with England after the civil war, France after the revolution and anywhere else that would back up their many-wrongs-make-a-right stance that such things are inevitable after revolution. The show trials, which they said were anyway in the business of trying true counter-revolutionaries, had to be expected and accepted. In her diary Beatrice confessed to 'an uneasiness ... [about] the continuance of the conspiracy trials and executions ...There is always the lurking suspicion that Stalin and his clique *may* have lost their heads!' Nevertheless, despite such doubts, she continued, as she ruefully admitted, to explain the trials away 'so plausibly to others'.[20]

The honour of socialist journalism was not saved by Barbara, either. In Autumn 1937, this 'keen young socialist with an independent mind'[21] was sent off to the Soviet Union to report on the condition of women and children for the *Tribune* and she did not deviate from the paper's line. The seven-part series, entitled 'Women in Russia', was pegged to the twentieth anniversary of the Bolshevik Revolution and the *Tribune* promised a Soviet Union seen 'through the eyes of someone free from rigidity'. Most of Barbara's *Tribune* pieces before and after her Russian series were criticisms, critiques, polemics against the state of education or the conditions of grinding poverty in Britain, which makes the tone of the Russian articles, one long paean to Soviet society, even more extraordinary. She could find nothing wrong anywhere and even if what she did find was not what it should be, it was better than it had been and was in the process of being made better still.

Barbara noted with pleasure that in the USSR women 'are everywhere', working as bricklayers, or tram drivers, or running government departments, that the 'women of the U.S.S.R. to-day don't cringe to anyone' as they had had to in the past. But there was the vexed question of Stalin's anti-abortion law, which came into effect in 1936, sixteen years after Soviet women had first got abortion legalised. 'Under Stalin ... family life is safeguarded,' she wrote, 'but in a different form from that to which we are accustomed.' Yes Stalin made abortion illegal, but the state also went after fathers who did not support their children; she argued that both of these things were to 'encourage the women to have children – not for cannon fodder, as in Fascist countries, but for factory workers'.[22]

Even the Webbs admitted that during the consultation period before abortion was outlawed, 'the opinion of the women (though not that of the men) seemed to be preponderatingly in favour of free abortion whenever desired'.[23] But to Barbara the fact that the birthrate in the Soviet Union was rising was 'proof, in my opinion that Soviet women are bearing children because they are happy and because they are secure'. No one but a 'Bloomsbury romantic' would suggest it was because abortion was illegal, because 'more than one person assured me that birth control instruction is given freely in the clinics' (something disputed in the letters columns of the *Tribune*). Women were having more children because of 'increasing material prosperity'. Moreover, 'there is justification for saying that, now facilities for ensuring a healthy motherhood are available to all women, a dangerous operation like abortion is better dispensed with'. The illegality of abortion was, Barbara concluded, part of 'the war on irresponsibility which must come when the chaotic period of a revolution ends' and was therefore acceptable, necessary and desirable.

When greeted with unmistakable signs of poverty and shortages, such as in Leningrad, where it was 'difficult to escape from the rarefied atmosphere of a people still in struggle', of ill-lit streets, dilapidated houses and half-empty shops, Barbara found examples that showed, 'despite superficial appearances', Russians having a better time than Westerners. The Park of Culture and Rest in Moscow had 'Blackpool and Coney Island beaten' and it wasn't as sleazy. 'Many a short-sighted visitor to Russia has been shocked by external evidences of poverty', Barbara wrote. 'But the Russians don't get alarmed ... they enjoy what capitalism can't offer its workers: security to-day, hope of abundance to-morrow.'

Like Sidney and Beatrice Webb before her, she seems to have found the 'combination of bureaucratic centralism with fanatical zeal' a highly attractive fusion.[24] She was impressed with the 'terrific drive to raise the standard of life by ever-increasing production [that] dominates all Russian life ... Here is no shadow of slump and unemployment – only an insatiable demand for more and yet more workers.'This production drive, she asserted,'explains the Stakhanov movement;* throws light on the Trotskyist trials; is the key to the anti-abortion law and the role of women'.

How the show trials were a derivative of the production drive was never explained. Although she wrote that she was 'warned' by 'the editor' not 'to engage in the Trotsky v. Stalin controversy', it permeates every page. She wrote, approvingly, of children being constantly reminded that they 'owe their happiness to Soviet rule'. But it was more than that:'At every turn they are warned of dangers from secret enemies.And such dangers do not seem unreal.Was not Kirov, one of the most genuinely beloved of their leaders, assassinated by such enemies?'

It was a provocative remark. Sergey Kirov had been Stalin's protégé, then rival. He was murdered, on Stalin's secret orders, in December 1934, an event that Stalin used to kick-start the show trials, which he claimed were to deliver the USSR from the vast Trotskyist conspiracy seeking to destroy the revolution.All kinds of people were implicated directly or indirectly in Kirov's murder. Over a hundred White Guards languishing in gaol at the time were taken out and shot. Stalin's political rivals went through various 'trials' and were executed for being part of the conspiracy to kill Kirov and/or Stalin on Leon Trotsky's orders (Trotsky had exiled himself in Mexico and was murdered in 1940).

The three big show trials for Kirov's murder, which began in summer 1936, wiped out the leadership of any potential opposition; thousands of prominent Bolsheviks disappeared between 1936 and 1938, including the people's commissioner for education,

---

*The Stakhanovites were worker heroes who achieved exceptional production.

Andrey Bubnov, one of the most prominent of the old Bolsheviks, who was removed as Barbara travelled home on the train clutching her bust of Stalin and a copy of the Soviet constitution.

Barbara's position in the polarised conditions of the late 1930s is comprehensible if not commendable, yet even sixty and seventy years later she still dissembled. In her autobiography she dismissed her Soviet articles as the products of journalistic naivety, of listening too much to the Intourist guide, of failing to write about what her unofficial contacts told her. Bizarrely, in a television programme broadcast in spring 2000, she defended her reporting on the upbeat mood of the people and insisted that there was no atmosphere of repression in Moscow. The articles, she claimed, were not too bad after all.*

In another account, via Michael Foot, Barbara's embarrassment was duly noted and her errors explained away because she 'was young and equipped with little background knowledge'.[25] She was 27 and had more background knowledge than most. Barbara wrote that she was curious to know what Bubnov had done to be removed from his post.† And she most certainly did not know everything about what was going on, but she did know details of the trials which were in the public domain: the sheer implausibility, the absurdities of both the accusations levelled by the Soviet State and the confessions of the accused were written about extensively in the West. Socialists were, for good reason, disinclined to believe much of what they read in the capitalist press about Russia, but Barbara, a member of the Socialist League's council, discussed the trials with her comrades in the League, in Unity and the *Tribune*, the cream of British Marxism, who, like many, but not all, on the left, decided to ignore, or actively justify, the inconvenient horror of what was happening in the Soviet Union.

Barbara had become quite well known through her activities in the Unity campaign and in November 1937, shortly after she returned

* *Tourists of the Revolution*, BBC2.
† He later died in prison.

from Russia, she was elected to the St Pancras Borough Council. She approached her job as councillor as she would all future political appointments, with high seriousness and feverish activity. Most councillors found serving on two committees quite sufficient. Committee work, if not always boring, is certainly time-consuming. In her first year Barbara sat on four main committees: Finance; Highways, Sewers and Public Works; Estates; and Contracts and Stores. Her male colleagues made the mistake of trying to co-opt her onto the Maternity and Child Welfare committee; she told them crossly that she hadn't got any children and knew nothing about child welfare. Although she often wrote about women's issues for the *Tribune*, she was not going to allow herself to be, as she said, 'enclosed in the antechambers of power'.[26]

Barbara already knew much of how local government worked – and didn't – from the pages of the *Councillor*, which she continued to produce. The polemicist had a deeply practical side. She really was interested in sewers, in the nitty-gritty of how things worked and how to get things done. She enjoyed poring over tenders for 'the removal and disinfestation of furniture and effects of tenants rehoused on the estates of the council'[27] and other exotic paraphernalia of council life. She had developed what became a lifelong interest in food production, which took her from St Pancras's co-delegate to the London regional conference of councils set up 'to encourage and facilitate allotments' to the Agriculture Committee of the EC nearly fifty years on.

The cultivation of allotments was part of the war preparations that went on in fits of panic and starts of chaos. The government had issued a booklet on war-preparedness as far back as 1935 but in St Pancras, as elsewhere, shelters were non-existent and or inadequate. The Special Air Raid Precautions (ARP) Committee, on which Barbara sat, set up a technical subcommittee, of which she was also a member; they ordered trenches dug in Regent's Park and had them lined with concrete, only to fill them back in again when the immediate danger had seemingly evaporated.

The ARP Committee searched for suitable basements to remodel into public shelters, for which the council was supposed to meet much of the cost. Converting commercial basements into public air-raid shelters ran into thousands and thousands of pounds. Barbara moved that the government be sent a message that it was its duty to meet the whole cost of the ARP measures. As the *Councillor* reported, many councils were in revolt over the crippling costs of civilian defence.

There were over 170,000 gas masks to be allocated to St Pancras's population of almost 180,000; alarmingly, none had been ordered for children aged 4 and under. (In the beginning there were no gas masks anywhere for babies.) The communists, who had supported the Labour candidates in the election, joined in badgering the Tory-controlled council. Where were the children's gas masks? Where were the deep shelters? Barbara was inundated with Home Office paperwork: procedures for dealing with civilian deaths due to 'war operations'. The dead had to be kept track of; they were to be buried in mass graves. There were procedures for evacuating children, as 'morale would be adversely affected if children were killed in large groups':[28] procedures for the unthinkable.

The Home Office chivvied the council over the lack of first-aid stations; this must receive urgent attention. Barbara was put on another special subcommittee to see that it did. There was a special Joint Welfare Committee for Manual Workers on which Barbara also sat and from where she was nominated to attend the trade unionists' conference in London 'to discuss ARP in relation to the Civil population' of London.[29]

Barbara, in a foretaste of what was to come in her ministerial career, became consumed by her work at the council. But she never lost sight of party politics. She needed to become a prospective parliamentary candidate for somewhere, and a bigger platform might help. She tried to get onto the London Labour Party Executive, being nominated first in 1938; she failed, and she stood in each subsequent election till she at last climbed aboard in 1944. She impressed Herbert Morrison,* 'the prime minister of London', as the first Labour leader of the first Labour-controlled London

---

* Morrison became home secretary in the wartime coalition government.

County Council (LCC) was tagged; he appointed Barbara to the Metropolitan Water Board in 1940, even though he was very much a gradualist member of official Labour, and she was very much not. (Shirley Williams once remarked that Morrison was one of the few men of that generation who would actively help women. He later helped her, but she was more to his political taste.)

Despite all the committee work and the journalism, Barbara seldom missed a general council meeting. In the new town hall, which had recently been built opposite St Pancras station, the enemy was in her sights. The town hall occasion is not quite the parliamentary occasion, but it's not a bad training in point-scoring and verbal jousting. She had a gift for the collar-grabbing phrase and she used it well. When the Tory mayor, yet again, called her 'the charming young lady', she was ready, wondering whether the question of 'sex attraction or no sex attraction' could be left out of council meetings. The forbidden word 'sex' guaranteed a headline, especially from such a red beauty. She made the national papers; she and her photo were a front-page story: 'The girl who refuses to be flattered!'[30] Bill was not amused. She'd gone for a cheap shot; it made politics trivial, he complained.

Bill was beset by problems. Cripps, having failed with a United Front, decided, along with Nye Bevan, Ellen Wilkinson and George Strauss, that a Popular Front against fascism was the only hope of ousting the Chamberlain government. This was unacceptable to Bill, who tried to explain why to Cripps. Cripps was 'obviously lost when ... Mellor put the Marxist case against the Popular Front', Brockway noted,[31] but Cripps's motives were mixed. The *Tribune* was leeching money as usual and Cripps wanted to mesh it with Gollancz's Left Book Club and its publication, *Left News*, to infuse it with more cash. As Bill was opposed to the Popular Front 'Gollancz advised (or demanded)' that he be ousted from the editor's chair. 'Cripps agreed without reluctance', firing Bill 'in a brusque manner which left many hard feelings'.[32] (The Labour Party did not take to the Popular Front, either, and expelled Bevan, Cripps and Strauss a year later; they were readmitted after a decent interval.)

Cripps asked Michael to take over the editorship of the *Tribune*, an attractive offer for a 25-year-old with just over two years' journalistic experience. But, tempted as he may have been, Michael agreed with Bill on the United v. Popular Front issue, and moreover he felt that Bill had been treated shabbily. He did the right thing and turned it down out of loyalty to a friend; he subsequently resigned from the *Tribune* and went to work for Lord Beaverbrook at the London *Evening Standard*.

More was to come. Town & County Councillor Publications was ailing and Cripps and his wife, Isobel, lent the company £2500 in the form of preferred shares, with Isobel owning 2000 of those shares. Bill now held only 250 ordinary shares. Barbara somehow managed to get £50 together to buy 50 shares of her own but the Crippses had taken over the company, leaving Bill in a humiliating position. He was profoundly despondent and went away on his own, hitching a ride on a banana boat.

He was 50, he had an 8-year-old son, a wife and an ongoing love affair with a woman little more than half his age. He had always walked where his conscience led him, and it had landed him in gaol, got him thrown out of the editor's chair of the *Daily Herald*, lost him two elections and a candidacy, lost him the editorship of the *Tribune* and forbade him to work for Beaverbrook and the other capitalist press barons. He was out of work and down on his luck; his ulcers bothered him and war approached: the slaughter of the working classes that he had predicted, feared and failed to prevent was about to occur. He knew he had to change his life, moderate it perhaps, compromise perhaps. He knew he had to do something.

Michael and Barbara went away, too, arriving in Veules-les-Roses, France, during Munich week, a holiday made famous by Michael's suggestive stories about it. They were given adjoining rooms and the *patronne* with a knowing smirk unlocked the connecting door. In the middle of the night Michael suffered an asthma attack, awakening Barbara, who ran to his assistance. Michael dined out on this holiday for years, telling party conferences, much to Barbara's irritation, that more than an asthma attack had happened that night.

Barbara often complained that she never understood why Michael said that.

Although he was deeply smitten with Barbara, Michael sometimes found her a trial. All through their holiday 'she never stopped talking, arguing, lecturing and delivering tirades against Hitler, Chamberlain and sometimes Stafford Cripps', a frazzled Michael reported.[33] What he found intriguing in small morsels turned out to be wearisome in one large scoop. They came back to Britain the day Chamberlain came back from Germany and announced 'peace in our time'. Michael liked to say that he turned to Barbara and said, 'I hope that goes for us, too.' Not that that stopped him trying to teach her to drive, something that perhaps nobody would attempt unless they were very fond of her. It was a terrifying and unsuccessful experience for all concerned, even by her own account, and Barbara, who later became Britain's first woman minister of transport, never did learn to master a motor vehicle.

'How horrible, fantastic, incredible, it is that we should be digging trenches and trying on gas masks here because of a quarrel in a far away country between people of whom we know nothing', Chamberlain had remarked, shortly before flying off to Munich to hand over Czechoslovakia to the Nazis. As the left in Britain had long urged, Britain had entered into tripartite talks with France and the Soviet Union – at the latter's request – to form an alliance against Germany.

But the Chamberlain government, still hoping that Hitler could be placated, and reluctant to deal with the Bolsheviks, 'decided not to embrace the Russian bear, but to hold out a hand and accept its paw gingerly'.[34] There was, as Churchill wrote, a 'long silence while half-measures and judicious compromises were being prepared'.[35] Simultaneously, the Soviets began to negotiate an alliance with Germany. The two countries signed a non-aggression pact in August 1939, which was a 'horrible thought for the friends of the Soviet Union',[36] Beatrice Webb, echoing Barbara's thoughts, wrote, a complete reversal of Soviet foreign policy. After the initial shock Barbara changed her mind, concurring with Nye, Michael and, for that matter, Churchill: Russia was simply looking after its own safety and its actions were prompted not a little by perfidious Albion, even though Soviet calumny was made worse by its subsequent invasion of Finland.

Ten days after the Nazi–Soviet Pact was signed, Germany invaded Poland and on the following Sunday, 3 September 1939, a glorious late summer's day, at quarter past eleven in the morning, Chamberlain came on the wireless to announce what had been true for fifteen minutes: Britain was at war with Germany. In London church bells rang out; at 11.27 they were smothered by the banshee wailing of air-raid sirens. People ran about the streets, trying to force themselves into buildings, dashing into hospitals; others stood immobilised staring at the sky, or dropped into their Anderson shelters or headed for the Underground. After a time the All Clear sounded. It was the first phony alert of what became known as the 'phony war'.

During that August and September, more people married than ever had in any equivalent period. Marriage was on Barbara's mind, too. Bill was still out of a job 'and deeply dispirited, so the last thing I wanted was for him to press for a divorce', she wrote.[37] Some seven years they had been together, and divorce was as remote as ever. Their relationship was an open secret, but she wanted more, a legitimacy. She would be 29 in October and she felt the clock ticking. The war added urgency: they could both be killed. Bill was too old for active service but there were always the bombs.

Barbara was utterly terrified by the prospect of aerial bombing. She, too, had heard the experts declare that Hitler would begin bombing Britain immediately and continue for sixty days and that 600,000 people would be killed. Barbara and Bill had already become ARP wardens, she in Brunswick Square, he on Primrose Hill, part of the citizens' army which was to include the Home Guard and the Observer Corps, the auxiliary police and firefighters, ambulance drivers, stretcher bearers and first-aid workers.

Despite expectations of immediate bombardment, the phony war continued for months. All was tedious anti-climax. The government had ordered places of mass entertainment closed, including all theatres and cinemas, 'a masterstroke of unimaginative stupidity', as George Bernard Shaw said. Only the pubs remained open in the blacked-out city and 'several million people [were subjected] to black boredom'[38] until Herbert Morrison helped get the cinemas reopened. Some people, more seriously, were subject to 'blackout blues' and committed suicide. The theatres and dance halls reopened in the New Year, with the Home Office proviso – often ignored – that no more than two hundred people at a time be gathered together. There was an insatiable hunger for entertainment, from Myra Hess's lunchtime piano concerts at the empty National Gallery (the art having been removed to an underground bunker in a disused quarry in Wales) to jitterbugging at the big public dance halls. From Hess the public got what they'd 'all been waiting for – an assertion of eternal values';[39] from the jitterbug, the relief of frenzied activity to assuage the tension and boredom of waiting for something to happen.

It was surreal. Life was normal and yet not. Buses ran, trains ran, people went to work. Barbara continued to freelance for *Picture Post* and various trade papers. She continued with her council work. Now on the Library Committee as well, she was delighted to report an all-round increase in book-borrowing (Trollope's mid-Victorian croquet lawns and country houses provided a soothing balm later during the Blitz). Barbara proposed that libraries be opened in the evening 'for purposes of literary discussion and collective study'.[40] She rowed with the Tory majority in St Pancras, especially over its tendency to use the war as a pretext for undemocratic practices. She spoke about this to a Fabian weekend conference on 'The Labour Party in Wartime'. She kept herself busy.

By the end of June 1940, Norway, Denmark, the Low Countries and France had fallen to the Nazis. The Germans were now twenty-two miles away on the other side of the Channel. Britain was alone. Let us ready ourselves, Churchill said, so it will be said that 'this was their finest hour'. The forces were on red alert, if not ready. The Home Guard, awaiting rifles, practised their manoeuvres with broomsticks. The war came home in July: the Battle of Britain. In the skies above south-east England the defence of the realm was often in the hands of boys, many of whom had only been amateur fliers before the war. It was reported like a sporting fixture: England 78, Germany 26; England still batting. A summer's worth of dogfights.

In August, the bombs began to fall on Newcastle, Yorkshire, south London, central London, Ramsgate. On 7 September, codeword 'Cromwell' was uttered: invasion imminent. At about four o'clock in the afternoon, hundreds of German planes flying in tight formation filled the skies above London. The Blitz had begun. Much of the East End and Thameside was destroyed: Stepney, West Ham, Bermondsey, Whitechapel and Poplar lit up the city. The bombardment continued without respite for the next twelve hours. For the following two months, every night bar one, London was blitzed. Barbara's feared personal Guernica was here.

The lack of sleep got to her, as it did to everybody; ditto the filth and the privations; the noise of the bombardment was nerve-jangling. A bomb had ripped out the gas main near Coram Street, so Barbara had no gas to cook with or to heat water. The street had a ghostly air, one increasingly common in parts of London; half-bombed-out buildings had been deserted; many people who could left the city. She was alone in her building, rattling around in her cold, dirty flat.

She learnt to cope with the physical discomforts and even with her fear. She found she could make do without good food, even much food, but when clothes-rationing came in in 1941 she was distraught. She had nothing to wear. There wasn't a thing she didn't need. Her wardrobe was bare; the few clothes she had were shabby. Her femininity was at stake. The importance of her appearance, her public face, was overwhelming. The lipstick in the air raid, the hair styled under the ARP tin hat, picking through the rubble in her well-pressed uniform. It was part of, but far beyond, the social mores of looking neat and tidy, of smartness as a visual form of manners, of owing it to others and later the public to look her best; it was part of, but far beyond, too, the vanity of a good-looking woman who likes to be admired. It was an obsession which, if anything, grew more all-encompassing with age.

Although many women had taken over men's jobs since the beginning of the war, they weren't officially mobilised until 1941. Barbara, given the choice between the services and the civil service, chose the latter. She did not want to be in an all-female environment as she had been at St Hugh's. Her dislike of such propinquity was rawly physical: 'I don't mind sleeping with men, but I will not sleep with women', she shuddered.[41] Moreover, a civil servant's job was a useful background for a would-be MP. She was assigned to the Fish Division of the Ministry of Food.

The Ministry of Food had been set up to manage food-rationing, and part of its function was continually to design and redesign a healthy diet, depending on what was available. Food advice centres were opened up all over the country and stocked with nicely spoken food advisers explaining exactly what could be done with such delicacies as a fish's head. Bureaucratic in the extreme, the ministry poked its nose everywhere, even into the Women's Institute, nationalising its jam-making operations with a myriad of rules and regulations. The ministry's motto was: Fair Shares for All, and in this it more than less succeeded. Much of the population had a better diet in wartime than they had had previously.

Bill had managed to get a job back on the *Daily Herald*, on the night desk. It was a long way from the editor's office but it was part of his comeback, this return to Fleet Street, as was his rapprochement with the Labour Party. The party had taken him back into the fold; he was accepted as one of the prospective candidates for Stockport. In February 1940, Bill stood on the same platform as Herbert Morrison in Stockport's Central Hall. He made a witty, clever speech, explaining how he had regarded the First World War as an imperialists' war and how he had been changed in his view that this war was much of the same not by Herbert Morrison but by Harry Pollitt, which got a laugh. He had decided it was necessary to fight for British grey capitalism, which allowed workers the right to free speech and representation, against Germany's black capitalism, which allowed neither. But fighting made sense only if the peace when it came was a socialist peace. The applause was sustained. Bill had found a way of being in the mainstream without losing his integrity. He was a Marxist, he told the crowd. But now he was a Marxist within, not without.

He had moved from Battersea Park across the river to Stanley (now Primrose) Gardens, more or less equidistant from Hampstead, Primrose Hill and Swiss Cottage in north London, not far from where the 'Grand Lama of Regent's Park Road', Friedrich Engels, had once held court. When his wife and son were evacuated, Bill went down to Coram Street to get Barbara and bring her back to his house. She stayed there on and off until, at the beginning of 1942, she found another flat, three minutes' walk away, round the corner in Belsize Park Gardens. She had the top flat of Number 44, a capacious detached house, with plantation columns holding up the porch, and tall, wide windows.

Barbara had a tranquil six months. The Luftwaffe had turned its attention to the provincial cities, leaving London in relative peace. She was enjoying her job and especially her nearness to Bill. She was as happy as she ever had been. Love had mingled with love for Barbara, as William Morris had promised. It had overwhelmed and possessed her. She and Bill were lovers, comrades, friends. She was not his protégée any more, she was not the ingenue, the graduate obsessed with her academic failure. This was a time of equanimity; despite the war, which perhaps would never end, she believed in her future; the life she had always imagined for herself would be possible. She would get there. She 'would have loved to get married and have [Bill's] child', she said, of course.[42] The one discordant note. But Barbara was an optimist. She trusted happiness.

When the end came it was sudden, violent. It was over within weeks. Bill was ill. She was looking at her life through the wrong end of a telescope. She had noticed how tired he was, how drawn. His duodenal ulcer could no longer be kept down by glasses of milk. The doctor told him he needed to rest, to take six months off or have an operation. A man of volcanic energy cannot do nothing for six months and besides he was afraid he would lose his job. He opted for the operation and went into hospital on 25 May. Two

72

weeks later, on 8 June 1942, he was dead, from complications following the surgery. It was a Monday. He would have been 54 the following month.

'William Mellor is dead', wrote a stunned W. N. Ewer, foreign editor of the *Daily Herald*. 'It just does not sound true to those who knew the vitality of the man.'[43] Barbara had watched Bill's vitality drain away. After he died she wrote a letter to his mother: 'Mom darling, when William died on Wednesday [sic] I hadn't seen or spoken to him for five days. When I saw him the previous week I knew I was helpless to do anything for him. So I told him I'm not going to see you again until you are stronger. That's not because I don't want to but because I love you. He smiled and nodded and we were as near as anything on earth could make us although I never spoke to him again.'[44]

Bill had 'dominated her life up to the time of his death', Michael said.[45] How would she go on? How could she? This was something she would not get over, not in any complete sense, not ever. He was the great love of my life, she said, again and again. His obituaries were many, but, owing to the war, they were terse. He left no diaries or memoirs. What could she hold on to? They cremated Bill at 10.30 a.m. that Wednesday at Golders Green Crematorium. Barbara was there, supported by a distraught Michael and two of their friends.

Afterwards it wasn't to her beloved sister, Marjorie, that she fled, nor to Annie, either, but to someone 'more competitor than friend'.[46] It was to Jennie Lee, the one person who knew from the inside out what she was going through. Jennie had felt the same terrible emptiness when Frank Wise died. Jennie could help this Barbara, vulnerable and fractured, she could feel for her, she could take pity. 'Jennie was kindness itself.'[47] Barbara stayed on with Jennie and Nye for part of that awful summer in their cottage in the Chilterns, mummified in the icy silence of grief.

PART II

Let Us Face the Future

Chapter Four

BARBARA'S CASTLE

By 1943 the course of the war had changed. What had seemed unendurable defeat began to look like durable success. It was, as Churchill said, perhaps the end of the beginning. The end couldn't come too soon. The British were war-weary: the papers were full of ads for products to ease exhaustion, strain and worry; others to cure depression and brain fag. There were tonics and blood purifiers from Bovril to cod-liver oil and something called Vitadatio to lift sagging spirits and weary bodies. But the future was the only real cure, thinking about the war's end, reconstruction.

The war had shaken things up. The British, ruled by an oligarchy for almost fifteen years, had, by VE Day, been 'bombed and burned into democracy'.[1] At home, power diffused. Leadership sprang up at ground level. The classes had not so much mixed as come upon each other, not only in the armed forces and the citizen militias but in their homes. It was said, often, that children evacuated from the slums into middle-class families screamed when shown a bath full of water, screamed worse when put into it, ate everything with their filthy fingers, and used the corner of the room as a toilet, so as to spare the rug.

The poor looked on equally askance. How much some had; how little most had. The revolutionary fervour of the 1930s dripped down into a determined popular radicalism, a grim refusal to return to the interbellum misery of Tory slump and slum, to what William

Beveridge defined as the five giant evils that would block the way to reconstruction. Want was only one of the five giants, he said. The others were Disease, Ignorance, Squalor and Idleness. His report, *Social Insurance and Allied Services*, was the blueprint for what became the welfare state, a safety net of comprehensive national provision, from the cradle to the grave. Barbara had been working on similar ideas with the Fabians. But Beveridge, she thought, was different. It wasn't a patch, it was a completed quilt. It was how Labour would win the peace, if the Labour ministers in the war cabinet could be so persuaded.

Beveridge proposed that the new schemes start almost immediately, in July 1944, with the first benefits paid out the following year, war or no war, a proposal backed by public opinion and Labour backbenchers, but not the coalition government – including the Labour ministers therein – who wanted to wait for the war's end. The Parliamentary Labour Party (PLP), led by Nye Bevan, revolted, censuring the government over its refusal to approve the Beveridge report. Five months later, it was Barbara's turn.

She had been nominated by her constituency party as its delegate to the 1943 party conference. First she addressed herself to the electoral truce. She was far from sharing official Labour's confidence 'that coalition for war emergency will not imperceptibly drift in to coalition for peace';[2] she called on the Labour ministers to act as Labour ministers, not tiny Tories. This was a deep concern on the left, and Barbara, Nye and others repeated the call the following year, with increasing urgency. 'There may come a point when coalition will become incompatible with conscience', Barbara said; then the Labour ministers should be willing to say, 'Thus far and no further.'[3]

During the Beveridge debate she listened to Arthur Deakin, a ruthless, irascible character who had taken over from Bevin as general secretary of the TGWU and proven himself equally right-wing. He attacked the PLP for its revolt in the House, for embarrassing the Labour ministers and violating the electoral truce. When it was Barbara's turn she rounded on him: 'We of the rank and file . . . say to the Trade Union Movement that this Beveridge issue is as axiomatic to us as the Trade Disputes Act* is to them.' Did the unions, she demanded, expect the PLP not to take up the union cause and say as they were saying about Beveridge, 'We are sorry; there is a war on; there is a truce'? Beveridge was 'the first attempt to translate into concrete terms the generalities' of 'Jam yesterday, and jam to-morrow, but never jam to-day'. She wanted 'some proof there is going to be jam to-day'.[4]

The door had been slightly ajar and Barbara kicked it open. It was a moment of concordance to which even Nye turned his head. The cameras clicked and the correspondents, seeing a headline, glanced up. Garry Allighan, who'd been in the Socialist League with Barbara, was covering conference for the *Daily Mirror* and was with the paper's night editor, Ted Castle. The next day a photograph of a bespectacled Barbara, dubbed 'the voice of youth', appeared on the front page of the *Mirror*; the bubble coming out of her mouth inevitably called for jam today.

Ted Castle had probably heard of Barbara from her activities in the league and the Unity campaign and now, watching her, he was intrigued. His eleven-year marriage had broken up a couple of months earlier and he was in the midst of divorcing his wife. Like Bill, Ted had a young child, born late in his married life, in this case after nine years. Like Barbara's, his recent emotional past was something he was trying to forget. He wangled an introduction. Ted and Barbara spent the whole of that afternoon together with Nye. I knew, Ted said, from 'that moment that this was a star'. It was the way she talked to Nye. Ted, like most people, had always deferred to Nye's superior political acumen. But not Barbara. She, Ted noticed, talked to him as 'an equal on a political plane'.[5]

Barbara wasn't impressed with Ted at first. She thought him 'the go-getter sort' which she found 'rather off-putting: the rather brash, successful journalist about Fleet Street' type was not of interest.[6] Bill's memory was still painfully alive; he had been dead for only just over a year and the dissimilarity between him and Ted was

---

* The Act, of 1927, among other things made general strikes illegal and weekened union power. It was repealed in 1946.

acute. Whereas Bill was awkward, unclubbable but brilliant and exciting, Ted, who at 36 was just three years older than Barbara, was 'affable, able, a clubbable person ... not the wildest of intellects' but 'a lovely man' and 'a great old cove'. Ted's 'character was extraordinarily similar to her brother Jimmie. They were both very extrovert, hard-drinking characters who really gave the impression of not giving a damn.'[7] Perhaps she found this redolence soothing because despite the fact that she was, she said, 'a bit mixed – a bit torn' about Ted,[8] she started to see him regularly.

Ted found a wary loneliness in her, 'a certain inclination towards being a solitary'.[9] What she found in him was someone with whom she shared values. Despite his man-about-town smoothness, Ted was political, a left-wing socialist, deeply committed to the Labour Party. He was also easy to get on with and – very important to Barbara – they both loved the countryside. She could, she thought, 'build on that ... think: this would be nice if it went on'.[10] And on it went. He grew on her. Ted was what Barbara needed, whether she knew it or not. She was to be very exposed as the sole woman in high politics and Ted proved her greatest, most loyal supporter, 'the secretary of her fan club',[11] in the years ahead, years that were not accustomed to seeing a husband take a back seat to his wife's career, gracefully or otherwise.

Barbara said that it took her some time before she came round to the idea of marrying Ted. But she did, as soon as they legally could, a month after his divorce became absolute, at the City of London registry office, on 28 July 1944, less than a year from their first meeting. If anything it seems hurried, as if both of them couldn't wait to get it over with, to move their lives on from death and divorce and despair. They held a celebration lunch at the Savoy with Nye, and Jennie (who had married Nye with similar reservations and in a comparable emotional state a decade earlier), Garry Allighan, and another friend of Ted's from the *Mirror*.

Allighan, who was almost thrown out of the league for leaking confidential information, had been sacked from the *Mirror* for playing loose with the facts in his column. Ted, thinking him wrongly accused, had resigned in protest. (The much-fired Allighan became an MP and was thrown out of the Commons in October 1947 for disgraceful conduct.) Luckily, Ted was hired almost immediately by *Picture Post* as assistant editor and Allighan's departure from the *Mirror* proved fortunate: in September Barbara took over his column, becoming 'Barbara Betts the Forces' Friend' with Question Time in the Mess. When Barbara took the column over the emphasis switched from answering questions from service personnel on the problems of life in the armed forces to addressing the problems the returning troops would face with retraining, jobs, housing, etc. Barbara also changed the format from the question-and-answer it had been under Allighan into expositions of what future government policy on these issues should be.

She went back to Blackburn in the hope of being selected this time as one of their two parliamentary candidates. It was still difficult for women to get selected to fight seats. Women, would-be women candidates were routinely told, will not vote for women; women of childbearing age were hardly ever selected and the few women who made it through often did so in unwinnable constituencies. But Blackburn was a double-member seat which already had had a woman MP, the biographer Mary Agnes Hamilton, and, like Bradford, it was a mill town, accustomed to working women. It was not without hope.

Barbara had been ill, first with shingles and then with acute appendicitis, which put her in hospital. She arrived at the selection meeting, still not in the best of health, to find that the other four contenders were men and trade unionists bearing union dowries for the constituency. She had continued to use her maiden name, which seemed to befuddle the introductions. She was introduced as Barbara Betts, or Barbara Castle of the *Daily Mirror* and Mrs Barbara Castle of the London County Council and Fabian Society. She opened her address to the selection committee with a bit of low cunning, telling them to forget she'd just come out of hospital, and that she was a woman. 'I'm no Feminist. I want you to judge me only as a Socialist,' she declared.[12] However they judged her, she won one of the nominations. John Edwards won the other. George Eddie, Barbara's electoral agent, was a tough old Scot, a jolly tyrant. The first

81

thing he told her was that there would be no more of this Betts nonsense. Henceforth she would be Mrs Barbara Castle, as Blackburnians didn't approve of married women keeping their own names.

On 30 April 1945 Hitler committed suicide in his Berlin bunker. A week later victory in Europe was declared. On 21 May the Labour Party conference rejected Churchill's request to continue with the coalition government until the war with Japan was won as well. As Barbara and her allies insisted, the coalition for war emergency was not allowed to drift into a coalition for peace.

For many Labour candidates, victory for the party seemed remote. Labour *qua* Labour had scant government experience. And Churchill, after all, had led the country to victory. But as the candidates began to campaign they realised that, although the public turned out in the streets to cheer Churchill, they were going to vote Labour. They wanted change. They wanted the future not the past. They wanted something better. It was enough that the Labour ministers had in effect run the home front during the war. They'd been judged successful and Churchill, having been stymied in his attempt to continue with a National Government, helped Labour's prospects further by saying that Labour would set up a Gestapo. No one could see Major Attlee as the commandant of the Gestapo.

Labour's manifesto, *Let Us Face the Future*, written by Herbert Morrison, Ellen Wilkinson and others, was bold and coherent in vision and purpose; it captured the electorate's dreams: 'The Labour Party is a Socialist Party, and proud of it. Its ultimate purpose at home is the establishment of the Socialist Commonwealth of Great Britain – free, democratic, efficient, progressive, public-spirited, its material resources organised in the service of the British people'. It was long on specifics: establishment of the National Health Service and the welfare state and national-isation of key industries. The nation's soul was also to be taken care of: concert halls, libraries, theatres and civic centres were to be built 'to assure to our people full access to the great heritage of culture in this nation', all to be paid for by 'full employment and the highest possible industrial efficiency'.[13]

Expectations were enormous. The party was expected to fix everything that anybody considered broken, and this mellifluous document was in almost perfect harmony with such a desire. It was about not just material progress, but spiritual; it was about who the British were going to be as a people. But, although Barbara agreed with this all-encompassing socialism, she thought some of the language used to express it too high-flown for the 'simple people for whom we fight', especially when addressing land nationalisation. This, she thought, 'was getting so statesmanlike that we are becoming a little obscure'.[14]

There hadn't been a general election for ten years and the postwar electoral campaign had an evangelical flourish to it. Each day Barbara spoke outside three or four factory gates, each evening she addressed two or three meetings. People crowded round. They wanted to know. This wasn't politics as usual; it was politics as it had never been before. On the eve of the election there were a dozen or so open-air meetings all over Blackburn, culminating in a crowd of ten to twelve thousand people in the old Market Square singing 'Jerusalem'. Barbara's eve-of-poll rally was held in St George's Hall, where several thousand people crammed in, filling every seat and aisle.

'Rejoice and Be Glad! For this is the Day of the People', the *Daily Express* exclaimed on 5 July 1945. The votes from the forces still abroad meant that the result would not be known until three weeks later, and wartime displacement had played havoc with the electoral register, leaving many people unable to vote. But the Labour victory when it came was unequivocal. The Labour government's outright majority, its first ever, was 146 seats. Almost two-thirds of the Labour intake were first-time MPs. At twenty-four, the number of women elected was a record: twenty-one of them were Labour. Barbara, at 34, was the youngest woman member, 'and quite the most glamorous with her auburn hair and colourful clothes'.[15] The class of '45 included the four new boys who were to lead the party for the next forty years after Attlee: Hugh Gaitskell, Harold Wilson,

James Callaghan and Michael Foot. There were future cabinet colleagues too: George Brown, Richard Crossman, Patrick Gordon Walker and Michael Stewart.

Nearly fifty years later, Barbara reached for Wordsworth to describe the overwhelming feeling that day:

> Bliss was it in that dawn to be alive,
> But to be young was very heaven.[16]

But her victory was not what it should have been. Her father was in a coma. He'd developed Parkinson's disease and just before the election had fallen over. When she took her seat she 'wasn't able to look up at the gallery and see the old bastard there'.[17] He died in August, aged 63, without knowing she had given him the one thing they had both wanted. It was Barbara *and Frank's* moment; the moment when she showed him she could do it. It was bittersweet; she luxuriated in singing 'The Red Flag' with her colleagues when the House first convened, horrifying the Tories. The officials continued with the opening ceremony, ignoring this breech of protocol 'much as a polite host continues the conversation after his guest has upset the soup', Michael Foot remarked.[18]

The left had reason to hope. In the cabinet were Nye Bevan as minister of health, Stafford Cripps as president of the Board of Trade and Ellen Wilkinson as minister of education. Then there was Hugh Dalton, originally destined for foreign secretary but switched by Attlee to chancellor of the exchequer, a man of the centre right, but one who adhered to left-leaning expansionist economic policies. And Attlee himself, once a member of the Socialist League and Zip, and the ILP before that, was prime minister. John Freeman, in moving the address to the King's Speech, made the first speech of the new House: 'It was a faultless act,' Dalton recalled, 'which I shall always remember. In the uniform of a Major in the Rifle Brigade, wearing several ribbons, very erect and astonishingly handsome', Freeman declared it was 'D-Day in the Battle of the New Britain'.[19]

Cripps was not what he had been. Perhaps two years in the Soviet Union as Britain's ambassador during the war had changed his mind. He had not so much swerved to the right as slipped into neutral, his Marxism shed like a snake's skin, his past transgressions forgotten by him and the party. Nevertheless, he continued to support the *Tribune* financially and he appointed Barbara one of his runners, parliamentary private secretary (PPS). The other was her fellow Blackburn MP, John Edwards. The appointment of two PPSS 'caused some surprise', as did the fact that one was a woman: 'There are few precedents for women as PPS ... their usefulness is limited by the fact that they are unable to retail to a Minister the Back Bench talk and the gossip of the smoke-room', the *Daily Telegraph* opined,[20] its correspondent apparently not having met the Smoking Room's soon-to-be most colourful habituée.

Women were not officially banned from the Smoking Room, but they didn't enter unless invited by a man, which rarely happened. It was not a place where 'women members were made very welcome', Leah Manning said: 'A freezing glance or a lull in the buzz of conversation was enough to make the boldest turn tail.'[21] But not Barbara. She wasn't subject to social opprobrium, to being frozen out by anyone. She had, in the best sense, too high an opinion of herself.

'Woman Board of Trade Home-Front Chief' was how the *News Chronicle* greeted Barbara's appointment, noting that this housewife was 'fair-haired [sic], blue-eyed ... She lives in a London flat which she cleans herself and she cooks her husband's evening meal when she gets home in time.' Much of the coverage made her sound like Mrs Miniver (film, not book), with her extravagant love of couture. Barbara encouraged them, of course: 'I love pretty clothes ... I've missed clothes more than food during the war', she trilled.[22] But unlike the *Telegraph* writer, who fulminated, darkly predicting the next office 'to fall to feminine assault', the coverage was more fascinated than hostile. The housewife for the Board of Trade was, on balance, a fairly good thing; at the very least, it could do little harm.

The war had intervened and it had taken Barbara longer than it might have to achieve her stated, and not inconsiderable, first goal.

This record number of women in the House was still minuscule and they 'had borne the brunt of long battles, many defeats, much victimization and bitterness towards' them, as the MP Jean Mann – no feminist – noted.[23] Three of their number got proper jobs: Ellen Wilkinson became the second woman to enter a British cabinet; Edith Summerskill was made a junior minister and Jenny Adamson a parliamentary secretary.

Women MPs were judged, and judged themselves, by harsher standards than those applied to men. Barbara was all too aware of this. She had to prove herself like anyone else but 'being a girl I was under extra-critical eyes', she said.[24] The press liked to ask whether the women MPs were worth the fight the suffragettes had put up. The women were not sure. In Jean Mann's view, even pro rata there were more outstanding men in parliament than women. Leah Manning agreed:'As for the women, we were very much run-of-the-mill, with two outstanding exceptions: Dr Edith Summerskill . . . and Barbara Castle, a young edition of Ellen Wilkinson, but much prettier and with good dress sense which poor Ellen could never achieve.'[25]

Barbara's obsession with her appearance became her trademark. The newly constructed women's toilet next to the debating chamber became known as 'Barbara's castle' and she its chief inhabitant. But she wasn't entirely alone. Most women members, even those who did 'not speak often' usually made 'a point of dressing well for the occasion'.[26] The men joined in the game with gusto, cheering on the women's outfits, whistling, yelling comments or laughing, as they did at Ellen Wilkinson's eccentric hat, forcing her from the despatch box in embarrassment, half collapsed with an asthma attack.

Women MPs were expected to stick to women's issues and were strongly advised to do so by Herbert Morrison, the leader of the House. No woman MP forgot to describe herself as a housewife, not even Barbara. 'Journalist and housewife' was her self-description. If women members did speak outside women's issues, they could do so only in ones. When Barbara, Leah Manning and Jean Mann wanted to speak in the Berlin Air Lift debate, Jean was confronted by one of the whips, who asked her, 'As Mr Speaker could not have three women in this debate, could I arrange with the other two which one of us would speak?' Jean shuffled along the bench to impart this news to Barbara and 'met a point-blank refusal'. She got more of the same from Leah. 'So Mr Speaker was informed that the ladies were unwilling.' The ladies may have been unwilling but the men, Jean Mann said, 'were disgusted' at their orneriness.[27]

Barbara, always more than willing to fight her corner, 'was not nearly as tough as she liked to make out', Leah Manning thought: 'In the early days of the 1945 Parliament she did not have an easy time.' More than once Leah 'found the girl ... vulnerable and in tears in the Lady Members' Room'.[28] Leah, like Ellen a survivor from the 1929–31 parliament, was what Barbara would have called a 'motherly body'. She was fiercely protective of Barbara and she saw a side of her that is seldom evident. Twenty-some odd years later, Bernard Ingham, also in his way a motherly body, saw this side as well during an embattled time; he found Barbara beset by 'innate insecurities and nervousness' and agreed that she was nowhere near as tough as she or anyone else made out.[29]

The Lady Members' Room was off the terrace, small, cramped, 'just seven desks ... a small powder room adjoining, not one wardrobe ... the pegs ... so close together ... that the place always looked like the hour before the Jumble Sale opened'. There were just 'two couches for rest, one small chest for storing things, and never enough waste paper baskets'. Work, if done in the House, was done in the library or sitting on the floor in the corridors. The only thing the Lady Members' room was good for was mucking about and gossiping, away from prying male eyes: Barbara and Megan Lloyd George, daughter of David, 'shocked the more staid women members by dancing a can can' on the desks.[30]

The majority of women MPs were professional middle-class people; most were married, few had children. Some, like Jennie Lee, unequivocally did not want children. Others were ambivalent. Some couldn't. And yet others still left it too late. Barbara said she had 'never been fond of a man without part of that being a feeling I should like his child'. Her childlessness, 'not for want of trying', padded doggedly beside her through the years, although what she wanted was never 'just a child in general' but 'the child of a particular person'.[31] It is something she talked of often and openly to almost everyone she knew. Not having children was, she said, one of her tremendous regrets.

But what would it have meant to her to have children in the 1940s or 1950s? Could she have continued her career as an MP? And if so, what kind of MP? One who embraced committee work and activist politics, one who wrote regularly for various newspapers, one who hoped for a government job? Her desire to have a child was in conflict with the life she wanted for herself – with the life she had. Yet the desire was strong and urgent, picking at her. Barbara, Ted said, really wanted children. In the beginning he had wanted more children as well, but 'with the kind of life that Barbara had ... the problem of bringing up a child as we would have wanted ... would have been overwhelming'.[32]

Ted was in many ways a man ahead of his time when it came to Barbara, but in the 1940s and 1950s the mere sight of a man pushing a pram was cause for hilarity; it would not have occurred to either of them that Ted could be, in turn-of-the-century parlance, a co-parent, even one who picked up where the nanny left off – if, indeed, such a person could be considered. 'It wasn't as if [Barbara] was young enough to give over seven years of her life and then come back into politics', Ted thought; having a child would have put her in 'an impossible situation'.[33]

For whatever reason, Ted's little girl, Judith, does not seem to have played much of a role in their lives and the Castles were left with just the dogs to lavish their frustrated parental desires upon.

By 1971 Barbara might have taken issue with Ted on whether motherhood would have put her in an impossible situation. When asked on the radio whether it was possible for women politicians to have both a successful career and children, she replied with an emphatic yes. But that was twenty years on. Perhaps she shared Ted's worries. By her own account she waited until just before the 1951 election before trying to get pregnant, which would mean she was around 40, shockingly old for the period; not the easiest time to conceive naturally in any era. Nothing happened. She sought what help there was at the time and then accepted the inevitable, taking refuge in her belief that her ovaries had been damaged by a bout of mumps she had suffered during the war.

Apart from time spent canvassing backbench opinion and planting questions for the minister, the work of a PPS varies considerably; some PPSS do very little, others, like Barbara, a great deal. She performed secretarial duties, wrote reports, did research, assisted with speeches, travelled around the country as bagwoman; whatever Cripps needed, Barbara crammed into her fifteen-hour days. Working for the former Red Squire was far from congenial: he was interested in the efficiency of industry and its workers now, not in making them socialist. It was a source of argument between them. But Cripps, famed for doing four hours of paperwork before breakfast, might have been expected to appreciate her hard work, if not her argument. She hoped it would pay off in the form of a junior ministerial post. It did not. John Edwards was promoted, but she was not. Harold Wilson was made a parliamentary secretary at once; Jim Callaghan was promoted from PPS to junior minister; but not Barbara.

Yet she was seen as bright and capable, even outstanding, and among a dozen or so others, including John Freeman, was given 'automatic access' to the chancellor, Hugh Dalton, 'whenever he was not at a meeting or in conference'.[34] She had friends across the party, managing to get herself on a cross-party jaunt of six MPs to visit the troops in Germany, on a parliamentary delegation to Paris, and selected twice as an alternate delegate to the UN General Assembly. Dalton put her on his hands-across-the-sea delegation to meet French and German socialists, made up of himself and Morgan Phillips, the general secretary of the party, and two older established Labour politicians Wilfred Burke and Mark Hewiston. This 'success as a young member caused jealousy'[35] but it did not add up to a job.

Dalton was an odd-looking man, almost bizarre, over six feet, with sharp light-blue eyes, the whites of which were often visible; top-heavy, pear-shaped, stooped, his bald head too large for his narrow shoulders; his arms short like a seal's flippers. He never spoke when he could boom. He was bisexual, leaning further to the gay side of the equation. His chief emotional attachments had been with Rupert Brooke at Cambridge and would be (unrequited) with Anthony Crosland at Westminster. His coterie were chosen not for reasons of ideology but for 'intellectual interest ... Intellectual interest reflected education which in turn, reflected class',[36] always important in the Labour Party. Most of Dalton's boys were the more comely members of the young male right, such as Hugh Gaitskell. The three left-wing exceptions were John Freeman, whom Dalton found attractive, Bill Mallalieu,* and Barbara, the only Dalton girl.

Barbara, who became an early member of the Ramblers' Association, accompanied Dalton on his annual three-day Whitsun treks, the first along the Pennine Way in 1948. Over the years the group, accompanied by carefully organised press coverage, marched through the Lake District, along Hadrian's Wall, and through other areas which were to become national parks or designated areas of outstanding natural beauty. Ted often joined them: 'The membership of the group changed little from year to year,' Dalton noted, 'the female component not at all; Barbara Castle never forsook us.'[37] Barbara often griped about Dalton, telling Dick Crossman that everyone hated him, but she never entirely forsook him; he continued to forgive what he considered her left-wing excesses and she continued to pump him for career advice.

Dalton's preferment of Barbara, coupled with his and Attlee's belief that PPSS were 'a deserving class which should never for long be left out of the flow of ministerial promotion',[38] were as nothing. On paper everything was in her favour. Her intelligence, her charisma, her capacity for hard work, her relationships with Cripps and Dalton and her background. Like Harold Wilson, she was one of forty-six MPs who had Oxbridge degrees, and also like him within this 'elite group ... had the unusual asset of a regional, non-public school background'[39] and benefit of a wartime Whitehall

---

* MP for Huddersfield, 1945–50, and Huddersfield East, 1950–79.

training. She was six years older than Harold, but still younger than the average Labour MP, many of whom were 'amateurs, dilettantes and semi-retired union officials'. Moreover, as Michael Foot often said, whatever criticisms could be made about Barbara, she was born to run things, as was seen subsequently in her various ministerial posts.

Michael blames Attlee, of whom he was less than enamoured, accusing him of a tight-lipped propensity to fish only in the public-school pond. But neither Nye nor Harold nor Jim Callaghan was a public schoolboy. Barbara would have been troubling to Attlee. Her star quality could be threatening. She was not only a woman, which was bad enough, but a *film noir* woman, exciting but dangerous. A heady mixture for someone of Attlee's celebrated recessive, laconic disposition; and she was also a rebel. She wasn't one to sit on her hands and let the Bills go through, as the party bosses wanted. If there was no one more elegantly dressed, there was no one more of a political nuisance. To Barbara, a political line was something not toed but tugged. At any sign of government drift, Barbara objected; and her objections were dutifully noted in the press. At a PLP meeting just three months after Labour had taken office, she announced that Bevin, who'd been made foreign secretary, was less than likely to carry out the socialist foreign policy to which he was committed by party policy, and so it was. As Chips Channon delightedly observed of Bevin's first speech on foreign affairs, 'It was almost a Tory speech, full of sense.'[40]

Barbara was one of the fifty-five signatories to a backbench amendment to the 1946 King's Speech which called for a 'democratic and constructive Socialist alternative to an otherwise inevitable conflict between American capitalism and Soviet communism'. She seconded an amendment to the National Insurance Act of that year, to delete Clause 12, which she said was a furtive effort to reintroduce a means test and accepted the Tory attitude that long-term unemployment was a man's own fault.* She also used her pen. Any inequities she found were at once displayed on the pages of the *Tribune*

---

* The amendment was defeated by 246 votes to 44.

or the *New Statesman*. When the government refused to pay family allowances to those receiving other benefits, she informed her readers that: 'To pay the allowance to the children of the bank manager and refuse it to the children of the barrow men on poor relief is to operate a fantastic inverted means test.'[41]

Michael, almost a public schoolboy (he attended Leighton Park, a private Quaker school), had similar tendencies, and was also kept out of government. So, too, was Dick Crossman, a Wykehamist. Major Attlee neither liked nor trusted him. 'Plenty of brains. Character's the trouble'[42] was the major's view. The dislike was mutual: the words 'contemptible' and 'odious' were never far from the word 'Attlee' in Dick's conversations.

Before he entered parliament, Dick had been an Oxford don. He came from an upper-middle-class family and was one of six children, all of whom were ministered to by a nanny, under-nurse, cook, three maids, a gardener and an odd-job boy. During the war he ran the German section of Britain's psychological warfare appar-atus. He was fascinated by both politics and players. He was a copious diarist, recording the machinations of his colleagues or reflecting upon the films he saw, the operas and parties he attended, his children's schools and the year that had just passed.

Unlike Barbara, who like Harold Wilson, had no interests outside politics, Dick had a distinct other life; he 'affected to see politics as a hobby', whereas Barbara 'treated it as a consuming passion and a vocation'.[43] Dick possessed a healthy ability to distance himself from himself, and a penchant for a ruthless determined analysis when writing of others. He doesn't appear to have gone in for much self-censoring, which gave him a reputation for being mercurial and inconstant; 'double-Crossman' was a popular epithet. He freely changed his mind about anything and held abundant contradictory ideas of people, especially Barbara.

Dick and Barbara soon formed a strong alliance. Throughout the years they 'hunted like two animals of incongruous shape and doubtful loyalty who were none the less inseparable'.[44] Dick, three years older, had had the usual Oxford fling with homosexuality - a wander round Auden, a dalliance with a scrumptious scrum half –

and subsequently married three times, first to a twice-divorced German morphine addict; second to a woman who divorced on his account; and lastly to Anne, with whom he had two children, the first when he was almost 50. Although he treated Barbara with chauvinistic condescension at times, he was entranced by her; she was like no woman he had ever known; he whittled away at her personality. She wanted power, often quite nakedly. She had more energy, more vitality than anyone he knew. Later, when they were in cabinet together she was 'the only person of Prime Ministerial timber';[45] but she was neurotic, petulant, pedestrian, infuriating and over-emotional.

Castle and Crossman were an unexpected but effective pair; together they became the centrifugal force of the left. 'They were very close indeed politically, but I don't think that either of them would ever totally trust the other', Gerald Kaufman said.[46] They differed violently on issues over the years, not least because he would shift position if circumstances or further thought warranted – and sometimes just for the hell of it. They both agreed that a characteristic difference between them was, as Dick noted, 'when a subject interests me I want to air it ... but she will say, "Don't talk about it just for the sake of airing it. Talk about it when you are ready to do something." '[47]

Dick wasn't a politician, he was a professor who relegated political thought to the art of 'deciding on the conclusion first and then finding good arguments for it'.[48] In contrast, Barbara, the Marxist-trained hedgehog, having come to a conclusion had concluded; which is not to say she couldn't change her mind, but rather that she didn't flip it like a coin. Dick could also be cruel. But cruelty, when served with lashings of wit and directed at others, can be a seductive quality; it is conspiratorial; a very English upper-class way of being clever together. Barbara was not entirely safe from establishment charms; nor from feelings and expressions of 'old-fashioned snobbery'.[49]

Most of the Labour backbenchers were, to begin with, a congruous bunch. In as much as they could coalesce around the manifesto, they were all socialists; and the younger generation, having put their youth on hold for six years, were as eager for a good time as they were for socialism. The Castles provided both. They loved parties, dinners, conversation and argument, wall-to-wall people and gossip and plotting. A few months after they married they had taken a flat at Number 32, Cholmeley Lodge, in Highgate Village, an elegant mansion block on the corner of Highgate Hill, and at Christmas gave enormous parties, overflowing boozy affairs in which future enemies cavorted and flirted with future enemies. Jim Callaghan, the most consequential of the future enemies, was a frequent and lively guest; his party turn was competing with Geoffrey de Freitas in trying to kick the shades off the chandelier.

Like Nye, Jim was a self-educated working-class boy – his constituency was Cardiff South – but this Portsmouth-born lad did not have Bevan's sheer Welsh brio, his carefree, and sometimes careless, self-confidence; Jim couldn't make his background work for him. 'He always grieved about the absence of a formal education', Neil Kinnock said,[50] feeling inferior to and not a little resentful of the educated elite. This was not an uncommon feeling. Another working-class boy, George Brown, 'eventually became unhinged [because] he was so bitter and jealous and envious' of his educated colleagues.[51] Callaghan and Brown were both union men, 'workers', from the industrial side of the party, intolerant of what was seen as the rarefied intellectual middle-class socialism of people like Barbara, from the 'brains' side of the party. Oxbridge attitudes didn't help. Barbara often adopted an 'elitist approach' when dealing with the union side: 'she thought she knew best.'[52]

The union side retorted that they, after all, had come from the world of work, from proper jobs, not journalism or languid professorial posts. They were from the people they claimed to represent. Their knowledge was born from experience, not books, and this had taught them, in Jim Callaghan's words, 'things which some of the people who come from university seem to know very little about'.[53] Class was a glacial fissure in country and party both.

Barbara and Jim got on well enough to begin with. He floated around the peripheries of the left, voting with Barbara and Michael against the American loan, joining them in sending a letter to Attlee urging reductions in military commitments, joining them in the Keep Left caucus. But somewhere along the way a switch was thrown. Barbara and Jim became antagonists. He drifted ever rightward. And 'like most men of his generation ... [he] held a broadly traditional view of the role of women'.[54] Professional women, opinionated political women, ambitious women like Barbara, did not fit in with his view of what the ways of the world and of women should be.

But Barbara and Jim's dislike of each other went beyond class or sex or even politics. It came upon them torrentially, like love. No one - probably not even them - knew exactly how or why it evolved. It was visceral, something jagged and immutable; their conflicts throughout the years mere sustenance. They carefully gathered up each other's crimes, political and temperamental, and kept them in a safe place. For thirty years they were never far from the glow of each other's enmity; theirs was a consuming inverse beguilement, which in the end did for Barbara.

The economic crisis that Labour inherited was severe. The war had cost Britain dearly; a nation that depended on exports to pay for the food it needed to import had made nothing but armaments. Gold and monetary reserves were near depleted; overseas debts were colossal; and then a week after Japan's surrender the USA cancelled the Lend-Lease* deal, forcing Britain to pay immediately for the goods it received. The only way this could be done was with an American loan, granted on less than favourable terms, 'a rough and harsh manner to hamper a faithful Ally', as Churchill complained. Barbara thought it should not be tolerated, that the government should 'say to the Americans - ruin us, then - go on - what do you think that will do to your economy?'[55] But the USA was 'concerned to consolidate the economic advantages'[56] that had accrued to it as a result of war, and determined to stop Britain re-emerging as a trading and political rival; it was deaf to entreaties or threats.

* Under the Lend-Lease Act, passed by Congress in 1941, the USA lent or leased Britain and its allies arms and *matériel*, in all worth some £5000 million.

The government accepted the American loan and put it to a vote in parliament in December 1945; Barbara and twenty-two other Labour backbenchers voted no in defiance of the whips. PPSS are not supposed to vote against their own government, especially when whipped, but it's usually left to their minister's discretion whether or not they resign. Jim Callaghan said, rather pompously, that he 'thought it right to resign if you voted against the government and you were a PPS'[57] and did so, but he was at least equally motivated by the prospect of the freedom of the back benches on which to await a proper job. Barbara, on Cripps's say-so, stayed on. Perhaps he, like Dalton, was one to welcome the dissent as an albeit muffled message of disapproval to the Americans.

For the populace, life continued to be hard and drab; the victors had got not the spoils but more more queues, ration books, austerity and spivs; any spirit of the bombsite was long since forgotten and 'grumbling might almost be said to be one of our national pastimes',[58] especially when bread and potatoes were rationed for the first time. The continuation of rationing, even before its expansion, was a cause of great and persistent complaint. Barbara dismissed the Housewives' League, who demonstrated against rationing and shortages, as 'one of the thorns in the side of the Labour Government'.[59] To her they were middle-class Tories, 'real viragos', all of which may have been true; but working-class women, too – and it was always women – were tired of standing 'patiently, often with their babies and small children, sometimes for the better part of a morning' in endless queues,[60] only to find what they were queuing for gone. Anger about shortages, restrictions and controls led to anger at the Labour government. In January 1947, Barbara wrote a booklet entitled *Are Controls Necessary?* in which she outlined, coherently and persuasively, the government's case for rationing, and explained why the need to export as much as possible to build up the coffers meant that luxuries, or as she preferred 'extras', had to be for export only – another cause of grievance.

The weather conspired to pile misery upon misery. The winter of 1947 was the worst since 1880: 'Roads became blocked with snowdrifts, and there were more and more power cuts. Whole villages in the Midlands became isolated and went for days without supplies.'[61] Coal shortages became so acute that in February, Emanuel Shinwell, the minister of fuel and power, turned out the lights for industry and consumers alike for several hours a day. Coal, the only form of home heat, was severely rationed in this deep-freeze, which blanketed London in snow for six weeks. Much of British industry came to a complete standstill and the fragile economy buckled. The American and Canadian loans drained away like dishwater as the country hurtled inexorably towards bankruptcy.

But it was foreign rather than domestic issues that prompted the most serious fracture in the PLP ranks thus far: Ernest Bevin's virulently anti-Soviet, pro-American foreign policy and his Palestine policy, which was keeping 100,000 Jews out of Israel. On May Day 1947, the loose left-wing dissent and discontent hardened into the Keep Left group which produced a pamphlet of the same name. *Keep Left*, by Michael Foot, Dick Crossman and Ian Mikardo (Mik), was a mixture of analysis, attack and alternate policy. The foreign policy section was written by Dick and called for a socialist European federation, independent of either the Soviet or the American bloc and with its own defence and security pact – a 'third force'.

Barbara, although not a signatory to the pamphlet, became a core member of the group and regularly attended the Keep Left meetings and lunches at La Belle Meunière in Charlotte Street, to which Jim Callaghan also went. The group was smaller than its successor, the Bevanites, and more concerned with party philosophy than with agitating over specific and immediate issues. It was an alternate party policy unit, its members writing pamphlets and articles for the *Tribune* and engaging in concerted efforts both to sway official policy and to garner support for their ideas within the Party.

The economic problems gave Cripps his moment. He sided with the Attlee Must Go movement – and he was the man to tell him, suggesting to the prime minister that Bevin take over from him. Attlee did what was necessary. He gave Cripps what he really wanted, mastery over economic planning by making him the first minister for economic affairs, a post the Keep Left group had called for (but not for Cripps to inhabit). Cripps stayed on as president of the Board of Trade (BOT) until the autumn, when Harold Wilson took over, becoming, at 31, the youngest cabinet minister since Pitt. In November, Dalton, who as chancellor had 'provided the resources and no small part of the drive behind Labour's great reforming measures',[62] resigned over a budget leak to a journalist, and Cripps became chancellor. Thus the most extraordinary relationship in modern politics, that between Barbara Castle and Harold Wilson, began. It lasted through frequent rows, intense political disagreements, contempt, despair, disappointment and a political suicide pact; in the end it helped ruin Barbara's career, but in the beginning it helped make it possible.

Although complaining to Cripps that she didn't go with the furniture, she stayed on at the BOT, becoming Wilson's PPS. Harold found her 'colourful, even flamboyant, with a sharp mind, endless persistence, and feminine charm which she used without scruple to achieve her ends'.[63] The young Harold, by contrast, was a roly-poly fellow with a scrubby moustache, seemingly as bland as blancmange with his dull recitations of facts and figures; 'Yorkshire pudding' was a familiar jibe. Politically he was the dedicated follower of fashion: you found him here, you found him there. You found him wherever you wished. Barbara found him on the left, although whether he was ever 'a genuine socialist or left-winger remains shrouded in ambiguity and blurred definitions'.[64]

'Harold was a very persuasive attractive political figure, an exceptionally able politician and Barbara was attracted to that.'[65] She saw something in him before their contemporaries in the party: a will to power and an ability to get it. Some political commentators had him as the coming man, but not his colleagues. It was Barbara who was the first to spot Harold, Michael Foot said; she did so even before he arrived at the BOT. Michael barely knew who Harold was; he 'had risen far and fast without any kind of Labour Party following within Parliament or out of it',[66] but Barbara had seen him coming.

Between them there was a frisson, chemistry of some sort. Her dangerousness appealed to him. Barbara was 'a great flirt and she would be coquettish, up to a certain point, with any area of political power'.[67] She flirted with Harold and he flirted right back, fuelling speculation that there was something between them. The rumour that they were or had been lovers had a malarial quality, flaring up regularly during their lives. Barbara admitted Harold gave her a fumbling kiss on a BOT trip to Canada, but only that. The rumour wouldn't go away because there was something ineffable between them; it looked sexual, and perhaps it was in one way or another, whether of mind or body. But their relationship soon matured beyond sexual attraction into almost a dependency, a symbiosis.

Barbara's primal and primary relationships were mostly with men. As lovers, friends or mentors, it was with men she fused as a rule, not women. There were exceptions. She loved her mother and she was extremely close to her sister, so much so that Marjorie's children resented it when they were young. But her mother and her sister were her protectors. They took care of her. Barbara brought out this tendency in other women too, in Leah Manning, for instance, to whom she was also close. Generally speaking, Barbara had more in common with men; women did not share her ambition, her drive, her will. During the years of her political ascendancy most women could not see where there was to get to; for most women there was nowhere to get to. Barbara had 'a loneness of purpose'.[68] And as Tony Benn's wife, Caroline, observed, Barbara was almost always the sole woman 'very much involved in a competition with the males'.[69]

She was said, by men and women alike, to have a masculine mind, a term she howled against; it was, she said, a 'piece of male arrogance which assumes that anything which works at all efficiently must be of the male gender'.[70] It was meant to be a compliment that explained an oddity: 'I never met *anybody* like her, let alone a woman', her secretary said in 1970. 'I never met a woman anything like' Barbara.[71] Few had. Not surprising, then, that Barbara's emotional home was where her life was lived: in the company of men. And her male intimates fused with her as she did with them, especially Harold.

Harold and Barbara were similar in obvious ways. They shared what Dick called her 'Girl Guide' and his 'Boy Scout' tendencies: 'this right and wrong attitude to life, this prissy rigour combined with an extraordinary power of self-deception'.[72] Barbara liked to say that their childhoods were similar, which they were in the broad sweep of a Northern nonconformist provincial grammar-school sense. She thought their Yorkshire upbringing gave them a supernatural sympathy. They spoke the same language. They shared a passion for detail, the need to have complete mastery over their subjects. Harold's powers of absorption were legendary and, in part because Barbara hadn't quite got that ease, there was a friendly rivalry between them, an I'm-clever-than-you jostling. Barbara had to work harder than Harold, be more diligent, but she got there in the end.

Barbara said that Harold reminded her of Ted. And Barbara, especially when they were both middle-aged, resembled a souped-up, more glamorous version of Harold's wife, Mary. Unlike Mary, who had no taste for political life, and even less ambition for herself or Harold – she loathed it when he was prime minister – Barbara was on all counts Harold's comrade in arms.

Her relationship with Harold was the foremost example of her capacity for loyalty to her friends: 'Once she's established loyalty with a person that's the overwhelming drive'.[73] And as Dick observed, 'loyalty to people and not ideas is universally regarded as the prime quality' in British politics.[74] It didn't matter that Barbara was often extremely critical of Harold; 'She never ever let him down, she never would. Harold could always rely on Barbara and in reverse she could always rely on Harold.'[75] But less so.

Barbara gave Harold politics and he gave her power. They put each other on the inside track. The balance of power within their relationship tipped this way, then that. Right from the start the pattern that was to dominate their lives was apparent. Just as later in cabinet Wilson couldn't bring himself to shut her up, now he tolerated her publicly attacking his 'bonfires of controls' policy.

By the end of 1948, the economy, boosted by Marshall Aid money, had made something of a recovery. Harold, mindful of public discontent over ration books and controls, decided it was time to get rid of them. Never one to shy away from a cliché, he began his conflagration that Guy Fawkes Day. Three weeks later Barbara was warning in the *Tribune* that the next election would be fought over the cost of living, and calling for more subsidies to keep prices down, as 'price rather than rationing is becoming the decisive factor in distributing supplies'.[76] Over the next three months hundreds of controls were dispensed with, and in March 1949 Harold tore up the clothes ration books, which was only possible, Barbara declared, because of the withdrawal of subsidies on clothes. Clothes were still rationed, but now they were rationed by price. As she told the party conference, 'Once it begins to dawn on the minds of ordinary people that price mechanism is coming increasingly into operation as the instrument of distribution, then we undermine our policy of wage stability.'[77]

Barbara wanted what she termed 'the present government' to go backwards, to 'make it perfectly clear' that what was needed for the successful governance of the country over the next five years was 'a greater measure, and not a less, of controls over the resources and the life of the people'. Controls were an agent of socialism, even more necessary when 'materials and necessities come into increasing supply [as] the only way in which we can carry out that policy of fair shares' was through equitable rationing.[78] The more that was produced the more that should be available to all, not just those who could pay for it. In the House, Barbara and Maurice Webb 'were two of the MPs most insistent that the housewife should be protected by delaying or abandoning the "bonfires of controls" '.[79]

During 1948, Nye fought his battle with the doctors over the establishment of the NHS. They absolutely refused to work within the confines of socialised medicine; they did not want to work for a flat salary. They wanted to hang on to private practice. Nye, as he put it, stuffed their mouths with gold. He cut a deal which allowed them to operate their private practice within the NHS in exchange for their employment (something Barbara tried to undo thirty years later in her last ministerial altercation). She herself had been embattled during that year. The *Express* had organised a series of debates after which the audience voted secretly Yes or No to the question: Does the country need a change of government? Barbara said on television that the Yes votes were rigged by the *Express*. The newspaper sued, and she unreservedly withdrew, paid the costs and donated 25 guineas to the Newspaper Press Fund.* This was the first of her frequent visits to the courts. Over the next dozen years Barbara was forever suing someone or being sued by someone else. She never let an attack go unchallenged, within parliament or without. She wasn't as paranoid about the press as a politician can sometimes (and sometimes justifiably) be, but she did, David Owen said, 'insist on everything being corrected.' 'You can't stop it being said but you can stop it being recycled', Barbara told him;[80] and as an act of policy she would correct every error.

The Keep Left group went into the 1950 election armed with a pamphlet, *Keeping Left*, written by Barbara, Dick Crossman and Michael Foot, a more or less constructive criticism of the government which the government would rather have done without. The government was drifting; the leadership was old, tired and sick (within the next two years Cripps and Bevin would be dead); and the vaporous Major Attlee behaved, at the best of times, as if 'communication between him and the public was to be conducted by telepathy'.[81] Attlee's pinched, spartan ways mirrored the country's ongoing condition. Even the policy statement, *Labour Believes in Britain*, seemed detached, as if Labour was looking benignly down at the child Britain. Jerusalem had slunk disconsolately away on all fours. The battle cry of the British revolution had turned out to be 'utility, priority, austerity'. Worse, the cost of living was beginning to go up on the back of Cripps's devaluation of the pound.

Attlee called the election for the greyest month of the British calendar: February. In this he had luck, as the weather was balmy and 84 per cent of the electorate turned out to vote. The Labour vote of 13.5 million was the highest polled by a single party, but, as

---

* A charity for the relief of distress among journalists and their dependants.

well as getting rid of undemocratic anomalies, such as the university vote and the business premises vote, the government had redrawn the boundaries and not in its own favour. Labour was returned, barely. The majority was five.

The double-member constituencies had also been abolished and Barbara now represented Blackburn East. John Edwards lost Blackburn West for Labour, an event that left her less than heartbroken. Edwards had become parliamentary secretary at the BOT, another infuriating appointment. But Leah Manning too lost her seat: 'Your defeat is one of the biggest blows of this election,' Barbara wrote to her, 'I miss you so; the Lady Members' Room isn't the same without you.'[82]

Left and right within the party blamed each other. A quarter of Labour's 1945 middle-class voters had floated back to the Tories. Herbert Morrison, presaging his grandson Peter Mandelson forty years on, argued that Labour had to broaden its appeal to get back the middle-class vote and especially 'consolidate' its nationalisation programme. Coal, civil aviation, the Bank of England, the railways, aspects of road transport, electricity, gas, and cable and wireless communication had, as promised in the manifesto, all been nationalised. Going into the 1950 election new targets for public ownership included sugar, cement, water and wholesale meat distribution.

But the dearth of coal emerging from the nationalised pits during the freezing winter of 1947 had left the electorate, not for the most part ideological, wary about, if not yet hostile to, public ownership. Nationalisation was to become one of the central left–right battles within the party over the next thirty years. To people like Barbara nationalisation meant what Attlee said it did in an interview with her for *Picture Post*. It showed 'quite clearly the difference between a Socialist and a social reform government'.[83] And she wanted a socialist government. Control over the commanding heights of the economy was essential.

Ted was assistant editor at *Picture Post* and Barbara, coincidentally or otherwise, got quite a lot of publicity from the photo weekly. The feature on a selection process was a feature on the selection at

Blackburn, featuring Barbara; the interview with the prime minister was given to Barbara, a freelance for the magazine. It appeared complete with photos of Barbara and Attlee. Her interviewing technique was, as might be expected from a member of the same government, mild-mannered, except for a couple of swipes at Bevin: 'You would not agree, then, that the Labour Government is less Socialist in its foreign policy than in home affairs?' she asked Attlee. 'Certainly not,' he rather unsurprisingly replied. The piece was attacked as Labour propaganda and her questions dismissed as lame in the letters page that followed.

Barbara always understood the importance of taking care of what she termed her personal publicity. She wasn't beneath the occasional stunt: 'M.P. To Be Mill Girl' was one. She took herself off to work in a cotton mill in Preston for a week in September 1947, accompanied by the reporters, who duly wrote that just like an ordinary working-class Lancashire lass she was awakened at 6 a.m. in the working-class home she was staying in, on Tennyson Road no less, by a knocker-up. Such stories were accompanied by pictures of Barbara wearing a jaunty hat and a rakish smile. She was a regular guest on the 'Ladies Night' edition of the popular television programme *In the News*, watched by half of all television viewers, and to balance these populist excursions she gave frequent talks and lectures around the country for the Fabian Society.

She also knew how to take care of her personal politics. Her colleagues on the Keep Left group, had, in her absence, omitted her name from their list of recommended candidates for the National Executive Committee (NEC), something she swiftly got reversed. The group agreed that a memo would be sent round, 'asking members to try and get their constituency parties to nominate her, and also to try and get union support for her candidature'.[84] Union support would be necessary. She would run for the five-seat Women's Section where, by custom rather than fiat, women MPS were confined. They were elected by the union block vote.

Remarkably, union support was garnered and at the 1950 Labour Party conference, Barbara was elected to the NEC for the first time. She was sponsored by Sam Watson of the Durham miners, that year's party chairman. She came bottom of the poll of the Women's Section, 2 million votes below Margaret Herbison* at the top, but she was on. She had a power base. The NEC was part of the decision-making machinery of the party. Constitutionally, its function was 'administration rather than of policy, but the distinction had never been maintained in practice'[85] and the NEC issued policy positions drawn up by its various committees.

Shortly after conference, the ailing Cripps resigned and Hugh Gaitskell was appointed chancellor. Gaitskell was almost by definition destined to become the *bête noire* of the left: an effete prototype yuppie, an Oxford-educated public schoolboy (he had been at Winchester with Dick) who had, in the left's view, done nothing to build the Labour movement in which he was now so rapidly ascending while attempting to 'turn it into something it was not, a social democrat party'.[86] He had been a member of Zip as a young man but had moved to the gradualist centre right. Gaitskell was an unyielding, unforgiving character; he became obsessed with Nye and what became the Bevanites, and Barbara disliked him intensely. He lacked poetry, she said. He was, in Nye's famous allusion, 'a desiccated calculating machine'.

Nye and Gaitskell were polar opposites and they loathed each other with a toxic mixture of personal antipathy, political dissonance and professional rivalry. The cabinet table was not big enough for both of them, a conclusion reached sooner rather than later through the medium of war. In June, what became North Korea had invaded what became South Korea, setting off the Korean War. The USA immediately leant on Britain to stump up men and money to fight for the South. Attlee announced to the House in January 1951 that the defence budget would amount to a staggering £4700 million over the next three years, £1000 million more than he had suggested just three months earlier, an immense burden for Britain – higher per capita than in the USA. Jim Callaghan, who had been promoted to a junior minister at the Admiralty, worked directly on implementing the excessive rearmament drive, an act of

* MP for North Lanark, 1945–70.

treachery in Barbara's eyes, of cynical careerism from someone who had so recently been part of the Keep Left group.

Gaitskell demanded that the NHS budget be cut and that charges be imposed on false teeth and glasses in order to pay for the defence expenditure. In cabinet, Nye and Harold argued, correctly, that the defence budget was so huge it could not be spent and therefore the health charges were unnecessary. But Gaitskell had Bevan where he wanted him. The minister of labour, as Nye now was, had told a dockers' meeting he wouldn't stay in a government that imposed NHS charges. Gaitskell was not going to back down. As he later acknowledged, it was a power battle between the two of them, which they both understood. Nye had little to lose. He had been passed over, as he saw it, for chancellor and also for foreign secret-ary, a job given to Morrison when Bevin became ill.

Gaitskell won this round, and on 21 April 1951 Bevan resigned in a maelstrom of publicity. Harold and John Freeman left the government two days later. Freeman, whose early political career was one of rapid progression from undersecretary to parliamentary secretary, had resisted Dalton's bribe of a cabinet job (the temptation of Christ, Dalton joked); Barbara, too, resigned her lowly PPS job. On the 26th, the three ex-ministers, accompanied by Jennie Lee, presented themselves at a Keep Left meeting consisting of Barbara, Dick, Michael, Ian Mikardo and Tom Driberg, among half a dozen others.

The alternative strategy group was now an alternative leadership platform. 'Overnight the word "Bevanite" went into the language' and the *Tribune*, now edited by Michael, who with Jennie Lee ran the editorial board, 'instantly became "must" reading for every political correspondent and commentator ... messengers from all the newspapers and news agencies waited every Thursday for the first copies to arrive' in the little red van.[87] The troubles, as Tony Greenwood aptly dubbed the Bevanite/Gaitskellite civil war, had begun, an internecine war for the soul of the Labour Party, with Barbara hoisted up as the Bevanites' Joan of Arc.

Chapter Five

THE TROUBLES

E very Tuesday, when parliament was sitting, Barbara, barring illness or catastrophe, walked along Millbank to Dick's house at 9 Vincent Square for lunch. There, in the long, comfortable drawing room, she would find Michael and sometimes Nye and other members of the Bevanite core: John Freeman, now assistant editor of the *New Statesman* as well as an MP, Ian Mikardo, Harold, Tom Driberg and Jennie Lee; sometimes others. There were in all about sixty Bevanites, many of whom turned up on occasion for lunch bearing position papers and the 6s 6d they chipped in for sandwiches and wine. Mik, who unless out of London never missed a lunch either, found the discussion much above anything he had ever experienced. But he noted an undercurrent among the core members, a 'subtle interplay, the delicate rapier-fencing, between some of these strong, sure-of-themselves characters ... the under-lying differences of purpose' which were bound to create tensions.[1]

The Bevanites as a group per se only existed for eighteen months, between the ministers' resignation in April 1951 and October 1952 when the Party forced them to disband, but they continued to cabal together throughout the 1950s until Hugh Gaitskell's death in 1963.

They were an audacious, sassy bunch. There were half a dozen writer-politicians but also fourteen future ministers, including a future prime minister in Harold and party leader in Michael. Most were great public performers and their talents were given full expression in the wildly successful *Tribune* Brains Trusts, modelled on the BBC's *Brains Trust*, an *Any Questions* predecessor. Almost every weekend Brains Trust teams of four or five made up of various blends of Barbara, husband Ted, Dick, Harold, Michael, Jennie, Tom Driberg, Mik (who usually chaired), Gavin Faringdon,* Fenner Brockway† and all, made their way in Faringdon's 'beautiful, rather ancient, pale green Rolls-Royce' (with the Faringdon arms discreetly etched on the doors) along the A roads and by-roads heading for the far corners of the land at a torpid 35 mph; his 'Lordship would never drive faster than that, and would not allow anyone else to drive'. Sometimes they took the *Tribune*'s more sprightly, if less commodious, little red van. The demand for the Brains Trusts 'seemed insatiable'. In the end they 'covered nearly every constituency in the country'.[2] There were big public meetings, too, addressed by Nye, Barbara, John Freeman, Harold, Dick and Michael. But the Brains Trusts were the heart of the Bevanite campaign.

Over a weekend the teams would do two or three meetings in as many towns. 'Even in high summer and even in Worthing, they could pull audiences of over nine hundred.'[3] It was a fund-raising activity for the *Tribune* as well as a propaganda machine. There was a charge to enter, but halls overflowed and the Brains Trusts were almost always sold out. They were very entertaining. There was no Bevanite line to be held, and the argumentative bunch often vehemently disagreed as much with each other as they did with the party bosses. On the bomb, for instance, it was quite common to hear Barbara or Ted claim that the issue of the bomb was all-important; Jennie to say that it didn't matter, only policies mattered; someone

* Lord Faringdon, a hereditary peer and left-wing member of the Labour Party. He lent his estate, Buscot Park in Berkshire, to the Bevanites for conferences.
† A prominent former member of the ILP, Brockway rejoined the Labout Party in 1946 and became a Labour MP in 1950. He was chairman of the Movement for Colonial Freedom 1954–67.

else say that if you banned the bomb you had to ban all weapons; another to favour the bomb; and yet another to want not only the bomb banned but Britain to be neutral.

Bevanite quarrels with the party were many and varied; as one weary observer plaintively put it, the conflicts 'come down to us now as a bewildering array of unconnected battles'.[4] Bevanites such as Barbara, Dick and Harold really were interested in trying to work out a coherent platform, to come up with solutions for real problems. And one of the underlying differences of purpose was that Nye was much more interested in leading the party than in formulating left-wing policy. He could never be persuaded to have a consistent or coherent strategy, Barbara and Dick complained. He was too much of an individualist for group thought and, although he dominated meetings largely through rhetoric, he liked neither to lead nor to organise the group. He was, as they both observed, a reluctant Bevanite.

The Bevanites' basic policies were for more nationalisation, less defence spending, more spending on the social services, and establishment of an unaligned, unified socialist Europe, the third force. They were anti-colonialisation and often anti-American. They were against the rearming of West Germany, on which Barbara, Dick, Harold, Nye, Mik and Driberg wrote a pamphlet, *It Need Not Happen*. (The party as a whole was ambivalent on German rearmament. Memories of the Nazis were live; and the public by and large took the Bevanite line. Dalton, too, was fiercely opposed; he had an intense dislike of the Germans, in part because Rupert Brooke, whom he had adored, had died from a mosquito-borne infection en route to Gallipoli.)

The Bevanites were against the American conduct of the Cold War, of which rearming West Germany was seen by them as an in-tegral part; they were for a level of détente with the Soviet Union and the admittance of China to the UN. On the nuclear issue some members, like Barbara, were unilateralists, some were multilateralists. Membership of the group was by invitation only. Not always successfully. Barbara recruited the MP for Pembroke, Desmond Donnelly, a motormouth with an eye on the main chance, who leaked information on the group to Hugh Dalton.

Outside of Parliament, there was a so-called 'Second VI' of people like Ted, who the *News Chronicle* claimed was the sinister-sounding 'national agent' for the Bevanites, a description more suitable for Mik. Many in the Second VI were, like Ted or Betty Boothroyd, say, either parliamentary candidates or would-be can-didates, and were also 'footsoldiers out in the constituencies',[5] according to Stan Orme, a party activist and would-be parliamentary candidate. Others were journalists who wrote for the *Tribune* anonymously as part of their political commitment, turning up at 'internal *Tribune* meetings where Nye and Jennie would be performing at 222 The Strand', the paper's offices.[6] 'The Second VI met regularly on Sunday afternoons in people's flats,' Ted said, 'our Highgate flat or Jo Richardson's* place in Hornsey.'[7]

The Second VI 'was very informal in the sense it was never a decision-making body. It was getting the message across and getting Bevanite MPs elected.'[8] There were four subcommittees: elections, contacts, policy and propaganda and conferences, and subcommittee members met regularly with each other and the First VI. We journalists 'might be asked to knock out a draft of a speech or keep the Bevanites informed of things they'd picked up on the intelligence grapevine', Geoffrey Goodman said, 'both inside the Labour Party and outside; it was that sort of very informal relationship. There were so many of us: [journalist] Jimmy Cameron was involved, [political cartoonist] Vicky was involved.'[9] But despite this level of journalistic support, the press on the whole was anti-Bevanite. Gaitskell and his ites had, as might be expected, the full support of the mainstream press, which portrayed the Bevanites much as it was to portray Militant Tendency in the late 1970s and 1980s, a wrecking-ball conspiracy out to destroy the Party.

They were indeed conspirators in the unsurprising sense that they were politicians: they wanted to get their own people into parliament and get their policies enacted. To this end, they met regularly, coordinated their tactics – some more successfully than

* Before she became an MP, Jo Richardson was Mikardo's secretary and kept the minutes of both the Keep Left and the Bevanite meetings.

others – and circulated their minutes. There was nothing baleful in this. Since as Peggy Duff* said, 'the main obstacle to left-wing policies lay in the right-wing majority in the Parliamentary Labour Party, the effective tactic, then as now, was to get more left-wingers in the House'.[10]

The Gaitskellites were a conspiracy as well, of course. They met regularly and secretly. The praetorian guard, Roy Jenkins and Tony Crosland among them, gathered at Gaitskell's home in Frognal Gardens where they succumbed to the aristocratic embrace of Gaitskell's duchesses:† 'the Frognal Set', the Bevanites sneered. As early as March 1952, Gaitskell, Jenkins, Crosland, Christopher Mayhew, Woodrow Wyatt (a signatory to *Keep Left* who had turned right), Patrick Gordon Walker and George Brown were caballing in order to bring down the Bevanites, and to fix it so that they chose the next leader of the party.

Between the Bevanites and the Gaitskellites, it was a war for hearts, minds and votes. It was fought on the NEC, in the House, in the constituencies, in the PLP, on political platforms, in the newspapers, at the universities, on the radio and television. The Bevanites had the edge with their performers. Barbara continued to be a regular guest on *In the News*, appearing often with Lady Astor on the monthly 'Ladies' Nights'; Michael was a favourite for the more frequent men's nights (on which Barbara also sometimes appeared). The Bevanites could justly claim to represent the sort of Labour Party its individual members wanted, real socialism; they had a mandate from the party in the country. The Gaitskellites tried to paint them as the enemy within; a 'party within a party' was the phrase put in Attlee's mouth.

As a Bevanite, Barbara knew that she would not be re-elected to the Women's Section of the NEC. Union patronage would be summarily withdrawn, so she decided to do what no woman had

---

*A left-wing campaigner, active in many causes, including the Abolition for Capital Punishment. In 1958 she became the organising secretary for the Campaign for Nuclear Disarmament (CND).

† A Bevanite reference to his love of high society and, by implication, his similarity to Ramsay MacDonald.

ever done before: run for the seven-seat Constituency Section, elected by the general membership of the party. She 'was the first to show that there was no need to sit tamely waiting to be crushed out of existence by [Arthur] Deakin's sledgehammer blows'.[11] (Deakin of the TGWU, Will Lawther of the National Union of Mineworkers, Tom Williamson of the National Union of General and Municipal Workers and the steelworkers' Lincoln Evans wielded nearly half the available conference votes, giving them the ultimate power in the party.)

She talked to Dalton about her plans on their annual Whitsun ramble, this one along the Pembrokeshire coast, and he encouraged her to go ahead and stand. Harold had other ideas. His resignation speech was the first political speech he had made in his ministerial capacity, one that was not following a departmental brief on coupons or shortages or the state of the British film industry. His resignation gave him more publicity than he had ever had, and he intended to make use of it. He would ride the Bevanite momentum and run for the NEC.

Harold was worried that two of them would be a Bevanite too far and Barbara was asked to stand aside for him. But it was Harold who was less likely to succeed. He was neither as popular nor as well-known as Barbara. And Barbara wanted to run. She went back to Dalton, who 'encouraged her to refuse' Harold's request.[12] Dalton's motives were mixed. He was fond of Barbara but he disliked Harold more. The youngest former cabinet minister had been a favoured protégé and he had let his patron down. He was now, Dalton said, just 'Nye's little dog'.

The 1951 party conference took place three weeks before the general election which Attlee, limping along with his wafer-thin majority, under siege from the Tories in the House, and the Bevanites in the party, had called for 25 October. But few at conference could get their minds round the general election; it was the NEC election that galvanised. The results were sensational. Barbara came second in the poll, topped only by Bevan, and getting more votes than Morrison, Dalton and James Griffiths, all of whom were cabinet ministers. Dalton was furious that both Mik and Tom Driberg had garnered more votes than he had, but for Barbara he had no anger. 'Of Barbara I felt quite differently', he told John Freeman; he was in fact 'rather pleased' by her success.[13]

Most sensationally Barbara had thrown the minister of defence, Emanuel Shinwell, a member of the party for nearly half a century, off the NEC. He had been 'replaced by this flibberty-gibbert of a girl'. Her 'good looks were an addition to the insult she had perpetrated on the established order'.[14] Shinwell did not take his ousting gracefully. Not for him sitting on the platform smiling and nodding: he cancelled all his engagements, packed his bags and stormed out of town. The right was incandescent. 'Barbara's victory was Labour's defeat,' Jean Mann said. 'She had removed the Minister of Defence from his seat on the National Executive and defied the trade unions.'[15]

'What annoyed [the unions] most was that, realising she would not get their votes, Barbara ... had had the audacity to find some elsewhere. They felt it monstrous that she ... should be proclaimed publicly on the eve of a General Election as more popular in the party than four Cabinet ministers.' Deakin, Lawther and Williamson met other union bosses and vowed that as soon as the general election was over they would 'squash the Bevanite movement and expel its leaders from the party'. After the election was over and lost, the impetus for action cooled. They did not see Barbara's 'victory for the portent it was'.[16]

The popularity of the Bevanites – the alternative leadership – had been resoundingly confirmed. They now held four out of the seven constituency seats on the NEC; 'the demand of the younger generation for something which the Old Guard apparently cannot deliver'[17] had found its focus. The focus did not extend to Harold, however. He remained ignominiously unelected to the Executive; he put it down to the fact that he had been listed by his initials, J. H. for James Harold Wilson. No one, he complained, knew who J. H. Wilson was.

From this first constituency election Barbara was never out of the top three spots until 1972, when her distinction with the constituencies began to wane; she was still voted onto the NEC until she left the House in 1979. For sixteen years, until Joan Lestor was elected in 1967, Barbara remained the only woman in the constituency section.

Three weeks later, Labour lost the general elction to the Tories by twenty-six seats. Winston Churchill was once again summoned to Buckingham Palace and asked to form a government. But elect-oral defeat was not all bad news for Barbara, as the NEC 'was an important focus of power in the party when it was not in office'; its influence 'especially over policy-making' was far greater when the party was in opposition.[18] The NEC could be used to put about the Bevanites' socialist agenda, to promote their ideas and themselves. Conference and the NEC became Barbara's power base, and the annual 'beauty contest' of the NEC elections of prime importance. As a left-winger, who could garner little support from the usually right-wing PLP, popularity with the constituencies was very import-ant, as was getting herself onto powerful NEC committees; that was how she could strengthen her position within the party.

Barbara had set her cap on becoming leader of the Labour Party and then, of course, Prime Minister. In her head she kept a mental snapshot, probably taken at around twelve years old: young Barbara outside Number 10, like the real snapshot that Harold Wilson's parents had taken of him. Certainly by her mid- to late teens her intention is becoming apparent and by the time she went to Oxford her fellow students were noting, with a mixture of awe and dismay, her enormous political ambition.

Nye was aware of Barbara's ambition and it didn't please him. He was aware of her popularity in the movement, of her oratorical gifts, of her comparative youth. Her election to the NEC had come a few days before her 41st birthday. Nye would be 54 in November: for him political time was running out. Perhaps he couldn't really see a woman leading the Labour Party, but he could see her deflecting his glory, making him look less than what he thought he was; perhaps he saw his younger self in her; both of them, as Dalton noted, had an eye to the main chance.

She had become one of Nye's 'dangerous people', a dedicated politician who cared for office. He took against her, loudly: 'Nye is anti-Barbara', Dalton noted. Dick saw it, too: there were ongoing 'terrible tensions between Barbara and Nye because Nye can't stand her'.[19] Harold thought Jennie Lee had something to do with it; that Nye resented, on his wife's behalf, Barbara's preferment in the party (which Jennie resented on her behalf as well). Barbara seemed less fierce about Nye. She was wary of him. She had distinct reservations about much of his intemperate behaviour and she tried to keep some distance between them. But she stuck to what he rep-resented. After all, as she said, 'the Bevanite movement was brought into being in spite of, rather than by, Nye Bevan'; he had 'inspired a faith but could not build a church'.[20] Barbara, on the other hand, could build that church.

In March 1952, the Bevanites, in defiance of a three-line whip, abstained on the Labour Amendment to the Tory Defence Estimates, which essentially accepted the defence budget, but doubted the Tories' abilities to administer it; the group also defied the whip and voted against the Tory Defence White Paper. Barbara and her friends could hardly have done otherwise, because the vast proposed defence expenditure remained unchanged, except that the £4700 million would be spent over four years instead of three. For the first time the Bevanite strength in parliament was seen. Fifty-seven MPs (inevitably dubbed the '57 Varieties', after Heinz), representing a fifth of the PLP, voted Bevanite.

The eruption in the party and in the press was cataclysmic. By the next day, the party was 'in the middle of its biggest crisis since 1931'. There were immediate calls for the core Bevanites to be expelled; Jim Callaghan was 'surprisingly strong on this', Hugh Gaitskell noted, and he himself 'was naturally quite prepared' for this to happen.[21] Arthur Deakin was sure that he could command at least a hundred Labour MPs to vote for expulsion. The Bevanite inner core assumed the worst, especially after Nye made a speech headlined 'I Refuse to Recant or Give Any Assurance', without consulting the rest of the group. This angered Barbara, Harold, Dick and John Freeman, who did not have a 'suicide mania', as Dick said, and did not want to indulge Nye's proclivity for gesture politics.

Whatever Nye said or did, battle had been joined. Barbara and Dick may have been worried about splitting the Party and provoking a 1931-like crisis, but the Gaitskellites seemed less concerned. Among those whom Dick saw 'voting for extreme measures'[22] at the PLP meeting that followed were Jenkins, Crosland, Douglas Jay, Patrick Gordon Walker, Woodrow Wyatt and the whole of the shadow cabinet,* which included Jim Callaghan and, of course, Hugh Gaitskell. But extreme measures were not to the taste of the bulk of the PLP and were rejected; the only punishment was a resurrection of the Standing Orders,† which had lain dormant since 1946.

The party limped on, two parties in one, social democrats versus democratic socialists with the twain meeting rather too often in the NEC and its subcommittees and on the party conference floor. The hatred between the two factions was boundless and became increasingly personal. Mik recalled Tom Driberg coming out of the monthly NEC meetings, 'wrung out like a dishrag and desperate for a large drink to get the taste of it out of his mouth'.[23] Edith Summerskill so hated Mik that she couldn't even spit out his name, calling him 'the man in the brown suit' if she had to refer to him at all. Barbara's particular personality better equipped her for this type of warfare. She was always 'prepared to use any argument at any time to win' on the NEC.[24] She could dish out the abuse when necessary.

'The bitterness between left and right ... was something tangible something you could almost feel when you walked into the tearoom', Judith Hart observed on entering the Commons in 1959.[25] And this feud, this battle over the soul of the Labour Party, remained feverish and clamorous for the thirteen years Labour was out of office; it outlived both Bevan and Gaitskell and slithered into the subsequent Labour governments. For the rest of her life, Barbara never trusted or allowed herself to get really close to

* Called the parliamentary committee at the time.
† Under Standing Orders, Labour MPs were not allowed to vote against majority decisions and could abstain only on grounds of conscience.

anyone who had been a Gaitskellite. And vice versa. Even as late as the mid-1970s, David Owen was shocked to find that there were people who 'passionately disliked Barbara from the old Bevanite battles. Tony Crosland had no time for her – no respect for her – on an ideas basis – on any basis. People's relationships were really forged in that time and I don't think they ever forgot.'[26]

There was plenty to remember. In October 1952, a few months after the Gaitskellites had tried to get the Bevanite core expelled, delegates arrived at the conference at Morecambe in the mood for a showdown, two battle-ready armies. A member of the Gaitskellite battalion, Douglas Jay, clenched his teeth: 'The town was ugly, the hotels forbidding, the weather bad, and the Conference, at its worst, hideous.'[27] The town had a four-mile promenade. The Grosvenor Hotel was at one end, the Winter Gardens in the middle and the Midland Hotel at the other. Delegates spent much of their time traipsing from one hotel to the other in howling winds and driving rain. By the end of conference, Dick noted, everybody had a cold and heartache. The cause of Barbara's heartache was simple. She had been kept off the platform, as had Mik and Tom Driberg; Nye was only given two small resolutions to speak too; he rejected one and it was given to Mik. This resulted in Dick staying up half the night trying to settle a tearful Barbara, who was being whipped into a frenzy by Ted, who kept repeating how intolerably she had been treated. What prima donnas we all are, Dick sighed, even us Bevanites.

If, as Ted saw it, the Bevanite 'problem was how we could get the unions to reflect what was going on in the party'[28] – which also meant getting the union leadership to reflect the desires of their individual members – the problem was proving insoluble. As it had been in the 1930s when the Socialist League tried to tug the party leftward, the union leadership was moving ever rightward. One constituency party delegate put forward a resolution calling for industrial action to bring down the Tory government, the sort of syndicalist sentiments guaranteed to inflame Arthur Deakin and Will Lawther. Deakin, present as a fraternal delegate from the TUC, and one who had already spoken, got up for an unscheduled rant:

'You know you would listen if you wanted to get money from the trade unions', he hollered when the floor objected.[29] He got his way. But the response was not the doffed cap a trade-union boss might expect when he slapped down a Labour MP but outraged, loud anger. The rank and file in the gallery bellowed and catcalled, they 'felt no inhibitions whatsoever about having it out with their industrial leaders';[30] howling dervishes, Deakin called them later. Lawther's contribution to the debate was 'Shut your gob!'[31] The union bosses were not going to let the rank and file tell the unions how to run their show.

The speeches of former ministers and lowly MPs were booed or cheered along factional lines. There was actual fisticuffs on the floor; both party and union leadership were 'stunned by the spirit of virtual insurgency amongst the constituency delegates'.[32] Most of these delegates had been mandated by the local parties to vote for every resolution that challenged the party and union leadership; and to vote the Bevanite ticket in the NEC elections. There was nothing of the usual desultory attitude towards voting. There was a scrum to pick up ballot papers. Everyone knew why they were there. Nye topped the poll again; Barbara was second with 200,000 more votes than the previous year; Mik and Driberg were back with increased votes, and Harold and Dick were elected for the first time.

Dalton was out, Morrison was out. The only non-Bevanite to survive was James Griffiths, a man in the unhappy position of being acceptable to all. The only Bevanite Dalton congratulated was Dick. He would 'have spoken a nice word to Barbara',[33] but he didn't run into her. The result 'produced something akin to a frenzy' among the party hierarchy; they 'had never before faced an unmanageable challenge'.[34] The results became international news, greeted by horror or awe, because, in John Freeman's anonymous view in the *New Statesman*, a 'non-Communist Left, based on individual Party membership, has succeeded in forging itself into a coherent group, gained a majority and used the constitutional machinery to register an effective protest and shift the Party noticeably Leftward'.[35] The Bevanites had won and were seen to have won.

Harold, delighted to be on the executive this time, if with far less support than Barbara, took to swinging over to her flat in Cholmeley Lodge on the mornings of the NEC meetings so that they could go together. She often kept him waiting, Harold's secretary, Marcia Williams said: 'She would wave from the window or dash out ... clutching ... her clothes, or with a piece of toast ... she hadn't quite finished, and throw herself into the front seat next to Harold and immediately launch into a long conversation, or an attack ... while fitting in a grumble about being late or warning Harold not to complain about having to wait for her', an entrance Marcia considered 'typically feminine'.[36]

The Gaitskellites were acting typically, too. Gaitskell raised the bogey of communist infiltration, declaring that what had happened was 'mob rule by a group of frustrated journalists' who had been elected because a sixth of the constituency delegates were 'communist or communist inspired'.[37] He knew what he was doing. Communism was almost as big a bogey in Britain as it was in America. In 1950 MI5 had told the government that there were a quarter of a million files on British citizens who might be Russian spies. To call someone a communist was, if not to shut them up, to move them beyond the pale, where they could not be taken seriously.

Jim Callaghan joined in, saying that the party must be 'aligned with forces who are against the insidious attempts of communism to break the democratic Socialist movement',[38] thus encouraging the whispering campaign that had dogged Labour in the previous election, the loudest whisper of which accused Bevan and the Bevanites of being fellow travellers. For Gaitskell the mob rule speech was a great personal success, establishing him with the king-makers, Messrs Deakin, Lawther and Williamson.

The Bevanites responded to the charge by Gaitskell, Attlee and others that they were a party within a party by announcing that their meetings – in the House, at least – were henceforth open to any Labour MP. But Attlee smelt the trap. This would create a rival party meeting, and the motion was put to the PLP that the Bevanites be disbanded. Barbara, John and Dick tried to get the vote put off until after the shadow cabinet elections in November;Attlee had no intention of postponing the agony. He put the vote to the PLP, who agreed to disband all unofficial groups within the party, on the usual penalty of expulsion. The Bevanites duly disbanded, but in name only. They continued to meet in one another's houses and gather round the big table in their corner of the Smoking Room:the smoking room within the Smoking Room, as Driberg quipped.They continued with the *Tribune* Brains Trusts.And the Second VI was, if anything, even more active.The real political battles were to come.

Chapter Six

SCARLET BOGEY

The Americans kept a wary eye and more on the Bevanites, who seemed to the USA much as they did to the right wing of the Labour Party: 'important, well-organised and machiavellian'.[1] Their activities were prominently reported in the US press and, although 'for reasons of national security ... the CIA can neither confirm nor deny the existence or nonexistence of any CIA records ... on British stateswoman, Barbara Castle',[2] they doubtless exist. Gaitskell's communist aspersions added credence to Washington's suspicions, and some Bevanites were more dangerous than others.

Barbara, 'an associate of Aneurin Bevan and his neutralist bloc', in the *New York Times*'s phrase,[3] was one of the most dangerous of all: an implacable unilateralist, a vociferous opponent of making, testing and retaining the British bomb, and a foe of the presence of American nuclear weapons on British soil. She sought assurances in parliament that such 'atom bombs would not be used by the United States without British consent' and expressed the view that 'Britain may one day be the object of Russian retaliation in a war precipitated by the United States'.[4]

She used her articles and speeches to attack America's disproportionate power, its immaturity, its love of brinkmanship, its failure to conduct real disarmament negotiations with the Russians. Britain was nothing more than an American aircraft-carrier. Churchill, once

121

the British bulldog sitting proudly on the Union Jack, was now the Americans' poodle simpering and snivelling on the Stars and Stripes. Barbara conjured up the spectre of the bomb; the prospect of atomic warfare inched ever closer as America and Russia spat belligerent threats at each other. The Cold War was feverish. American planes flew to the edge of Russian territory,* a sure act of provocation, a near act of war.

The bomb became one of Barbara's central issues. The fact that the government had decided that Britain would manufacture its own H-Bomb galvanised her. This weakens 'our biggest source of strength: our moral leadership', she told the *Sunday Times*.[5] Britain's moral leadership had always been part of her armoury, as it had much of the left's. Her utopian socialism remained strong all her life. She always believed that you could teach people to do what was right and to want what was good for them. She believed she could take the crucial issue of the bomb and fight the next election with it. She talked to Dick about it; the longer she talked, Dick noted, the more it became obvious that her 'only real argument was that we must appeal to morality' by refusing to enter the nuclear arms race. It was not a point of view he accepted or understood. 'To run a campaign against an accomplished fact is difficult at the best of times', he grumbled;[6] and it may not have been an issue to fight the 1955 election on, but Barbara was right. Very soon the bomb was going to be *the* issue for country and party alike.

By the mid-1950s, Barbara had become a well-known public figure. The Brains Trusts alone had proved to be a great promoter as much of the personalities who appeared on them as of the ideas promulgated, and none more so than Barbara. But Barbara had also 'carved out her own position inside the party', distinct from the Bevanites per se. She had her own agenda, which was 'quite rightly to be leader of the party', Richard Clements said.[7] She continued to

---

* And into it, but this was not known until the 'U2 Incident': on 1 May 1960, an American U2 reconnaissance plane was shot down over Sverdlovsk. A few days later, Krushchev used the incident as a reason to walk out of a Paris summit meeting with Eisenhower.

attend to her personal publicity, appearing frequently on television and keeping herself on the lecture circuit, talking on such subjects as 'The Cost of Living' or 'Living in the Cold War'.

Apart from her articles in the *New Statesman* and the *Tribune*, she also wrote for mainstream publications, most lucratively and effectively her column in the late fifties for the *Sunday Pictorial*. Through all this she had managed to create a public image of herself that was vivid and familiar. There was scarcely an article written that did not portray her as a fiery redhead, or the red-haired conscience of the Labour Party; Red Barbara, like Red Ellen before her, red in hair and spirit.

Being a 'bit of a rebel is far from being a handicap to an attractive, zestful redhead who looks younger than her forty-three years', the *Sunday Times* noted,[8] when Lancashire's likely lass was actually 44, the year of her birth being consistently misreported as 1911.

Barbara being the first woman MP 'to achieve distinction as a leading member of a ginger group', her sayings and doings were watched and recorded; she was 'a first-class broadcaster', an accomplishment deemed 'rare among women Parliamentarians', a fearless, glamorous controversialist who could not be ignored. 'Whatever we think of her opinions, we have to think of them,' the *Sunday Dispatch* sighed. Barbara and Bevan, 'the two Bs', as they were sometimes called, with all that implied, were talked of in one breath. She had become 'one of the very few political superstars that we have ever had in this country', Gerald Kaufman said, 'certainly one of the very few political superstars' in the last half of the twentieth century. 'She was extraordinarily charismatic.'[9]

Charisma was stoked by fear. Barbara was afraid of being afraid. That fear of fear had not gone away. It egged her on. The more afraid she was of doing something, the more she had to do it. She was afraid of letting herself down, of being a coward. Publicly she never seemed afraid. Publicly she seemed ready to take on all comers. To be courageous and to be seen to be so was vital to Barbara. She had 'felt compelled' to continue her lawsuit against the journalist and broadcaster Godfrey Winn until he retracted his comment that she was afraid to debate with him over Cyprus, holding out until he unequivocally stated that she was 'not a person who would hesitate or fear to engage in any such debate with any adversary on a public platform'.[10]

The friendlier cartoonists portrayed her as Joan of Arc; the more admiring columnists dubbed her a 'woman of courage'. And she was willing to go out on a limb and champion causes likely to be less than popular, such as justice for the eleven Mau Mau* prisoners beaten to death in Hola, a British detention camp in Kenya, a case she 'exposed with splendid courage'.[11] To the right-wing media, issues such as this made her the red bogey, the political scarlet woman.

Even though, as Michael Foot observed, Barbara made herself into probably the best woman parliamentarian ever, she did not like being a backbencher. She found it a frustrating experience. She didn't like having only words with which to influence people. But she worked extremely hard and she got things done. She sat on standing committees to do with finance, social insurance and restrictive trade practices, and she took up issues. In 1950, she introduced an amendment to the Criminal Law Bill, again under the ten-minute rule, to protect prostitutes, hitherto outside the law, from misuse and abduction, a significant piece of civil and women's rights legislation. One of her most famous backbench campaigns was that of turnstiles in women's toilets. Again, under the ten-minute rule, Barbara submitted a Bill calling for their removal, a) because they were difficult for the old, handicapped and pregnant to manoeuvre through; and b), as men did not have to pay to visit the Gents, they were discriminatory.

Turnstiles and toilets were a giggle to the House and for the press; this issue got the most publicity and generated stacks and stacks of approving correspondence. Eventually, perhaps to her chagrin, it was Patricia McLaughlin's Bill which finally got turnstiles abolished, two years after Barbara had begun her campaign.

'In attack she provides one of the most awesome sights the House of Commons has to offer', the *Manchester Guardian* observed. Her usual seat in the House was far back, below the gangway, 'but you

* An insurgent group whose members belonged to Kenya's Kikuyu tribe. Its aim was to expel all immigrant races from Kenya; it killed thousands of people, most of them Black Africans it considered collaborators.

always know when she is there, pale and vivid and watchful'. Her stage presence had, if anything, become greater. So had her sense of theatre. Her entrance was always 'the sartorial moment of every parliamentary day ... as with Royalty, it has come to be a point of principle that Mrs Castle must not appear more than a few times in any outfit, however smart'. Her clothes, and what was seen (despite the 'masculine mind' tag) as her ultra-femininity continued to be remarked upon throughout her career. As one columnist mused, political women were accepted as politicians only if they 'un-sex themselves as they pass through the gates at Westminster', with the exception, he added, of Barbara.[12]

She did the opposite, and more than got away with it. 'She alone ... is a woman MP who is securely plugged into the high-voltage circuit of political power.' While the chaps were gawking, Barbara was crouching ready to pounce. 'She would use that piercing voice to question [Harold] Macmillan', Tam Dalyell said, often putting Supermac on the back foot; 'he was more flappable to her than to anyone else',[13] especially over colonial and race issues, which Barbara passionately made her own.

She was a member of the Commonwealth and Colonial Affairs Group and on the NEC's Commonwealth Subcommittee, which wrote Labour's colonial policy and was a left-wing enclave. Dick, Tom Driberg and Tony Greenwood were also members, as was her brother, Jimmie; home from Africa, he had become assistant secretary of the Fabian Society Colonial Bureau.

As the sole woman in Labour's high politics, Barbara was subjected to rumours of affairs. The only man she was close to whom nobody appeared to suspect her of sleeping with was Dick Crossman, and Dick, as his diaries suggest, was more than a little obsessed with Barbara and saw as much of her as Ted did, if not more, during the thirty years they knew each other.

Tony Greenwood, whom Barbara had known since their Oxford days, had been elected to parliament in a by-election in 1946 and was elected to the NEC eight years later. He was not a Bevanite, but was on the left of the party and, like Barbara and Mik, a unilateralist and an anti-colonial activist. Barbara and Tony were politically at one on most issues. They worked closely together and saw a lot of each other which provoked much gossip at Westminster.

Barbara considered Tony a 'lightweight with more charm than principle' and patronised him shamelessly, pulling stunts such as thanking him for a 'sweet article' he penned, which 'incidentally ... was very well written'. He was, she purred, 'a natural journalist'.[14] Neither she nor Dick considered him intellectually over-endowed, nor politically astute. Dick wrote him off as a 'clothes horse'.

Barbara, who was appointed honorary president of the Anti-Apartheid Movement (AAM) in 1960, was a sponsor of the Movement for Colonial Freedom (MCF), another left-wing enclave to which two-thirds of Bevanite MPs subscribed, and of which Jim Callaghan, in a variation of the language the right always uses to vilify the left, called 'a well-intentioned but essentially unreliable, if not unstable, group ... whose views of colonial matters were simplistic'.[15] Simplistic or not, imperialism was high capitalism, and decolonisation, although arguably historically inevitable, became the left's tangible success.

While Britain's fifty-plus colonies continued to exist, Barbara concerned herself with exposing any abuses by the British authorities, becoming a thorn in the side of the Colonial Office. She visited Kenya in 1955 to investigate the case of a Kikuyu chief who had been found dead in suspicious circumstances. She criticised the government's handling of the affair, and the colonial secretary, Alan Lennox Boyd, attacked her in the House saying that she had gone to Kenya 'to support conclusions at which she had already arrived'.

Barbara covered, and campaigned against, the South African treason trial, which went on for over four years (1956–61) and ended in acquittal of all 156 suspects, including, that time, Nelson Mandela. On her trips to Rhodesia, she 'consistently shocked and annoyed Rhodesians by her open association with Africans', especially when she went into a whites-only dining room in a Salisbury hotel 'with an African by her side'.[16] The African was Wellington Chirwa, a member of the Central African Federation parliament. It was headline news: 'Shocked Diners Walk Out.' The sight of a white woman and a black man, even accompanied by the very white and Scottish Reverend Andrew Doig, had proven too much.

She was a raucous opponent of the Central African Federation, which originally grouped Northern Rhodesia, Southern Rhodesia and Nyasaland* together under white domination. Her pro-black-African views kept her off the Monckton Committee set up to look into the Federation and African opposition to it; the Federation's white prime minister, Roy Welensky, a former heavyweight boxing champion, insisted that all the committee's members be privy councillors just to keep her – and Jim Callaghan – off. Jim was not opposed to a federation per se, but as Labour's colonial affairs spokesman he had angered Welensky by reiterating the party's position that any federation had to be acceptable to black Africans.

Labour's Colonial Policy: The Plural Society,† co-written by Barbara, 'was regarded within the party as the most significant' of the three colonial policy statements; it was embraced by the 1956 party conference with Julius Nyerere, the future president of Tanzania, watching from the gallery. In the country it aroused wide interest, not, as it was ahead of its time, all favourable. Barbara and her co-authors had had the temerity to suggest that the 'principles of democracy are no less valid' for colonial societies 'than any other type of society'. Moreover, the British first-past-the-post unitary parliamentary model was not sacrosanct. People in the colonies 'have the right to determine which particular form of constitution (perhaps some entirely new form)' best suited them; but adult universal suffrage was a must, with minority rights protected, and it was Britain's responsibility to stay on until the 'conditions for the establishment of full democracy exist'. Such rights were not dependent 'on colour, race, religion, ability, experience, influence, education, wealth or power', Barbara and her colleagues wrote, startling news to the establishment, which bemoaned the passing of an Attlee or a Morrison and accused them of being 'a donnish circle' lacking 'hard experience'.[17]

* Now respectively Zambia, Zimbabwe and Malawi.
† What would now be called a multiracial society.

The following year the donnish circle produced *Economic Aid*, which, once adopted by conference, committed the next Labour Government to 'an average of 1% of our national income' in aid without shirking from the fact that it 'may mean some delay in increasing our own standards of good living, but the poorer areas must have priority and we have a special obligation to our own colonies and to the other members of the Commonwealth'.[18] Barbara, Tony and some of the other committee members also accepted the even less palatable fact that aid had to be accompanied by export opportunities free from sectional interests, such as those of her constituents in the Lancashire cotton industry, who sought to block cheap cotton imports produced under what they considered 'unfair competitive conditions'.

Barbara believed in expansionist economic policies for the world, not just for Britain. There was no such thing, she argued in the *Tribune* and elsewhere, as overproduction of cotton at that moment; the problem was underconsumption caused by a lack of purchasing power. Aid coupled with buying the exports of the backward countries, as they were called, was not only natural justice but enlightened self-interest. 'The fight for exports [from the developing world] has become part of the fight against world poverty', Barbara wrote. 'Unless we lift the standards of the backward peoples, we, too, will slip into depression and poverty.'[19]

For Blackburn's MP this was a stance of considerable courage. She stuck to it, even in the face of a mass demonstration in London by Lancashire cotton-workers and mill-owners. Although sympathetic to her constituents' plight of short working and unemployment and mindful that the 'Labour movement came into existence to fight for full employment against the inhuman economics of the free market', she argued that this must be applied to the whole world: 'To offer aid instead of trade is to condemn the under-developed countries to be perpetual remittance-men.' The world had to work out an equitable trading system because 'the traditional solutions of quotas and tariffs, designed to meet purely western needs, provide no remedy'.[20] Lancashire needed redevelopment rather than protectionism. She promulgated a temporary scheme under which the state would buy Asian cotton and resell it at prices that wouldn't immediately destroy Lancashire, so that the transition from one industry to others could be, if not painless, at least less than an-archic.

As Barbara's parliamentary career glittered, Ted's would-be parliamentary career floundered. Like Bill Mellor before him, Ted was an MP manqué. Throughout the fifties he tried to get selected to fight half a dozen seats and failed and the seats he was selected to fight were hopeless. The fact that he was Barbara's husband drew unwanted and sometimes nasty press attention: 'For years and years he has been rejected everywhere like an author's first novel', the *Sunday Express* sneered.[21] Although Barbara was probably anxious to get Ted in the House, many people assumed the opposite. By now, the Castles' marriage had become *the* subject of the Westminster rumour mill, and what Barbara supposedly did or did not do to help or hinder Ted was pure grist.

It wasn't just Barbara's supposed affairs that were chewed over. Ted, too, caused raised eyebrows during the 1953 Abingdon by-election he was contesting, for supposedly chasing a young woman. (He lost the by-election; the Tories increased their majority.) The belief that Barbara and Ted went their own ways became more and more entrenched the more successful she became.

Barbara had a close friendship with John Freeman that set tongues wagging: enigmatic John, fiercely intelligent, self-effacing, was a man of tremendous feline charm, as Dalton put it, elegant, exceedingly attractive, a recipient of an MBE at 28 and five years younger than the ever-youthful Barbara.

They were so different in many ways that their friendship is surprising. The much-married John had something of the invisible man about him; he was, thought Dick, who knew him well, a 'strangely secretive person'; a man of the utmost rectitude, for whom, Nye Bevan said, 'form is all-important'.[22] Barbara would have found any kind of relationship with an emotionally remote man difficult. She was an emotional woman; she liked the volume at full blast; she liked engagement. She was easily moved to tears or laughter or anger. There was nothing once removed about Barbara.

As he was a television interviewer on *Face to Face*, John's cheerful, intelligent face was known to millions, despite his famous technique of remaining out of the camera's eye during interviews, a technique which Barbara thought summed up his reticent personality. He was one of the few who, having licked the edges of power, moved on without a backward glance. He preferred the role of disinterested analyst. He was, Barbara concluded, 'afraid of giving himself too fully to anything or anyone'.[23] Polite, disciplined, he slipped in and out of the shadows. The grimy world of parliamentary and party intrigue offended. He resigned his seat in 1955, going from assistant editor of the *New Statesman* to deputy editor to editor within the next five years.

Barbara and John saw a lot of each other through the *New Statesman*, the house organ of the 'Oxford Bevanites'. She was writing as much for the more mainstream and measured *Statesman*, on whose editorial board she sat, as she was for the *Tribune*. The *Statesman* was, and had been for many years, Dick's home, too; it was more centre left, intellectual left, more where she and Dick and Harold were moving.

Every Monday, Barbara dashed over to the *Statesman*'s offices for the editorial conference, always late, always flustered, always rushing into the conference room, always interrupting someone in mid-sentence, flopping down and launching immediately into a litany of complaints. She had been up so late. There was so much to do; too much. All her committee work, all her journalism, all her speeches, and then her diary, which she scrawled down, more intermittently than later, in an old school notebook. (Barbara often took notes all through meetings and conferences, 'simultaneously recording the proceedings and taking an active part in them', as Mik archly noted.[24]) 'This is my pension', she told a young and very amused Anthony Howard, waving her notebook at him. Howard would watch her during the two hours of morning conference as she ran the gamut of emotions: laughing one minute, tearful the next, roaring with anger a moment later. It was, he recalled, 'a marvellous dramatic display'.[25]

Such displays were unremarkable for Barbara, especially as she moved towards the height of her powers. She came at everything with gusto. She roared, she hummed, she bristled with intensity, she was lustily ravenous for life, operating at her best at this high voltage and in the starring role. She was, for the most part, enjoying herself. She had, as Michael said, a 'great capacity for enjoying life',[26] but she wanted the big prize, which was somewhere (or nowhere) down the road.

She could be tetchy, irritable, self-obsessed; 'she gets herself into tight neurotic knots', Michael said. She was never an easy friend. She had, Roy Hattersley observed, 'an infinite capacity for annoying people'.[27] Barbara was capable of bursting 'out into great invective against people around her', appalling Michael, who could be rough but was seldom vicious; he found her behaviour at times outrageous. He would watch her at dinner parties, turning on her friends and deriding them 'contemptuously'. She lived on her nerves; as they used to say, she was highly strung. 'Barbara is taking too much benzedrine, or is very strained',[28] Hugh Dalton wrote; pill-popping was not unusual at Westminster in the 1950s. Benzedrine tablets, called 'bennies', were amphetamines, widely prescribed by doctors at the time, the perfect antidote to a life in which sleep was a combination of nuisance and luxury.

Her self-absorption made her ill-mannered. Dick angrily watched her walk out of one of his dinner parties because there was something she needed to look up for a forthcoming speech. Nothing could stop her; she left without even saying goodbye. 'If she wants to know why she is unpopular, I could tell her', he fumed. This kind of reaction seemed to puzzle her, as if she expected to be indulged. 'I'm told that I have made many enemies', she said. She admitted she had, like her father, a hot temper. She knew that when roused she could 'lash out – even at my friends',[29] but she expected them to understand there was no malice in it.

Barbara's temperamental difficulties were nothing compared to

Nye's. In the course of one year he stalked out of the shadow cabinet, without consulting his friends, and then decided to run against Gaitskell for treasurer of the party, which meant resigning his safe NEC seat. The treasurer's position is courtesy of the union block vote and Nye could not hope to win against Gaitskell, who was not only a man of the right, and a man whom the unions promoted, but a former chancellor of the exchequer. Nye had de facto resigned from the NEC as well. Not even the NUM voted for this miner. He went into 1955 without a power base. Barbara blamed Jennie for encouraging these antics, for bringing out the worst in Nye, his self-indulgent side; Jennie's 'Nyedolatry', she called it. It was the last thing Nye needed: 'more men are ruined by doting wives than anything else!'[30] Barbara told the *Daily Herald*.

Harold, with Dick's support, had taken Nye's place in the twelve-seat shadow cabinet, as he was automatically entitled, having come thirteenth in the previous shadow cabinet election; it was an act of apostasy to some of the Bevanites. Barbara, just back from a holiday in Scotland, was initially opposed to Harold's alacrity, even though she disagreed with Nye's resignation. Nye refused to give Harold his blessing, which left her with a conflict of loyalties. Whatever she thought of Nye, he was the titular head of their group. But she gradually changed her mind. Barbara was not a resigner: she believed in staying put, digging in, fighting from within. Resigning once had been proper and necessary. Resigning once, twice, thrice, was becoming an ineffectual habit.

In March 1955 Nye was almost expelled from the party for questioning Attlee in the House over Labour's attitude to the bomb. Unlike Barbara, Nye was not clear-cut on the issue of the H-bomb; he was ambivalent about a British independent deterrent and had not resigned from the 1945 cabinet when the decision to manufacture the bomb had been taken; he didn't see nuclear weapons as a *particular* evil, distinct from, say, saturation bombing. Nevertheless, he pushed Attlee to clarify whether Labour's amendment repudiated using the H-bomb in response to conventional non-nuclear aggression. Attlee did not clarify Labour's position to anyone's satisfaction. And Nye, after accusing him of being unable to give a lead, joined Barbara in abstaining on the amendment; Barbara wished he hadn't, as he lacked 'moral scruples' on the issue. Other Bevanites, such Harold, John and Dick, who were not unilateralists, had voted for the amendment.

Nye's public attack on Attlee was a gift to the Gaitskellites. Attlee's retirement could not be far off and the anti-Bevanite inquisition was in full swing. Two months earlier, Barbara had been censured by the party for her comment on a *Tribune* Brains Trust platform that there had been 'dirty dealings' backstage at the 1954 party conference when the woodworkers' union had switched its conference vote and voted for German rearmament. And now here was Nye, throwing down, in Gaitskell's words, 'a direct challenge to the elected leader of our Party'. It was, Gaitskell fluttered, nothing short of 'an affront to the Party which elected him'. The shadow cabinet voted to withdraw the whip from Nye. The whip withdrawn, Nye faced a meeting of the full NEC which would decide whether or not to expel him. Most people, 'even his fellow Bevanites, thought Nye had gone too far' in openly challenging Attlee.[31] But Nye was still the leader of the party in the country, the leader of the left, and he had to be saved, if only from himself.

After he had savaged the party leader, Nye went down with flu – with or without quotation marks – and swanned off to Asheridge, the Lee–Bevan farmhouse in the Chilterns. Barbara, Dick and Tony Greenwood followed, to try and talk some sense into him before his NEC trial. They found him sitting up in bed, 'wonderfully obstreperous', Dick said. Barbara told him he *must* issue a statement apologising to Attlee. Nye was having none of it. He 'shouted, like a petulant child, I won't! I won't!'[32] But he did in the end, stating that what he had said was not a challenge to Attlee's leadership but a difference of policy. The NEC voted fourteen to thirteen not to expel him. He was saved by Jean Mann, an implacable anti-Bevanite right-winger, but one who had known Jennie since she was a girl; she put personal loyalty before politics and hoped that the specially convened subcommittee would sort Nye out.

Barbara was the only Bevanite on this subcommittee, which consisted of Attlee, Gaitskell, James Griffiths, three union leaders, and Edith Summerskill in the chair. Attlee was interested in holding the party together and was as anxious as Barbara that Nye not be expelled. Together they drafted a motion which called upon Nye to give them assurances as to his future conduct as a member of the party, which, taking Barbara and Dick's advice, he did. They had saved Bevan from himself once again, but it was beyond being the last straw. Barbara, Dick and Harold had, as Dick told Dalton, 'practically pulled out' of the Bevanites per se. Their left-wing orbit would increasingly be round each other.

Barbara and Mik were still convinced that Ban the Bomb was enough to win the election, Dick noted, three weeks before the May 1955 general election. And indeed the opinion polls put the H-bomb and the cost of living neck and neck at the top of the public's chief concerns. But there were other worries, too, notably the state of the Labour Party. Nye's near expulsion, and the cavernous split it once again exposed, came two months before the election and was brought up at every opportunity by the Tories, led since Churchill's retirement in 1955 by Anthony Eden; the Tories' Johnny Ray, as Barbara chided, their mindless matinée idol. Matinée idol versus ageing silent-film star in the personage of the 72-year-old Clement Attlee. Publicly, Barbara's line was usually the rather inevitable, Splits, what splits? We are separated by words or emphasis, not meaning or policies, and so on. But it was difficult to explain why the party had almost thrown out the man thought of as the architect of the beloved NHS.

Rab Butler, the chancellor, tried to buy the election in the usual way by reducing taxes and increasing personal income-tax allowances. His decision to cut purchase tax from 50 per cent to 25 per cent on goods produced by Barbara's ailing Lancashire cotton mills did not help her campaign efforts to blame the parlous state of the industry on the Tories; nor did the future Cardinal Basil Hume's denunciation of the Bevanites as evil incarnate gather her votes.

Right: Barbara at fifteen, romantic and rebellious.
© Hulton Getty

Below: The newly-elected member for Blackburn, July 1945.
© Hulton Getty

Right: Bill Mellor, Barbara's mentor and first love.

General Election, 1931.

ENFIELD DIVISION of MIDDLESEX
Polling Day: Tuesday, October 27th, 8 a.m. to 9 p.m.

WILLIAM MELLOR
The LABOUR Candidate

Below: The 'Prime Minister of London', Herbert Morrison, appointed the St Pancras Borough Councillor to the Metropolitan Water Board.
© Kurt Hutton/Hulton Getty

Above: Interviewing Prime Minister
Attlee for *Picture Post* in 1946.
© Haywood Magee/Hulton Getty

Left: En route to the United Nations in
New York, 1949 – Barbara's success as a
young MP caused jealousy.
© Popperfoto

Below: With Hugh Dalton in 1951 – he
encouraged her to run for the constituency
party section of the NEC.
© Hulton Getty

Above: The first woman ever elected by the constituencies on to the NEC. Barbara stands with fellow Bevanites (right to left) Tom Driberg, Ian Mikardo and Nye Bevan. Harold Wilson was not elected. ©Popperfoto

Below left: Barbara's presence in the House was 'the sartorial moment of every parliamentary day'. Here she is emerging after a record 23-hour sitting in 1952. © Popperfoto

Below right: It would take another twenty years for Barbara to get equal pay for women. © Hulton Getty

Above: Campaigning in 1955. She won by only 489 votes – one of the smallest majorities in the country. © MSI

Right: Barbara was one of the first to spot Harold Wilson's talents. 1955. © Popperfoto

Below: Barbara and Dick Crossman with spouses Anne and Ted looking on. At the Labour Conference in Scarborough, 1958. © Hulton Getty

Above: The Chairman of the Party, with Hugh Gaitskell and Nye Bevan in 1959. © MSI

Below: Barbara and Tony Greenwood in 1960. He had the job of deterring her from making a leadership bid. © Hulton Getty

Above: Barbara and Ted in Fanny and Johnny mode. © Popperfoto

Above: Barbara and
Jim Callaghan in
1960 – an inverse
beguilement.
© Hulton Getty

Left: The Minister of
Overseas Development
was the first woman
in cabinet for ten
years and the fourth in
British history. 1964.
© Hulton Getty

Blackburn had a sizeable minority of Catholic voters who Barbara would later assiduously win back by championing state support for Catholic schools, with which she disagreed.

In the lead-up to the election, Gallup showed the two main parties with no more than two or three points between them. But the Tories won, increasing their majority from seventeen to sixty; the result was judged as Labour's failure rather than the Conservatives' success. It was the safe Labour seats that were hardest hit, including Blackburn. It never occurred to Barbara that she might lose Blackburn, Abbot Hume, Rab Butler and Labour splits notwithstanding.

She had always been an excellent constituency MP, conscientiously taking her surgeries and following up her constituents' concerns. The time and trouble she took were legendary. There were many stories about her lavishing care and attention on people. She sometimes visited sick constituents and spent time talking to them, and then went off and sorted out their benefits, pension, or housing problems. When she was a minister, Barbara kept up with her constituency work; too much so, some people thought: even when she was under the most appalling pressure she insisted on making time to deal with what many felt were not especially significant personal problems. She would have considered anything less an abrogation of duty.

It was a worried George Eddie (her electoral agent) who hurried across the room to tell Barbara she'd lost her seat. His back-of-the-envelope calculations put her out. She froze, keeping an equally frozen smile on her face. What on earth would she do? This was political death, one of the worst moments in her life. Ted stood beside her, waiting as the vote was recounted. She was down, but not out. She scraped in by 489 votes, a majority of 0.9 per cent, one of the smallest in the country. It wasn't as bad as Mik's 238-vote majority, and it was infinitely better than what had happened to Michael Foot: he lost his seat to Joan Vickers by 100 votes. Dick saw his majority halved, to a relatively healthy 6000, but halved none the less. Dalton and Attlee also suffered vote losses. The party was in trouble. Bevanites and anti-Bevanites had suffered defeats and near misses in equal measure. The electorate was disgusted with a rudderless party at war with itself.

Attlee, who had been party leader for twenty years, had now lost two elections. His retirement was inevitable, but it was not welcome to the Bevanites, because Gaitskell was the likely successor. Barbara went to talk to Attlee, who told her that he would be willing to stay on for another year. Dick was not convinced: 'With Barbara one is never sure whether Attlee hadn't merely grunted at intervals while she told him what to think.'[33] Attlee resigned three months later.

Barbara tried to mobilise against Gaitskell, of course, tried to drum up sympathy for Herbert Morrison (anyone but Gaitskell), passionately explaining to journalists that although she had disagreed with Herbert in the past – somewhat of an understatement – he had earned the 'right to a short period of leadership'. Attlee, she said, was 'crazy' if he thought the party would accept Gaitskell. At the pre-conference rally, Barbara pulled out all the stops. Attlee had just come out of hospital and she rejoiced at his return; 'her voice breaking with emotion', she pleaded that the old sick man not be rushed off the scene at the behest of right-wing forces and right-wing papers. 'We still need Clem's wise leadership', she declared. 'Let us decide in his interests, and ours, when we shall thank him and say good-bye.'[34] She was mobbed afterwards, as she often was, by the audience seeking autographs. Barbara considered this speech one of the best of her life, and she was especially pleased with a David Low cartoon depicting her as Joan of Arc defending Attlee, the doodling dauphin.

The goodbyes were said and done and Nemesis was now at the wheel, despite Bevan's cackhanded attempt to cook up a secret deal with Morrison whereby Nye would morally force Gaitskell to stand aside by doing so himself, thus allowing homespun Herbert a clear run. After a decent interval, in this scenario, Morrison would himself step down, allowing Nye to step up. Barbara and Dick were appalled when they found out. Not surprisingly, Gaitskell refused to step aside; he thrashed Bevan and Morrison gaining 157 votes to their respective 70 and 40; a third of his votes came from the trade-union-sponsored MPs, who, almost to a man, were solidly behind him.

'When Gaitskell was a prospective premier who might soon be appointing Ministers ... his critics like Barbara ... had been carefully loyal or effusively friendly', his biographer wrote.[35] No one wanted power more than Barbara did, and she was willing to smile and try to be pleasant, even ingratiating, but she would not cut her conscience to fit into the Gaitskellite pattern. In the first year of his leadership Barbara was attacking him for his initial support of the Tory government over the Suez crisis precipitated, in July 1956, by President Nasser of Egypt nationalising the Suez Canal Company in which Britain and France had enormous financial interests.

Half of the oil consumed by Britain, Scandinavia and Western Europe was transported from the Middle East through the canal and Gaitskell supported Eden in the Commons when he condemned Nasser's illegal act. Gaitskell had let the Labour Movement down by such support, Barbara declared, and she, along with a couple of dozen Labour MPs, formed the Suez Emergency Committee to oppose any war with Egypt.

She fought Gaitskell all the way on his anti-unilateralist stance and on his attempts to abandon Clause 4 of the party's constitution which was inscribed on Labour Party membership cards and committed a Labour government to 'secure for the workers by hand or by brain the full fruits of their industry and the most equitable distribution thereof that may be possible upon the basis of the common ownership of the means of production, distribution and exchange'.

Although she was never elected to the shadow cabinet,* Gaitskell gave her work. She followed pensions for the party, and he made her shadow minister of works in 1959, which meant that she was responsible for the very popular cause of getting MPs better facilities. However reluctantly, Gaitskell saw the necessity of making the

---

*The only left-wingers elected to the shadow cabinet between 1951 and 1963 were Tony Greenwood and Dick Crossman, the latter once and briefly replacing Tony, who'd resigned. After replacing Nye in 1954, Harold was continually re-elected.

popular Barbara part of his team and she could have used that to ensure her place in any future Gaitskell government. But a year later, she was sacked for publicly opposing Gaitskell's stance on the bomb and Clause 4. She derided his refusal to abide by conference decisions and made 'public declarations that she would not wish to make herself available to serve on the front bench under Mr Gaitskell'.[36] Not the actions of a careerist. Barbara was a conviction politician. She wanted power, yes, but on terms that were acceptable. Perhaps Gaitskell respected this, because even after all their contretemps he repeated to Frank Cousins* in 1962 what he had told journalist George Gale a decade earlier: Barbara and Dick were the two left-wingers he would have in his cabinet (along, now, with Cousins).

In spring 1957, Britain tested its own H-bomb off Christmas Island. In response the H-bomb Campaign Committee was set up within the party and a hastily arranged protest rally was organised in Trafalgar Square, addressed by Barbara, Tony Greenwood and Mik. The bomb was now foursquare on the agenda of the forthcoming party conference in Brighton: 120 resolutions were tabled, almost all of them calling for the party to support unilateralism. They were merged into three composite resolutions; the unequivocally unilateralist one was the Norwood resolution.

Nye, whom Gaitskell had made shadow foreign secretary, got to his feet at conference to speak to the resolution. He began almost gently, softly, especially when compared with the ardour of the previous speakers for the resolution. But Barbara knew something was coming. She'd been at the NEC meeting the night before at which Nye had performed, in Dick's phrase, one of his 'intellectual emotional somersaults', reversing his stance at the earlier NEC meeting and putting himself in opposition to Norwood. She had

---

* A unilateralist, Cousins became leader of the TGWU in 1956, the first of the big left-wing union leaders; he was made minister of technology by Wilson and he resigned in 1966, in protest at the government's prices and incomes policy.

tried being emollient, tried to 'attempt a last-minute rescue operation', tried to postpone that which couldn't be agreed upon 'with a
proposal that Norwood ... remit the resolution on the basis that the
question of renunciation [of Nuclear weapons] would be left open
for the Executive to decide later',[37] thus endeavouring to hold all
doors simultaneously ajar. But she was voted down.

Nye explained to conference why he did not like Norwood, its
vagaries on certain issues, and then, as Michael observed, when he 'was
nearly halfway through his speech – something stirred his animosities
and awakened his belligerence, and he turned to crush his opponents
... with a cold hate'. The road to Brighton pier had been a long and
arduous one for Nye, one of continual opposition and near exile from
the party. He had tried to be both rebel and official Labour leader, an
impossible quest. He had been brought back into the fold and now, at
60, was potentially the next foreign secretary, the high office of state
that he had thought his due ten years earlier. He was in the Last Chance
Saloon and perhaps reflected that Gaitskell was unlikely to employ a
unilateralist foreign secretary. If the delegates passed the Norwood
resolution, he contemptuously told conference, they would 'send a
Foreign Secretary ... naked into the conference chamber'. There were
cries from the floor of 'Oh no!' and 'Don't say it, Nye', but he wasn't
finished with them yet. 'You call that statesmanship,' he spat, 'I call that
an emotional spasm'.[38]

Michael felt as if he had been horsewhipped, as did many delegates. Perhaps it was the cold hate, the contempt for all the love
and admiration Nye's followers had shown him that was so upsetting, the pain of personal betrayal, because Nye had never been
consistent on his attitude to the bomb. Delegates had read more
into his opaqueness than was there. They expected him to be a
unilateralist. He had sometimes been a unilateralist or appeared to
have been one, or been one in certain circumstances or something.
Barbara, too, although she knew full well that Nye lacked 'moral
scruples' on the bomb, was 'heartbroken' by his speech, his public
disavowal of so many of his followers. She couldn't believe what he
had said; or perhaps more the way he said it, the sheer gratuitous
nastiness of the whole thing.

The Norwood resolution was lost, sunk under the weight of 6 million mostly block votes. Delegates were in tears, not at the loss of Norwood as such, but at what they thought of as the loss of Nye. A paralysing sense of despair pervaded the auditorium without which, as Michael said, the 'whole place might have broken into uproar'. Barbara and Mik 'attacked [Nye] immediately afterwards ... He was flustered and flurried [but] did not concede to them in any way.'[39] As Barbara, Michael and Mik wandered around they were constantly stopped by bemused delegates and asked over and over again: 'Why did he do it?'

Cynics took it to mean that Nye had simply dumped his principles for power. The *Daily Express* ran a cartoon of an imperious top-hatted Bevan curling his lip at Barbara and Mik who were both wearing 'Ban the Bomb' badges and holding banners calling for more socialism. 'Ugh, Bevanites', Nye was saying.

A few months later the Campaign for Nuclear Disarmament (CND) was born; it subsequently became the biggest mass movement in British history. At Easter 1958, CND endorsed a ban-the-bomb march between Aldermaston and Trafalgar Square; it became an annual event, attracting up to 150,000 demonstrators at its zenith. On the first march banners were carried which read: 'No H Bombs, not even Nye's'. Selwyn Lloyd, the foreign secretary, speaking on *Woman's Hour*, said that a good deal of this agitation was Soviet-inspired in order to stop Britain emerging as the third nuclear power; to which Barbara's well-publicised 'feline comment' was 'Selwyn must have thought he was talking on *Children's Hour*.'[40]

Barbara joined CND, briefly and not happily; she marched and called her cocker spaniel Aldie, short for Aldermaston, but to her the danger of a single-issue campaign was that you might become marginalised, lose sight of the big picture, the context, capitalism, and the solution, socialism. To her it was all about what the next Labour government would do about the bomb. It was about moving the party with her. Barbara identified 'herself with the party as de Gaulle did France'.[41] What needed to be done would be done within the party and with the party, even if led by Gaitskell, even if the official Labour Party line was opposed to all she thought right and necessary; her loyalty to the party came first, last and always.

Anti-nuclear campaigner Pat Arrowsmith remembered Barbara 'quite vigorously attacking one of the Direct Action Committee (DAC) campaigns'[42] for its Voters Veto policy, which encouraged people not to vote for non-unilateralist candidates, whether they were Labour or anything else. DAC was a radical precursor of CND, and Barbara not its only opponent. The Labour left could not countenance this 'anti-Labour Party anti-politics element'[43] within the peace movement and nor could the CND leadership. The H-bomb Campaign Committee had become the CND Labour Advisory Committee and the CND leadership regarded the Labour Party as the only potential vehicle for its policies.

DAC was people's politics, a movement in favour of direct action, suspicious of parliament and parties and especially politicians; the first of the new libertarian left movements, anti-hierarchy, pro-collectivism, regarding the means as important as the ends; it wanted its power to come from below: its aim was 'to work from the bottom up more',[44] as Pat Arrowsmith said. Barbara, a proponent of left-wing orthodoxy, was for top-down government, statist, people politics channelled and organised and controlled and pyramid-shaped. Ted was much more active in CND than Barbara, as was Michael, who was a founder member of its executive council. But nevertheless Barbara continued to identify herself with, and champion, unilateral disarmament.

The issue of Cyprus almost did for Barbara. The island had been a crown colony since 1925 and was considered of strategic importance because of its location and the presence of British military bases. The islanders were predominantly Greek and the National Organization for Cypriot Struggle, EOKA, was engaged in armed insurrection against colonial rule and for *enosis*, union with Greece, to which the minority Turkish population and Turkey were violently opposed.

The Tories trusted the Turks more than the Greeks and sought to partition Cyprus as a way of securing the future of the British bases.

141

The Labour hierarchy, including Nye, went along with all this as a matter of expediency. Barbara did not. She reminded the 1957 annual conference that party policy on Cyprus was for 'democratic self-determination within an agreed period with safeguards for minority rights'.[45] Moreover the party was not, 'like the Tories, talking of a vague and misty future' when this would come about, but would 'endeavour to complete this ... during the lifetime of the next Labour Government'. Partition was not an option. 'We have no intention of dragging Cyprus through the tragedy of a partitioned Ireland', she said.

This 'statement had greatly cheered the Greeks, though it seems to have embarrassed' the Labour party leadership.[46] Thus cheered, Archbishop Makarios, the spiritual and political leader of the Greek Cypriots, and *bête noire* of the British, contacted Barbara through an intermediary and invited her to Athens to meet him. Barbara accepted. She took the precaution of meeting Foreign Office officials and the Greek and Turkish ambassadors in London before departing in September 1958, but what she said to Gaitskell, Bevan or Callaghan* about her impending freelance diplomacy is not clear.

John Hatch, the party's Commonwealth officer, had worked out a simple plan under which Cyprus would be a self-governing Commonwealth country, and it was this that Barbara put to the 'wily prelate': no *enosis*, no partition. He agreed; it was the first significant concession in the dispute. 'Staggering news that transforms the whole situation',[47] Tony Benn (then a man of the centre) noted.

Barbara did the rounds in Greece and Turkey, feeling like a foreign secretary-elect, she said, going on to Cyprus and meeting the governor, Sir Hugh Foot, brother of Michael, who told her that he didn't mind if the British soldiers got a bit rough when in hot pursuit of terrorists, as long as they didn't do it in cold blood. Having listened to a litany of complaints from Greek Cypriots about the brutality of the British troops, Barbara put the two things

* Now shadow colonial secretary.

together and told the press that the troops were 'permitted and even encouraged by the authorities to use unnecessarily tough measures' in circumstances of 'hot pursuit'.[48]

The words 'even encouraged' sent the media into a chorus of righteous indignation. She returned home to a deluge of hysterical denunciation. She was set upon by one of her trade-union foes on the NEC, Jim Matthews, who said her remarks were 'deplorable'. Much outraged comments were directed at the fact that she was the upcoming chairman of the Party, making, according to much of the press, this 'latest piece of political mischief-making . . . the most disgraceful episode in Barbara Castle's political career'.[49]

Barbara was summoned to a meeting with Gaitskell, James Griffiths, Nye and Jim Callaghan, from whom she did not get a word of praise for her deal with Makarios, just frosty and united disapproval over her comments. Jim thought her an 'unduly one-sided advocate of the Greek Cypriot cause', although he himself had attacked the governance of Cyprus, saying that 'many of the aspects of the regime . . . conducted in the name of the people of Britain are totalitarian'. Perhaps he objected to her muscling in on his colonial territory or worried lest she wrecked the deal he had covertly set up, committing the party to Hugh Foot's plan, which would have left Cyprus's status unchanged for seven years and was 'incompatible with . . . a belief in self determination' for Cyprus[50] – official party policy. She was also summoned back to Blackburn to explain herself to her constituency party, where, by a mixture of sweet reason, rhetorical persuasion and cajoling, she persuaded most of them of her argument.

Gaitskell was not so forgiving, cajoled or easily persuaded. He issued a statement which totally dissociated the party from her remarks, in effect publicly repudiating her, without paying tribute to her diplomatic achievement. His actions were an abrogation of loyalty and leadership, a 'poor demonstration of the Gallup poll mentality',[51] as an indignant Tony Benn pointed out; whatever Harold Macmillan's faults he had 'never allowed a colleague to be downtrodden without rising firmly in his support'. Gaitskell's stance made it appear as if he agreed with the *Daily Telegraph* in its opinion of the settlement plan: that the 'manner of its presentation – an interview with Mrs Barbara Castle – scarcely encourages belief in the Archbishop's seriousness of intent'.[52]

Barbara's agreement with Makarios, however unbelievable or inconvenient it was to government and opposition alike, had indeed transformed the whole situation. In February 1959 a settlement was reached on Cyprus. Its 'essential basis was the one proposed by Makarios in September',[53] which is to say the one proposed by Barbara. Nevertheless, her comments on 'our boys' dragged after her. She was booed and jeered, her life threatened. She ended up suing the Tory MP Christopher Chataway for his remarks over what she had said, and Godfrey Winn, and an outraged letter writer called Major Pope. She lost badly to Chataway and a Barbara Castle Fund was set up by party's general secretary Morgan Phillips to help pay her legal bills. 'Thank God,' she tactlessly told one contributing MP who had no secondary income and a young family, 'otherwise we would've had to sell our country cottage.'*[54]

With the 'uproar over her remarks' on Cyprus 'still faintly audible', Barbara became chairman of the Labour Party for the 1958–59 session. The word 'chairwoman' was not in the party's lexicon, but, as Barbara liked to say, she didn't care whether she was the chairman, the chairwoman or the chair, so long as she was *in* the chair. Being chairman is a ceremonial but prestigious appointment allocated to some members of the NEC. It was, as Dalton had said on becoming chairman himself, 'a high honour, a climax in the life of a Labour leader'.[55] (Jim Callaghan did not step down from the NEC when he was chancellor because he wanted his turn as party chairman and Tony Benn gloated that he would be chairman before him.) For Barbara, if anything, it had even more importance.

One of her last jobs as party chairman was to chair the 1959 annual conference, and she did so after Labour's third successive electoral defeat, each more devastating than the last. The Tories had managed once again to increase their majority, this time from sixty

* The Beacons in Buckinghamshire.

to a hundred (a result that brought Margaret Thatcher into the House). The mood at conference was part wake, part autopsy. Was the party too class-based? Were Gaitskell's tactics and leadership wrong? For once, Barbara didn't seem to think so; she not only praised his 'brilliant leadership' in her chairman's address, which might be expected, but privately 'sent him a warm tribute',[56] praising the way he had run the campaign. His one mistake had been to pledge that Labour would not increase taxes, which, in the more exacting environment of 1959, was beaten up by the Tories as a shameless bribe.

Many party members thought the defeat lay with Britain's increasing affluence: was it possible for a Labour Party to win in an affluent Britain? 'Tory voters are far more afraid of another Labour Government than Labour voters are afraid of another Tory Government', Dick Crossman wrote,[57] even though Labour had run on a very moderate programme designed to appeal to the aspiring classes: no more than thirty children in any classroom, primary or secondary, and the right of council tenants to buy their properties were two of their pledges. What was to be done? Jim Callaghan and others nearly lost their seats over steel nationalisation and to the revisionists, as those who wanted to remove Clause 4 from the constitution were called, this was the central problem. Labour's traditional supporters had completely reversed their opinion on nationalisation. In 1949, 60 per cent had been in favour of more public ownership; by 1959 almost the same percentage was opposed.

The revisionists' answer was not just to mobilise to scrap Clause 4, but to reinvent the Labour Party as something other than a working-class party; perhaps, as Douglas Jay suggested in *Forward*, even change its name in order to appeal to middle-class voters, an idea posited at the very moment when working-class culture was becoming youth culture – something desirable and vital – through the media of fashion, photography and pop music, and the brio of such books and films as *A Taste of Honey*, *The Loneliness of the Long-Distance Runner*, *A Kind of Loving*, *Billy Liar*, *Room at the Top*, etc, etc, apparently entirely unnoticed in the parallel universe of party politics.

The battle in conference focused on Clause 4. Gaitskell wrote a speech demanding its repeal. Barbara wrote a speech defending it as part of an economically moral system. They did not show each other their speeches. These two discourses of and on party policy were 'personal statements, deliberately uncorrelated and ... highly competitive'.[58] Barbara's effort was, Dick thought, 'a brilliant doctrinal speech', which took on Tory affluence and its contradictions.

For Barbara, there was to be no backtracking and no bystanding. If the problem was that socialism was not attractive to the newly rising and aspiring, who 'came from a class that owed its chance in life to us', they were not to be pandered to, they were to be taught 'the lessons of the new age in which we now live' in a 'commercialised society in which the customer is bombarded every day with advertisements persuading him that his highest happiness lies in acquiring more and more immediate satisfactions and consumer goods'.[59]

Barbara loathed the commercialisation of Britain, the 'Americanisation', as it was often called, and thought of; she opposed the introduction of commercial television and radio, stating that she did not buy any product advertised. We must, she told conference, convince the people that they 'and not a few private interests – should control their economic lives' or we will shrink into 'an impotent appendage of the windfall state'. This was the 'real case for public ownership'. The public had recoiled from nationalisation because in its present form it wasn't true public ownership. Nationalised entities needed to be made 'responsible to us all', she said; until then 'they are not Socialist'.

And if socialism had, as the pundits said, been resoundingly rejected, the solution was to educate the public about what true socialism was: a moral philosophy, a spiritual condition in which 'economic and social morality go hand in hand'. That you cannot separate moral from economic issues was one of her oldest arguments. It was, she said, part of her Marxist training, and it was a 'fallacy' to believe otherwise.

'The morality of a society is not created in a vacuum,' Barbara

146

said; 'it springs from the way it organises its economic life and distributes its rewards.' Socialism is about a way of life, about who we are as a people. Barbara, anticipating the 1960s, believed that the young were waiting 'for a call to public service; a call to idealism; a call to comradeship between all peoples ... Let us be big enough to give them that call: to show them that a prosperous Britain need not be a selfish one', she said.

Michael thought her speech the 'most telling chairman's address ever delivered'. The delegates, expecting the more usual conventional and uncontroversial chairman's opening remarks, had been 'offered the Socialist answer to the affluent election; an answer as deep in Labour Party tradition as the writings of R. H. Tawney, as up-to-date as the hovercraft'.[60] The hyperbole can be, if not forgiven, understood. Even centrists such as Benn thought Gaitskell's speech a 'ghastly failure';[61] his perspective on the Tory economy was, Dick said, one of 'apparent complacent accept-ance';[62] he offered nothing in its stead and Barbara offered a return to the promised land.

Her speech confirmed the worst fears of the Gaitskellites, people like Roy Jenkins who were already 'alarmed' by people like Barbara; especially Barbara, because she was so effective as part of what Jenkins thought of as the 'minority within the party who clung to extreme, socially divisive and utopian ideas of socialism'. Crosland and others claimed she had 'smugly and self-righteously' blamed the voters by saying that Labour's defeat was because 'our ethical reach was beyond the mental grasp of the average person'.[63]

The speech hit an off-note with some left-wingers, too. Wealth, as J. K. Galbraith pointed out, 'is not without its advantages and the case to the contrary, although it has often been made, has never proved widely persuasive'.[64] To millions of people in the country, freed from the privations of war and its long grey aftermath, affluence was a good thing, and Barbara's speech could be seen as attacking the working classes for enjoying what the middle classes had long taken for granted.

To the 17-year-old future leader of the Labour Party, Neil Kinnock, sitting in his parents' prefab with its newly fitted carpets and fridge and first television, 'the idea that these people for the first time in their lives could accumulate consumer durables and somehow that had diverted their minds away from the realities was bloody astounding'.[65] Barbara would argue that she wasn't attacking wealth per se, working class or otherwise; she was attacking private afflu- ence accompanied by public squalor, the result of free enterprise and the unplanned economy, crass commercialism, a privatised society in which looking out for Number One was the only morality. It was an immensely powerful speech, which is why, forty years after its delivery, Neil Kinnock could recall it so vividly. She carried a 'fearsome array of six-shooters', as the *Sunday Dispatch* put it. 'Not another woman in politics wields even a sharp hatpin by comparison.'[66]

Barbara was in tune with her party over Clause 4. The unions disliked tinkering with the sacred texts as much or more than the Bevanites. Gaitskell couldn't win and he would spend the next six months proving it. At the crucial NEC meeting it was Barbara who rewrote the constitution, amending Gaitskell's phrase that the party 'believes that further extension of common ownership should be decided from time to time' to read, 'through an expansion of common ownership substantial enough to give the community power over the commanding heights of the economy'.[67] Barbara's amendment was accepted by the NEC 22 votes to one.

There were to be three significant deaths for Barbara over the next four years. The first, in July 1960, was of the man who had completed her political education, Nye Bevan, the man who, despite all the bad feeling that was often between them, ran with Frank Betts and Bill Mellor, like 'a golden thread through my political life', as she said. Nye had died of stomach cancer and Barbara wrote that she was 'overwhelmed with despair – and with love'. Her obituary of Nye, written for the *New Statesman*, is one of her best pieces of writing. She had, she confessed, 'been frequently dealt with by him in scath- ing terms'. She had 'been politically abandoned by him, too, more than once' and yet there he was, 'an outsize individualist with an outsize social sense';[68] for this, his friends would forgive him much.

Dick, too, felt a huge, gaping sadness. And Tony Benn simply noted in his diary: 'Nye Bevan died this afternoon.'[69] That corner of the Smoking Room would never be the same.

Nye died the same year unilateral disarmament became official party policy, the same year as the U2 Incident as well. The 1960 conference, against Gaitskell's wishes, accepted the Amalgamated Engineering Union (AEU) motion calling for 'the unilateral renunciation of the testing, manufacture, stockpiling and basing of all nuclear weapons in Great Britain'. The unions had swung their block votes behind the resolution for several reasons: the public debate and concern over nuclear weapons and increasing tension between the two big nuclear superpowers had a profound effect on union members as much as anyone else; strong leadership from Frank Cousins, a vocal left-wing unilateralist and general secretary of the TGWU; and residual anger over Gaitskell's high-handed attempt to remove Clause 4.

The Labour Party had voted against its leader, an act without precedence in the party's history; Gaitskell refused to accept its decision. Lip-service to the supremacy of conference was fine when the right-wing union leadership was in accord with the right-wing PLP, the usual state of affairs, but not otherwise. Gaitskell made his famous 'fight, fight, fight for the party we love' speech; the vote, he said, had been engineered by 'pacifists, neutralists and fellow travellers'; he vowed to get it overturned; it was a declaration of war.

The NEC meetings that followed were if anything more vile than the ones in the 1950s. Barbara took the lead, relentlessly challenging Gaitskell to accept the democratic decisions of conference. Gaitskell's avowedly undemocratic refusal to do so led to the formation of the Unity group, founded to 'unite progressive sections of the Labour and Trade Union Movements behind a policy of broad democratic control of the Labour Party by its rank and file members'. Barbara, Tony Greenwood, Mik, Tom Driberg and Judith Hart were founder members.

A few days after the 1960 conference, there was a meeting at Barbara's flat with Michael, Jennie Lee, Lena Jeger, the former Labour MP for Holborn and St Pancras South, Dick, Tony Greenwood,

Harold and Mik. Tony started off by announcing that he intended to resign from the shadow cabinet and read out a letter of resignation, delineating all of Gaitskell's many faults. With Bevan dead, Harold had decided to run for the deputy leadership, but George Brown threw his hat in the ring making the outcome less certain. Now Tony said he wanted to stand for the leadership itself, but Barbara insisted that if anyone was going to challenge Gaitskell it was to be Harold. Harold 'this little spherical thing kept twirling round in dismay',[70] he didn't want to challenge for the leadership because he knew he could not win.

'But oh dear, dear, dear', Dick said, as the evening drew on and more drinks were drunk. Barbara revealed that she wanted to run for the leadership herself. Suddenly, Dick wrote, 'it became clear that Barbara's one ambition was to immolate herself and thereby to establish that women can be Leaders and Prime Ministers. She was nearly in tears insisting that she had the right.' Barbara had never hidden her ambition from her friends: 'there was nothing underhand about it,' Richard Clements said, 'indeed the last thing about Barbara is underhandedness.'[71] And she had tried to plant in the public mind the idea not only that women should have high office, but, as she told interviewers, that this particular woman wanted to be prime minister, being chancellor or foreign secretary en route.

To challenge Gaitskell now, after he had defied conference, and with Nye dead, seemed as good a time as any. She wouldn't win this round and she knew it, not with this right-wing PLP who had never voted her into the shadow cabinet. Yet if she didn't challenge, she would never be considered. Dick was waspishly appalled and the others, too, were loudly dissuasive. She would be crucified, humiliated, made a laughing-stock.

Barbara was devastated by the ferociously negative reaction. Tony Greenwood took her out into the kitchen to talk to her calmly. Tony had 'the uncomfortable job of deterring a termagant from suicide', Dick said acidly, thankful for Tony's powers of persuasion, as Barbara's candidature would be 'a farce'. Arguably, Nye's challenge for the leadership five years earlier had been a farce too: he'd got only seventy votes. There was a core of left-wing MPs whose votes she should get. But of course there was another factor. She wasn't just an ordinary scarlet bogey; she was that, and in Dick's telling word, something much worse, a termagant: an overbearing woman, a virago, a scold. When it came to women, the Labour party was deeply conservative. The horny-handed sons of toil were sons, not daughters. Barbara might be 'something of a mascot in the party',[72] its copper-haired, copper-bottomed Joan of Arc, but she was not to be the dauphin.

The next day Tony declared his candidature, forcing Harold's hand. Harold thought he now had no choice. If he didn't stand, he would be accused of cowardice. He asked Tony to stand aside but Tony declined, even though Barbara and Dick made it clear they would vote for Harold. Harold, now panicking, methodically bullied Tony into submission. Tony stood aside and Harold got 81 votes to Gaitskell's 166, pretty much what he had expected.

Gaitskell, his authority re-established with the PLP at least, travelled around the country to put his anti-unilateralist case to not necessarily friendly audiences. He was facilitated in this by the Campaign for Democratic Socialism (CDS), an organised group of centre-right and right-wing supporters such as Tony Crosland and Roy Jenkins, who worked at persuading the unions to vote for Gaitskell's anti-unilateralist *Policy for Peace* document, which was to be submitted to the 1961 conference. CDS 'adopted the same techniques of grass-roots entryism and mobilization traditionally exploited by the left'[73] and it worked, in part because the urgency of the unilateralist case had been softened by the abandonment of Blue Streak, Britain's de facto independent nuclear deterrent, and in part because of the unions' desire for party unity. *Policy for Peace* became Gaitskell's triumph, his trumpet-laden return; the 1961 conference made it party policy and rejected unilateralism as last year's model.

Barbara and Tony decided they could not let this pass. There had to be another left-wing challenge to the leadership. This time it was agreed that Tony would challenge Gaitskell and Barbara would challenge George Brown for the deputy leadership. There was still a chronic shortage of rooms in the House, which led to various ribald remarks to the effect that people should vote for Greenwood and Castle, because they could share a room as they shared a bed. They didn't get to share that room or the leadership. Tony got 59 votes to Gaitskell's 171, and Barbara 56 votes to Brown's 169. (The following year, Harold challenged Brown for deputy, doing considerably better than Barbara but still losing, getting 103 votes to Brown's 133.)

In August 1961, Macmillan's government formally applied to take Britain into the Common Market, launching Barbara's eighteen-year anti-Common Market crusade. Her objections were twofold. First, it was inherently anti-socialist, set up for the convenience and claims of big business and against the needs and interests of ordin-ary people; second, its fortress trading system would seriously harm the Commonwealth, to which Britain owed special allegiance, by keeping out its goods. The issue of British membership, she argued, was something that should be agreed to by the whole of the Commons *and* a special conference of Commonwealth prime ministers. In this, for divergent reasons, she found common cause with right-wingers such as Douglas Jay, with whom she set up the Anti-Common Market Committee, and Hugh Gaitskell, who famously remarked that entry would be 'the end of a thousand years of history'.

There was an element of nationalism in Barbara's objections, too, a moral nationalism which championed the cause of sovereignty, democracy, free people in free nations determining their own futures, and objected to democratic control being removed to unaccountable bureaucrats. She foresaw the inevitable logic of federalism inherent in the European project, wherein national governments would lose more and more control over the running of their own economies and societies. A socialist Britain could not exist in a federal capitalist Europe. It was a battle postponed. Britain's application was rejected in January 1963, two weeks after Hugh Gaitskell died.

Gaitskell's death at 56, of a rare immunological illness, transformed everything. The old political adage that 'Where there is death there is hope' had never been truer. This time Harold would run for the leadership against George Brown, and Barbara was the one to nominate him. The Gaitskellites were not prepared to be led by Brown, a 'neurotic drunk', as Tony Crosland complained. He was too unstable. It wasn't on. So, although the Gaitskellites considered Callaghan 'intellectually lightweight',[74] they drafted him in as the third man. For the party the choice between a drunk and a dolt was neither. Harold won on the first ballot, with 115 to Brown's 88 and Callaghan's 41, forcing the latter out and on Valentine's Day 1963 Harold Wilson beat George Brown, 144 votes to 103.

From that moment Barbara and Dick knew that they would be ministers under Harold. With Gaitskell, despite all he had said about putting Barbara and Dick in his cabinet, and despite the fact that he would have, for party unity's sake, appointed one or two left-wingers, they could never be sure it would be them. With Harold they were sure. Labour was riding high in the polls: by late February and early March its popularity was the highest since the immediate postwar period – even before the Profumo affair, the scandal that seemed to define the period, and which was credited, at least in part, with Labour's 1964 election victory.

John Profumo, secretary of state for war in Macmillan's government, was, like many a minister before him, sleeping with a call-girl. This one was the 20-year-old Christine Keeler. This might, as one MP put it, have been a matter for congratulations, if another of her clients hadn't been the Soviet assistant naval attaché and spook, Colonel Yevgeniy Ivanov. Most of the action took place at Cliveden, and this new set of mysterious foreigners and social climbers, 'the scruffier sections of upper-class society', provided 'one long glorious summer of vicarious excitement, novelettish intrigue and sexual titillation'[75] in a country balanced precariously between the end of the ban on *Lady Chatterley's Lover* and the Beatles' first LP.

Barbara, Dick and Harold learnt of the affair from another Labour MP, George Wigg, a do-it-yourself MI5, who had amassed a bulging dossier on Profumo and blabbed about it at one of

Barbara's dinner parties. Wigg, a lugubrious, ambling, damp carp of a man, was a 6ft 4in ex-army colonel, a self-appointed Mr Findit, Mr Fixit and Mr Hideit of the Labour Party, the faithful retainer who retained everything, including files on his colleagues. Barbara, Michael, Ted and Dick all advised Harold not to touch it; it was sleazy, tawdry, and would make Labour look bad. But Wigg understood the case for how it could be sold: not as private sex but as national security.

Until she had found her way into the musty ossuary of Cliveden, Christine Keeler had been living with a West Indian man (adding further titillation to the affair), who, suspecting Keeler's fancy had turned elsewhere, arrived on the doorstep of Stephen Ward, osteopath and procurer to the gentry, and emptied his gun into Ward's door. In the trial that followed Keeler was called to the Old Bailey as a key witness. She didn't turn up. She had disappeared. Rumour had it that Profumo had helped her do so. This gossip was picked up and apparently believed by Barbara.

On the evening of 21 March, Barbara came into the House planning to blow the Profumo scandal wide open. Four Labour MPs addressed the issue that evening, first Ben Parkin, with an indigestible pigeon stew of double entendres and circumlocutions about sewers, pipes and models of buildings, understood only by the cognoscenti; then Wigg, who called for a select committee to look into the still-unspecified 'rumour upon rumour involving a member of the Government Front Bench', then Dick, who echoed Wigg, both careful not to say anything they could not repeat outside the House; and then Barbara, who went much further.

She insinuated that Profumo was mixed up in Keeler's disappearance: 'Mr Paget* said that if it is just a case of a Minister having been found with a pretty girl good luck to him, but what ... if it's a question of the perversion of justice that is at stake? ... If accusations are made that there are people in high places who do know [Keeler's whereabouts] and are not informing the police is it not a matter of public interest?'[76]

---

* Reginald Paget, Labour MP for Northampton.

Dick and Wigg were appalled. The statement was slanderous. It could not be repeated outside the House and it had the added disadvantage of being untrue. Profumo had nothing to do with Keeler's disappearance and could quite truthfully deny the accusation, which he did the next morning, hiding behind the smoke Barbara had provided. But, luckily for Barbara, he hanged himself with a skein of arrogance. Macmillan sat next to the secretary of state for war and patted him on the back after his personal statement which gave voice to the arrant lie that 'There was no impropriety whatsoever in my acquaintanceship with Miss Keeler', a statement later retracted when, upon resignation, he apologised for lying to the House.

The public and press fascination with the grainy glamour of the Profumo affair went on for about six months; it was followed by the revelation that Kim Philby was 'the third man'. The first two members of the Russian spy ring, Guy Burgess and Donald Maclean, had defected to the Soviet Union in May 1951, and the existence of other members had hitherto been strenuously denied by the government. This was followed by revelations about Rachmanism, the slum landlord Peter Rachman's nefarious extortion of his tenants: Rachman, too, had been involved with Keeler and her 18-year-old friend Mandy Rice-Davies. It all added up to a portrait of the Tories presiding complacently over slum and sleaze. Macmillan, who proved himself inept over Profumo, was condemned by the Denning report into the affair for his indolence; ailing, he left office in October 1963 and was replaced by Sir Alec Douglas-Home, a grouse-hunting Tory grandee, the 14th Earl (who in a flash of wit described Harold as the 14th Mr Wilson); an Old Etonian, proud of his upper-class-twit qualities, he bragged that he employed matches to work out economic problems.

What was to be Labour's last party conference before the next general election was held the same month. Harold sought to portray the Labour Party as everything the Tories were not. The Tories were inept dilettantes, moribund upper-class buffoons who had presided over real industrial decline. Labour was whiz-bang and up-to-date and would bring about a classless society, a merito-cracy, a 'New

Britain' through the white heat of technology and science and modernity. Whereas the Tories had reached back into the eighteenth century for their new leader, the Labour Party had reached forward for Harold, the twentieth-century techno-pol in the Gannex mac.

It was not a good conference for Barbara. She was 'almost in tears because Alice Bacon* had been given a major speech and she had not', Tony Benn noted. 'She was outraged Shirley Williams should have been put on the TV presentation team' for the election and she had not. Dick, Tony Benn, Jim Callaghan, George Brown, even Megan Lloyd George, a Labour convert, made broadcasts, but not Barbara. She had been sidelined. 'Harold . . . always sold the Left down the river', she told Tony Benn; 'she would quit politics if she did not get a major Shadow Cabinet appointment . . . It was almost hysterical', Benn thought. He tried to calm her down. Harold did not put her in the shadow cabinet. It would, he told Tony, be simpler to 'make his own appointments in the Government than in the Shadow Cabinet.' He saw no reason to cause trouble by impos- ing 'people unacceptable to other members of the Shadow Cabinet.'[77] Barbara was made opposition spokeswoman on over- seas development, outside the shadow cabinet. As she later remarked, 'The language of party unity was the religion of Harold Wilson.'[78] And party unity came even above her.

Six months before the 1964 October election none of this seemed important to Barbara. The very worst had happened. Her sister, Marjorie, who was chairman of the London County Council's Education Committee, had collapsed at a meeting and been rushed to hospital . Marjorie, who had hypertension, had had a stroke; she never recovered. She died a week before her 57th birthday.

Barbara sat in her room in the Commons, sobbing and sobbing. No one knew what to do with her. As Frank had died without seeing her into the House, now Marjorie had died without seeing her into cabinet. Marjorie had always protected Barbara and given

* Labour MP for Leeds South-East.

her advice and comfort; they had remained close all of their lives. It was Ted whom Barbara would turn to now. It was on him more than anyone she would rely for counsel and support.

PART III

The Most Powerful Woman
in Britain

Chapter Seven

HIS LITTLE MINISTER

When Barbara answered the phone at The Beacons, her country cottage in Buckinghamshire, and was told the prime minister wanted to see her, she 'feigned surprise . . . Does he? she said, What for?'[1] It was unnecessarily coy and scarcely convincing. Within two weeks of becoming leader Harold had told those closest to him that they would have jobs, and he had worked out the core of his cabinet at least four months before the election. From the moment the votes were counted on 16 October 1964, ten days after her 54th birthday, Barbara knew she was going to be a cabinet minister, only the fourth woman in British history to achieve that rank.

The portfolio was Overseas Development, a new ministry for which Barbara, working with the Fabian Society, had recently drawn up the blueprint. For the last year she had been opposition spokeswoman on overseas development, and it was the obvious job for someone who had made herself an expert on Africa and had been a chief architect of Labour's colonial policy. She was, as Hastings Banda, president-for-life of Malawi, wrote to Harold, 'well known to most of us in Africa' and 'very popular with Africans', to some of whom she was known as 'Lady Barbara, the Great Mother'.[2] Praise from Banda, a dictator, was praise Barbara would rather have done without, but what he said was true.

The Ministry of Overseas Development, called ODM lest it be

confused with Denis Healey's Ministry of Defence (MOD), although close to her heart, had to be somewhat of a disappointment. Barbara had always desired one of the high offices of state, foreign secretary or chancellor. But she had the ability, and the egotism, to treat whatever she was doing as the most important thing because she was doing it: 'her extraordinary excitement and exhilaration that at last she'd got something to do' were infectious. Her parliamentary secretary, Bert Oram, remembered her creating and maintaining an atmosphere of 'tremendous excitement' at ODM.[3]

After nearly twenty years on the back benches Barbara had at last swallowed 'the vitamin of power' on which, she thinks, 'women in particular' thrive. She was 'in love with power and with herself',[4] a state she later observed in Margaret Thatcher. At a *Financial Times* lunch shortly after the election, journalist Christopher Tugendhat watched her 'sparking off the young men. She is a flirt but it wasn't just that she flirted, it was that she liked being an important woman still attractive to younger men who were subordinate. She used her sexuality and rather enjoyed the fact that she was the one with the power.'[5] There were few powerful women in 1964, fewer still who behaved like Elizabeth I, enjoying both their power and their sexuality as an adjunct of it.

Press lunches and interviews were plentiful. Barbara was 'amazing with the photographers, she knew how to handle them, how to get the best possible photographs of herself taken. In that sense she was just like a film star,'[6] Gerald Kaufman said. And, like a film star, she wanted the biggest role. There was no reason why a woman shouldn't be prime minister she told the *Telegraph* a week after her appointment. The idea, 'perhaps preposterous itself', seemed natural enough even to the *Telegraph*, because it came from a woman 'entirely feminine as well as entirely efficient'. It was a rarity, the paper declared, that 'blue stockings go with blue eyes, burnished copper hair and high heels' and Barbara was that rarity.[7]

Power may be the ultimate aphrodisiac, but to Barbara it was also fuel for her legendary vast reserves of physical and mental stamina. She was a detail-obsessed workaholic, who worked fanatically hard and worked equally hard at letting everyone know how hard she worked, making, as Roy Jenkins memorably put it, 'exhaustion into a political virility symbol'. Barbara the minister was proudly pummelled, satiated by weariness, dizzy and reeling with fatigue, forever 'dragging herself to early meetings, crawling with exhaustion out of cabinets and finally creeping home to a tired bed',[8] managing on five hours' sleep or less, rolling her eyes at the slovenly work habits of Jenkins, who left his ministry at 7.30 in the evening, when she was beginning her second shift. Jenkins retorted that he didn't believe in the Castle dictum that 'decisions were best taken in a state of prostration'.

Anything they could do she could do longer. As Bernard Ingham, who a few years later became Barbara's chief information officer (a decade before he was Thatcher's), observed, 'she grossly overprepared' for everything, which he thought 'a woman's failing in politics', this overcompensation, this need to prove and prove again that, yes, she was as good or preferably better than any man there.[9]

Her plans for her new ministry were extensive. The budget was a modest £175m, £27m more than the Tories had managed the previous year, but only 'as much as might be spent on a weapon that is going to be obsolete before it even exists', Barbara said;[10] and at 0.6 per cent of GNP scarcely more than the overseas aid allocation immediately after the war. The *raison d'être* for ODM was, she said, echoing her familiar theme, that you cannot expand world markets without expanding world wealth. It was to be not merely a department for allocating aid, but, as its name implied, a ministry for facilitating development, a quasi-independent foreign office for the developing world. ODM representatives were to be put in every high commission and embassy in countries receiving British aid, to ensure that it was spent on the people not the palaces.

Barbara set about empire-building, trying, as she said, to snatch 'powers from anybody who had a bit to do with aid – from the Foreign Office, the Board of Trade, Technical Assistance Bureau, Treasury' and the Commonwealth and Colonial offices, which 'provoked a major internal Whitehall battle'.[11] It was a battle she only half won. The Colonial Office kept complete control over budgetary aid for the dependent territories, and ODM had to consult it before discharging development aid. The Treasury kept control of relations with the International Bank for Reconstruction and Development; and ODM had no control over military aid, which remained under the authority of the Foreign, Commonwealth and Colonial Offices. In the end ODM was 'simply a ministry for allocating aid',[12] but Barbara remained its most memorable minister.

The lone woman in the 23-member cabinet sat at the furthermost left of the elongated oval cabinet table. Dick Crossman, the minister of housing and local government, sat at the furthermost right. Holders of the senior cabinet posts, Chancellor Jim Callaghan, Foreign Secretary Patrick Gordon Walker, Home Secretary Frank Soskice, and Herbert Bowden, the lord president and leader of the house, were grouped in the centre of the table around Harold, who faced the window overlooking Horseguards Parade. Down from them were three other Gaitskellite faces Barbara knew well: Douglas Jay, the president of the Board of Trade; George Brown, the first secretary and the head of the newly created Department of Economic Affairs (DEA); and Lord Longford, the lord privy seal.

Only half a dozen people around that cabinet table had voted for Harold to be leader of the party. His two rivals in the leadership contest, Callaghan and Brown, were, it was hoped, to be kept busy cancelling each other out with the 'creative tension' inherent in, as Harold put it, attempting to achieve 'unity in diversity of economic policy'.[13] Harold liked to say that he was trying to run a bolshevik revolution with a tsarist cabinet. Except for Barbara, Dick, Tony Greenwood, who was colonial secretary, and Frank Cousins, the minister of technology, the ministers came from the right and centre right of the party, so much so that if 'Gaitskell had been distributing portfolios he could scarcely have favoured the Left less'.[14] Cabinet business was conducted with formality. Former enemies called each other by their ministerial titles not their names, part of the reason, Barbara thought, that cabinet meetings seemed stiff, unreal and curiously unpolitical.

Barbara, delicate, still very lovely, at least a foot smaller than her colleagues, used 'every womanly wile' to get her way in cabinet, and every other kind of wile as well. She flirted, she cajoled, she bullied and she charmed. Her flirting could be heavy-handed to the point of outrageousness. Frank Cousins was 'somewhat taken aback at her unabashed use of her feminine charm to get her way within the Cabinet' and commented to his biographer on her constantly 'flirting and being coquettish with him'.[15] She could go too far and she did. There were scenes, 'a great row with Nance', Frank's wife, about Barbara's over-the-top flirtation with him on the dance floor.

Barbara soon began to be a dominant presence in cabinet, beating her fellow ministers about the head with the concerns of her ministry, or her preoccupations, pounding the table. She was 'immensely self-centred'[16] and she never shut up, 'achieving her many successes by boring the cabinet to death; they very often went along with things just to shut her up.'[17] Barbara was by temperament and design the self-appointed socialist conscience of cabinet, Harold's conscience. It was to be Barbara who raised the issue of Vietnam and its repercussions; Barbara who fought (but lost) to have the government insist that the Royal Navy visits to South Africa be cancelled unless the multiracial crew were not subjected to the apartheid laws; Barbara who continued to berate Harold over Rhodesia.

Gordon Walker sometimes ran a sweepstake when Barbara 'was expected to speak for a long time', taking bets on the length of her oration. Tony Crosland and Jim Callaghan once devised a 'party game to be played during Barbara's speeches',[18] running a book on who would still be around the cabinet table the following year. This sort of thing went on through the eight years of her ministerial life. There was a lot of note-passing in cabinet, commentary on what was going on, bad jokes, games, and critiques of colleagues.

Barbara, of all people, thought it the 'most talkative Cabinet in political history'.[19] She busied herself when others babbled on, writing notes for her diary in shorthand, drawing up shopping lists ('Buy new lavatory seat'), composing departmental minutes, topping and tailing White Papers, writing speeches, doing any urgent departmental work, or just doodling. Harold's cabinets were long, lazy affairs, enervating as a sultry summer's afternoon.

Letting his ministers talk themselves out was part of Harold's cabinet tactics. His way of dealing with controversial issues without having to resort to confrontation or outright decision-making was to allow cabinet 'to bore itself into exhaustion.'[20] But with Barbara it was more. He really 'couldn't bring himself to shut her up. It was certainly very odd. He just let her go on and on and on.'[21] If she had a question, it would be Harold himself who sprang up and answered her. He affectionately called her 'my little minister'. She was, he liked to say, the 'best man' in cabinet. He was her prime minister but the balance of power in their relationship was mer-curial and often swung in Barbara's favour.

Edmund Dell remembered on one occasion sitting next to Ted Short, the chief whip, when 'Barbara was orating and Harold was just letting her go on and on and Ted, exasperated, cried: why doesn't he stop her!' He seldom did. Barbara, as one minister put it, had only to 'waggle that bottom of hers' to get all her own way, but usually not even that. She had an 'extraordinary ability to get Harold to do what she wanted Harold to do'. Decisions taken by cabinet committees, which were supposed to be final, were brought by Barbara, with Harold's indulgence, to cabinet for further argument. Other cabinet committee decisions 'would be reversed because Barbara had got at Harold and no one could quite work it out except by the gossip'.[22]

The gossip was about sex, still, the supposed affair with Harold, past and or present. The prime minister, a somewhat unlikely Lothario, provoked excited sexual speculation. He was rumoured to be involved not only with Barbara but with his self-titled personal political secretary, Marcia Williams.

Harold was said to love women. Barbara said so. Marcia said so. But behind their backs he could be as viscerally sexist as the next man: 'Bloody Barbara – she only menstruates once a year – and that's just before the NEC elections', he growled at Joe Haines when she was in one of her tight neurotic knots.[23] The man who loved women seemed to love being dominated by at least these two. Marcia's public relationship with Harold was similar to Barbara's. She, too, chivvied and bullied the prime minister; she, too, was a self-appointed socialist conscience. Whereas Barbara was given leave to thump the cabinet table and drone on and on unstoppably, Marcia, in the private office at Number Ten, was free to yell and shout and slam doors for all to hear: the prime minister 'seemed to be seeking his assistant's approval, rather than the other way round'.[24] The prime minister seemed to be seeking his little minister's approval as well.

He often didn't get it. Even before Harold became prime minister, Barbara confided in Tony Benn that she had 'grave reservations' about his leadership qualities, especially his inability to confront his colleagues and give a lead, reservations Tony shared. For much of the time Barbara didn't approve of Harold's way of running cabinet or country; she told Jim Callaghan two and a half years into office that there wasn't one major plank of government policy that she agreed with. She was 'always attacking' Harold, Tony said, but nevertheless she continued to follow him 'absolutely faithfully'.[25]

Within her ministry Barbara 'always in the end got her own way',[26] most of the time, but not without a fight with the civil servants, especially Andrew Cohen, her permanent secretary, who she said was always 'trying to wear me down ... He would be in my office about seven times a day saying Minister, I know the ultimate decision is yours but I would be failing in my duty if I didn't tell you how unhappy your decision makes me.'[27]

Barbara, and the 'mountainous Mr Cohen', who had once 'volunteered the view that whatever fate might overtake him he could never see himself working for a woman',[28] were collectively known as the Elephant & Castle. Cohen, who got off to a bad start with Barbara by being 'shamefully' not in attendance for 'that great moment of the act of appointment',[29] could be a decidedly rogue elephant, although he broadly shared her politics. The problem was systematic, rather than personal.

The civil service, Barbara found, was operating as a state within a state. All her years of party in-fighting and politicking on and around the back benches and the NEC had not prepared her for what she called the 'companionable embrace' of Whitehall: 'politicians do not take on board until they become Ministers ... the extent to which ... the Civil Service takes over [their] life', she said. She felt isolated 'cut off from the political lifeline', insulated from the world, with every minute of her day controlled by her private office, even having to lie 'like a trooper' in order to go out for a walk across St James's Park.[30] Dick called this the 'bureaucratic embrace'. He, too, was struck by the 'tremendous effort it required not to be taken over' by the mandarins, 'this astonishing Whitehall hierarchy [which] ... takes you into itself and folds you into its bosom.'[31]

On Barbara's first day at the ODM offices at Stag Place in Victoria she found in her in-tray a 'pile of documents which the civil servants had prepared telling us what form this new ministry should take'; it was more than advice and she found it presumptuous. She dispatched a government messenger on a motorbike to the Fabian Society to bring back six copies of their blueprint for ODM. She brought in outside advisers, economists and experts to counteract the civil servants. She set up her own economic planning department within the ministry, headed by Dudley Seers, a former Keep Left colleague, who most recently had been a director at the UN's Economic Commission for Africa. By the time she left ODM, seventeen economists had been brought into the economic planning department and there were twenty-nine professional advisers in all. The orthodox objected to these advisers at first but they soon absorbed them, Barbara said, making them 'a specialist appendage to the administrator and not to the Minister'.[32]

Sometimes she found her civil servants deliberately malign; they could and did, as Tony Benn said, use 'their power to undermine ... and influence events'.[33] A minister would give instructions that never evolved into action. This was experienced and complained about by most of the ministers some of the time. The civil servants' 'loyalty is to each other rather than to the Government', Tony noted; to the ministry, not the minister, a bauble temporarily entangled in its hair, who, having come, will go.

Civil servants horse-traded interdepartmentally; based on these deals and without her consent, they made decisions, even changes

to her White Paper. The 'administrative function' always took precedence over the 'political function', Barbara concluded. She moved
to get on top of this, instituting her own systems, such as the weekly
meeting at which her ministerial line was firmly laid down, trying
to make it difficult for the civil servants to act autonomously or pre-
empt her at the meetings they alone attended.

But, despite her critical attitude to the way the civil service
worked, most of her civil servants, in all four of the ministries she
served in, deeply respected her; many liked her enormously. She
was often a difficult cabinet colleague, and 'she could be madden-
ingly obsessive, vain and coy', as Roy Jenkins said,[34] but she was, for
the most part, a superb departmental boss. She was, her civil servants said, 'the kind of minister a civil servant likes: one who knows
his or her own mind'.[35]

'She had strong personality and the ability to push through
essentially what she wanted,' said John Burgh, who worked for
Barbara at the Department of Employment and Productivity, 'but
she listened.' Richard Bird, who worked for her at Transport,
concurred: 'She listened widely to views' and was a natural manager
of people, 'enormously considerate, she forgave genuine error,
appreciated good and well executed endeavour' and she was
extremely capable; she 'mastered the detail as necessary and was a
very conscientious minister'.[36]

Barbara 'got immense loyalty from civil servants who wouldn't
have given the time of day for her politics', said David Owen, later
Barbara's minister of health and social security. Bird agreed: 'She
won a lot of things because she got most of her staff working for
her.'[37] She worked her staff almost as hard as she worked herself,
often keeping them late into the evening but equally often producing a bottle of whisky after the day's work was done. Some of her
staff found her humorous. Others found her utterly humourless. At
times she could be difficult, but she was often disarmingly ordinary,
human, sitting on the couch with her shoes off and her legs curled
under her, smoking one of her many cigarettes and chatting away.

Her ministerial 'qualities took Whitehall by surprise'. All they had
to go on was 'the shrill headline image of the fiery-haired opposi-

tion MP – an image to which [she] ... certainly lent weight'. The woman they met was at odds with this strident spectre; she was willing to think things through; she could change her mind and 'leave behind her political preconceptions'.[38]

That she sometimes shed, or gave the appearance of shedding, not just her political preconceptions but her politics as well, was not a cause for celebration within the party. To Paul Foot, who was left of the Labour left, Barbara was, for the most part, 'a very progressive minister as the ministers go'. But some in her own party 'pointed the finger at Barbara', Neil Kinnock said,[39] at the woman who had spent her backbench years making trenchant left-wing cri-ticisms of her government and party, who had passionately set the left-wing agenda, was now part of a rightward-listing government which she was equally passionately defending.

It didn't help that the policy issues that bedevilled the government had been Barbara's causes, which as a backbencher, and as a member of the Movement for Colonial Freedom and chairman of the Anti-Apartheid Movement (AAM), she had constantly spoken out on: Rhodesia and its unwillingness to move towards black majority rule; on arms to South Africa; on the war in Vietnam; and on the presence of British troops in the colonies.

A month after he became party leader, Harold, addressing an AAM rally in Trafalgar Square, had pledged that the next Labour government would put an embargo on the export of arms to South Africa. Barbara had reiterated the pledge at the pre-election party conference, where she pronounced herself 'proud that we have taken an unequivocal stand on this question of an embargo on the export of arms'.[40] As for the sixteen Buccaneer bomber planes being manufactured for South Africa, 'we say that a Labour Government would cancel that order', Barbara said; the planes could be usefully employed elsewhere.

Five weeks into office, economic exigencies triumphed over morality. The planes were on their way to Pretoria; there was no MOD requirement for such aircraft, nor any other acceptable foreign buyers who could afford them and to cancel would cost £25 million, plus compensation to South Africa, *and* domestic redundancies. 'African opinion would probably understand', Harold optim-istically told cabinet,[41] after all they would not accept any new orders from the apartheid regime.

The AAM did not understand, however. David Steel, its president, declared the Labour government's record on South Africa one of 'disappointment, retraction and evasion',[42] and not just over the sale of arms, but its continued 'economic and political co-operation', and its refusal to back international sanctions against Britain's fourth biggest trading partner, or to remove the Commonwealth pref-erences from what Barbara had called a 'slave state'.

No one on the left expected anything of Jim Callaghan or the Gaitskellites but they expected much of the party's Joan of Arc. Tam Dalyell was absolutely furious with Barbara, who 'had been on every platform for the Movement for Colonial Freedom' and yet did not stand up to Harold over the East of Suez policy, most especially the British military presence in Borneo. 'If she had displayed her usual guts, Wilson would have withdrawn earlier', he said, still angry thirty-five years later.[43] He confronted Barbara over this, and Tony Greenwood too: she was 'spitting with rage' at being so challenged, Tony was merely embarrassed.

Barbara would become accustomed to attacks from former colleagues and supporters. The left-wing Unity group, of which she and Tony Greenwood were founder members, now wanted them off the NEC, because as ministers they were representing the government, not the party as the NEC was supposed to do, which is to say they were no longer publicly representing the left. It was 'quite impossible' for either Barbara or himself, Tony wrote to Unity, to 'make any sort of pronouncement that conflicted with our collective responsibility as Members of the Cabinet'. As cabinet ministers, they were, Unity complained, isolated from the very people who gave them power. (A view Barbara was not unsym-pathetic to; she later tried to counteract political isolation by employing her own political advisors inside her ministry.) But she and Tony wanted to be taken on good faith. 'People must just accept that we are still the same people that we have always been', Tony wrote; a 'little more trust would not come amiss.'[44] Trust that

171

they were, as Barbara often was, fighting for the old causes behind closed cabinet doors.

Both Barbara and Tony were terrified that they would not be re-elected to the NEC in 1965. All through that conference weekend, Barbara kept telling Dick that all the ministers would be thrown off. 'What shall we do?' she kept asking him. 'What shall we do?' The NEC, Dick thought impatiently, dominated her life like a 'chronic disease'. He and Tony Benn reassured her that they wouldn't be thrown off, which they weren't. Barbara came top of the poll that year with the two Tonys and Dick scrambling after.

In April 1965, six months after Labour had taken office, London was declared the most swinging city in the world, 'the most cooly elegant city in the world', as one American journalist put it. Cool Britannia with manners. Bankrupt Britannia with style. On his first day at Number 10 Harold had been confronted by civil servants bearing bad news. The economic situation was much worse than even he had claimed it to be during the election campaign. 'Not since 1945 ... had an incoming administration faced so severe a crisis.'[45] The balance-of-payments deficit would not stand at £400 million, as Labour had contended, but by the end of the financial year would be nearer to £800 million.

Everything Labour had said about the Tories was nowhere near as bad as the reality. Treasury and Bank of England officials told Harold that the Tory economic mismanagement had amounted 'to criminal negligence'.[46] There were three immediate options: devaluation, import quotas or tariffs on imports. Barbara and Dick were for immediate devaluation, but Harold, out of a 'mixture of economics, politics, and bad memories from the 1940s', when the Attlee government had devalued the pound, decided, with the agreement of Callaghan and Brown (the three formed the troika who ran the government), on import tariffs of 15 per cent.

Britain was still paying off the postwar American loan; further loans from the central banks were arranged, as was a standby line of credit from the IMF, and Harold went to Washington to drum up support for sterling. The 'pound was seen as the first line of defence for the dollar'[47] by the Americans, whose support came with the precondition that 'under any and all circumstances devaluation of the pound is unthinkable'. Another American precondition was that Britain maintain its expensive and anachronistic military presence east of Suez. President Lyndon B. Johnson and his aides were 'particularly insistent on the value of the world-wide military role played by the United Kingdom and on the importance of our continuing to discharge that role', Harold told cabinet.[48]

During the following eighteen months, Harold came to a series of 'understandings' with Washington in exchange for continued financial assistance. He gave the Americans much of what they wanted, except for the one thing they wanted most: British military involvement in Vietnam. They needed to make sure 'that the British get it into their heads that it makes no sense for us to rescue the Pound in a situation in which there is no British flag in Vietnam', McGeorge Bundy, LBJ's principal aide, told the president.[49] But, although the Americans immediately and continually pressured Harold and Denis Healey to send troops to Vietnam, even a symbolic pipe and fife regiment, 'we continued to resist their pressure', Harold told cabinet.[50]

At first most ministers were uninterested in Vietnam, bogged down by domestic concerns and the problems of their own ministries. Dick, after four months of government and much discussion of the subject, noted that he nearly always had his mind elsewhere while Barbara, Harold's most vociferous and persistent critic on the war, talked on. When she got the full cabinet discussion on foreign policy she'd been badgering Harold for, Dick wondered whether it was worth it, as they were all so preoccupied with their own slither of government. What impact could they have on foreign policy?

The party, however, felt differently. The PLP was in uproar over the cabinet's Vietnam policy. 'The Vietnam war,' Barbara said later, 'struck at the very soul of the Labour Party. It was so barbaric, it was so unnecessary, it was so wasteful, it was so cruel ... but [Harold] wouldn't condemn the Americans not even when they were bombing in the most appalling way.' He did dissociate the UK from specific actions, such as the bombing of Hanoi and the invasion of Cambodia. And of course keep Britain out of the war. But if he had done otherwise, Barbara remarked, there would've been 'a revolution' in the streets and most of the Cabinet 'would have resigned'.[51]

Michael Foot refused to join the cabinet as home secretary in the 1965 reshuffle because of the government's continued support of the Americans over Vietnam. Barbara felt as strongly as Michael did, but the only issue in her first two jobs that she ever seriously contemplated resigning over was Rhodesia. She had made a pact with Arthur Bottomley, the minister for Commonwealth relations, that if the principle of black majority rule was breached they would both resign from cabinet, and she made Harold aware of her plans.

Barbara did not want to return to the aridity of the back benches; she did not want to give up her work or her power; and perhaps she would not have resigned had the crunch come. She turned it over in her mind. Could she give up the 'sheer intoxication of administrative responsibility'? she asked herself.[52] She thought she could, rather than have a bad conscience over Rhodesia, her personal line in the sand. She went out on a limb, briefing her PPS, David Ennals, in a 'weak moment', she said, on conversations that had taken place in cabinet on Rhodesia. Ennals, Tam Dalyell and two other PPSS put down a motion in the House, based on what Barbara had said, calling for safeguards for the black majority.

In the cabinet that followed, Harold complained about Ennals but refused to rebuke Barbara for leaking, or even acknowledge that she had done so. The prime minister, in official Whitehallese, was concerned that PPSS were not 'always content to observe the necessary discretion in situations in which strong feelings were engaged and emotions tended to run high'. No harm done, Harold said; the motion was all in all a good thing. But, given the government's tiny majority, from now on PPSS 'before they intervened publicly'[53] in government business were to consult not only their own ministers but the chief whip.

On Rhodesia, especially, Barbara's conscience 'haunted [Harold] and made him uneasy and unsure of himself', Dick thought: 'She got under his skin in a quite extraordinary way.' Barbara knew she had Harold on this: he keeps 'looking at me for approval' she confided in her diary. But he could be slippery. Opposing Harold, she said, was like 'playing blind man's bluff'. She tightened the screws. And it was her 'powerful one-woman campaign against concessions to the Smith regime* [that] checked any temptation Harold may have felt to backslide'.[54]

Barbara's hard work and high profile raised the status of overseas development; 'the fact that she was doing it made it a significant job'[55] and the way that she did it made it more so. Her 'spectacular' achievement was the granting of interest-free loans to the poorest countries, which, 'given the state of the economy at the time ... was a remarkable tribute to [her] negotiating powers'[56] and to her talent for presentation. The Tories had previously waived up to the first seven years of interest on loans to the poorest countries. Therefore, Barbara's completely interest-free loans, while helping the poorest more, and achieving acclaim on the left and in development circles – the World Bank commended the British lead – had little immediate impact on the balance-of-payments ledger, something of great concern to the chancellor.

Within cabinet, aid was treated with indifference or contempt; in the perilous economic circumstances it was a politically easy target for cuts. That 1 per cent of GNP should be allocated to overseas aid was something Barbara had helped commit the party to in the 1950s, but the majority of cabinet, uninterested in and irritated by the subject, wanted all commitments forgotten, and the public felt a 'growing resentment ... towards the coloured Commonwealth',[57] where the aid for the most part went.

Since 1955, the number of immigrants to Britain had grown to 600,000, with 330,000 more on the waiting list. Racial tensions had evolved from implicit to incipient to obtrusive. Gordon Walker had been brought into cabinet without having been elected to

* Ian Smith was the white prime minister of Rhodesia. In November 1965 he promulgated a unilateral declaration of independence from Britain.

parliament because he had lost in an overtly racist campaign at Smethwick. (He then lost the hitherto safe seat at Leyton, on which he had been foisted, making his continuation in office untenable, and simultaneously reducing Labour's knife-edge majority to three. He was replaced as foreign secretary by Michael Stewart.)

Barbara said she received a 'little stream of correspondence that always linked race and sex' of the 'Why are you giving our money away to sex-mad Orientals?' variety, much of it less mild than that, as her secretary remembered:'She used to get some horrible letters from people ... Revolting.'When Hastings Banda was photographed hugging Barbara enthusiastically, her correspondents went to the trouble of cutting the photo out of the newspapers and sending it to her with 'obscene comments' scrawled over it. Some letters wished the 'nigger-lover' dead; one man said he prayed 'every night that you will die screaming in agony'; another told her it was 'cheap cows like you that let the nation down'. It was, Barbara said, a 'shoal of the filthiest letters I have ever received'.[58]

As late as February 1961, not even a Conservative Home Office could contemplate legislation 'which might restrict the historic right of every British subject regardless of race or colour freely to enter and stay in the United Kingdom'.[59] The following year, the Tories brought in legislation which consigned this historic right to history. Labour, which had condemned the Conservative legislation lock, stock and barrel, now mindful of the white backlash, was drawing up a policy which would further restrict the number of 'coloured Commonwealth citizens' entering Britain, cutting quotas at a time when there was a shortage of labour. It was agreed that, despite the 1962 controls, black and Asian immigrants were 'now entering the country more rapidly than was consistent with their absorption into the community'.[60] In Cabinet Barbara agreed with some cuts in immigration, ('if the electorate is saying "control them, control them" you have to listen,' she said later[61]) but she argued that the right of unskilled workers to enter should be restored. As Dick noted, no minister was a hundred per cent pro-immigration any more.

*

Much of the last ten days of July 1965 was taken up with wrangling over Barbara's share of the public-sector spending allocation and the contents of her forthcoming White Paper. Both Callaghan and Brown insisted she remove from it the statement that overseas aid would eventually amount to 1 per cent of GNP, because, they said, such projected largesse would have a detrimental effect on international confidence in sterling.

Barbara wanted more money, £250 million for 1966–67, not the £216 million Jim had offered; she explained at great length why she needed the extra £34 million to avoid major changes in overseas policy. Harold backed her up. She had spoken to him the night before and had agreed to accept his offer of a £10 million increase in foreign exchange, which he now suggested to cabinet. Callaghan and Brown turned on Harold 'like wolfhounds in at the kill'.[62] There could be absolutely no further increases in foreign exchange, they told him; he was undermining the work of the Public Expenditure Committee, which had concluded this matter. He was reversing the committee's decision.

Barbara had got to Harold and they knew it. Harold held on. He decreed that aid would be the exception: shortfalls in overseas aid could not be defended by his government or Britain. He declared that the matter of overseas aid was to be kept back for further consideration. At the end of cabinet, Dick noted acidly, Harold had the whole row removed from the official minutes.

A week later, Jim Callaghan announced that because of the financial crisis many election promises would be postponed indefinitely, among them the income-guarantee scheme and the abolition of prescription charges. The planned construction of hospitals, schools and council houses was halted. But the discussion on aid went on, producing an explosion. Tony Crosland, who'd taken over from Stewart at Education, was appalled: hours and hours discussing ODM when higher education had been cut.

The amount Jim had finally agreed upon for aid was £225 million for the next financial year, £9 million extra, but, unlike monies allocated to other ministries, it was to be on a cash basis (it would not increase by the amount of inflation). This did little to cool tempers.

Brown and Frank Cousins were outraged: where was this extra money to come from? After lengthy argument in which it was suggested that any further increase would mean 'borrowing additional money abroad in order to finance the aid' – borrowing to provide soup kitchens for Africans – Barbara 'reluctantly accepted this proposal', with the proviso that subsequent years were reviewed to take inflation into consideration.[63]

Even though financial committments were left out of the White Paper, Callaghan and Brown wanted Barbara to postpone its publication until after the summer recess, to coincide with publication of the National Economic Plan. Once again, they claimed anything else would damage international confidence in sterling; for the Treasury and the Department of Economic Affairs the very fact of even an unspecified amount of aid was too expansionist. She refused to concede and took the matter out of the Ministerial Committee on Public Expenditure and into cabinet, where she played her ace.

Within the party reaction to the new immigration controls had been less than sanguine. Restricting immigration for racist reasons was yet more evidence to the left that the Labour government was not a socialist government. Her White Paper, Barbara said, should be published at the same time as that on immigration, in order to 'to take the bad taste of the latter out of our people's mouths'.[64]

Overseas Development: The Work of a New Ministry and the immigration White Paper were both published in the first week of August. As she had been forbidden to put in any hard commitments, Barbara's introduction necessarily waffled: 'The basis of the aid programme is therefore a moral one ...Aid is not a means of winning the friendship of individual countries, though we are glad to offer aid to our friends';[65] but at least the interest-free loans were intact.

Barbara would be gone from ODM by the end of 1965. Harold had decided on a mini-shuffle in order to remove Frank Soskice from the Home Office and Tom Fraser from the Ministry of Transport (MOT); neither had proved up to the job. He moved Barbara to Transport, the Gaitskellite, Roy Jenkins, was brought into the cabinet as home secretary and Tony Greenwood was given ODM, an appointment with which Barbara only reluctantly agreed. Tony was 'weak', she thought. Harold thought he had 'no brains', but gave a shrug of the shoulders; someone had to run ODM and it wasn't going to be someone he needed elsewhere. ODM was import-ant to Harold for as long as it was Barbara's ministry and no longer.

Barbara left a 'Department of State truly dismayed at her going and wondering if life can ever be the same again'.[66] It would not. ODM would have four ministers in three years. When Arthur Bottomley took over from Tony eight months later, he found the ministry in a deeply demoralised state:'They felt that they no longer had a mission and the inspiration of Barbara' was gone, he wrote.[67] By January 1967 ODM was out of cabinet altogether, returning briefly in 1975 as a favour to Roy Jenkins, to keep a pal in cabinet. When Labour left office in 1979 ODM ceased to be a separate ministry. There was not another cabinet minister for overseas development until Clare Short in 1997.

Dick thought Harold had been anxious to move Barbara out of ODM because 'he didn't want her formidable, old-fashioned, left-wing conscience there preventing him finding some kind of settlement with the Smith regime'.[68] She would no longer routinely see the overseas telegrams and be apprised of the nitty-gritty of Harold's seemingly endless talks with Smith. This way she wouldn't be such a well-informed nuisance, but she would, as the prime minister must've known, still not let him backslide. Harold was at least equally motivated to move her to MOT because, as he told Ted Short (who thought little of her abilities and considered her totally unfit to be minister of transport), 'she always got her way and would be able to control those so-and-so Civil Servants who had controlled' the hapless Fraser;[69] she would, he was sure, be able to get the integrated transport policy, promised in the manifesto, onto the books.

Chapter Eight

SOCIALISM IN ONE MINISTRY

'I want a tiger in my tank', Harold told Barbara when offering her Transport, and she was the only tiger he'd got.* Dick agreed: if there was anybody who could get an integrated transport policy it was Barbara. Barbara described herself as heartbroken at leaving ODM. Transport was the last job she wanted. Not surprisingly, because the MOT had become the politicians' morgue; and integrating road and rail transport, while also attending to the demands of the motorist, would be almost impossible. Barbara would be vulnerable to criticism and carping, and she knew it.

But it was a promotion and she would be the first woman minister of transport, and the first since Oliver Stanley in 1933 who couldn't drive a car. Michael Foot had tried valiantly to teach her to drive in the 1930s, but Barbara had more or less conceded defeat. She belonged to the driven classes and, like Stanley before her, was to be attacked as unfit for the job because of it.

Her appointment was a sensation. Never before had the naming of a transport minister caused such a flurry of media activity, in part because she was the first woman, in part because she could not drive, and in part because she was Barbara: scarlet bogey and It Girl

---

* A play on the catch-phrase used in ads for Esso petrol: 'Put a tiger in your tank.'

rolled into one. Mobs of photographers jammed the road outside the MOT offices so that she had to fight her way into the building. Once inside the photographers swarmed after her. They wouldn't go until she let them take the pictures they wanted. For an hour Barbara posed this way and that. There were so many cameramen they had to photograph her in relays.

At her first press conference a week later two-hundred-plus rapturous journalists were stuffed into the room. Barbara 'made almost a film star's entrance', the *Guardian*'s reporter gushed, attired in 'a bright red frock, and wearing a necklace of chunky old-gold costume jewelry ... photographers flashbulbs going off all around her'. There was applause as she entered; the hard-bitten hacks put their hands together and clapped briefly before succumbing to embarrassment, while Barbara, 'eyes flashing, chunky necklace flashing', was winsomeness itself. 'I want to give you a chance to have a look at this woman who cannot even drive,' she said demurely. And, no, for the sake of matrimonial harmony she was not going to learn to drive: 'One family one car means one husband one car', she said, gaining the approval of 'every man in the room' although the 'women there bristled slightly' at this display of little womanhood.[1]

Transport was heavy lifting, a man's job, roads and railways. How would men react to this 'woman who cannot even drive'? Barbara, with her genius for self-presentation and her ability to manipulate an audience, did what had worked so well for her in the past with a predominately male and potentially hostile crowd: she applied her femininity with a trowel. She hammed it up for the gallery, swathed in red and gold, draped with a garland of coyness, playing the role Quintin Hogg ascribed to her: 'the Pussy Galore of a Goldfinger Government'.

It was a strategy not without risks. She was the 'Tigress with red hair, a rare animal in the political jungle ... a frighteningly feminine figure'. Some commentators made remarks to the effect that she couldn't be both tough and feminine. Others aired the bitch model: 'Queen of Her Castle', stated the *Evening News*, 'How close are the scratches to the purring?'[2] But at this stage of her career, in particular, she had most of the pressmen (and they were mostly men) on her side, mesmerised by her glamour and mindful of her entertainment value. Barbara could spot a front-page photo op at fifty paces: jumping on a desk and wrapping her arms round the neck of a lorry driver and road haulier who had been demonstrating against her, for instance, or reaching up to kiss a group of angry workers.

Being the only woman in cabinet, and now with this high-profile domestic job, she became the most-photographed member of the government. No politician before or since has been covered in quite that way. The paparazzi trailed after her. They snapped her on horseback, at family weddings, on holidays, and walks with the dogs, and having a drink in the pub, as well as in her 'with it' hat opening the Severn Bridge; clambering aboard the new Red Arrow bus; laughing in a helicopter; waving out of a train window, testing the newfangled seatbelts. Fashion and outrage in motion. She bowed, not curtsied, to the Queen; and that hat was rather outré. She got coverage befitting a Hollywood star cum royal favourite.

Barbara spent her first few days as transport minister locked away from the cameras in her new country cottage in the Chilterns. This was her first Christmas at Hell Corner Farm – not a name she chose: it was already called that. She called it 'HCF' and it was, she said, the best thing that ever happened to her. It was a gorgeous old house, ramshackle, L-shaped, snuggled into a ridge. The view over the valley to the hills beyond was exquisite. From her bedroom she could see the apple trees in her hundred-year-old orchard. The garden was triangular. It was picture-book perfect, a faultless slice of rural England, peaceful, seemingly remote, accessible by car only along a narrow lane, yet no more than an hour from Westminster or the Castles' Islington flat. And, when Barbara could spare the time, there was good walking to be had in the surrounding Chiltern hills.

The woods behind the cottage led to the Wormsley Estate (subsequently bought by John Paul Getty) and the tiny, sedate, well-heeled village of Ibstone, where Barbara and Ted took Aldie, their cocker spaniel, for walks, often popping into the Fox for a drink. This was Tory country, a true blue shire, beautiful but with hidden troubles, like a Singer-Sargent lady, and it was here that Barbara, at 55, found her real home; the one her brother Jimmie, who never married, came to for Christmas, the one her mother lived in towards the end of her life; the home her nieces and nephews and their children visited for the annual Guy Fawkes bash or for Christmas dinner or part of the summer holiday. The home she would have for the rest of her life.

A dense, consuming political life such as Barbara's precluded in-timate friendships outside politics; family was therefore very important to her. A house full of children, greatnephews and great-nieces to whom she was 'Gabby' (short for Great Aunt Barbara), the presiding matriarch, a fabulous cook and entertainer, a perfectionist here, too. She thought children great, especially the boys; she was wonderful with them, wonder-full for them. Olive Shapley, whom Barbara saw occasionally after Oxford, noted Barbara's way with her own children, how they loved her outrageousness. Dick thought she was lovely with his children. And her niece, Sonya, marvelled at Barbara, up to her arms in cooking and yet entertaining Sonya's grouchy two-year-old son, whereas Jimmie was intolerant, waspish, of the seen not heard school.

Jimmie could be foul-tempered with adults too. He drank and sometimes he drank a bit more than his temperamental difficulties allowed. He'd gone back to Africa to work, for Oxfam this time, as the field director for East Africa, operating out of offices at Wilson Airport in Nairobi. He travelled extensively in this job, all round Uganda, Burundi, Rwanda and Tanzania, often just with one or two other people. In this setting he could be 'autocratic' and 'insensi-tive to Africans', pulling rank and sometimes being downright rude if he was the worse for wear.[3] In Africa he kept quiet about being Barbara's brother; perhaps he thought it invidious. Having a famous sibling can as easily cast a shadow as illuminate in reflected glory.

Barbara's importance, rather than her fame, was increasingly diffi-cult for Ted. In 1964 he'd become a GLC alderman, a poor relation

– no matter how he and Barbara tried to present it – to a cabinet minister. Ted, who was on the GLC's Transport Committee, now also worked on the *Sun*, a left-of-centre paper when, before Rupert Murdoch acquired it, it was owned by Odhams. His colleagues found him a marvellous companion, gregarious, garrul-ous, wonder-ful fun. He could be a bit pompous but there was not much side to Ted; he was always willing to pitch in. But no one could get close to him. There was no possibility of building an in-timate friendship with him. He kept himself apart, one friend and colleague thought, to protect Barbara, because of his assumption that 'if you got close to him you were getting close to Barbara', to whom he was 'abso-lutely loyal to a fault'.[4]

Ted still went to the pub with the lads as he always had, prop-ping up the bar at the Radio Arms at the back of Endell Street, where Barbara sometimes swung by in her ministerial car to pick him up. He seemed much the same as he always had, but he felt increasingly isolated. 'It must be hell to be a Cabinet Minister's husband', Tony Benn thought during dinner with Ted. Ted had told him that Barbara said nothing of what went on in cabinet and that he felt shut out.[5] He told others the same. Barbara, he said, treated her privy councillor's oath of secrecy with 'such fantastic sanctity'. Under the same regime it would be hell to be a cabinet minister's wife, too, but it was more than that. It was seen as emasculating to be the male appendage of The Boss: 'We girls have got to stick together', as Ted remarked to Tony's wife, Caroline.[6]

'Ted wears the trousers at home' was a message frequently promoted by both Castles, even before Barbara became a minister. But it wasn't always believed. That 'there was a switch in that family with Ted playing the motherly womanly supportive role and Barbara being the aggressive, sharp, career-building person', as one observer said,[7] was not an uncommon view. During most of their marriage their relationship was the stuff of seaside postcards. In these incarnations female power is drawn or writ large. The huge, bosomy wife nagging the frail, small, henpecked husband half her size, the stuff of sitcoms and Carry On films. Or the thinner, sharper-tongued version, such as the scold Fanny Craddock, the first TV chef, with husband and partner Johnny as put-upon pina-fored poodle de la cuisine.

Barbara was the most powerful woman in Britain, 'the first lady of the land', as she was often introduced. 'In an age when distinction in politics was very very rare for women', Ted coped pretty well with life as second fiddle and the sideswipe glances of knowing pity, and patronising smirks that went with it. 'He gave no evidence of being resentful', Neil Kinnock remembered, a fact which 'in the 1950s, 1960s and even the 1970s was quite remarkable. I always found this bloody impressive: it said a lot for the size of the man.'[8] And Ted was, in Mik's view, 'even more ambitious for Barbara than she was for herself, which was more than somewhat'.[9]

At home Ted did wear the trousers. Barbara, despite her exalted status, and her often exhausted state, considered herself totally responsible for the domestic organisation of their life, moaning quietly, albeit often, about it in her diary. 'There really isn't any escape from the extra chores that fall on a woman', she noted with resignation. When they moved to HCF Barbara remarked wearily that she doubted whether the 'Chancellor has to do his own removing', and when the housekeeper was off, it was Barbara who spent the weekend doing the housework and cooking; no one knew the 'problems of a woman Minister!' she exclaimed. There were just 'so many things to do a man doesn't have to do (my dress to press, the housekeeper's journey home to organize, the dog to see to)'.[10]

Her friend Mary Hepworth, spending a weekend with the Castles at HCF, was astonished not only at the punishing schedule of Barbara's supposed weekend off, which included ploughing through her red boxes and dictating to her secretary for over five hours on both Saturday and Sunday (as it would for many ministers), but the fact that at 9.30 on Saturday night, after dictating since 4 p.m., Barbara made Ted's supper. Mary offered to do it for her, but she refused, saying it 'was her job, she always did it and she was always going to' do it.[11] Just as she was always going to iron that blouse (which would be invisible under her jacket) and spend hours in the toilets of the land attending to her hair and make-up, leaving her male staff, as Bernard Ingham joked, feeling like the biggest 'perverts in Whitehall' having 'spent more time than anyone waiting outside ladies loos'.[12]

Barbara's preoccupation with fashion was undiminished. She was forced, as she complained, to open a by-pass coatless in the rain because she hadn't had time to buy a new coat or get her own shortened. 'Men just don't know!' she said, unaware, perhaps, that it was possible for women just not to care so much. No wonder Barbara, the original superwoman, preparing a speech for the fiftieth anniversary of women's suffrage, mused that she was 'too busy exercising my emancipation to have time to celebrate it'.[13]

Barbara's first impressions of MOT were of an 'intimidatingly masculine' organisation, a grim, grey culture, intractable, intransigent. Even the lift operators were sullen. She was the first minister anyone could remember who actually smiled while in the building; but she was smiling through gritted teeth. The atmosphere was one 'of ill-concealed hostility' both to herself and to the concept of an integrated transport policy. It took 'several months to get my civil servants even to be able to mouth the words', she said.[14] They simply didn't believe in it. Many didn't believe she needed a women's loo and bathroom near her ministerial office, either. Barbara had one installed. As the smell of freshly applied Lanvin's L'Apèrge drifted down the corridor, mumbles could be heard along the lines of what a nuisance women were!

Getting control of the ministry and instituting her own systems were a top priority. This being an established department, the staff and their bad habits were entrenched. The first thing Barbara wanted to do, as she had told Harold when he offered her the post, was to get rid of Sir Thomas Padmore, MOT's permanent secretary. (She could have anything she wanted, said Harold gaily.) Barbara wasn't alone in holding Padmore responsible for the indolent culture at the ministry. His recent career had been one of slow, painful descent from Treasury knight to cabinet secretariat to MOT. He would get in the way and be seen to get in the way, and his *Yes, Minister* unctuousness when they met hardened Barbara's resolve to get rid of him. Not one week in the job and her plan to remove

Padmore had been leaked to the *Guardian*, perhaps by Christopher Foster, whom Barbara had appointed her director-general of economic planning.

The civil service panjandrums were outraged that a mere minister should seek to remove a permanent secretary, and in such unseemly haste. Ministers who were 'only temporary . . . could not interfere with staffing'.[15] No minister had ever tried to remove a permanent secretary before. Who did she think she was? Sir Laurence Helsby, head of the Home Civil Service, suggested that little could be done quickly, if at all. He wasn't saying that it was impossible, merely improbable: another regrettable first. Maybe in a few months, when, if nature took its course, another suitable position would open up and Padmore could be booted sideways.

Barbara was persistent. Padmore had to go and, just in case nature's course was slower or more obstacle-strewn than it should be, she made his life as disagreeable as possible, sending handwritten 'manuscript minutes to him, great long minutes saying this, that and the other is a cause of reproach'.[16] She lost this battle, though; she was indeed only temporary, and could not be seen to be interfering with civil service management. The 'totally dispensable' Padmore stayed on.

Whereas Tom Fraser had presided over, in the words of a senior civil servant, 'stagnation, had done, as far as anybody could judge, absolutely nothing for fourteen months', the MOT under Barbara 'was a moment of go'. She wanted her first White Paper to be published within six months, 'quite something by MOT standards'.[17] She flew around, changing everything she could as quickly as she could before the cement hardened round her ankles.

The ministry was divided into three divisions, of which twain seldom met. When they did, they did so round Padmore's table. She instructed him that from now on the heads of all three divisions would meet round her table each and every Monday morning. Whereas there had been only a single part-time economist for the entire ministry, now there would be a team under Foster. Foster was an economist, an expert on traffic and a fellow of Jesus College,

Oxford. His job was to solve such mysteries as what it actually cost to move freight around on road or on rail, and to present the cost-benefit arguments for closing or not closing stations and, among other things, to forecast future transport demands and their costs.

Barbara set up a political policy group, and expanded research and development. Her boffins came up with wonderfully futuristic schemes. One was for driverless taxis which would travel along a guided track and look something like four-seater bubble cars; another was for overways built and reserved for Minis.

The workload was much heavier at MOT than at ODM and Barbara made it more so. She was inundated; there was not enough time in her much-trumpeted sixteen-hour-plus working day to review everything as she would have wished. Big projects like the Channel Tunnel and the Victoria Line for London's Underground, with their seemingly uncontrollable costs and movable-feast completion dates, jockeyed for her attention against the priority of building an integrated transport policy.

There were meetings, meetings, and damn meetings, some days one every thirty minutes. Eight months into the job, and she had never felt so exhausted. Although she determined still to write her own introductions and conclusions to her White Papers, and ensure that the bit in the middle was written in English, not Whitehallese, there was certainly no time for niceties such as rewriting official speeches, as she had done at ODM.

Any speeches she did write were written during cabinet. She gave a speech at a formal dinner at least three times a week: to engineers, road people, rail people, freight people, public transport people, almost all of them men, many of them gawking, curious to see the Woman Transport Minister. It was usual for Barbara to be the only woman at these events, a tiny dot of colour in a profusion of black, white and grey.

Her social life was what it had always been: political. Barbara and Dick continued to have dinner every so often with their left-wing colleagues: people like Michael Foot, who was still on the back benches, and Judith Hart, who would soon come into government as the postmaster general, and the other Bolshevik in Harold's tsarist cabinet, Frank Cousins. But there was less and less time for friends and family.

Despite the punishing schedule, Barbara was never prepared, 'except in extremis, to miss an NEC meeting. That was as important in her diary as almost anything else.'[18] She continued to fear that she would be bumped off the executive, and decided to pre-empt any possible ousting by standing down – if, that was, she could get the other ministers to follow suit. Tony Greenwood agreed in principle. Dick thought about it, then thought better of it, then resigned anyway the following year and regretted it always. But Jim Callaghan and Tony Benn told Barbara they had no intention of going. Both wanted their turn as chairman of the party and neither wanted to abandon the power base of the NEC.

Barbara was afraid she was 'losing her role as leader of the Left', Tony Benn noted.[19] It was a fear she would have to conquer. There was no way she would leave Jim Callaghan on the executive when she was not. She steeled herself to resist the continual grassroots pressures for ministers to stand down, defending 'her foot-in-both-camps with one of her clanging barrages of amazonian bellicosity', as Mik boisterously put it.[20]

Necessity made Barbara's work habits even more fanatical. Saturday working was de rigueur; so were early mornings and late nights. 'The only time I had a proper night's sleep in the course of the week was Thursday when she went straight into the cabinet meeting from her flat', recalled Richard Bird, her principal private secretary. The standard of dedication and hard work she set was awesome. When she had pneumonia during the all-important public expenditure negotiations – during which a minister argues for his or her share of the budget – 'she was fetched every day by car to come and battle this stuff out'. The doctors ordered her to rest but she refused, attending all seven of the cabinet meetings during that ten-day period. 'She was very very ill,' Bird said, 'but she was simply not going to let it go. Indomitable, indefatigable: words like that come to mind.'[21]

Other words come to mind, too: compulsive, foolish, driven. But despite being under such pressure, Barbara was once again seen as 'without reservation, a very good boss'. Her junior ministers and special advisers were treated as vital allies in the running of the department. She conducted weekly meetings with all her staff, tried out her speeches on the whole office, and dealt personally 'with people down the hierarchy – as a sensible minister will'.[22]

Paul Rose, her PPS at Transport, who had been 'in love with Barbara at fourteen like other people are in love with the Spice Girls' today, found being PPS to his 'idol heavenly – although she was very tough to work with as most strong people are and she could sometimes be difficult'.[23] She was a very inclusive boss, letting her most junior staff, such as Rose, sit in on meetings so that they could learn how government worked, something neither Cripps nor Harold had done for her when she was their PPS.

She was 'very motherly in some ways', Rose said. She sometimes, quite unselfconsciously, ran her fingers through his hair when they talked.[24] When he voted against the government over the East of Suez policy, she gave him the same leeway Cripps had given her and refused to accept his offer of resignation. As she told him, she believed that the function of the Labour left in parliament was to 'guard the conscience of the Party and insist that the Government, which was always in danger of being swamped by administrative compromises, did not lose sight of its principles';[25] a role she herself had played. She believed her job now was to produce a transport policy, 'consciously as a fundamental socialist measure, perhaps the brightest jewel in her left-wing career', as *The Times* observed.[26]

But first there was the politics. A knife-edge majority meant that at any moment, owing to accident or illness, the government might fall. Harold needed to call a general election sooner rather than later. Most immediately there was a by-election coming up in Hull which had to be won, and Barbara was the one who could win it by the time-honoured method of scraping the pork barrel. Photographers in tow, Barbara swept up to Hull to speak to packed houses for Labour's candidate, Kevin McNamara. Her appeal was simple, a variation on the theme of the election address she'd scrawled on a scrap of paper as a six-year-old: Vote for Kevin and I will build you the Humber Bridge (although never the world's most-travelled thoroughfare, it was the longest suspension bridge of its day, both an engineering and an electoral miracle).

Labour did more than keep Hull. It increased its majority to almost six thousand, a 4.5 per cent swing, the largest by-election swing to a government in more than ten years, a result that 'created a completely new political situation', as Tony Benn noted.[27] Labour had gone from losers to winners overnight in public perception. Harold agreed. The general election was called two months later, on 31 March. Labour won that as well, returning with a healthy majority of ninety-six.

At Transport, Barbara made a point of meeting all the relevant unions and was surprised to find that she was the first minister to do so. She found the executive of the National Union of Railwaymen (NUR) deeply unimpressive, busy covering up their insecurities with pomposity and elaborate formality; within three weeks of her taking office they had threatened to strike over a recommendation by the Prices and Incomes Board on pay and conditions which held their members' increase to 3.5 per cent.

Barbara, as the minister responsible for the railways, Ray Gunter, as the minister of labour, and George Brown were the negotiating team. Their first meeting at Number 10 did not augur well. George was missing. He was unwell, Harold told them. (Like Jeffrey Bernard, George Brown was unwell frequently; more and more frequently as the pressures of work collided with his overarching frustration that he was not prime minister.) He came in later, thick of speech and lolling of head.

Sober, Brown was an ebullient man, an amusing character; smart and dynamic, an able minister, he stood up for the ordinary working-class person in cabinet. But he was a repulsive drunk, belligerent, intolerable, with all his many and assorted chips spilling off his shoulders. The poverty of his childhood was cankerous within him. It was an 'inhibiting bitterness', he knew, but like his resentment of the educated he could not shake it off. He loved to pull rank and was capable of such objectionable acts as sending his civil servants out for booze. He often went AWOL, disappearing on benders, out of phone contact, out of control. He pawed at women, even trying to unbutton Barbara's blouse in the division lobby. But nevertheless she preferred him to Ray Gunter, whom she thought 'despicable and dangerous'. The dislike was mutual. When polite, Gunter referred to Barbara as 'leather knickers', rather than his more usual 'bitch'.[28]

This crack negotiating team spent much time negotiating ways round each other, with Brown not returning phone calls or telling Barbara of meetings he had convened with the NUR.

Matters regarding the strike were eventually settled at a marathon beer-and-sandwiches fiesta at Number 10, with Harold in impresario mode. He thought Barbara, who 'took an almost parental interest in those who worked within her ministerial sphere ... most helpful. With little encouragement she spoke for twenty minutes, weaving a web of hope: higher productivity and higher wages in the not very distant tomorrow.'[29] The strike was called off.

Eleven months at MOT and Barbara was the coming person. She had moved further to the centre of the cabinet table, both literally and figuratively. She was, as Dick said, doing 'extremely well' and was seen to be doing so. She had inherited two controversial issues from Tom Fraser: the breathalyser and the 70 mph speed-limit trials on the motorways, both part of his Road Safety Bill announced the day before she took office. Under the Bill the breathalyser was to be administered randomly. The RAC and AA strongly objected, on the grounds that women drivers would be stopped by rapists pretending to be police officers. Over the next eighteen months Barbara's 'regime at Transport was subjected to vigorous and often extravagant attacks' by these organisations, which claimed that she was anti-car and anti-motorist; the result was a state of 'almost total war' between themselves and the ministry.[30]

The Tories, too, painted Barbara as anti-car and anti-motorist and claimed she was indulging in the politics of anti-individualism and socialist envy. Because 'she does not drive a car herself, she does not see why other people should', one Tory MP absurdly said, as if she didn't own a car. This was all part of the ongoing 'traditional Tory attempt to present Labour as ideologically opposed to wide car-ownership', whereas the 'Conservative utopia' was one in which 'twenty million motorists could drive their cars wherever and whenever they chose'.[31] (This four-wheel nirvana was surpassed in 1996, when twenty-one million cars were driven wherever and whenever, a figure that had risen to over twenty-eight million by the turn of the century.)

There were around nine million private cars on the road when Barbara took office. But eight thousand people were killed that year on the roads, compared with less than half that number in 1999. The proliferation of motorbikes and scooters was in part to blame for the death toll, but few cars were fitted with seatbelts, and motorists could drive as fast as they liked as drunk as they liked. Both the speed-limit trials and the proposed drink–driving legislation were attempts to control the carnage, which was costing £250 million a year, the price of ten new hospitals in the mid-1960s.

It was Barbara's job to defend the introduction of the breathalyser, which she did with gusto, calling drunk driving 'criminally selfish behaviour' and finding herself portrayed by some as antediluvian and anti-civil-libertarian. Her record postbag ran 50:50, with opponents abusing her as a bitch or worse and supporters telling her how brave she was. Her life was threatened more than once, and on one occasion the threat was taken seriously enough for her security to be beefed up. There were occasional bomb scares, too; and she was discredited with losing Labour the Leicester South West by-election, which the Tories fought and won on an anti-breathalyser platform.

She 'was reviled by all these chaps who thought it laddish to go and drink and then drive a car', Paul Rose said. The people of Leicester 'bitterly resented the breathalyser – and they resented her because she couldn't bloody drive'. Barbara 'came under an enormous amount of attack and a lot of anti-feminine attack', Rose said. She 'showed enormous courage' in the face of such opprobrium,[32] but Fraser's Transport Bill didn't get through all its stages before the 1966 general election, and it was killed. She had to start again and cut a deal with the AA and the RAC: if they wouldn't oppose her new breathalyser legislation she would remove the clause that allowed the police to stop and breathalyse motorists at random; motorists would not be stopped without due cause. The definition of 'over the limit' was a bacchanalian 80 milligrams of alcohol per 100 milligrams of blood, a level recommended by the British Medical Association – the equivalent of six pints of beer or six double whiskies!

Barbara produced her first White Paper in July, almost within her self-imposed six-month deadline. It outlined her policies and the reorganisation of the department, and set the course of transport policy for years to come. Her plans overlapped into other domains, which caused rows about her legislating for other ministries. Such encroachments 'might provoke demands for further White Papers in those fields', the Cabinet Conclusions dryly recorded, which would make her White Paper 'a precedent'.[33] Her fellow ministers objected to what they regarded as empire-building and, despite her plea that the White Paper had already been extensively redrafted by the relevant ministerial committee, a further eight lengthy alterations were insisted upon.

Such major changes in cabinet to a draft White Paper were not unknown, but neither were they common. It was said of Barbara that some of her White Papers came to cabinet still in need of work, because of her rush to get them out. Sometimes it was simply a technique to ram through something she knew was not acceptable, as was the case with her draft White Paper on freight, which she brought to cabinet for approval even though 'a number of specific policy issues had not yet been satisfactorily resolved between Departments'.[34] Even Harold balked at that, postponing consideration of the draft until the following week and instructing Barbara and the other parties involved to sort it out.

In the lead-up to her Transport Bill, Barbara published an additional five White Papers laying out in more detail her policies on road safety, canals, freight transport, reorganisation of the railways, and public transport and traffic. The control of traffic had begun to be recognised as a major problem, especially in cities. Until the early

1960s it had been assumed that private cars would never become universally available. Owning a car was a middle-class luxury. At the time of the 1959 general election only around 5 million people did so, and 60 per cent of them said they voted Tory. But falling prices and rising wages had rapidly begun to democratise car ownership, something Barbara wanted to extend, half toying with Tony Benn's idea of getting people to rent rather than own cars.

Democratising car ownership would mean building new roads and spending more on existing ones, of course; but 90 per cent of passenger traffic and 60 per cent of freight was carried on the roads, and Barbara accepted that you would not get people out of their cars and 'onto railways which could not take them where they wanted to go'.[35] An accommodation with the car had to be found: ring roads, restrictions on cars in the centres of towns and cities, and subsidised public transport were obvious beginnings. But, as she wrote, the overall 'aim of a rational transport policy must be to solve ... [the] paradox' of the benefits of the car and the problems of congestion, noise, fumes, dangers, and a despoiled environment in both town and country.[36] It is a paradox that remains unresolved.

Barbara extended the 70mph speed limit – an issue she became 'strongly identified with' – for an additional two months. This angered the car industry, which claimed it would 'discourage the development' of fast cars and tight brakes.[37] Lorries and trailers were banned from the fast lane of motorways for fifteen months. The time lorry drivers spent at the wheel was reduced to a maximum of nine hours a day, down from eleven, and was to be monitored by tachograph, which became known as the 'spy in the cab'. She also ruled that all cars manufactured after 1967 had to be fitted with seatbelts, and later extended the ruling to cars which came on the road from 1965. She introduced an official driving manual, a new edition of the *Highway Code*, and a compulsory register of professional driving instructors.

Vested interests attacked fiercely, accusing her of running a nanny state. This was all a 'gospel of defeatism and despair' to the AA. After the short respite while she was at ODM, Barbara had the word 'controversial' appended to her name again. The London

195

Evening Standard wondered whether the 'controversial minister of transport' was 'the imaginative planner of Britain's mobile future ... or a skirted socialist despot'. To the Tories she was the latter. She 'must be watched', the *Daily Telegraph* had warned upon her appointment: 'She is a nationaliser, both by temperament and by inclination.'[38]

Barbara's efforts to fit the private car into a coherent national transport policy meant that she had to improve the commuter's lot. Half the population lived in large towns or cities, and around 80 per cent in urban areas. She reprieved six commuter lines that had been due for the chop, saying that she was not going to adhere to the 'commercialisation gone mad' philosophy of Dr Beeching, who had closed over two thousand stations deemed uneconomic. Although she was not prepared to keep each and every station and line open, something often overlooked. Barbara was an expert on spinning at a time when the word was applied only to something in a cotton mill. She was, she chuckled to her diary, 'delighted to see that the rejigged press release on railway closures ... had the desired effect ... the press has concentrated on the refusals of closure as they were intended'.[39]

But nevertheless 'commercial viability is important, but secondary', as she said.[40] Transport was a social service. It was necessary to 'get away from the concept of paying our way'. She wiped out British Rail's annual £130 million running loss, allocating grants and subsidies. She drew up plans for local passenger transport authorities (PTAS) to integrate public transport in large urban areas such as Greater Manchester, Merseyside, Tyneside and the West Midlands.

The idea was to coordinate and control not only bus and train schedules but road-building and railway maintenance, traffic and parking, to centralise such things locally but with reference to, and coordination with, the overall national policy. Like road-building, which received capital grants of 75 per cent, public transport would be grant-aided. And as much freight as possible was to be got off the roads and onto rail. To this end the National Freight Corporation, directly responsible to the minister, was to be set up, and goods going more than a hundred miles would be required to go by rail, not by lorry, if the costs were at least equivalent.

Barbara's labyrinthine Transport Bill was the longest non-financial Bill in parliamentary history and the longest Bill of any sort since the war. The experts and the media, for the most part, were impressed. She had, said the *New Statesman*, set out 'to reform practically the whole of the internal transport system ... by a nice blend of traditional socialism and up to date technocratic intervention'. The Bill was often called a pantechnicon – a bazaar and a receptacle containing many miscellaneous objects, as well as a removal lorry – it was 'stuffed with all the radical proposals for reorganising British transport that have been maturing under that neat crop of fiery hair for the past eighteen months', wrote *The Times*.[41]

As she told Dick, 'if you want to impress people you must make things unreadably long'. The Bill caused him, as leader of the House, 'endless trouble'. But he thought it 'a serious effort to reorganize transport ... as nobody has dared do before'; and the *Journal of Transport, Economics and Policy* wrote that her policy was 'the first since the war to try to grapple with the overall market situation and to use all means of policy'.[42] Market measures such as taxation and subsidy were combined with administrative measures such as licensing and new institutions. She had even, said the journal's editor, a reader in Transport at Nuffield, tried to grapple with the problem of the private car, although she had not solved it. Barbara had rejected the concept of supplementary licensing for motorists commuting into inner London as being too difficult to enforce. It would also have been highly unpopular with London motorists, who might have taken their anger out on London Labour councillors.

Little that moved was left uncontrolled by the 169 clauses and 18 schedules in the Bill's two hundred pages. The PTAs, although bureaucratic and unwieldy, 'laid the foundations of a comprehensive urban transport policy';[43] the railways were also dealt with, and the National Bus Company was set up. Barbara had even persuaded the NUR to accept the opening of freightliner terminals for container trains, which meant allowing private hauliers access, something it had been violently opposed to. She had negotiated with the union for three days almost non-stop, using 'techniques and methods which would have shocked her to the core if used by anybody else'. She eventually threatened to starve the railways of funds unless they agreed. It was a 'tremendous triumph', Dick thought; she had more than earned her *Question Time* applause.[44]

The Bill was regarded by Barbara, and by her friends and enemies alike, as the 'socialist centrepiece' of the Labour government, the most important Bill of the parliamentary session. It was seen as a declaration of war by the Tories and powerful special-interest groups such as the Road Haulage Association and the right-wing Aims of Industry. The Tories howled that it was a tyrannical extension of state power; Aims of Industry produced its own booklet on Barbara and the 'economic consequences' of her policies.

Awaiting her in the House was something 'no Labour minister so far has faced ... a near military campaign that was to be rough, tough and sustained',[45] led by the shadow transport minister, Peter Walker, who marshalled the Young Conservatives as his footsoldiers throughout the country. He divided his team into three sections, each of which was to pick holes in one of the Bill's three main components (Michael Heseltine was in charge of destroying the section that dealt with the PTAS); six economists, eight lawyers and six shorthand typists were signed up to the Tory campaign at a cost of £10,000, some of it paid from Walker's own pocket.

Barbara spent many exhausting hours getting her Bill through the House; sometimes she was there all through the night. By February 1968, as the Bill reached its final stages, she was absolutely exhausted, so much so that she fell asleep for the first time ever in cabinet. Unfortunately it was during the crucial debate on the Kenyan Asians, British passport holders who had been thrown out of Kenya. About a thousand were arriving in Britain each week to live and Jim Callaghan, then home secretary, was in the process of rushing through legislation which denied these people their right of automatic residence, legislation Barbara strongly opposed. 'I struggled to keep awake,' Barbara said later, 'but it was Jim Callaghan's droning on ... I just couldn't stay awake. That haunted me the rest of my cabinet life.' Barbara knew all too well what her enemies would say: see, 'she never said a word'.[46]

As if this wasn't enough warfare for one woman, Barbara opened a second front by launching 'Operation Getting Rid of Raymond', (Stanley Raymond, chairman of British Rail). Though in her diaries her remarks about him run from the temperate to the noncommittal, there was more than bad chemistry between them: 'he loathed her and she didn't like him'.[47] Raymond thought Barbara 'was interfering too much' in the railways and 'that the whole system was coming far too much under the domination of the ministry'. Barbara thought, 'Raymond wasn't running the railways as she wanted.' He was, she thought, a bully to his staff, a man incapable of delegating and one who was unwilling to put into practice the recommendations of the report on British Rail which had found the management wanting.

She began a propaganda war against him briefing 'eminent journ-alists' – many of them her friends, or friends of Ted – on his faults. Ray Gunter, the minister of labour, got wind of the fact that she intended to sack Raymond and leaked it to the *Daily Mail*, which in turn told Barbara they were going to run the story, thereby forcing her hand. Raymond was deep in negotiations with the NUR over another threatened strike. He was in the middle of a meeting when she unceremoniously fired him. After his 'resignation' had been officially announced, Raymond made no comment except to remark, ex gratis, in a pre-arranged speech, that he had never understood women and wondered whether that had been his undoing.

Jim Callaghan was enraged. He and Raymond went back to the 1930s together: as young men they had both worked at the tax of-ficers' union. Like Callaghan, Raymond had had no middle-class advantages. He'd grown up in an orphanage; he was a self-made man, who'd risen on his own merits to become chairman of British Rail; but then, Jim recorded mournfully in his autobiography, he 'fell out with Barbara ... a fate he shared with me'.[48]

Barbara had worked closely with Dick Crossman when he was at Housing, setting up a joint MOT/ Ministry of Housing committee to integrate transport into town planning and vice versa (characteristically, they both claimed credit for initiating this). It evolved into a cabinet committee on environmental planning, one of the stages en route to what became the Department of the Environment. Once Dick became leader of the House in August 1966, with Tony Greenwood taking his place at Housing, Barbara took the reins and the focus of planning shifted from Housing to Transport: as she said, transport is the key to a good environment.

It was no longer enough to plan transport as a unified system, Barbara told the 1966 party conference. 'We must plan transport now as an integral part of all our other planning – our planning for national economic expansion, our planning for regional development, our planning to protect and improve our environment.'[49] And she, the ultimate planner, the one minister who held onto the concept of a planned economy long after George Brown's National Economic Plan had slipped into oblivion, was the right woman for the job.

She was praised by the Royal Institute of British Architects for seeing transport through the prism of planning; and the Town and Country Planning Association gave her a standing ovation for her speech to their conference in 1966. Of her Transport Bill the *Journal of Transport, Economics and Policy* wrote that 'for the first time there is a real grappling with the relations between all forms of urban transport and overall planning of city regions'.[50] She was the darling of the press, she basked in professional praise, her popularity with the backbenchers and the party had never been surpassed, and she had become the most popular minister with the public.

Barbara was featured by Marjorie Proops in the *Daily Mirror* as top of the ministerial pops, a full-page spread complete with a photo of the minister astride a pony, wearing culottes and delicate, beautiful shoes. It was, Harold declared, the sexiest snap he'd seen for many a year, and he promptly affixed it to his shaving mirror. She was probably 'the only Transport Minister who could top a popularity poll during her own term in office', *the Sunday Mirror* marvelled.[51]

On 9 October 1967, the day after Clem Attlee died, the breath-alyser came into force; it was the rocket that was to carry Barbara into the stratosphere. The immediate effect was that the takings in country pubs went down by a third – more at weekends – which, as Barbara pointed out with her 'unique verve and energy', only went to prove that people had been drinking far too much to drive. More death threats arrived, but she shrugged them off. The media were with her and so, soon, was the majority of the population.

The breathalyser saved lives, measurably and immediately. In the first five months of operation, road deaths were down by 22 per cent and serious injuries by 15 per cent. In the first year, deaths fell by between 8 per cent and 33 per cent each month, 40 per cent over Christmas. To the public, the name 'Barbara Castle meant not the Transport Bill but the breathalyser'.[52] She had, in popular perception, stood up to special interests without blinking or flinching. She had 'taken on two of Britain's greatest vested interests – the motor industry and the brewers – refusing to flinch against the enormous and expensive campaign which they launched against her', the *Tribune* wrote admiringly.[53] She was now being seriously canvassed by the press as the next prime minister. She was at the epitome of her career, at the absolute zenith of her popularity; she'd even joined Harold in wax at Madame Tussaud's. (Her effigy was 'absolutely horrible', she said to Ted: a 'raddled face under a red wig, [and] with a mouth like Edith Summerskill's'.[54] He assured her she didn't really look like that.) In politics, guts is all, Barbara said over and over, and she had been proven right.

Harold was under siege. Ever since the general election victory of March 1966 things had started to go wrong. The parliamentary party, confident in its majority of ninety-six, had grown more belligerent in its criticism of its own government. The situation in Vietnam had gone from bad to worse. Foreign Secretary Michael Stewart's statement in the House, a month before the election, that the government understood and supported the resumption of us bombing in North Vietnam had violently angered the Labour Movement. And the Rhodesian fiasco continued.

After Ian Smith's unilateral declaration of independence in 1965, Harold tried a mixture of talks and sanctions to bring Rhodesia back into the fold and get Smith to agree to the concept of black majority rule. He succeeded only in making himself look weak, Barbara thought. The oil sanctions were busted by the big companies and Smith kept him dangling. All those 'endless negotiations – his *Tiger* talks and *Fearless* talks – all these warships and silly meetings. I found it so undignified,' she said.[55] And so wrong. The terms he offered Smith on HMS *Fearless* were a sell-out. She threatened to resign. The last thing Harold needed was his most popular minister decamping. He tried to reassure her he would not sell out the black majority. Luckily for them both, Smith rejected all Harold's offers.

In May the seamen went on strike. Harold, cheered on by Jim Callaghan and George Brown, had decided to oppose their wage claim, not on its merits, which were undeniable, but on the grounds that to break the prices and incomes policy, which froze all wage increases for the next twelve months, would put pressure on sterling. The strike did that anyway. It closed the docks. Nothing came in and, more importantly, nothing went out. The pound sank. Barbara had told cabinet that it would be insanity to get into open conflict with the TUC, and in conflict with the TUC the government now was. Concessions had been made to doctors, civil servants and judges, but would not be made to the seamen. Labour's supporters were disgusted. The government was taking an anti-union, pro-boss line. It had rewarded the well-off, but was penalising the working class. What kind of socialist incomes policy was that? And what kind of Labour government was this? The government's definition of socialism, Bertrand Russell fumed, included 'penalising ... the poorest, capitulating to bankers, attacking the social services, banning the coloured* and applauding naked imperialism'.[56]

Harold's biographer wrote that 'his most precious asset, self-assurance, died in July 1966'.[57] He no longer believed he was the man who had the answers to Britain's economic woes. And nor did anyone else. Unemployment shot up by 200,000 in six months to just over half a million, unacceptably high for the 1960s. Industrial

*A reference to Labour's control of the number of black and Asian im-migrants.

unrest grew on the back of frozen wages and less than frozen prices: strikes, go-slows, work-to-rules. But it was not only his economic grip Harold felt slipping through his fingers. He had lost his political grip, too.

Harold smelt plots everywhere, and not without reason. The party was no longer with him. It might actually rise up to throw him out; it might even make Jenkins or Healey leader. Brown and Callaghan were plotting against him. They were after his job, and Callaghan, for one, would stop at little to get it. Harold retreated to the safety of Number 10. He unravelled. He listened too much to the reports of George Wigg, his spymaster general, the 'Ear-Wigg' who confirmed his fears; 'Harold's Rasputin', Barbara called him.

The press, which had been indulgent of Harold during his first three years, now predictably turned against him, in part because of his reaction to an article written by the *Daily Express*'s defence correspondent, Chapman Pincher, claiming that there was widespread vetting of private communications. Harold said the article breached the D-notice code, a voluntary agreement between press and government over what was or was not secret. Pincher was vindicated by the Radcliffe Inquiry, set up to look into the affair, but Harold bellicosely rejected its conclusions.

His standing with the press was also not helped by his ill-fated attempts to act as honest broker over Vietnam, while still supporting the American position. Nor by his handling of the seamen's strike, or of Ian Smith, or of any number of things. He was beginning to look like a man not waving but drowning.

By November 1967 economic reality could no longer be postponed. The pro-devaluation group in cabinet – the odd bedfellows of Barbara, Dick, George Brown, Tony Crosland, Roy Jenkins and Tony Benn – were proved correct: there was another sterling crisis. Harold was told by the Americans that, reluctantly, 'they would have to see us go down';[58] later they wobbled, fearful of the effect on the dollar, but they were not going to prop up the pound any longer. It was to be devalued from \$2.80 to \$2.40. Harold went on television and delivered his unfortunate statement that devaluation did not mean that the 'pound in the pocket' was worth less.

The decision had already been taken to withdraw at last from East of Suez some time in the early 1970s. This was now brought forward, with withdrawal from the Middle East and cancellation of an order for American F1-11 fighter planes, too. George Brown, whom Harold had made foreign secretary (the best foreign secretary ever till about 4 o'clock in the afternoon, Harold liked to say), was left to have what he called a 'disturbing and distasteful discussion' with Dean Rusk, the US secretary of state, who was openly appalled that Britain was opting out of its responsibilities. 'For God's sake act like Britain', he implored a rather flabbergasted Brown; and he went on to say that 'the acrid aroma of a fait accompli' that hung around the British decision would have grave consequences for US–UK relations.[59]

After opposing devaluation for so long, Callaghan felt he could no longer stay on at the Treasury and defend it. Harold happily obliged. At the end of November he made a direct swap with Roy Jenkins at the Home Office, after considering and rejecting Tony Crosland for the Treasury, in good part because he and Callaghan were friends; Jenkins had the advantage of being 'barely on hissing and spitting terms' with Callaghan.[60] He had another advantage too: unlike most home secretaries, Jenkins had been a success; his liberal reforms on homosexuality and divorce, his shepherding of David Steel's private member's Abortion Bill, the Race Relations Bill he put in train and the scrapping of theatre censorship had made him popular in the party. He would be the breath of fresh air the Treasury needed.

Roy Jenkins, like Barbara and Harold, was the product of a regional grammar school, unusual for a former habitué of the upper-middle-class Frognal Set. His background was unusual, too. His father, Arthur, had been a Welsh coalminer who worked his way up in the Labour Party, becoming an MP, a member of the NEC and Attlee's PPS. In party terms, Roy Jenkins was, as he liked to remark, a member of the squirearchy. A clever squire, he went to Balliol, where he moved effortlessly around the Oxford establishment. His manner was fey, upper-class, dandyish. He spoke without a trace of a Welsh lilt, but with a lisp that turned his Rs into Ws, as in Woy. He was clever in that nonchalantly aristocratic way of being effortlessly, carelessly so. He affected to consider politics something put on for his amusement, and wandered around the House like a Regency buck sauntering through Vauxhall Gardens. But this languidness caged a watchful ambition.

Barbara would not have been best pleased by Jenkins's promotion. She had long concluded that being one of Harold's usual hunting companions had its drawbacks. He had no problem giving his enemies high offices of state, while she and Dick were relatively sidelined. She had earlier suggested to Harold that he make her foreign secretary, trying to sell the idea to him as the smartest and most audacious move he could make. He smiled benignly and did otherwise. She thought Harold only listened to people he was afraid of. He leaves his friends on the margins, she told Dick, he takes us for granted and placates our adversaries. Both she and Dick had conspired and campaigned with Harold, stuck by him; and Barbara, for one, wanted her loyalty and all her hard work rewarded with a top job.

Devaluation did nothing for Harold's public approval ratings, which sank to 30 per cent, the same as the Tory lead. More austerity had followed devaluation, accompanied by rising prices. Jenkins brought in a budget which promised the electorate two more years of 'hard slog'. Industrial unrest evolved into tumult. Nineteen sixty-eight was the 'Year of the Strike', as well as the year of revolution. In the first eight months, 3.5 million workdays were lost to strikes, half a million more than in all of the previous five years.

Many strikes were unofficial: tools down, everyone out, over whose job it was to flip a switch. The shop stewards blew the whistle. In the previous ten years there had been over two thousand unofficial strikes and just 82 official ones. There was a 'new mood of impatience with authority and the ossified structures' of many trade unions.[61] Shop stewards engaged daily in detailed bargaining over bonuses and special payments, all of which served to raise wages, on a factory-by-factory basis, above nationally agreed rates; it was known as 'wage drift', and wildcat strikes were used as a local bargaining tool.

Unions competed for members and control on the shopfloor. There were dozens of different unions in companies, each jealously guarding its members' rights. The unions were out of control, the press shrieked. Harold had already concluded that it was the seamen's strike that had blown the government off course; now, he concluded, the unions were blowing the nation onto the rocks. He had to do something: about the unions, about his falling popularity.

First, he would reshuffle the cabinet. He would remake the government. It was Dick who came up with the idea of calling it the Mark II cabinet. It sounded like a new Jaguar, sleek, streamlined, with leather seats and elegant passengers. It sounded as if it were going places. Harold was delighted. Then he had a brainwave: he would put his most popular minister in charge of the Department of Economic Affairs (DEA). They wouldn't have had the trouble they had with the unions if Barbara had been in charge of the hated prices and incomes policy; she at least could get it adhered to, if not loved, could convince the unions of its necessity. She was a left-winger. They would trust her.

Roy Jenkins was appalled. 'I could not possibly accept that', he told Harold. He 'admired many aspects of Barbara, although ... [he] was occasionally put off by her obsessiveness, but there could be no question of ... allowing such a strong minister to reactivate the Department of Economic Affairs'. He had seen what 'creative tension' had done for Callaghan while George Brown was at the DEA. Jenkins told Dick he was going to 'jolly well run the show ... without a rival'.[62] Barbara tried to convince him that she would see her work at the DEA as underpinning his at the Treasury. He didn't believe a word of it. He knew her too well. She would try to run the government's whole economic policy.

Edmund Dell thought Harold would have done better to make Barbara chancellor, rather than putting her at the DEA. The country 'needed an "obsessive" Chancellor', and there was no minister more obsessive than Barbara: 'there would have been no dallying', he

wrote.[63] Time did not change that opinion. 'She was very determined, very courageous and I think she would have done what was
necessary. Despite Barbara's left-wing politics, when she saw a need
she tended to fight for it rather hard. But it would've been quite a
shock to everyone that such a left-wing personality should have
been put in charge of the Treasury. It was not an additional risk
Wilson was willing to take.'[64]

Politics, too, according to Dell, 'prevented such an appointment.
Callaghan would not have been the only colleague to be outraged.'[65]
So Harold came up with another idea. He'd make Barbara lady
president of the (Privy) Council and leader of the House. He'd give
her Dick's job – she would be the first woman to hold the post, he
emphasised. With no departmental duties, she would have time to
think about strategy, and of course she would be a member of his
new inner cabinet (something Callaghan tried to block, saying she
would talk too much, about foreign left-wing causes, 'particularly
about Rhodesia, South Africa, etc.'[66]).

Harold was inordinately pleased with himself, in almost exact
proportion to Barbara's displeasure. She was utterly dismayed. She
could not immediately think of anything she would less like to do
than hang around the House all hours of the day and night as Dick
did. She wanted to run another department. She wanted a proper
job. Look, she told him, 'my real talents lay in getting on with the
trade unions and with the working-class rank and file'.[67] It was a
fatal statement. It sank lazily into Harold's consciousness, like a rock
sinking into a bog.

He would make her minister of labour – with responsibility for
prices and incomes. In that way he could shift the present incum-
bent, Ray Gunter, from what the latter termed his 'bed of nails'. A
right-winger, Gunter was abhorred by the powerful left-wing unionist leaders such as Hugh Scanlon, of the Amalgamated Engineering
Union (AEU) and Jack Jones of the TGWU, the future 'terrible twins' of
the tabloids. Gunter also had poor relations with George Woodcock,
general secretary of the TUC. Barbara, with her portfolio of left-wing
credentials, was politically on the same side as the union men. She
could persuade them to do the right thing. She would 'make the

whole difference by taking over relations with the trade unions', Harold told Dick,[68] a Panglossian view echoed later by some papers: 'Nobody will question her dedication to social justice ... She can insist on restraint ... with the promise that fair shares will be guaranteed in better times to come,' said the *Guardian*.[69] Harold sent word he wanted to see Barbara. It was late. She was at home in her Islington flat, in her dressing gown, drink in hand, fagged out from the long day, when the phone rang. She got dressed, and Ted drove her down to Number 10.

Leader of the House and minister of labour? Barbara saw the ghost of Margaret Bondfield, the first woman cabinet minister; she'd been minister of labour in the MacDonald government, and had gone down in ignomy. Barbara did not want to be Maggie Bondfield Mk II. Moreover, the Ministry of Labour – which, said the wags, 'operated in the manner of an embassy to a foreign power – the working classes'[70] – would not, even with prices and incomes, necessarily ensure her a position at the heart of government. Harold offered to change the name; she said she wanted it to be Labour and Productivity, to which he responded 'that with a lady minister this might lead to bar-room ribaldry'.[71] She left Number 10, saying she would sleep on it.

It was Dick who made up her mind by offering her the position of first secretary (which Harold had offered him), for the rather eccentric reason that he wanted to keep the job of lord president, or, rather, the really 'lovely room in the Privy Council' that went with it. In Harold's administration the title of first secretary carried with it status and power. It was the power Barbara was after. As Dick told a rather bemused Harold, who questioned whether she was so 'status conscious', she was 'power conscious and quite right'.[72]

Barbara was in her bunk on the night sleeper to Blackburn when the news came, via a porter bearing a message, that she was to ring Number 10 from the next station. The first lady of the land recorded in her diary that, bare-legged, nightgown tucked up in knickers, coat over the top, she made her way across a draughty platform to the station master's office to make the call. A cheerful

Harold told her he had decided that she would be not a mere minister of labour, but first secretary *and* secretary of state for employment and productivity.

Chapter Nine

THE GAME'S AFOOT

On 5 April 1968, Barbara Castle walked into 'the Cabinet's inner power circle'. She was now, as the *Guardian* put it, 'within hailing distance of the premiership'.[1] The door to Number 10 had blown wide open, but she knew it could just as easily slam shut on her fingers: 'I am under no illusions that I may be committing political suicide', she confided in her diary. She knew what she was going to have to do. Mrs Secretary Castle, the first woman minister to qualify for this official style of address, had effectively become the 'economics boss'.[2] She would be responsible not only for managing the compulsory prices and incomes policy, loathed by many Labour MPs, but also for 'doing something about the unions'.

When asked how she saw her new job, Barbara told the assembled journalists that she saw it as a 'springboard', revealing, perhaps, more than she intended. She made a joke of the fact that she had meant not a springboard to the premiership but the fact that the Department of Employment and Productivity (DEP) would be a springboard for government policy, rather than Gunter's bed of nails. The two things were not unconnected. Both Harold and Dick thought that everything – the whole future of the Labour government – depended on her success; if she failed, she went down with it.

Barbara dropped a note to her old friend and protector, Leah

Manning: 'I may not succeed. But you know me, I'll have a bash.'[3] Not everyone liked her chances. 'The fact that Mr Wilson has decided to throw a glamorous woman to the wolves is unlikely to stop them from howling', the *Telegraph* said. And the *New Statesman* pointed out, 'Although a springboard is a thing you take off from, the final objective is down rather than up.'[4]

Until now Barbara had been ruled out of the leadership by the PLP because she was too left-wing and because she was a woman. The scarlet termagant – Dick's revealing term for Barbara when she had the audacity to say she wanted to challenge Gaitskell for the party leadership. Dick knew, as he often noted, that if she weren't a woman she would be a natural number one, and now, he mused, it could happen. She could 'quite conceivably be the first lady Prime Minister'.[5] Barbara had never ruled herself out on either grounds. Left-wing is as left-wing does. The public certainly would not care about her sex or her politics if she could organise and control the industrial chaos, and nor, therefore, would the party.

She had already got further than any woman in British parliamentary history. She was the first of the (by then) four women cabinet ministers to have held more than one portfolio, and the first to have survived in office for more than two years. Now she was the first woman in the inner cabinet. She was the deputy prime minister in all but name. Her place at the cabinet table reflected her new importance. The first secretary sat in the centre, directly opposite the prime minister; if she kept her nerve, she might in due course, sit in Harold's chair.

Not that she would try to eject him from it. Although she badmouthed Harold and disapproved of much of what he did (or didn't do) as prime minister, she would never seek to usurp him as Jim Callaghan would, as Roy Jenkins might. Barbara knew that the rank and file of the party had, like the public, lost confidence in Harold. They wanted him replaced, but by whom? 'What about you?' Joan Lestor asked her over lunch. 'I shied away from that one', Barbara said.[6] She and Harold had walked together too far and too long for that. She was too loyal; too inextricably, and sometimes inexplicably, bound to him. She was 'the only member of the

Cabinet who ever felt a really human sympathy' for him,[7] and even if, as *The Economist* speculated, his senior colleagues got together and told him to go, Barbara might 'find it impossible for sentimental reasons ever to join any such junta';[8] which isn't to say she wouldn't feel able to exploit its success. Whatever happened had to happen soon. She would be 58 in October. She was getting too old for the leadership.

Jim Callaghan, only two years younger, was getting too old as well. He was seething that Barbara had been 'over-promoted because of her special relationship' with Harold, while he was moving in the wrong direction. Proceeding from the Treasury to the Home Office to Number 10 was 'like travelling from Birmingham to London via Newcastle-upon-Tyne'.[9] His chancellorship had not been seen as a success. His economic measures had proved so unpopular with the party that he had feared losing his NEC seat in 1967, and had been saved only by the vacancy for party treasurer, a post elected by all the party, which is to say by the union block vote, his natural constituency.

At first he was not considered an impressive home secretary, either, rolling down hill with both feet in his mouth. He made howlers, such as telling the House that this murderer and that murderer had been arrested, lamentably failing to distinguish between an arrest and a conviction. His fuddy-duddy (a favourite self-description), avuncular, Farmer Giles style looked reactionary at worst, unimaginative at best, especially when compared with the style of his deft, libertarian-inclined predecessor.

But Jim tapped into something in the Labour movement, its deep bedrock of conservatism, its sense rather than sensibility. He conveyed soundness, the comforting slowness of a Suffolk Punch dragging the party wagon steadily behind him. But he was more cunning than comforting, and his desperation made him more so. Just under two months into the Mk II government, he made his first move. He gave a speech to the Fire Brigades Union conference and told them that the prices and incomes policy would have to be voluntary by 1969; this was a direct breach of cabinet policy, which was to adopt a wait-and-see approach.

It wasn't so much a shot across Barbara's bows as a direct hit.

Harold had already shown that he was afraid of Jim, putting him on the Parliamentary Committee, his new inner cabinet, after telling Barbara that he would do no such thing. He thought Callaghan safer in than out. The home secretary had the prime minister on the back foot. Reports that Callaghan's political career had waxed and waned were premature, but for the moment it was Barbara and Roy Jenkins who were the rising stars. Barbara, Roy and Harold were now the troika that ran the government.

Barbara saw the competent, erudite, lucid and urbane Jenkins as a worrying rival. She jotted down reasons why he could not successfully lead the party. There was a frigidity at the heart of the man, the acclaimed icy aloofness; he did not have the natural bonhomie to be a Labour Party leader. And he was helplessly exposed up there with his two years of 'hard slog'. Being chancellor under those conditions was, he said, like living through 'a long Arctic night'.

The rub was that Barbara, too, was now inexorably part of the management of the hard slog – 'right at the heart of the economic equation', as she noted in her diary[10] – although a month after her appointment she thought this a good thing; all her initial misgivings about committing political suicide had been washed away by her essential optimism, her buoyant self-confidence, which could melt into self-deception.

In the long fourteen months that began in April 1968 and ended in June 1969, the three most powerful people in the government, the prime minister, the chancellor and the first secretary, had too much to lose and too much to gain: Harold his premiership, Barbara her chance and Roy his chance, too. But Jim Callaghan had the least to lose and the most to gain. I did not 'number the years 1968 and 1969 among my happiest political memories', he wrote later.[11] Nor did Barbara.

In 1965, Harold had set up a royal commission under Lord Donovan to look into trade unions and employers' associations, in the hope of staunching public criticism of strikes and bolshie unions, and to pre-empt the Tories' predictable calls for anti-union legislation. Harold had little faith in the commission's ability to come up with a solution; they will 'take minutes and waste years', he mumbled lugubriously, and indeed they did. In June 1968, the long-awaited, and long, 145,000-word Donovan Report fell onto Barbara's desk.

Donovan acknowledged the obvious: there were 'two systems of industrial relations; the formal system, operating at industry wide level ... and an informal system, operating at company, factory or shop-floor level ... The two systems were in conflict.' The second 'was the more important and more powerful'. What they meant was what everyone knew and refused to admit: that, as Barbara more pithily put it, 'power has passed to the shopfloor'. Donovan's solution was 'voluntary self-reform' by unions and management. He decreed that 'reform through legislation was quite impracticable'.[12]

Barbara could not have disagreed more. All her experience with the trade unions had confirmed her belief that they needed to be radically reformed. Her meetings with George Woodcock and Vic Feather (the latter now deputy general secretary of the the TUC), to discuss Donovan and future industrial relations legislation, did nothing to dissuade her. Woodcock, who had sat on Donovan, kept reprising the same old song: sanctions against unofficial strikes would not work, although a voluntary policy would not work, either. But what could you do?

She could do what she had already decided. As she had told Denis Barnes, the permanent secretary at DEP, they needed to work out their own industrial-relations policy, deciding how much, if any, of Donovan they wanted to retain, and if necessary to 'propose our own sanctions'.[13]

Vic Feather watched Woodcock and Castle and he listened. He had assiduously worked himself up the TUC ladder and had been Woodcock's deputy for fourteen irksome years. Woodcock had gone to Oxford and did not wear his learning lightly, and Feather intensely disliked him and what he considered his pompous ways. He wanted his boss out, off to the new industrial relations committee called for in Donovan. His dislike of the first secretary was bitter and longstanding. She was 'ready to go to any lengths to get herself publicity or acclaim', he told Cecil King, editor of the *Daily Mirror* and lately

214

arch-enemy of Harold.[14] He wanted her out, too. Who did she think she was, this bloody woman who knew nothing about the world of work, poking her nose into TUC business. 'I knew Barbara Castle when she had dirty knickers', he liked to tell everyone.[15] He had been watching her posturing on the political stage since their Bradford days. He'd bring her down a peg or two yet.

Victor Grayson Hardie Feather, named for the socialist heroes who had gone before, was not a man to have as an enemy. Cunning, calculating, utterly ruthless, he was a 'machine politician, a scarred and decorated hero of the smoke-filled room and the midnight formula'.[16] He had come a long, hard way since he'd sat in the Bettses' sitting room discussing 'the world and its books'. He had written for the *Daily Herald* for a brief period before, in 1937, joining the organisation department of the TUC, where he became the communist-finder-general, a role in which he excelled.

Feather was a natural antagonist to Barbara. Politically they were at odds. He'd been opposed to the United Front because it opened up opportunities for the communists; he had supported the POUM in the Spanish Civil War and yet he'd been close to right-wing union bosses Arthur Deakin and Tom Williamson, Barbara's old foes from the Bevanite days. But his dislike of Barbara was more human than political. He envied her. He was jealous, the poor boy who had had to leave school at 14, while she had been bought a grammar-school education and gone off to Oxford. She had had every opportunity – and he had had none – and as a result she had got further than she deserved. Feather 'was utterly disparaging of Barbara', said Bernard Ingham.[17] Even Jim Callaghan was shocked at the language he used to denounce her; it was, he said, 'frankly unprintable'.[18]

As well as being a member of the inner cabinet, Barbara was also a member of the key cabinet committees: the Economic Strategy Committee; the Overseas and Defence Policy Committee; and, once Roy Jenkins had been persuaded to give up his objection to her membership, the inner circle on monetary policy, MISC 205, where the unthinkable was regularly thought in preparedness lest the economy go belly up.

While she was still at Transport, Barbara had been 'woman enough to admit' to the *Evening Standard* 'that, in the full light of Ministry knowledge, she has taken decisions that, as a backbencher, she would have criticised'.[19] Now she was operating in the full light of government knowledge which made her intolerant of what she called the left, something she had come to see as separate from herself. This left was a hard left to her soft left. It was something she neither approved of nor understood.

On her first full day at DEP she had met the left-wing Tribune Group of MPs, which included her old friends Michael Foot, Ian 'Mik' Mikardo and Fenner Brockway, together with new left-wingers such as Stan Orme and Eric Heffer.* The Tribune Group had already concluded that Barbara's appointment, as far as prices and incomes were concerned, would not mean a change in policy. She told them they didn't understand what desperate straits the economy was in. (The only five people who did were the members of MISC 205: Harold, Barbara, Roy Jenkins, Tony Crosland, now president of the Board of Trade, and Peter Shore, head of the DEA.) The choice for the government was stark, she told the group. A statutory prices and incomes policy had to be maintained, which meant risking a breach with the unions and, yes, she was willing to put trade unionists in gaol and go with them, if that's what it took to maintain the wage ceiling. If it was not maintained they were looking at another devaluation, 'which would put social democracy out of office in Britain for the next twenty years'.[20]

Barbara told them she was going to operate a truly socialist prices and incomes policy, which would not be about crude wage restraint; wages could rise in exchange for increased productivity; moreover, she would run a tough prices policy, too, using the Bill's powers to force prices down. But that was not what they wanted. They wanted the Bill repealed. Her policy, they told her, was 'no change of policy, only a change of phraseology'.[21] As Mik, who was

---

* Not all the Tribune group was hard left. Michael, like Barbara, was part of the so-called soft left, as were others.

excessively fond of this kind of groaning analogy put it, 'Hemlock served in a golden chalice by a goddess is still hemlock.'[22]

The Tribune Group was, in Barbara's disparaging term, the Bevanite rump. But it was also home to a new left-wing breed of trade-union-sponsored MP, and in a reversal of the Bevanite experience the Tribune Group held regular dinners with politically sympathetic union officials. The Bevanite dream of getting 'the unions to reflect what was going on in the party' was at last coming to fruition. But Barbara was not rejoicing. In her view, the Tribunites and the unions were thinking no further than the next wage claim. They came at everything from the negative. They were mere wreckers.

A central tenet of Barbara's social democracy was that the free market is an inequitable and inefficient way to organise economic relationships. To her, the Tribunite-union devotion to free collective bargaining was a devotion to that inequitable and inefficient system; it was simply a form of capitalism. True socialists did not act out of their own narrow selfish interests, striking at the drop of a spanner; they acted in the interests of all. Wildcat strikes were not socialism; socialism was solidarity. She was not alone in this view: 'Since when has free market bargaining been a fundamental prin-ciple of socialism?' the *New Statesman* asked its readers.[23]

Free market bargaining was a fundamental union right, as Hugh Scanlon said, especially when there was no public ownership of the means of production, distribution and exchange. They were not prepared to act like socialists until there was socialism. To Barbara this was anarchism. It would all end in tears and chaos, with a bankrupt country and even more capitalism, in the form of everlasting IMF control. Barbara was still very much a believer in the corporate socialist state; in economic and social planning; in centralised control; she thought, fundamentally, that the socialist man and woman in Whitehall really did know best.

Her beliefs showed. Barbara conveyed a sense that she was talking to worthy but not very bright subordinates. Her dealings with individual unionists and union-sponsored MPs were often tainted by class and by the mother-knows-best attitude they seemed to bring out in her. She was seen, in that cherished left-wing epithet, as elitist. She was, Jack Jones recalled, 'anxious to do things *for* the workers but not *with* them', an attitude 'not all that unusual', in his view, among middle-class left-wing politicians.[24] Stan Orme agreed. 'She knew best. She'd tell you how to do things because she knew what was in your interest – my interest as a trade unionist',[25] a sentiment echoed by Eric Heffer and other union-sponsored MPs and union officials. Jones said she had a patronising style of address which left him 'often feeling like a schoolboy'.[26]

Not all union leaders felt like that. Moss Evans found her warm and 'exceptionally charming' with individual union negotiators. He did not find it patronising that she put an arm round a man's shoulder during negotiations and said things like 'Come along, love, you know it makes sense – you're not going to lose anything', when trying to persuade them to do what she wanted.[27]

But others did. The fact that she was a woman made it worse. Most union men were 'male chauvinist pigs at the best of times',[28] and one man's charming woman was most others' hectoring shrew. To them Barbara's sex was more than an irritant. The 'old trade union boys who hate nagging women always trying to get their way' were beside themselves at having to deal with her:[29] this 'bloody woman', this 'daft woman – doesn't know a bloody thing about' trade unionism; she 'couldn't even spell it', Feather said. Marie Patterson, one of only two women on the TUC's forty-strong General Council – and no Castle fan – said her male colleagues' attitude was that 'the statutory woman politician was all right as Minister for Education or something, not interfering in things they knew nothing about, like the horny-handed sons of toil'.[30] Some unions, such as the AEU, had had women members for only twenty-odd years, and now here was this woman telling them what to do.

Her gender not only offended individual unionists but 'alienated the TUC', Joe Haines said. 'They were anti-feminist to a man, so macho. She would lecture them and some of them would say that was the sort of thing that happens when you go home. Your wife might tell you off, but you're not going to be told off by Barbara Castle. They really were pretty dreadful.'[31] With few exceptions, the trade-union leaders Barbara encountered were 'abysmal beyond her belief ... selfish, petty, intensely limited, and in some cases rude or unpleasant'. They 'could be absolute shits', she said later, especially to her.[32]

Over the summer of 1968, the TUC laid out the case for the Donovan Report, the voluntary code they wanted enshrined in any future industrial-relations legislation. They were anxious to get in, they said, 'before senior civil servants could convince ... [Barbara] to take the much harder line'. They were, they said, 'worried that she would be especially susceptible' to bringing in compulsory measures 'because she was inexperienced in industrial relations', being a bloody woman. But they were too late. The bloody woman gave them to understand that she would not stop short of 'sanctions against unconstitutional industrial action'. She in turn was warned that 'she must not attempt to prescribe union behaviour'.[33] According to Woodcock, the TUC leaders were 'horrified by what they heard'. Barbara 'seemed fixed already in views that would inevitably lead to serious conflict'.[34]

Barbara talked to the Tribune Group and union-sponsored MPS about Donovan, too. She was 'cagey' over what sort of legislation she had in mind, Eric Heffer said. Not cagey enough, perhaps, because she let them know that trade unions would have to put their own house in order or risk having someone else do it for them. Stan Orme, already incensed that Barbara would not allow the builders their extra penny increase because it broke prices and incomes norms (which angered much of the PLP because it seemed so petty), had an immediate and vehement reaction to Barbara's comments. He drew up a memo itemising cooling-off periods and sanctions; it was 'designed to impress on Barbara that we would not support her' if her White Paper called for such measures.[35] 'Some of our left are just anarchists', she sighed.[36]

Particular industrial disputes – such as that at the Girling brake factory, where twenty-two workers walked off the job over a member of a rival union switching on an oil-supply valve, an act which laid off five thousand car workers; or the women machinists at Ford's Dagenham plant being negotiated for (or over) by half a dozen unions – provided her with more ammunition for a tough industrial relations Bill.

Barbara personally reconciled the Ford women's dispute, which was essentially about equal pay, by famously inviting them to her beautiful offices in St James's Square on which she spent 'hundreds of pounds on the most lovely decorations, new wallpaper, new furniture, new carpets and curtains'.[37] She was photographed and filmed sipping tea with them, in an all-girls-together giggling photo op. It so incensed Ray Gunter, already seething because the 'bitch' had his job, that he resigned from the government, announcing that he was, as he put it, returning to 'the folk from whence I came'.

Reforming the trade unions would, Barbara and Harold had decided, be 'the focus of the Government's radical intent'.[38] Barbara's radical intent owed little to her hard-line civil servants. Nor did she become unduly influenced by the industrial disputes going on all around her, or even decide to take revenge for all the grief the unions had caused her and her friends throughout the 1930s, 1940s and 1950s. What she was going to do was simply try to make the unions into what she always thought they should be: a responsible part of a socialist planned economy.

'Economic planning in a democratic socialist economy cannot operate successfully if wage-fixing is left either to the arbitrary decision of a wage-stop or the accidents of unco-ordinated sectional bargaining', Barbara and her Bevanite allies had written in *Keeping Left* in 1950. The business of the unions and the TUC was everybody's business, they said, as the ILP had said before them. What the unions needed to do was refashion themselves so they were 'not merely a defence-mechanism against the instability of capitalism but a positive and powerful contributor to the successful functioning of a planned socialist society'.[39]

Barbara wrote in her obituary of Nye Bevan that he had been haunted by the question that ought to 'haunt us all: how can we build a society in which men freely choose to put restraints on their own greed and give their government power to direct the resources of the country for socially honourable and nationally desirable ends?'[40] Was it possible for people freely to choose restraint? In her pamphlet *Are Controls Necessary?*, published in 1947 to put the government's case for rationing and a planned economy, Barbara ended by asking how far workers were willing to make central planning work under Labour's 'revolution by consent'. The problem was that 'If there is to be no control over labour, there must be self-control by labour. Are we ready for it yet?' she asked.[41] She had since concluded that we were not.

In October Barbara asked John Burgh, her DEP under-secretary specialising in industrial relations, to set up a conference to discuss future legislation. She wanted, she said, everything to be examined, nothing excluded. The conference was held at Sunningdale, the civil service staff college, over the weekend of 15 November. Those attending included Peter Shore, Campbell Adamson, soon to become director-general of the CBI, industrialists such as George Turnbull of Leyland, Aubrey Jones, head of the Prices and Incomes Board, and academics and civil servants.

On the Saturday, the team read and discussed various position papers. After listening, Barbara had dinner and went to bed. 'The next morning,' recalls one participant, 'Barbara came down that sweeping staircase at Sunningdale into the room where we were all sitting and said, "We are going to do the following," and she outlined the skeleton of the policy.' What she wanted was made 'clear and authoritative – it was Barbara's policy' and it changed very little in the writing.[42]

Peter Shore went to Chequers immediately after the conference for a meeting with Harold and his kitchen cabinet of Marcia Williams, Gerald Kaufman, the party's parliamentary press officer, and the economist Tommy Balogh, an old Bevanite adviser who was now economic adviser to the cabinet. Also present were Tony Benn, the new woman in cabinet, the left-wing postmaster-general, Judith Hart, and one or two others. With the exception of Hart, who thought it impossible to get trade-union legislation through in the teeth of what would be virulent opposition from the unions and the PLP, everyone agreed that the White Paper should include strike ballots and a cooling-off period, because 'in this way we would say we were going to control the trade unions by democratising them', as Tony Benn said.[43]

Barbara's White Paper on industrial relations was written more or less within a month after Sunningdale, in secrecy and looked over by a special small hastily convened committee known as MISC 230, which included Barbara, Harold, Roy Jenkins, a couple of other ministers and a handful of legal officers such as the solicitor-general. This was done in order to present cabinet with a fait accompli and to circumvent, in Barbara's description, the most 'disloyal and damaging' member of the government, Jim Callaghan, who sat on both the Industrial Relations and the Economic Strategy committees. She put her civil servants 'under direct instructions not to discuss the proposals with anyone at the Home Office. She knew Jim would be against it; that was in the nature of their relationship.'[44]

The White Paper was without a title. Nothing the civil servants thought of was right. It was Ted, just about to leave hospital after having a non-malignant tumour removed, who came up with *In Place of Strife*, on the very morning the Paper was going to the printers. Barbara considered it one of his 'strokes of genius'. It was a reference to Nye Bevan's book *In Place of Fear*, and was meant to suggest the socialist nature of the project. '*Strife*' came from the title of John Galsworthy's play about a strike, the very play Barbara's father had produced in Pontefract in 1920 in which she had made her stage debut. She had played a maid who was supposed to come in and announce a works deputation but had tripped on the stage and fallen flat on her face; perhaps not the best of omens.

Through its title, the White Paper offered hostages to fortune. Harold Lever quickly christened it *In Chase of Strife*; Barbara naturally became 'Trouble and Strife'; its opponents said they wanted something in place of strife in the party; and it caused the government nothing but strife, coming 'closer than almost any other issue, domestic or foreign, to forcing the Prime Minister's resignation'.[45] *In Place of Strife* began with words written by Barbara herself: 'There are necessarily conflicts of interest in industry.'[46]

*

A 'Labour Government couldn't survive giving itself statutory strike-breaking powers', Barbara had said in July 1966, when the possibility that a trade unionist might be fined or imprisoned under potential prices and incomes legislation was under discussion. But she thought it could thrive by giving itself powers to prevent strikes. *In Place of Strife* laid out her 'dream of a new political equilibrium'.[47] She described it, and wanted it to be understood, as a charter of trade-union rights. Workers would, for the first time, have a statutory right to join a union; protection against unfair dismissal; protection of the closed shop; the right to certain in-formation from the company; and a promise that industrial democracy would be extended. Companies would be compelled to recognise and negoti-ate with unions, but when there were dozens of competing unions, the Commission on Industrial Relations, backed up by the statutory powers of the secretary of state, would decide which unions would be recognised.

There was nothing unambitious here. She sought to change the entire system of industrial relations. The preamble analysed the 'serious deficiencies' on both sides of the negotiating table, includ-ing bad procedural agreements and lack of consultation or forewarning on job losses on the management side. She wanted to set up a register, soon to be mandatory, for companies to submit their collective agreements, including rules and policies on this, that and the other thing. And for the unions there would be another register, in which they had to enrol themselves and their rules and regulations; failing to do so would result in a fine.

The White Paper stated that the forthcoming Industrial Relations Bill would have twenty-five proposals. Only three, the so-called 'penal clauses', incensed the Labour and trade-union movements. The first gave the secretary of state the powers to order a strike ballot if she judged a strike would be especially harmful to the economy (and she would phrase the ballot question). The second gave her the power to order a 28-day conciliation pause before unof-ficial strikes. The third concerned the power of the Committee on

223

Industrial Relations or the secret-ary of state to decide which unions were recognised where. The *coup de grâce* was the fact that disregarding any of the above would result in fines for individual trade unionists, trade unions and/or companies.

When rumours of the penal clauses began to circulate in parliament, they were brushed off with incredulity by left-wing MPs. They 'could not believe that Barbara Castle would lend her name to such proposals',[48] the same proposals which were, in the minds of the first secretary and the prime minister, 'a very skillful weapon for defeating Heath'* at the next election. Barbara recalled Harold 'chuckling and saying, Barbara hasn't so much out-heathed Heath ... [as] outmanoeuvred him'.[49]

Harold knew *Strife* would not be popular with the unions or the Labour movement, but, he told Dick, that was irrelevant, 'because this was going to be a great popular success'.[50] As a *Times* leader rejoiced on Strife's publication, public 'demand for action ... had been clamorous' to rid the country once and for all of workplaces full of 'restrictive practices, excessive overtime, leap-frogging workgroup wage increases, incessant guerrilla warfare, and an excessive number of small unofficial strikes',[51] and at last that demand for action had been heeded. It would be a vote-winner, Barbara told Jack Jones. The polls showed that the majority of the population favoured making unofficial strikes illegal and three-quarters wanted compulsory strike ballots.

With most of the cabinet still blissfully unaware of what the White Paper contained, Barbara set out to sell it to the unions. She put it first to a small group at Chequers in mid-December, to four union leaders (including Frank Cousins, who had left the government), Roy Jenkins and, as 'a silent witness', Edmund Dell, Crosland's deputy at the Board of Trade. After dinner they gathered in the library around a roaring fire and Barbara broached the subject of her proposals. 'The reaction of the trade union leaders – except for Jack Cooper – was immediate and forceful,' according to

* Edward 'Ted' Heath, the Member for Bexley since 1950. He became leader of the Conservative Party in 1965 and was Prime Minister 1970-74.

Dell. 'They were all against – it was not the sort of thing a Labour government should be doing, et cetera.' After a while Jenkins fell asleep; but not before he had heard the reaction. 'None of us who were present at that meeting could've been under any illusions', Dell said.[52]

Under a week later, Barbara decided, on 'impulse', to take Woodcock into her confidence and tell him what she had in mind for the unions. She said he 'wasn't really basically opposed' to her proposals, and that he thought she had 'let the trade unions off very lightly'.[53] Peter Jenkins, in his contemporaneous account of the affair, *The Battle of Downing Street*, quotes Woodcock as saying, 'I don't think there is anything in this to which the unions can fundamentally object',[54] but Woodcock later denied it, claiming to have merely said the very different 'There's nothing here that surprises me'; or, more expansively, that seventeen of the twenty-five clauses were acceptable to him, five were not accep-table in their present form, and three 'were totally unac-ceptable'.[55] Perhaps everyone heard what they wanted to hear. Certainly Barbara later thought Woodcock had 'misled' her; but he had always been well known for his opposition to legal sanc-tions.

Woodcock suggested to Barbara that she show *Strife* to the TUC in December – before she showed it to Cabinet. Barbara was anxious. She knew she should put it before cabinet first, but Woodcock convinced her that bringing the TUC in from the begin-ning would pay off. She agreed, and on 30 December, sleepy from her Christmas holiday, she went to talk to the Finance and General Purposes Committee. She swore them to secrecy, of course, but inevitably what was said appeared in the newspapers the following day. (When Barbara then went to talk to the CBI, she was assured that *they* did not leak.)

The following evening the Castles went off to Geoffrey Goodman's New Year's Eve party at his home in Mill Hill. The place was full of left-wing politicians, journalists and union people, including Jack Jones. Jones was a self-educated man, the son of a docker, and like Barbara had been baptised by 1930s left-wing politics; as a boy he had worked on the Liverpool docks, marched with the hunger marchers. He became active in the TGWU and the Labour Party before going to Spain to fight in the International Brigade.

Barbara thought Jack was a man she could do business with. She considered him intellectually superior to other trade unionists on the NEC and when she had first gone to DEP, it was 'Jack this and Jack that and "I'll have a word with Jack",' Peter Jenkins said, adding that there was another side to Jack she seemed not to have seen: the 'hard-boiled union man ... a rough customer in a negotiating clinch, even with a lady'.[56] Barbara decided to talk to Jack about *Strife*, and the two of them went off into a corner and almost at once began to argue violently: Jones was absolutely outraged. 'I can still see Jack exploding in that corner', Geoffrey Goodman said, thirty years later.[57]

As many have observed, Barbara did sometimes have a tendency towards self-delusion, never more so than in the matter of *Strife* v. the Labour movement. In her diary her encounter with Jack sounds a jolly affair. He, like everyone else, would be fixable. The next day Barbara told Dick, hitherto kept in the dark, that although she was having 'difficulties' with the TUC, the White Paper would 'be popular, [and] there will be no real opposition in the Party'.[58] Barbara's conviction that she was operating from political strength was strong. She was sure that she could get cabinet to support her and that she could win over the majority of the TUC's General Council, because national union leaders were fed up with having their authority usurped by the shop-floor. She believed both government and union leaders had this converging stake in restoring centralised authority to the unions, even though she had just been told by most of those leaders that penal sanctions against the unions or their members were totally unacceptable.

Barbara believed in the power of her oratory; in the persuasive-ness of her personality; in the currency of her left-wing reputation. She was convinced by her own rapturous receptions, the autograph hunters, the mobbing crowds, the cheers, the sound of her name being called, the policemen parting the crowds, the applause that rang heavy and true seemingly no matter what she said. She could and would talk to 'our own people'. She would explain to them how things worked, how it was for their own good. They would come round in the end; they would listen to reason; she could reason with them. She believed she could not fail. She would get them to accept what she needed them to accept: ministerial control.

Copies of *In Place of Strife* were sent to ministers a few days ahead of the first cabinet on the subject. Barbara's intention was to publish it six days later, on 9 January 1969. The fact that she had discussed the matter with the TUC first 'created a tremendous row' in cabinet, Tony Benn said. Barbara had 'made a lot of trouble for herself ... by not consulting us earlier'.[59] Ministers deeply resented having read in the papers the contents of such a serious policy document, about which they had not been consulted. And now there was to be 'no proper discussion'. Richard Marsh, who had taken over from Barbara at Transport, complained, 'It was a classic ploy: Let's bounce it through Cabinet.'[60] Dick concurred. In a letter to Harold six months later he told him that his ministers felt he had deliberately bounced them into accepting *Strife*, and the consequent 'appalling risks'. Barbara affected to think that Dick's grumpy and continual criticisms of *Strife* were because he had been left off MISC 230 – discretion not being any part of his valour; and because he was going through the menopause!

Dick was fuelled by a mixture of pique and pragmatism. Yes, he was miffed he'd been left off MISC 230 by his friends, as Barbara would have been in similar circumstances, and he was angry that his pensions White Paper would be eclipsed. But he also thought her proposals would cause more trouble than they were worth. He did not think his constituency party, in the car-manufacturing city of Coventry, would accept another piece of anti-union legislation on the back of the prices and incomes policy. Like Judith Hart, he did not think the White Paper was politically acceptable to the Labour movement.

Jim Callaghan was one of the few who said he had no objections to her unorthodox approach of talking to the unions first. As well he might not: he had already discussed it with them. 'They're all old friends of mine ... we are bound to discuss it', he explained. After all he was treasurer of the party, the TUC's representative on earth. He said at once that the penal sanctions were 'absolutely wrong and unnecessary', and told Barbara and Harold that they should accept Donovan and put the TUC 'on their honour', to which they predictably replied that that would make the government a laughing-stock with the public.[61]

Jim Callaghan knew what he knew. There was no way the TUC would accept *In Place of Strife*. Nor would much of the PLP. Out of 363 Labour MPs, 127 were union-sponsored; they would be naturally opposed. The Tribune Group, union and non-union, and the unaligned left would also be naturally opposed. Many other MPs would simply accept Callaghan's line that legislation to curb the trade unions was 'not *our* issue', as he told the MP for Birmingham All Saints, Brian Walden: 'if it is so inevitable, let the Tories pass it'. Jim was going to be the 'keeper of the cloth cap'.[62]

From the outset those vehemently opposed were Judith Hart, Dick Crossman, Richard Marsh and Jim Callaghan. Tony Benn was in favour, for White Heat of Technology reasons, into which restrictive union practices did not meld. Denis Healey backed it, on the nation-before-class ticket. Peter Shore, who had helped draft it, was actively in favour. Tony Crosland, motivated in part by his rivalry with Roy Jenkins, who strongly supported Barbara's proposals, wanted to produce more papers. And Harold was Barbara's enthusiastic cheer-leader.

The first cabinet of the New Year discussed the White Paper for six hours. At the end Harold summed up, agreeing to Dick's wish that Barbara tell the TUC no final decision had been taken, nor would be until she talked to them again. In the meantime, said Harold pointedly, both eyes on Jim, 'Other members of the Cabinet should refrain from entering into any discussion of these matters with the TUC or CBI and if approached about the First Secretary's proposals they should avoid saying anything which might weaken her position in her own discussions with them.'[63]

Jenkins, mindful that the Labour and TUC autumn conferences would coincide with *Strife*'s becoming law, wanted to act quickly and produce a short interim bill, at which Barbara demurred. She told cabinet on 14 January that 'when her proposed measures were seen as a whole she believed that the trade unions would accept that they were directed to strengthening the trade unions and not weakening them. It would be politically most unwise to forgo this advantage by selection for early enactment, in order to satisfy public opinion, those parts of the bill to which the trade unions were particularly hostile; to do so would emphasise the penal aspects of the legislation.'[64]

It took three full cabinets, one of which lasted for two days, and rewrites by another hastily formed committee – which included the White Paper's two biggest critics, Dick Crossman and Judith Hart – before *Strife* was approved. It was published on 17 January 1969, to a 60 per cent public approval rating.

Two hours before publication Barbara had convened a meeting with the trade union group of MPs, attended by Douglas Houghton, chairman of the PLP. She hoped to get over her point that *Strife* was a charter for trade-union rights beneficial to the trade-union movement. It was a false hope. The White Paper had the same effect as a 'bomb thrown by a Women's Lib fanatic into a quiet front parlour while Dad was having his high tea'.[65] Barbara's proposals were evil, despicable, unworkable, trade-union MPs told the newspapers. Coming after the prices and incomes policy, this was the living end. The trade-union group had already taken as much as they could, they said. Only Jack Ashley* supported her. Many union-sponsored MPs decided to oppose *Strife*, even at the risk of losing their seats.

The Tribune Group, meeting three days later, did agree that 'there was much that was good, and overdue, in the White Paper', but added that 'it should be opposed because of the inclusion of three anti-trade-union proposals'.[66] Other MPs, too, were uneasy

---

*The MP for Stoke on Trent South. Barbara appointed him as her PPS in 1974.

about the proposals, considering that a Labour government had declared war on the unions which had helped to give birth to the party. Barbara was chipping away at the icons of the Labour movement. The TUC's foundation and the formation of the Labour Party itself 'owed much to union defence against the judiciary',[67] and here she was bringing the judiciary to bear upon the unions. But to Barbara all this was to miss the point. It was as the Bevanites had said two decades earlier: 'If the partnership between Political Labour and Industrial Labour means anything, it should be be strong enough to fashion a new and more responsible place for workers' organisations in the planning and operation of a socialist economy.'[68] And that was what she considered she was doing.

The TUC's General Council could not have agreed less. Frank Cousins wanted to reject the White Paper in its entirety, but Woodcock prevailed, getting the council to agree to a statement accepting the nice bits of *Strife* and rejecting the nasty bits. The compulsory strike ballots were 'completely misguided and quite unacceptable'; the 28-day conciliation pause, or any kind of cooling-off period, were 'neither practicable nor desirable'.[69] And fines? Absolutely not. The sanctions, pronounced Vic Feather, 'introduce the taint of criminality into industrial relations'.[70] Not one to find himself short of a soundbite, he later came up with 'Law courts do not make exports'. For over a hundred years, except in wartime, there had been no criminal law in industrial relations, and the TUC flatly told Barbara and Harold they would 'not co-operate with the operation of legal sanctions'.[71]

In Place of Strife was greeted by, in Barbara's own words, a 'sense of alarm and outrage' from her own people,[72] not least from her oldest political friend, Michael Foot. It was Michael who brought a deputation of Labour MPs into her office, telling her she had to retreat while she could. Michael had found that a friend in power was a friend lost indeed. Over the following six months he put away all his personal feelings for Barbara and relentlessly attacked her in the House, in the PLP, on the front pages of the *Tribune*. The fiasco over the Bill was, he wrote, 'the maddest scene in the modern history of Britain'.[73] He and Barbara argued passionately. They screamed. They shouted. She told him that he had grown 'soft on a diet of soft options';[74] he had never once had to make a choice. The language of priorities was not one he had ever learnt. These slanging matches left them both profoundly distressed and often close to tears.

Shortly after *Strife*'s publication, George Woodcock suffered a heart attack. Vic Feather became the acting general secretary of the TUC. He immediately set about writing highly critical articles about Barbara's White Paper for obscure publications which somehow always found their way onto the desks of Fleet Street editors. He tore at it in public while remaining affable, at first, with Harold and Barbara in private, sipping brandy with them in the prime minister's study. His only negative comment to Barbara about her proposals was a lugubrious 'Why did you do it, luv?' He did not, of course, wait for the answer.

The only question that interested Feather was how he was going to win the Battle of Barbara's Bill. And he already knew the answer: with a little help from his friends Jim Callaghan and Douglas Houghton. They would form the decisive triumvirate whose purpose was to destroy Barbara and her proposals, and perhaps replace Harold with a prime minister who would drop them: Jim Callaghan.

In the Members' Dining Room in the House, there were two tables where the cabinet and the top brass of the party divided along class lines: Harold's table and Jim's table. Houghton sat at Callaghan's table. Houghton and Callaghan went way back. Like Stanley Raymond, Houghton had worked with Jim in the tax inspectors' union in the 1930s; he had gone on to become a member of the TUC's General Council in the 1950s, and was now chairman of the PLP. Sitting with them were other, usually self-educated, union men, the working-class lads, the George Browns, the Ray Gunters.

Whereas at Harold's table 'you'd got to have not just an Oxford Degree but a bloody First – it was for the real high flyers', people like Roy, Dick, Tony Crosland and Barbara. She was renowned for 'swearing like a trooper – fucking this and fucking that'[75] – shocking for a woman then, shocking to the diners at Callaghan's table. No self-respecting working-class woman would swear in public.

The people on Harold's table were 'alienated from working-class thinking', Houghton snorted, 'removed by education and life's experience from the great mass of the Movement'.[76] Although he did not share Callaghan and Feather's brute animosity towards Barbara, Houghton was not disposed to find palatable anything she said about working men.

In one of the biggest party rebellions since the war (although not quite as big as many of those Barbara had taken part in), fifty-three Labour MPs voted against *In Place of Strife*, and forty abstained. At the crucial NEC meeting that followed three weeks later, on 26 March, Joe Gormley, the miners' president, slapped down a resolution that the NEC would not agree to 'any legislation' based on all the suggestions in *In Place of Strife*.

It was time for Jim Callaghan's second move. He suggested that, by way of maintaining bliss and harmony in the party, they remove the word 'any' from the resolution. Barbara could see Jim's trap closing but was powerless to do anything about it. Having rearranged the wording, Jim now voted for the Gormley resolution, a senior cabinet minister contravening the policy of his own cabinet and seen to be doing so. Gormley's resolution was accepted by sixteen votes to five, the first time the NEC had rejected a government proposal since the Wilson government came into office.

But that wasn't all. Jim also voted against Tony Greenwood's amendment that the NEC welcome Barbara's assurances that there would be the fullest consultation with the trade unions before legislation was framed. Jim, and the majority of the NEC, neither welcomed nor accepted her assurances: the amendment was rejected by fifteen votes to six. Jim, with ponderous Victorian deliberation, had poured another vial of poison into her political blood.

The meeting became public, of course. Headline news. Barbara was done for. She had long known that Jim was 'capable of anything'; this was just another reason why she should 'despise'

232

him. She wanted Harold to ask for Jim's resignation on the grounds that he clearly did not regard himself as a member of the government. She could almost feel Harold shrink back at the suggestion. He couldn't do it, he told her, not when he was just about to leave the country on a trip. But he promised he would get tough on Jim when he got back. 'I'll believe that when it happens', Barbara muttered.[77] Harold was going to do what he usually did about Jim: nothing.

Barbara decided she would have to go ahead with a Short Bill, as Roy Jenkins had originally proposed. If she didn't get something on the books soon, she would get nothing. In Callaghan's words, '*In Place of Strife* was suddenly to be turned into instant government',[78] largely to stop him becoming the government but also because the White Paper had focused press attention on strikes. The public was now inundated with images of (usually unofficially) striking workers. The fact that Barbara's proposals were designed to stop this was far from raising the government's popularity, as she and Harold had assumed; the government was merely seen to be talking and not doing.

The cabinet for telling Callaghan off was nothing of the kind. He, showing who was boss, strolled in ten minutes late to listen to Harold talk of some ministers' growing tendency to disregard government policies and let this be known to outsiders, 'particularly the Trade Unions, with whom their colleagues were often conducting difficult and delicate negotiations in the name of the Government as a whole'.[79]

The some minister in question said he couldn't see what the problem was. Had not the first secretary herself said the proposals were up for discussion? Harold, of course, allowed him to get away with this nonsense. The prime minister said he was 'more concerned with the future than with the past ... [and] he did not propose to take any further action', provided it did not happen again. Harold got the cabinet to reaffirm 'their endorsement of the proposals' in *Strife*, though with a 'but': that endorsement was 'subject to further consideration ... of any alternative proposals which might be brought before cabinet'.[80] He then told the press that he had excoriated his home secretary, when he had done no such thing. Jim was winning and seen to be winning.

After Barbara had dropped her objections to his doing so, it was Roy Jenkins who announced the forthcoming Short Bill in his budget speech, along with the sweetener that prices and incomes legislation was to be dropped. The statutory right of every worker to belong to a union, was included in the Short Bill, as were powers to compel an employer to recognise a union. Nevertheless, stripped down like this Barbara's argument that *Strife* was a charter of trade-union rights with a small counterweight of responsibilities could not, as she had known, be sustained. The Scottish TUC's response was to pass an emergency resolution saying that the White Paper could no longer be debated on its merits and the hasty legislation had to be rejected out of hand. And unions such as Hugh Scanlon's AEU voted to forbid Barbara from speaking to their conferences.

The strain on Barbara was becoming intolerable. The intensity of resistance to *Strife*, the breadth of the opposition to it, had caught her off balance. Friend and foe alike opposed what she was doing. There were few enthusiastic takers for her legislation, even in cabinet. Nothing that had worked for her before was working now. She could not convince anyone of anything, it seemed. After listening to yet more critical diatribes from Michael and other former left-wing allies at a PLP meeting, she retorted that they could reject her Bill if they wished but 'they could not take away from me my right to destroy myself'.[81] She was getting close to breaking-point.

Enter Harold. With impeccably bad timing, he 'mistakenly – one of the silliest moves he ever made – replaced John Silkin, the chief whip, who was totally loyal, with Bob Mellish, who was never loyal to to anyone, not even his own Party'.[82] Mellish, a 'yapping terrier', was a *bête noire* of Barbara's, a right-wing union man, who opposed *Strife* in long or short form. Harold, with whom she'd had a lengthy conversation earlier that day, had done this without giving her the slightest hint of his intention, and in the middle of her negotiations with Silkin over the passage of the Short Bill.

Barbara's rage was icy, hard, controlled. She was going to destroy Harold, she told Dick over dinner. She was through with him now.

He had to go. Barbara and Dick discussed who should replace him. Only either of them was acceptable to the other. Dick said he didn't want it; Barbara said that although she 'wouldn't shrink from leadership', she thought *Strife* had excluded her. She was, she said, looking for an excuse to get out from under the whole bloody mess, and Harold had handed it to her.[83] She had had enough. Enough of Harold allowing Jim to undermine her. Enough of the PLP and the TUC and the unions and the left. Enough of her friends shouting at her. Part of what this whole thing had been about was to save the government, to save Harold, as well as to secure her a chance at the leadership. None of the above had come about, nor was it likely to.

Barbara went back to DEP and wrote Harold a resignation letter which pulled no punches. She could not believe she had done it: it was 'a more blistering letter to Harold than I would ever have believed possible'.[84] She swung past Downing Street on her way home from St James's Square and dropped it off. It was 11.30 p.m.

Shortly after midnight a near-hysterical prime minister was on the phone to Dick, terrified that the one true staunch political ally he had, the one of all his ministers he could trust utterly, his totally loyal little minister, was really going to resign. 'I have never in my life heard him so frightened', Dick noted. He tried to reassure him that Barbara would not actually resign. Harold phoned her at home: 'She pretended to be out. It was like a lovers' tiff.'[85]

The next morning Harold came running after Barbara with endearments and promises, apologising for his precipitous action, assuring her that Mellish would help, not hinder, the passage of her Bill. Barbara, still absolutely furious, was unforgiving. She flounced off to the shops and bought herself some clothes.

There had been half a dozen stormy meetings with the PLP at which Barbara and Harold had vigorously defended *Strife*. Harold had told the party on 17 April that the Short Bill was an 'essential Bill. Essential to our economic recovery. Essential to the balance of payments. Essential to full employment . . . an essential component of ensuring the economic success of the Government.'[86] The passage of the Bill was, he concluded dramatically, 'essential to [the government's] continuance in office.

Barbara and Harold's continuation in office was looking increasingly shaky. The PLP was in open revolt. The Harold Must Go movement was split into Callaghanites and Jenkinsites. About a hundred MPs had signed a petition calling for a full meeting of the PLP to discuss the leadership question. Others wanted a secret vote of confidence in the leadership. Opposition to Harold and/or Barbara and/or Barbara's Bill now ran from left to right and back again, merging and mingling.

It was May Day. The unions had called their workers out to protest against Barbara's Bill, and Harold had told the London May Day rally, 'I know what's going on. I'm going on.' But he doubted it. He was now seriously alarmed; he was mentally battered and bruised by the extreme political pressure. He summoned Barbara and Dick to his room. There they found the 'great India-rubber, unbreakable, undepressable Prime Minister ... crumpled in his chair'. All the rage Barbara felt towards him drained out of her. 'My God, we want to help you Harold,' she said. 'Why do you sit alone in No 10 with Marcia [Williams] and Gerald Kaufman and these minions?'[87]

The announcement of the Short Bill had sharpened everyone's game, especially that of the Callaghan, Houghton and Feather team. The leader of the parliamentary party, the leader of the trade unionists and the cabinet's snake in the grassroots (operating 'like a caricature of an old wheeler-dealer', Tony Crosland remarked[88]) were the ones who really knew what was going on; and at this rate it wouldn't be Harold or Barbara.

Houghton kept Feather informed on where the votes were likely to fall for Barbara's Bill; Feather kept Houghton informed on his endless chats with the prime minister and the first secretary; and Callaghan discussed matters industrial and political with his old friends at the TUC and with his old friend Houghton, too. Their collective view covered every angle; between them they could conjure a 360-degree view of the state of play.

Houghton stepped up to bat in the first week of May, telling the
PLP that party unity and purpose mattered more to the country than
the marginal damage done by unofficial strikes. He warned the
government not to introduce the Short Bill; the PLP would not
support it and they risked 'disintegration' of the party. As Harold
pointed out in the cabinet that followed, this implied that the
government could no longer govern and must face a dissolution of
parliament, or, if they continued to govern, 'must do so on suffer-
ance and in the knowledge that there were certain policies which
they must not pursue, however necessary in the country's interests
they might consider them to be'.[89]

In reply Jim coolly remarked that the proposed Industrial Relations
Bill involved 'issues of principle' which had 'strained the loyalty of the
PLP and of some Ministers to breaking point'. The benefits Barbara
claimed would accrue from the Bill were not 'worth the destruction
of the Labour Party'. He strongly urged the cabinet to 'consider how
they could withdraw from the brink of disaster', and equally strongly
urged that the Short Bill be held back until the TUC special congress
on 5 June, so that the TUC could offer alternative proposals 'which
would afford a way out of the impasse'.[90]

In all the meetings Barbara and Harold had with the PLP not 'half
a dozen voices were raised to support the Government's so-called
penal clauses', Houghton said. Yet when Barbara, in 'her most impassioned manner', got up to speak, she was still greeted with applause.
On one occasion in particular, Harold said that in all his experience
of PLP meetings he had never seen such an ovation: 'the applause
went on and on and she had to rise to her feet to acknowledge it
. . . almost every sentence being cheered'.[91]

At the joint NEC–cabinet meeting after Houghton's move, Dick
watched Barbara speak, immaculately turned out despite her
exhaustion. She was 'immensely moving' he said, and 'everybody
there cheered their redhead'.[92] She made a 'passionate and brilliant
speech', Tony Benn marvelled: 'Barbara really pulls it out of the
hat.'[93] She had, she said, 'moved in systematically for the kill', effectively picking her critics off one by one. For Jim Callaghan, whose
calculating speech was received in stony silence, she had organised

'one of those premeditated bursts of anger',[94] which left him shielding his eyes from the blast. However, hugs and applause notwithstanding, Barbara did not change a single mind. They were applauding her guts, her sheer bravado; her brilliant speech-making, her performance. They were cheering for battling Barbara.

That sort of thing gave her an Alice in Wonderland sense of the political reality. She was still convinced that what she was trying to do was correct. Her policy would give the 'injection of effectiveness' into the trade union movement that the Bevanites used to discuss. The opinion polls showed 70 per cent of the public behind her; her postbag was overwhelmingly in favour, as was Harold's – and, for that matter, Houghton's. Many ordinary trade unionists she met wished her well. As late as mid-June she received a standing ovation from a NALGO conference, which had tabled hostile amendment after hostile amendment to *Strife*.

She suspected organised union opposition of being pro forma; she thought she heard 'reinforcement for her optimism from several moderate union leaders' who met her privately.[95] She looked at the disintegrating PLP and reached for Freud: party opposition to her White Paper was transference, displaced dissatisfaction at the government's overall economic strategy.

It was with such lullabies that she soothed herself. But Houghton's disaffection had changed things utterly. Barbara and Harold suddenly appeared in cabinet desperate to cobble together some sort of settlement with the TUC. Even the anodyne official minutes show them scrambling for the lifeboats. Their tone changes from the cabinet of 7 May, from we're-going-to-have-the-smack-of-firm-government, to cabinet the following week, when there was suddenly very-little-between-the-government-and-the-TUC.

Harold had set up a new inner cabinet, this one called the Management Committee, consisting of Barbara, Harold, Dick Crossman, Roy Jenkins, Denis Healey, Michael Stewart, and, yes, Jim Callaghan. His presence meant that Harold had to cabal with Barbara and Dick and Roy separately, in a secret inner inner cabinet. Harold did eventually throw Callaghan off the Management Committee after he had made a well-leaked speech to the NEC, two days after Houghton's escapade, saying in effect that the government had no right to impose Barbara's Bill, long or short, unless they could prove it was necessary. He was reinstated five months later.

Barbara agreed to postpone the Short Bill until after the TUC special congress; to do otherwise would undeniably be not listening to the TUC. Some unions were now calling for the replacement of the cabinet with MPs committed to socialism; others wanted to disaffiliate from the party or suspend dues until the Bill was dropped. But generally speaking the leadership of the unions, even Scanlon and Jones, did not want an irrevocable split with the Labour government; they were at least motivated this far, if no further, to pulling everyone out of the void.

The TUC sent Barbara and Harold a copy of its *Programme for Action*, the unions' answer to Barbara legislation, wherein the TUC gave itself powers to intervene in strikes and make affiliated unions inform them in the case of unofficial strikes, which they would discourage by persuasion, something Barbara thought a 'vague, pious hope'. What were the unions going to do to ensure their members returned to work during negotiations? she wanted to know. She had come up with a deal to freeze or suspend the penal clauses, put them in mothballs, if the TUC would harden its promise to persuade into a commitment to make unofficial strikers go back to work. If they would 'agree to legislate, the Government would agree not to legislate'.[96] But in Jack Jones's view this was to 'draw up rigid rules, apply harsh discipline and take measures which might well have destroyed the organization altogether'.[97] The TUC told Barbara and Harold that they were not prepared to swap sanctions.

In the last week of May, with the Labour Party in tatters, the unions in uproar, and the first secretary and the prime minister on the brink of being thrown out of office, Barbara set sail across the Mediterranean for a fortnight's holiday on the *Maria Luigi II*, Charles Forte's yacht.* Forte had generously lent the 'ridiculously

---

* Forte was a millionaire restaurateur, owner of, among many other establishments, the Café Royal.

expensive . . . toy' to the Castles after meeting them in Italy the previous year. Despite the fact that she and Dick had been rowing non-stop since January, Barbara, Dick's 'Girl Guide', invited Dick, his wife, Anne, and their two children, Patrick and Virginia, to join them. There were a cook, a waiter from the Café Royal and a crew to see to their creature comforts.[98]

Nothing could have been more firmly guaranteed to bring sneers and hoots of derision from the TUC than the knowledge that the minister of labour – or whatever she called herself – was cavorting on a millionaire's yacht while readying an about-to-self-destruct Labour government to enact legislation which would bring about the ruination of the working classes. Barbara could see that sneer, hear those hoots of derision, and not just from the TUC. She was desperate to keep whole thing secret.

Harold would keep her apprised of events and, to facilitate secret ship-to-shore communications, they were given code names by civil servants, doubtless Avengers fans: Barbara was 'Peacock', Harold 'Eagle', Dick 'Owl', Jenkins 'Starling', Callaghan 'Sparrow' and Healey 'Pigeon'. The cabinet was 'the Aviary'. The TUC was mammalian: Feather was 'Rhino', Cousins 'Bull', Scanlon 'Bear' and Jones 'Horse'; the General Council was 'the Zoo'. If Harold wanted the boat to dock, the message would be 'Auntie has mumps'.

Dick, according to Barbara, had the hump. He bullied Patrick and Virginia like a Victorian father. He wanted all his own way and sulked. But all was not lost: when he got his own way he was good company. Life aboard the *Maria Luigi* seemed like a set-up for a murder mystery. There they were, out to sea, 'the two members of the cabinet most deeply committed to two measures each of which is condemned by the other as fatal and catastrophic'.[99] Surely only one would leave alive.

Ted and Anne had merely walk-on roles. Everyone climbed Mount Epomeo, and everyone knocked back the wine at the top, but it was Barbara and Dick who did the screaming. Barbara's Bill would bring about another 1931 crisis, Dick yelled; the PLP was in revolt, the party split, the government would lose the next election and so on, back and forth, forth and back, the argument ceasing only when the restaurant closed and the happy band tripped tipsily back down the mountain.

Peacock took time out of her holiday to fly back from Naples (in a specially converted military transport plane) for secret talks with Rhino, Bear and Horse at Chequers, on 1 June, four days before the TUC special congress. Harold had offered to send Roy Jenkins in her stead, 'as a sort of guardian of her intransigence', he said, but she had refused.[100] Perhaps Harold forgot to tell Scanlon, Feather and Jones. They certainly had not expected 'the queer one' to be present. It was quite a shock. Feather ran to and from the door, pre-empting the butler, in order to let the others know that *she* was here.

In the union boys' opinion, Barbara was the stubborn, intractable one: it was *her* policy and she would not compromise. 'I got all the blame in the eyes of the unions', she said later; they forgave Harold. It was an understatement. The men had cast her as the villain of the piece. 'Why is she so bitter against our people?' Jones dolefully wondered. Her presence, he was sure, would 'inhibit the chances of getting an understanding'.[101] But what was to be understood was simple. Not only would the TUC not accept penal powers, not even in mothballs, or in suspended or frozen form, but they would not accept any legislation over their affairs. As Ernest Bevin had told the 1927 party conference, socialism was all right in its place but not if it poked its nose into union affairs.

Jones thought 'Barbara was rather shrewish' as they went round and round the argument; he thought she came on like a headmistress, trying to put Scanlon and him 'in our place'.[102] Both she and Harold were academics, the men complained, they could not see life from the angle of the shopfloor. The only angle Barbara and Harold were after was for the TUC to state unequivocally what it would do about unofficial strikes. As Feather recalled, 'Barbara Castle's repeated and specific question was: What will you do?'[103] What they did was to continue to say they would not accept legislation over their affairs. Harold told them, sotto voce, that he would not preside over a government that was not allowed to govern and that he would not be a MacDonald or a Dubček and issued to Scanlon his legendary demand: 'Get your tanks off my lawn, Hughie!'*

Peacock flew back to the Mediterranean and told Dick that the 'greatest quality in politics is good nerves'. He wasn't so sure. He thought a little wisdom might not come amiss. She was relying too much on what had succeeded in the past. She was relying on taking the TUC to the brink and watching it pull back.[104] Harold too. Once more to the brink, he liked to say. 'Brinkmanship is essential.' The more unlikely they were to succeed the more they egged each other on. Theirs was a Boy's Own heroism, a recitation from Kipling's *If*; the *folie à deux* to end them all.

The TUC's Special Congress at Croydon came and went. *Programme for Action* was ratified, with its vague pious hope intact and an emphasis that the TUC was not prepared to trade sanctions with the government but was prepared to help secure settlements. Congress passed a vote of 'unalterable opposition' to the penal clauses and the provision for fines embodied in the Bill; it heartily welcomed the trade-union rights therein.

Barbara and Dick flew home the next day. Her civil servants met her at the airport. The press coverage of the Croydon congress was remarkably friendly and favourable, full of praise for how much the unions had moved, which, in Barbara's view, gave the government the opportunity to suspend the Short Bill and say they were willing to give the unions a chance to put their own house in order. She was therefore astonished, and initially furious, to discover that Harold had, without consulting her, 'issued a statement over my name',[105] rejecting the TUC's proposals on unconstitutional strikes, provoking 'Barbara Castle Snubs Unions' headlines. Harold had bricked up the door marked 'Exit'. He had upped the ante. He told Barbara that if the unions had moved thus far he could get them to move further.

---

* In spring 1968, the Czechoslovak premier, Alexander Dubček, had implemented a policy of political liberalisation and reform of communism. In August, Leonid Brezhnev sent in Soviet troops and tanks, and all dissent was crushed.

'Harold certainly seems very firm', Barbara marvelled, as she walked over and joined him back at the precipice.

Between the special congress and the denouement thirteen days later, Barbara and Harold met the TUC's negotiating committee almost daily for a mélange of argie-bargie, arcana, warm beer and doorstop sandwiches. The TUC made it clear that it would withdraw *Programme for Action* unless the government withdrew its legislation, and the government would then get nothing. It was not willing to accept the Bill, even in cold storage. Barbara and Harold put through various alternatives for hardening up *Programme*, especially the aspects dealing with unofficial strikes. The TUC was happy to discuss model rules, or word changes, or tinkering with this rule or that, and eat and drink and be merry, but whatever Harold and Barbara said, it was going no further than *Programme*, which it considered far enough. There was no need. As Houghton told Feather, 'The Prime Minister would have to accept whatever they offered.' The TUC, Roy Jenkins observed, 'dug in and waited for the investing forces to disintegrate'.[106]

Barbara was beginning to disintegrate. She was not sleeping and she was smoking too much. She was restless, agitated; she was disproportionately upset at the snide coverage of her cruise on Forte's yacht, which had, of course, got out. She felt permanently sick and could barely eat. She vacillated between misplaced optimism – she could do it, she could do it – and overwhelming despair. If the party rejected the Bill she would have to resign; what else could she do? Harold, too, perhaps even Roy. For God's sake, Dick told her, don't resign; that would be to play right into Jim Callaghan's hands.

Was it over? She couldn't decide. She never knew whether something was over or not. 'The game is never finished' her father had hammered into her, and he would not have expected her to give up. But he had drummed the same lesson into Vic Feather, and, as Denis Healey pointed out, it was Feather who had manoeuvred everything perfectly. The game is never finished. Except when it is.

After Croydon, Roy Jenkins, hitherto Barbara and Harold's keenest supporter, suddenly wasn't. Roy 'slid elegantly onto the fence'.[107] He looked 'shifty', Barbara noticed, uneasy; he couldn't quite meet her eye. That was on Sunday, 8 June; by Tuesday the papers had the story. Roy's support was weakening. He had been told by his fans in the PLP some months before that the only thing standing between him and the premiership was *In Place of Strife*. A few days later, Douglas Houghton made his next move. He sent a letter to Harold. The prime minister would never ever get penal sanctions through the party, he wrote. Never. He gave the press a copy of his missive.

It was the 'most traumatic day of my political life', Barbara said of 17 June.[108] She had come up with another plan: to fine only the unions, not individual unionists, over unofficial strikes. But what she and Harold wanted was cabinet backing to say that sanctions were still on the table if the TUC wouldn't harden up its proposals. But cabinet had simply had enough. What was the point in going on like this? As Barbara and Harold both said, the TUC had moved further and faster in the previous two weeks than in all the past forty years. They were not going to get the PLP to accept penal sanctions anyway. The chief whip, Bob Mellish, never one for formalities, spoke up without waiting for the prime minister to ask him. You can't get this Bill through the House of Commons, he barked, echoing Houghton. Forget it.

Programme for Action was as much as they were going to get. Why not ask for a letter of intent from the TUC, declare victory and go home? That was unacceptable to Barbara; that was peace without honour; that was retreat. Her colleagues were 'vultures' and 'wreckers'. Then Peter Shore, who had been at Sunningdale and helped to draft aspects of *In Place of Strife*, gave an impassioned speech against trying to ram the Bill through the House: it was a 'complete misjudgment' not to accept what the TUC had offered. Shore's defection was a bitter blow for Barbara and Harold. Cabinet was falling away: 'by lunch-time, a majority of the Cabinet had expressed either their opposition to the Bill, or at least strong reservations about it,' as Harold, the master of understatement, put it.[109]

Before Barbara's most devastating cabinet meeting resumed late in the afternoon, Roy Jenkins came to see her. He had been, in his own view, almost the last on the burning deck. He was sorry, but he was jumping off before his trousers caught fire. She accepted the news, he said, 'like St Sebastian receiving another arrow'. She wearily told him that she and Harold could not back down now. If they could not get an acceptable compromise, they 'should both resign'. Roy, looking mournful, told her that it was her resignation that would have a detrimental effect on party morale, 'if I may say so'.[110]

Abandoning Barbara is something Roy still 'regrets'; it was, he said, 'humiliating to desert them', but nevertheless, it was politically expedient. In cabinet, he wrote, 'Wilson behaved with a touch of King Lear-like nobility. He sounded fairly unhinged at times and there was a wild outpouring of words ... [Nevertheless] he and Barbara Castle emerged with more credit than the rest of us.'[111] As Edmund Dell observed, this was a 'splendid example ... of a method of making an apology that incorporates its own excuses'.[112]

Only Cledwyn Hughes and George Thomas* continued to back Harold and Barbara enthusiastically. Barbara 'was frantic in the usual Barbara sort of way', Tony Benn sighed;[113] he, too, had gone. Barbara and Harold 'became extremely bitter'. Harold was coming undone. He threatened several times to resign, which left most of cabinet unmoved. If it was a question of saving the movement and the government with Barbara and Harold's resignation, so be it. He and Barbara were due to meet the Trade Union Group of MPs at 7 p.m., and Harold was due to address them. What was he supposed to tell them? Cabinet had approved *In Place of Strife* and the Short Bill, Harold said. They were backing off because the measures were unpopular: 'You're soft, you're cowardly, you're lily-livered', he spat.[114] Barbara and Harold now '*despised* Cabinet'.[115] Outside, Harold told Joe Haines: 'I don't mind running a green cabinet, but I'm buggered if I'm going to run a yellow one!'[116]

Barbara went to bed that night wondering if it might not be the last time she would do so as first secretary of state and secretary of

---

* Ministers for, respectively, agriculture and Wales.

state for employment and productivity, yet the next day she had a
burst of optimism. Perhaps they could still get a majority in cabinet
to back them in whatever they thought right. She started jotting
down names of those she thought would back them when the chips
were down; they included Tony Greenwood and Tony Benn, the
latter having spent much of the previous cabinet explaining why he
regrettably had to withdraw support.

Harold and Barbara held their final meeting with the TUC at Number
10 on 18 June, the anniversary of the battle of Waterloo, aboard 'HMS
Fruitless', as a wag in the cabinet secretariat said. That very morning
the Tory lead had been cut to a mere seventeen points, in good part
because the public felt that the Labour government was showing
itself more resolute in dealing with the unions.

In the meeting Barbara faced the General Council. She 'was tense
and white and she was gripping – I can still see her knuckles
shining white – as she gripped the edge of the table', Len Murray*
said, 'and she made one last impassioned plea, and the plea that she
made was so odd; she said a Labour government must be able to
control these people in the City, we must be able to control the
owners of industry, we must be able to exercise control over work
people who threaten what we are doing – and it sent an appalled
quiver around our side of the table'.[117]

Harold tried to bluff Feather and the council, threatening them
with the legislation cabinet had rejected if they did not agree to a
rule change. They would not. Harold and Barbara were trying to 'go
pontoon with a three and a two', whereas the TUC 'held an ace and
a king'.[118] They knew what had and had not been agreed to in
cabinet. Harold knew it was over. He was not going to trade his
career and the future of the party for a gesture. He was not going to
resign. He was ready to cobble together some sort of face-saving
formula. It was Jack Jones who suggested the solution. He told
Barbara that she 'probably did not understand' that under TUC rules

---

* Lionel Murray, the assistant general-secretary of the TUC. He succeeded Vic
Feather in 1973.

a binding agreement was just that and had the same form as the 1939 Bridlington Agreement.*

The TUC was willing to give a 'solemn and binding undertaking' to do its utmost to resolve unconstitutional strikes if the government was willing to scrap the Short Bill and promise that it would not during its lifetime bring forth any Bills with penal clauses or sanctions. Barbara wanted everyone to sign the TUC's undertaking in the presence of the attorney-general, but the unions refused. Mr Solomon Binding, as the agreement was instantly baptized, was to have a short and not notably eventful life.

Cabinet had been called for midday, and postponed, and postponed. Then at last, at 5.30 p.m., Harold and Barbara dragged themselves in to explain the deal they had accepted. According to Harold, there was great excitement, 'even cheers', as he read out the agreement, although loud rejoicing seems to have been limited to George Thomas, who was relieved to the point of being histrionic. After showering Harold with Kiplingesque compliments, he dropped Barbara a note which began, 'Oh! you beautiful doll!'

After Harold had finished addressing cabinet, Barbara 'insisted on intervening', he recalled, dressing 'down the whole Cabinet for placing me in this position: they had left me without a card in my hand', but nevertheless, she told them, Harold 'had taken the ace'. Afterwards Barbara and Harold held a joint press conference until he asked the press to 'release Barbara, as a prior hairdressing appointment was a categorical imperative prior to her television appearance with Vic Feather'.[119]

On the way to the studio Barbara felt 'deflated to the point of tears'.[120] But, the battle lost, she and Harold soon rallied. They convinced themselves and each other that victory was theirs. Their integrity intact, resignation was rendered unnecessary. In her first solo press interview, Barbara told Geoffrey Goodman, 'Harold and I have won this battle.' 'She put on a fantastic front,' he said, 'but it was pure pretence. She knew that she had been defeated; she knew that it was a devastating blow to both of them, but she said the TUC

---

* A code of practice on inter-union relations which prohibited poaching.

would never have agreed to do all these things they have agreed to if we hadn't pushed them. That's how she rationalised it. But I don't think for a moment she believed it.'[121]

To the unions, the prime minister's rapacious lady had always been the problem. The fact that she was a woman, and, as Hugh Scanlon said, 'she had been to university, she'd got a degree, she'd never been in a factory or a working environment',[122] were all used against her. She had been a Bevanite and a silver-spoon Bevanite at that; her political past, her flamboyance, stridency, elitism – all were used against her. But no one at that time could have got onto the statute books an industrial relations bill that sought to control the unions.

'To be quite frank,' Scanlon said, 'in those days when there was still a greater demand for labour than there were jobs to be filled, I don't think anything other than unbridled collective bargaining would've have satisfied the trade unions and I would have gone along with that. When the economic boot is on your foot you tend to use it and that would've been true whatever Barbara tried to introduce.'[123]

PART IV

The Future's Not What It Was

Chapter Ten

POWER RESIDES
ELSEWHERE

When Barbara had first arrived at the Department of Employment and Productivity (DEP), she told Hugh Scanlon that she wanted to be remembered for her work there. 'She used to get really ruffled when we said what a courageous woman she'd been in introducing the breathalyser,' Scanlon said; 'she said she didn't want to be remembered as a Minister of Transport, she wanted to be remembered as Minister of Labour.'[1] Fourteen months into the job and she had got her wish: all her successes at Transport and at Overseas Development forgotten; her twenty years on the back benches fighting for unpopular causes forgotten. Barbara, the scarlet bogey of the right wing, the Joan of Arc of the Labour Party, the woman recently canvassed as the one most likely to become Britain's first female prime minister: no more. If I ever had any chance of being leader of the party, that ditched it, she said over and over again. The right had always loathed her and now the left loathed her more. Barbara was in that most invidious position for a politician: isolated within her party, without either supporters or a base. She was blamed for bringing her party, her government and her prime minister to the very brink of destruction. She was, in Jack Jones's vividly painful phrase, totally politically discredited.

How would she go on? How could she go on? She was exhausted, physically and psychologically near collapse; she'd been working almost non-stop, and when she went to bed she couldn't sleep. She'd barely eaten and had smoked incessantly. The strain of the last few months had been almost unendurable – would have been unendurable for most people. But Barbara bore the tremendous stress 'astonishingly well'. Moreover, she was now enduring, 'from apparent appearances remarkably well', the worst failure of her life. She seemed unfaltering in her grasp of herself as the bloodied but unbowed heroine; like the singer of the Impossible Dream, she reached for her last ounce of courage. She had known Triumph and Disaster: 'Treat those two impostors just the same' was, she said, still her 'favourite philosophy'.[2] Life as an everlasting, rip-roaring recitation of Kipling's 'If'.

The papers on 19 June, the day after her Waterloo, were merciless. 'Surrender 69!': she and Harold had capitulated to the unions. *In Place of Strife*, *The Economist* witheringly splashed on its front cover, had been replaced by 'In Place of Government'. The more she read, the more angry she became at the commentators, the pontificators. When attacked, Barbara instinctively counter-attacked; she didn't wilt, she hardened. My God, she noted in her diary, couldn't the 'illiterate and prejudiced' press understand that the blame lay with a cabinet of cowards, that the fault lay with cabinet's refusal to support her and Harold when the going got tough, to support the measures they had collectively approved? Why was it that she and Harold were taking all the flak for cabinet's spinelessness?[3]

She was shell-shocked, reeling, but she was already on the move, beginning a desperate offensive to rehabilitate herself. A week was too short a time in politics to judge 'consequences', to judge 'results', she said. With extraordinary bravado she went and had her hair done and threw a champagne party for her staff at DEP. It wasn't their fault, she told them, that the 'pulpit' they had built for her to preach her 'sermons' from had turned into a 'scaffold'.[4]

Barbara wasn't alone on the scaffold. Harold was there, fumbling with his blindfold; politically they still had each other, perhaps only each other; the severed head of the Labour Party rolling in psychic lockstep. You and I must stick together, Harold told her. 'I am the only friend you have and you are the only friend I have.' He was like an elephant, he said; he never forgot. It was a declaration to Barbara of 'his own deepest feelings about friendship, loyalty, trust and betrayal'.[5]

When she went to the House to answer the Tory censure motion on *Strife*, Harold was next to her on the front bench. He stuck close, wittering in her ear about Ted Heath, perhaps trying to help her relax. Dick came into the House just in time to see her rise to speak, 'trembling as she got up, nervous, tense and tiny and somehow pathetic'. Diminutive Barbara could only just see over the top of the despatch box, and her 'high-pitched woman's voice' was drowned out by the boos, cheers and catcalls, the 'post-prandial, alcoholic clouds of noise', emitted by the Honourable Members. The angrier she became, the more effective she became, but the House was in 'ferocious and violent' temper and in the end 'she got through very little'.[6] It was, she said, the roughest ride possible.

The ride was long and harsh. A week after *Strife*'s defeat, Tony Benn went over to Congress House to see Vic Feather. The general secretary kept him waiting an egregiously long time, 'an indication of how powerful he felt', Tony noted; 'he didn't have to bother very much about Cabinet Ministers' and he was 'very pleased with the way things had gone last week'.[7] Reports that Vic Feather and Barbara were at each other's throats, and that she was persona non grata with the unions, continued apace. The trade unionists now 'loathe the sight of Barbara', Fred Peart, the lord privy seal, told Dick; every time she saw them 'she lectures them with one of her emotional tirades'. Feather did not bother to hide his feelings from Barbara. He told Harold in front of her that when it came to industrial relations she was a 'liability'. Dick thought the fact that she was a woman and had failed put her at an 'appalling disadvantage', much worse than if she'd been a man.[8] It confirmed the old trade-union boys' prejudices and brought out the worst in them. They had always said the bloody woman wasn't up to the job.

Newspapers called for her removal from DEP and Harold, too, thought she would be better off elsewhere. A month after the solemn and binding agreement, he offered her a new superministry to run. He would combine Transport, Housing and Planning under one roof. In this way she could revisit the scene of her greatest triumph; in that way she could play to her greatest strengths. But Barbara turned it down. She could not be seen to be running away from DEP; there could be no suggestion whatsoever of that. Fear of acting in a cowardly fashion, and of being seen to do so, still haunted her. There could be no suggestion, either, that Harold blamed her. It would, she rationalised, be bad for both of them. She would stay on and pick through the ashes. Harold shook his head and let her do as she wished: 'She is nursing a dead baby', he told Tony Benn. It was an analogy he was fond of: 'Poor Barbara,' he told Sir William Armstrong,* 'she hangs around like someone with a still-born child. She can't believe it's dead.'[9]

But Barbara didn't mope. The point of staying on was to try to rescue her reputation as the secretary of state for employment and productivity. Almost immediately she was on the move. She came up with the idea for a Bill merging the Prices and Incomes Board and the Monopolies Commission into a Commission for Industry and Manpower (CIM), so that she could be seen to be controlling industry as well as unions, prices more than wages. Her original idea was to call CIM the Public Accountability Commission, because the concept was to bring forth 'the public accountability of industry', both private and state. It would engage in the 'positive promotion of efficiency and productivity' in industry. But the reaction from her colleagues was ferocious. The policy, was asymmetrical, they said. Controlling prices but not wages would infuriate business; so would the commission's overweeningly wide-ranging powers to poke about in every corner of industry. As she had alienated the TUC, she would now alienate the CBI.

Tony Benn at the Ministry of Technology (MinTech), and Tony Crosland at the Board of Trade (BOT), both thought she was trying to take the whole of the government's industrial policy into DEP, sticking her fingers into their ministries' business, a not unfamiliar

* Head of the Home Civil Service.

254

complaint about Barbara from her cabinet colleagues. There should be 'no derogation from the existing powers and responsibilities of sponsoring Ministers', Harold told her.[10] She was an empire-builder by nature but her actions this time were as much engendered by an external threat.

Harold had vastly increased the power of Tony Benn's MinTech, giving him the Ministry of Power, the regional and industrial policy of the BOT (now essentially the ministry for exports) and certain functions of the Department of Economic Affairs, which was wound up. 'The responsibility for industrial policy, outside of course the very wide functions carried out by the Department of Employment and Productivity, will be concentrated in a single Department', Harold told the lobby.[11] Although he had not removed any existing powers from DEP, he had centralised industrial policy under the MinTech. Barbara's CIM was industrial policy; she was remarking her territory.

Getting CIM through cabinet was agonising, Barbara griped. Her colleagues complained that she droned on and on even more than usual. Tony Benn objected that, 'as usual', there was no documentary back-up: 'Barbara believes that if you give information to the Cabinet, Ministers won't agree with what you want to do, so she tries to get through a presentation orally, always under tremendous pressure because of a press conference which is just about to take place, for which she has to leave early to get her hair done.' She tried, he added, to 'railroad stuff through Cabinet and it infuriates everybody'.[12] Dick agreed. 'The more she does this, the more irritated Cabinet becomes', he noted.[13] The generalised complaint was that, once again, 'inadequate collective consideration had been given' to the proposed legislation.[14]

She had more luck with her proposed equal-pay legislation. They could not deny or obstruct her over this. Pressure for equal pay was rising in the country and she told cabinet that, of the seven workers' rights promised in the 1964 manifesto, equal pay was the only one on which nothing had been done. They had, she said, run out of delaying excuses: 'It was no longer possible to stall; they must either fulfil the expectations which had been aroused or say publicly and firmly that they could not go ahead in the present economic situation.'[15]

The unions could no longer resist the end to the male–female differential even if they wished. Union attitudes had been historically 'equivocal if not hypocritical' on equal pay, Barbara said, but now they were almost solidly behind it: it was going to happen, and the government might as well take credit for it, in 'a controlled operation in which the economic disadvantages were minimised'. It would put an upper limit of 1 per cent on the wage bill per annum if phased in over five years,'the maximum [amount of time] we could get away with', said Barbara,[16] the long-time equal-pay ad-vocate hanging on to her ministerial hat.

The CBI's and TUC's reactions on timing were predictable, Barbara told cabinet.The CBI wanted it delayed for nine years, whereas the TUC wanted it implemented in two, although they 'know very well that this is unrealistic' and privately Vic Feather told her that 'they would regard a three or perhaps four year period as reasonable'.[17] Labour and union women made noises about the dilatory phasing-in schedule.Why couldn't women have equal pay in two years? This cry, Barbara, in full rhetorical flight, told the National Conference of Labour women, 'was part of the divine impatience which had got the Labour Movement where it was, but she would point out that impatience had not got the movement [for equal pay] very far in eighty-two years, and it would not have got it anywhere if it had not been that a Labour Government had decided, at a moment of great economic difficulty, that, whatever the cost, it was going to give women the justice so long overdue'.[18]

Barbara also needed to introduce a new Industrial Relations Bill, which she would base largely on the Donovan Report, of which the TUC had previously approved. But Donovan called for the compulsory registration of unions, with fines for those who failed to do so, of which the TUC now did not approve. Nor did it approve of the right of individuals to appeal to an independent review body over expulsion from, or refusal of membership of, a union. To these clauses, the TUC, had an 'implacable and emotional opposition', Barbara said.[19] It had no intention of accepting anything that involved sanctions or interference in its business. Why should it? It had won.

She accepted there was no fight left to have with the TUC. Her new Bill would indeed be a charter of trade-union rights and nothing else. As she told the TUC, she had seen to it that it contained nothing offensive to them. She convinced herself that this was the right approach: 'One often produces one's best results obliquely, as the fall-out, for instance, from apparent defeat on a major issue', she noted.[20] However, such apparent defeat and subsequent apparent capitulation would, she knew, make her the butt of jibes. As one scrap of ministerial graffiti had it: 'She attempts intercourse with the previous non-participants.'[21]

Barbara, who had 'always been a supporter' of the prices and incomes policy, because she believed 'it leads us to the heart of a social-ist society', revamped it to act as a bridging mechanism until CIM came into force. Whatever her beliefs as to its efficacy in bringing about a socialist society, as she saw it she had little choice, 'not only because of the Government's commitment to the International Monetary Fund [to do so], but also because the Government could not retreat further from their declared policies in face of trade union pressures'. As she told cabinet, 'we certainly cannot now draw back.'[22]

She, of course, would have to be the one to lean forward. At the 1969 party conference she once again defended the necessity for a prices and incomes policy, to catcalls and boos and angry shouts, especially when she said it was not a 'curtailment of basic trade union rights' (to which conference had declared its 'unalterable opposition').[23]

Barbara was supposed to be replying for the NEC, which was opposed to any statutory prices and incomes policy, but she had given the government position. This ended up in a midnight brawl between Barbara, on the one hand, and Jack Jones and Hugh Scanlon, on the other, in Harold's hotel room, with Harold playing the role of emollient referee. The prime minister issued a tortuous explanatory statement to the effect she wasn't expressing the NEC's position, as in whatever capacity a minister speaks a minister speaks as a minister bound by collective responsibility.

While accepting that such silky ministrations were an integral constituent of leadership, Barbara felt sickened by Harold; the more so when she thought he was suggesting she should backpedal from the agreed cabinet line. Moreover, she was furious that prices and incomes had stolen the spotlight from her announcement of her forthcoming equal-pay legislation, which had earned her prolonged applause. There was only so much she could take, she warned Harold. He soothed her. He was not asking her to backpedal. Nothing was further from his mind.

Yet despite Barbara's rough ride at conference, despite the lacerating endless arguments over *Strife* still echoing in everyone's mind, despite the fact that most constituency parties had been anti-*Strife* and opposed prices and incomes legislation, Barbara, to her monumental relief, came top of the poll for the NEC constituency section again. Being the progenitor of equal pay helped, but it was as much a tribute to Battling Barbara, whose courage, if perhaps misguided, had to be admired; she still had the affection of the party in the country, even though they disagreed with much of what she was trying to do, the only minister for which this was true. The public, too, was still with her. She had gone down fighting for something they had believed right, and they admired her for it. She was still their favourite, top of the ministerial pops.

Barbara's White Paper, *Productivity, Prices and Incomes Policy*, was accepted by cabinet on 8 December 1969 and published three days later. Pay settlements had to be between 2.5 and 4.5 per cent, the higher end for low-earners and equal-pay purposes. Real wage increases continued to be way ahead of that (the average was close to 9 per cent), many on the higher end awarded to stop the unofficial strikes that proliferated. Barbara and Harold thought they might go to the TUC 'to obtain their assessment of the extent and reasons for the deterioration in industrial relations, including the growth of militancy on the shopfloor, and to examine with them the reasons for their inability to live up to the undertakings which they had given in the summer'.[24] Mr Solomon Binding was impotent.

The TUC meanwhile rejected *Productivity*. The PLP, a 'politically irresponsible rabble' in Barbara's view, was predictably, and variously opposed: 'not one question put to Barbara ... had been favourable', the Tribune Group noted of the December meeting.[25] Many in the PLP were willing to defeat the government on this. Houghton this time sought to rein in the dissent. He told them that defeat would force a general election at the worst of all possible times.

On the day of the prices and incomes debate, many MPs, more Labour than Tory, were at home, suffering from flu. Everyone who could be was forced into the chamber. Roy Jenkins was dragged out of his sickbed to speak for the government and threw 'all his considerable prestige' behind Barbara. 'Barbara Castle Face-saver (Number Two) Bill', jeered Robert Carr, the shadow employment secretary. It was a kiss-and-make-up gesture to atone for selling her down the river over *Strife*, 'a high price for chivalry!' When Barbara reached the despatch box, 'Labour's most desperate house since devaluation had come'. Determined 'to uphold her reputation as a fighter at her best with her back to the wall' she rose to the occasion, first deriding the Tories for their 'incomes only' policies and then turning to her own rebels, the bevy 'below the gangway'.[26] She won by twenty-eight votes.

On 28 January 1970, the day after a conference on women's history at Ruskin College, Oxford, spontaneously became the first national conference of the women's liberation movement, Barbara introduced the Equal Pay Bill to the House. It received an unopposed second reading. Although some MPs from all sides of the House came up and congratulated Barbara on what was after all a historic piece of legislation, the response from the party as a whole was lacklustre. This, she sighed, was just one more illustration of how the Labour movement was 'so schooled in protest that it doesn't know how to celebrate victory'.[27] The party had a 'constitutional inability' to enjoy success. The Equal Pay Act was one of the last pieces of legislation to make it onto the statute book before the general election.

Harold had decided to hold the election on 18 June 1970, the anniversary of the defeat of *In Place of Strife*. Perhaps he had forgotten the Labour government's failure, or hoped to expunge it by the certain Labour victory. The pollsters were putting Labour anywhere between 3 per cent and 12 per cent ahead of the Tories. Ted Heath, wooden and uncharismatic, compared unfavourably to the old nurse everyone knew. Barbara was not convinced. It did not feel right. There was a strange detachment among party activists and within the audiences she addressed. Perhaps it was the weather. The weeks leading up to the election were warm and sultry; voters' minds were elsewhere, on their forthcoming holidays or the foot-ball World Cup, which England, winners of the 1966 title, were defending.

Harold was sure of a Labour victory and hopeful of an England one, as were most of his ministers. Not only were the polls in Labour's favour, but so were the facts. By August 1969, the balance of payments had turned round, and when the figures for the year as a whole were released, Britain's balance of payments was shown to be in the black. Labour's economic management seemed justified and a few days before the election the bookmakers had Labour the favourites at 20:1.

Then, on Sunday, 14 June, England was knocked out of the World Cup by Germany, after leading 2–0 at half-time. The next day the weather broke. June became less than flaming; and the monthly trade figures were announced, registering a £31 million deficit for May – the first month-on-month deficit for nine months – £18 million of which was accounted for by the purchase of two jumbo jets. Combined with rumours of a rise in the jobless rate and Heath's disinformation about a possible further devaluation, this gave the Tories the break that had so long eluded them.

Harold was joking with reporters in Liverpool's Adelphi Hotel when the first result came in from Guildford at 11 p.m., showing the Tory candidate with a hugely increased majority. Within fifteen minutes, Harold and Barbara knew that Labour was defeated, in this, the first election in which the newly enfranchised 18-year-olds could vote. Even Jennie Lee and George Brown lost their seats.

Many things were blamed for the defeat: Barbara had wanted a grand budget of largesse and vision, which she did not get from Roy Jenkins, and an autumn election, which she did not get from Harold. She blamed Roy for the defeat. Others blamed the government's failure to increase real living standards over the past six years, the 'widespread feeling that in many occupations family men who did a conscientious job of work were only marginally better off than those who preferred to remain unemployed'.[28] The general shambolic nature of Harold's leadership was also blamed, as was the bad luck with the weather, the World Cup and the jumbo jets, the fact that working-class women were seduced by Ted Heath's promise to halt rising prices 'at a stroke', et cetera, but the 'dominant interpretation' of why Labour lost was 'because traditional working-class Labour voters, alienated by wage restraint and anti-union proposals, had stayed at home'.[29] In other words, it was Barbara wot lost it.

Almost a decade later, Jim Callaghan, by then prime minister, was still blaming Barbara for the 1970 defeat: 'trade unionists did not turn up to vote because of what they thought was the attitude of the Labour Government to them', he said.[30] Ironically, a month later the trade unionists' attitude to Jim Callaghan began Labour's eighteen-year sojourn in the wilderness.

A year after her defeat over *Strife*, Barbara's ambition to lead the party had returned with force and conviction. George Brown's departure from the House meant that the position of deputy leader was now vacant and Barbara decided to run. It was an extraordinary decision. It was true that she had proved it possible to retain political strength in government 'not merely in circumstances of lack of success but in failure', as Dick put it,[31] and that she had maintained her popularity with the constituency parties and the public, but the votes would come from the PLP, the honourable members with whom she had been in mortal combat for six months, returning for a rematch with the post-*Strife* prices and

261

incomes legislation. Perhaps she believed that she had worked her passage back home with the Equal Pay Act, and her proposed conciliatory Industrial Relations Bill (which never made it on to the statute books).

Harold wanted his new running-mate to be more compatible and less trouble than the previous wild inhabitant. Barbara would be the former, but not the latter. And, as Harold was seen to be of the left, his deputy, in his view, must be seen to be of the right. He needed the balance to keep the party together and he liked to keep his rivals and enemies within his sights. He thought of Callaghan. He thought of Jenkins. He certainly did not think of Barbara.

Consequently it was a 'moment of terror' for Harold when Barbara appeared in the leader of the opposition's room (where he sat surrounded by packing cases from Number 10) and informed him of her plans. She came straight to the point; so did Harold. She was going to do no such thing, he told her. 'Barbara was adamant. She had to do what was right, she said, everyone was free to do what they liked.' They argued. They shouted. Harold told her he would resign 'rather than lead a rabble'. She stormed out. 'As she was leaving Harold added brutally – and what's more you won't get fourteen votes!'[32]

A contest between Barbara and Roy would be a contest not only between Bevanite and Gaitskellite but also a contest between anti- and pro-European. Harold wanted neither split to become cavernous at the beginning of his period of opposition. He prob-ably had the spirit of the numbers right, too. Barbara would only just scrape into the twelve-member shadow cabinet with ninety-eight votes, compared with 178 for Callaghan, who topped the poll.

Barbara was furious. She decided to fight Harold, to ignore him, to do what she had to do. At a dinner in her flat for Dick Crossman, Tony Benn and a few others, she fumed that she was tired of everything being carved up. 'Why should I go on just accepting the Number Three position? Harold never helped me. This is the moment to stand up and fight', she said. Dick, who had taken over

Above: The Minister
of Transport was
the most popular
minister in Harold
Wilson's government.
(By permission of the
National Museum of
Labour History)

Right: The Cabinet's
It Girl emerges
from talks with the
National Union of
Railwaymen in 1966.
© Hulton Getty

Above: Fashion and outrage in motion. © Hulton Getty

Below: The first lady of the land is appointed first secretary of state and secretary of state for employment and productivity. © Hulton Getty

Above: Tea and publicity – Barbara with the Dagenham women after resolving their strike against Ford. © MSI

Below: Meeting her Waterloo with Harold Wilson and Vic Feather in 1969. © Hulton Getty

Above: The secretary of state for health and social security with her team. From left to right: David Owen, Jack Ashley and Brian O'Malley. © *Daily Mirror*

Below: Harold giving Barbara flowers for her sixty-first birthday. Ted was already seriously ill with heart problems. © *Daily Mirror*

Above: Anti-Europeans make strange bedfellows. Barbara with Enoch Powell campaigning for a 'no' vote in the upcoming referendum on Europe in 1975. © Hulton Getty

Below: The Blues brother and sister at the 1971 Conference. © Hulton Getty

Above: Putting on a brave face with Tony Benn at her first Party Conference after Jim Callaghan sacked her. September 1976. © Hulton Getty

Below: The Pearly people – Barbara with Neil Kinnock in 1984, shortly after he became Party leader. They were bringing down the butter mountain by handing it out to pensioners. © Popperfoto

Left: Old comrades at the 1992 Party Conference. Barbara and Michael Foot. © Steve Eason/ Hulton Getty

Right: The moment of terror for New Labour – the immaculately turned-out blast from the past waits to speak to the pre-election conference. © John Giles/PA

Above: Labour's Queen Mother, it's only elder stateswoman. © *Daily Mirror*

the editorship of the *New Statesman*, said the magazine would support her in her bid against Roy or Jim Callaghan. But, as Tony Benn noted, 'there was a general feeling that Barbara really shouldn't stand ... that it was an explosion of feeling rather than a sensible decision, because ... her reputation in the Party had dropped very sharply'.[33]

Later Harold went after Barbara to sweet-talk her and 'after long hours of talk (mostly late at night) he persuaded her' not to run.[34] Everything had indeed been carved up. Harold made his 'grudging mating offering' to Roy Jenkins, tendering support for any bid the former chancellor cared to make for the deputy leadership. In the end, it was Michael Foot, a figure of 'far lower political stature at that time' than Barbara, who challenged Jenkins.[35] He lost decisively, getting sixty-seven votes to Jenkins 133; Jenkins's other challenger, Fred Peart, polled forty-eight votes.

Harold had, for his own reasons, stopped Barbara making a fool of herself by getting a similarly derisory vote. Perhaps, having refused her one thing, he felt he could not refuse her another. He allowed her to shadow Robert Carr at the Department of Employment, which put her in the invidious position of leading the charge against the Tories' Industrial Relations Bill. The Carr Bill, although more draconian than the Castle Bill, was not all that dissimilar. ('It is only when the Bill is examined line by line that a different picture begins to emerge', as Barbara herself put it.[36]) Harold, foreseeing the absurdity of Barbara opposing that which she had so recently proposed, had been 'reluctant' to let her take on Employment, Joe Haines remembered, but she insisted and he went along with it because if 'he had dropped her it would have looked as if she was being blamed for *In Place of Strife* – the headlines would have been "The TUC force Barbara out". Harold wouldn't have that. He'd suffered enough from the TUC.'[37]

Barbara was to suffer more. 'Within minutes of Heath taking office', Vic Feather made a statement in which he 'hoped that the DEP would now revert to being the Ministry of Labour – the right place for conciliation.'[38] The Tribune Group were opposed to her shadowing DEP because of her 'doubtful credibility' caused by her attempts to 'foist legislation on the country',[39] and at the post-election party conference she was told by Stan Orme that, if she was going to fight the Tory Industrial Relations Bill, she would 'have to reject her past policies'. He said that 'one cannot but admire her courage; whether her judgement is right or not you will have to judge for yourselves'.[40]

Barbara spoke at length to conference, defending her record rather than apologising for it. Answering Orme, she asked if he wanted her to forget the 90 per cent of her Bill which had been 'the biggest charter for trade unionism in this country's history'.[41] She had, she said, always known voluntary action by the trade unions was preferable, and that was why 'Harold Wilson and I reached that understanding' with the TUC. Even though it could be said that it wasn't very effective it was more effective than imposing unwanted solutions on a 'violently protesting trade union' movement. The soundbites snowballed. She lambasted Carr for running a department dedicated to 'laissez fight'. The Tory Bill was 'In Place of an Economic Policy' and so on and on.

Barbara needed to separate Castle from Carr. She started with his motives. They were different, and she explained why at great length to the shadow cabinet. As she had reiterated up and down the land, her White Paper had sought to strengthen the unions; Carr's purpose was to weaken them. She wrote a series of articles for the *New Statesman* elucidating this point.

Carr's 'proposals encroach on our traditional concept of free trade unionism', she wrote, something the 'TUC will protest with vigour – and some justice' against.[42] Her penal sanctions, she insisted, were not like Carr's. Her fundamental philosophy was not his. Dick indulged her, giving her space to develop her drawn-out, microscopic accounts of some of the most unpalatable (to the unions) of Carr's clauses, such as the right not to join a union, which would inevitably lead to the destruction of the closed shop. To her friends it was mortifying. She'd become defensive and contorted.

On the one hand, Barbara adopted an I-told-you-so attitude to the unions, telling them that if they had cooperated with her and not opposed *Strife* the Tories could never have never introduced this Bill. On the other hand, she was busy playing to their gallery. Eric Heffer, who ascended onto the shadow front bench to help fight the Carr Bill, seemed ready more or less to forgive if not forget: once she 'understood that trade union unity with the Party was essential for our future success no one fought harder or with greater courage that she did', he said,[43] which was unfortunately true.

Barbara had to shout loud to make herself heard; and shout louder in order to believe what she was saying; by the time the Bill reached the floor of the House, she had lost all political judgement and much of her dignity. It didn't help that Ted was now quite seriously ill with heart trouble, and so she was 'working under terrific stress', said Paul Rose, who was also part of the Shadow Employment team.[44] She 'opened her frenzied attack' in Parliament by accusing Carr of treating the House with 'intolerable discourtesy' and accused him of practising 'dishonest salesmanship'. The Bill was a 'document written by lawyers for lawyers', a theme she returned to again and again. 'It is not only a lawyer's breakfast: it is his dinner and tea as well!'[45]

She pledged to fight the 'blackleg's charter . . . tooth and nail, line by line; and however long it takes we shall destroy the Bill'.[46] For Neil Kinnock it was like standing helplessly at the scene of a motorway pile-up: the Tories 'just kept on quoting her throwing her words back at her – we're only doing what you didn't have the guts to do – which was extremely unpleasant for Barbara'.[47] *In Place of Strife* was 'raised in every debate' on the Bill, Eric Heffer recalled; he had continually to 'point out that it was the Government's Bill we were discussing, not *In Place of Strife*'.[48]

Her main tactic of opposition was unrelenting guerrilla warfare, which both left and right found uncomfortable. Every clause was opposed by Barbara making 'the most passionate speeches, attacking this Bill as if it was the work of the devil, totally oblivious to the fact that most people saw it as more or less a carbon copy of *In Place of Strife*'.[49] She had, Roy Jenkins said, spun 'round in a way that made a squirrel in a cage look consistent'. He thought her

actions 'deeply damaging, not only to her own reputation, but to
that of politics generally', and accused her of making 'a most appalling ass of herself, and of the Labour Party, by frenziedly opposing'
the Bill, as a 'monstrous piece of class oppression, despite the fact
that it owed about 80 per cent of its inspiration' to her own White
Paper.[50]

Ted Heath sought to damn her with loud Tory praise, paying
tribute to her 'remarkable courage' in attempting union reform
while in office. Heath and Carr assumed that Barbara intended
nothing but obstruction, and therefore dispensed with the custom-
ary consultations and moved the committee stage onto the floor of
the House instead of in the usual upstairs committee room, almost
immediately introducing their own timetable – a guillotine motion
– the usual channels of communication and consultation on such
matters between the parties having broken down at the outset.

Barbara was told that the allotted time would be ten eight-hour
days, to which she rather predictably replied that she would need a
a minimum of thirty ten-hour days. The Bill's passage 'was remarkable for the intensity of emotion evinced by Labour MPs' still smarting
from the 'trauma' of Barbara's Bill and now spending all night tramp-
ing through the lobbies.[51] The first two all-night sittings dealt only
with clauses one and two: six words were removed and twenty-nine
added, a feat that took eleven divisions.

'The bare statistics of the proceedings are staggering',
Parliamentary Affairs wrote: the Report stage took five days, culminating with a sitting of 21 hours and 41 minutes, 'the longest
since 1881', and involving 63 divisions, breaking the paltry record
of 43 achieved in 1907. In the House there were 21 sittings on the
original Bill with 238 divisions; the Lords had 30 sittings and 138
divisions and a committee stage which lasted for 150 hours, 'an
unprecedented experience for their Lordships' which 'astonishingly
for a legislature used to rising in time to change for dinner ... once
actually sat through the night'.[52]

There were a further thirty-four divisions when the House
considered the nearly 350 amendments from the Lords. Barbara and
her team concerned themselves with debating the principle of the

legislation and 'failed to carry out' the parliamentarians' role of effecting 'improvements in the legislation proposed by the Government'.[53] The result was that all the real work was left to the Lords, 'where the small contingent of Labour peers suffered considerable stress through a number of all-night sittings'.[54] Their Lordships, Lord Shackleton complained, were at the end of their tether.

During a debate on a timetable motion in January 1971 the sitting was suspended after forty backbench Labour MPs surrounded the speaker's chair and blocked the gangway, chanting and shouting. The mace was inadvertently dislodged from the table and was 'carefully replaced' by one MP, in 'a strange deference to constitutional symbolism in the midst of so much partisan excitement'.[55]

The first guillotine fell three days later and Barbara led her troops into twenty-two consecutive votes, which took five hours. In between, Labour MPs played chess, read old copies of *Hansard*, gossiped and, egged on by Tony Benn, broke out into song – 'The Red Flag', 'Cwm Rhondda' and 'We Shall Overcome' – while the Tories 'derisively flicked coins to them across the Chamber'. The party was 'purging itself of Government', Benn noted, meaning the previous Labour government.[56] Eric Heffer was moved by the singing if not the money. 'We had lost the vote, but we were not defeated', he recalled.[57]

But not all the shadow frontbench team were so sanguine. 'We all agreed on the amendments and things', Paul Rose said, 'but in retrospect, that sort of strategy – taking twenty minutes to march through the lobby night after night – I don't think it impressed people outside.' It was of course ridiculous, Tony Benn acknowledged: 'anybody from outside would have thought we were mad', but in his view it was psychologically necessary. It 'did the Party good'. The team could enjoy themselves talking 'about St Crispian's day and fighting the Battle of Agincourt and all that', said Rose,[58] but everyone knew the protest was ritual.

The absurdity in Parliament was amplified outside. The Angry Brigade blew up Carr's house (injuring no one). The unions held a series of one-day political strikes, bringing one and a half million workers out. The TUC held another special conference and a massive rally in Trafalgar Square, attended by an estimated 150,000 people, to which not one member of the previous government was invited to speak.

On 24 February, time ran out on the Industrial Relations debate, leaving 111 of the 150 clauses still not debated. Barbara, making the last speech as the clock inched towards midnight, proclaimed that 'British employers are not saints'. They were almost her last words as the final guillotine fell, accompanied by Tory shouts of 'Gabble, gabble, gabble!' After eight months of operatic opposition it was all over, bar the usual sound and fury.

Barbara thought her opposition to the Bill had been less successful than it might have been, because of Ted's heart problems. She had been tearful, tense and distracted. Shortness of breath now dogged him and he was in and out of hospital, eventually undergoing open heart surgery at the National Heart Hospital. Barbara had been terrified she was going to lose him. They 'quarrelled almost every day of their life', Michael Foot said; it was the way they handled each other. Barbara needed Ted. Ted was always there to have a glass of whisky with after a long day. Ted was always there to listen, to support her, whether she was right or wrong (he had plenty of practice with the latter, Michael joked). 'How could I ever face life if I lived a solitary, self-contained widow's life?' Barbara anxiously confided in her diary.[59] Joe Haines visited her once when she herself was ill, 'coughing so badly that she cracked her rib'. He was astounded when 'suddenly she put her arms around my shoulders and began to cry' because she was so worried about Ted's health.[60] Thinking of Ted's death was staring into the abyss. She could not imagine life without him.

Ted had had a terrible time recently. Rupert Murdoch had taken over the *Sun* and fired him; and, worse, he'd been humiliated when the Labour group on the Greater London Council had not re-selected him as an alderman, in part because of his support for motorways in London, in part because of his age (he would be 63 next birthday). Barbara had come home to Hell Corner Farm one Friday to a broken man, weeping and railing: 'Everywhere and by everybody I am rejected.' She had no idea what failure was like. Her career had gone from strength to strength whilst his went nowhere. He had failed at everything he had tried to do. She could not understand what he was going through, how could she? And what was he supposed to do now? Hang around their flat waiting for the few minutes she could spare him? She had 'never seen him in a more desperate state', she said.[61] He was, he told *The Times*, 'deeply humiliated'. Barbara went to Harold the following Monday and asked him to help Ted; without a moment's hesitation he promised he would. He would make him a peer, he told her, he would do this for Ted; but there hadn't been time before the election.

The Industrial Relations Bill now a done deal, Barbara turned her full attention to the Common Market. A fortnight after the election, the Heath government had begun negotiations to take Britain into Europe (conversations about the whens and wherefores of this second application had been going on during the last term of the Labour government). Barbara's opposition was longstanding, consistent, virulent and public; she had recently become a patron of the newly formed Common Market Safeguards Campaign, along with Ian Mikardo, Peter Shore and Jack Jones.

To a greater or lesser extent, within the Labour Party to be 'pro-Commonwealth was, ipso facto, to be anti-EEC',[62] and this was one of the central planks of her opposition. A decision to enter was a decision to destroy the Commonwealth, not only because Commonwealth countries would lose the UK's preferential treatment for their goods but because immigration priority would have to be given to citizens of the Community: France, Germany, Italy, Brussels, the Netherlands and Luxembourg. Her other main objection was that a Britain in Europe would have to abandon socialist planning and principles.

Harold had been an anti-marketeer in the early 1960s, as indeed had Gaitskell – he would think differently now, his supporters claimed. Midway through his first term as prime minister, Harold had changed his mind, converted to the European way, he liked to say, by an *Economist* article he read on the train. He had tried to take Britain into Europe but had been greeted with a French veto, and he would certainly have reapplied had Labour been re-elected. He was now in an awkward position. Jenkins, his deputy and rival, was maniacally pro; his political base maniacally anti, as were the majority of the party. His other rival, Jim Callaghan, had come up with the neat solution of opposing not entry itself but the Tory terms of entry. There were no acceptable terms of entry for Barbara; she was against the EEC on principle.

The NEC had decided to hold a special conference on EEC entry if parliament had to vote on the issue before the recess. It did not, but Barbara, mindful of the speed of the negotiations, wanted a special conference as soon as possible. In June, she submitted to the NEC a resolution calling for a 'take note' (rather than a decision-making) special conference, to occur after the publication of the White Paper on European entry. Both Harold and Roy Jenkins voted against, but Barbara persuaded a number of people, including Shirley Williams, to vote with her in the name of democracy – after all, this was a merely a 'take note' conference. Shirley's was a 'democratic defection', Jenkins noted, eyebrow arched. The resolution was accepted by thirteen votes to eleven.

The special conference, only the second in the party's history, was held on 17 July at the Central Hall in London. It was carried live on television and Harold came out against joining the EEC on the offered terms. It was, Jenkins said, like 'watching someone being sold down the river into slavery, drifting away, depressed but unprotesting'.[63] Harold had done what he felt necessary, despite the flak he knew he would get from the press: 'he feels he has warded off Jim Callaghan's assault on the leadership', which he almost certainly has', Tony Benn noted.[64]

At the next PLP meeting the following Monday, in one of the House's larger committee rooms, packed with about two hundred and fifty MPs, Barbara and Roy conducted their set-piece debate on entry. Barbara wanted to speak second, the more favourable slot, but Jenkins would not allow it. He pulled rank: he was the deputy leader; he would speak second. Barbara made her case against entry, arguing in part that the objective of the EEC was federalisation, which was never discussed. The EEC ministers had agreed the previous February on economic and monetary union, something which was a long way from a Common Market as it was usually understood. But it was an uncharacteristically bad speech, and Roy's 'demolition of Barbara ... was greeted by such a drumming of desks by the Jenkinsites that the [anti-entry] majority rumbled with rage'.[65]

Barbara saw Jenkins's powerful pro-Europe speech as a direct attack on Harold. 'I used to respect you a great deal,' she snarled at him afterwards, 'but I will never do so again as long as I live.' She told him she would never speak to him again, either. That sentiment, in Jenkins's less than unbiased view, was delivered 'in a voice of controlled hysteria'.[66] Afterwards Tony Benn went down to the Smoking Room and found Barbara making a call to arms to the assembled left-wing anti-Marketeers. 'We must organise, we must fight', she implored. 'It took you right back to 1951 or 1961 – the Party at its worst', Tony said,[67] which is exactly what the Common Market issue had done.

With some notable exceptions, over Europe the party split to either side of the Gaitskellite–Bevanite fault. The most prominent pro-Marketeers were Roy Jenkins, Shirley Williams and Bill Rodgers. (A 'new political party under the surface', as Tony Benn, then pro-entry, observed a decade before they became three of the four founders of the short-lived Social Democratic Party.[68]) The Labour anti-Marketeer leaders were the old Bevanites: Barbara, Michael Foot and Mik, and Peter Shore, a left-winger of a younger political generation.

Even at her closest to Roy Jenkins, during the early days of *Strife*, Barbara had reflected that she could never really trust him because of their mutually incompatible Bevanite–Gaitskellite past. The past was now the present. Common Market entry produced bitterness and divisiveness of the depth and breadth evidenced in the 1930s and 1950s and Barbara was once in the front line. Harold, too, reignited old fires. He attacked the pro-Marketeers, who tended to meet in fashionable watering-holes, by reviving a phrase once slung at the Bevanites. 'A party within a party is no less so,' he said, 'because it meets outside the House in more socially agreeable surroundings.'[69]

The pro-Marketeers were accused of looking at Europe through wine-splattered spectacles. Their propensity for 'working lunches and meetings habitually held in the Reform Club' was evidence that the Market was a rich men's club wanted by rich men (and women). Roy Jenkins, the most prominent example of the breed, was an habitué of fashionable society, a man almost constitutionally uninterested in the workers, 'aloof and superior ... [and] unwilling to swill beer with non-intellectuals'.[70]

The issue of Common Market entry, coming especially as it did after the attacks on the organised working classes by prices and incomes legislation, *In Place of Strife*, Robert Carr's Industrial Relations Bill and the former Labour government's failure to improve the people's lot significantly, strengthened the left within the party. More MPS swung to the left; those already on the left became more so. The Tribune Group saw its membership double in the few years after 1970. The left within the unions was also strengthened, and both the leading left-wing trade unionists, Scanlon and Jones, were anti-Marketeers.

Barbara's outspoken opposition to the EEC, much more than her embarrassing leadership of the opposition to the Carr Bill, put her back in favour with the people she had so alienated. A week after the special conference, she spoke at the Tribune Anti-Common Market rally; as 'a resolute opponent of entry', she was 'glad at last of the opportunity to speak out with absolute freedom'. She used her freedom to attack Jenkins and his allies as people who 'have been trying and plotting to get into Europe for many years'[71] and without whose influence opposition to Heath would be unstoppable. Barbara became the first name on the Tribune Group's recommendations for the 1971–72 shadow cabinet. The 'common ground of all the nominees had been agreed as opposition to entry'.[72]

At the end of July, the NEC voted, by sixteen to six, to oppose entry on existing terms, and the annual conference, which had swung decisively left, carried the resolution by a margin of five to one, calling on all Labour MPs to vote against entry. Public opinion was running 70 per cent against entry and the lead-up to the Commons vote in October was wall-to-wall television coverage, culminating in a three-and-a-quarter-hour programme called *The Great Debate*. It took the form of a mock trial, with David Steel, Christopher Chataway and Harold Lever proposing the motion 'that Britain should now join the Common Market', and Barbara, Peter Shore and Edward Taylor opposing. Witnesses were called; Jack Jones against, Michael Stewart for; and so on. This time, and in 'forensic terms, there was little doubt that the cold, determined passion and fierce intelligence of Barbara Castle won hands down'.[73]

The debate in the House lasted for six days; a hundred and eighty MPs spoke, often to a full gallery and half-empty chamber. When the vote was taken, in defiance of a three-line whip, sixty-nine Labour MPs, including Roy Jenkins, voted with the Tories to approve Britain's entry 'on the basis of the arrangements which have been negotiated', and twenty abstained. The Bill was passed by 112 votes. Feelings ran high. There was 'shouting at Roy Jenkins as he went through the Lobby. It was awful,' Tony Benn noted.[74] Roy Hattersley was so convinced that Jenkins would be physically attacked by 'some of the more aggressive members of the Labour left' that he organised a bodyguard and a getaway car to spirit the deputy leader to a safe house.[75]

The cry went up that the Labour rebels had clinched the vote. If the eighty-nine had obeyed the Labour whip, Heath would have been defeated. Barbara felt violently against Jenkins and the others – but especially Jenkins – because she believed that Heath had indeed only carried the day through Labour support. If the rebels had obeyed the whip, the Labour vote would have been 287, against the Tories' 282, which to be fair presupposes that the Tory anti-Market vote of thirty-nine against and two abstentions would have held if Labour had been united. The Labour pro-Marketeers did not vote with the Tories on the Common Market legislation that followed, but they often abstained, missing several opportunities of

defeating the government as it limped off to Europe with its majority in single figures no fewer than sixteen times during the
committee stage.

That year, 1971, did not end well for Barbara. The left might have
been willing to be pragmatic and get behind her but the interest of
the right was contrary. At the NEC meeting before the annual conference in Brighton in October, the trade-union members of the
Executive, led by her old enemy Joe Gormley, ganged up to prevent
her from winding up the conference debate on the Industrial
Relations Bill. She arrived late, and so did not hear Gormley tell the
NEC that she had 'lost all credibility with the trade union movement'
because of *In Place of Strife*.

Two months later she lost her place in the shadow cabinet, the
only member not reselected. It was front-page news. Ted Short
came first, Michael Foot second; Barbara came fifteenth. It was a
humiliating snub. Jim Callaghan was given DEP to shadow. Michael
was appointed shadow leader of the House, and the 41-year-old
Shirley Williams was made shadow home secretary, the youngest
member of the shadow cabinet. Harold at least came through. He
put Barbara on the Common Market team and gave her Social
Security to shadow, making her the only non-elected member of the
shadow front bench.

Before the election, Dick's idea had been that in the next Labour
government Barbara should be secretary of state at the Department
of Health and Social Security (DHSS). It would be big enough for
her, and she would bring 'panache and drive and imagination' to it,
he told Harold. Win or lose, Dick had decided to edit the *New
Statesman* and write books and he couldn't 'think of anybody
who could replace [him at DHSS] and do the job as well as she
could'.[76]

Shadowing Health and Social Security was a position from which
Barbara could continue to rebuild her left-wing power base. She
certainly had not abandoned the idea that she might become leader
of the party one day. On *It's Your Line* on Radio 4 in November
1971, she was asked whether she would be able to serve under Roy

Jenkins if something happened to Harold and he took over. 'I should have thought that if anything happens to Harold, I might be a candidate myself', she said.[77]

The Industrial Relations Bills, with Major Barbara leading the attack, the retreat and the counter-attack, further radicalised the unions. The Bills 'created a feeling of persecution ... Penal sanctions and industrial militancy fed and justified each other.' In the party it brought class conflict to the fore once again and sharpened class consciousness; there were calls for more working-class MPs. Heath's resolve to force through Carr's Bill did more than anything else to put the party back together. As Barbara remarked dryly, Heath 'had driven the unions back into the arms of the Labour Party'.[78] The political and industrial wings looked close to flapping in left-wing synchrony.

It was Barbara as much as anyone who worked to bring this about. Whether out of necessity or conviction, or conviction born of necessity, she concluded that for a Labour government to be successful it had to share power and responsibility with the unions. It was her old argument recast, the Bevanite argument for a political trade-union movement. She had found – to her considerable cost – that it could not be imposed from above; now she knew it had to be mutually created. 'The most urgent need in the next few years is to develop a new dialogue between the trade union movements and the political one', she wrote. Yes, 'we have to turn a Labour government into a socialist one. But we can't do that unless the trade union movement is socialist, too.' What was needed was to bring about, 'a radical transformation of society, in which we share power as well as responsibility ... The time has come to forge a common strategy.'[79]

Barbara was a member of the NEC group that regularly met the TUC during 1971. The TUC had been in day-to-day consultations with Barbara's parliamentary team and the House of Lords team on the Carr Bill, and in November the party formally invited them to form a joint TUC–Labour Party Liaison Committee, with a 'view to closely involving Trade Union representatives in the shaping of our next Election programme'.[80]

This was first time since the MacDonald rout that there been a formal attempt to bring all the sections of the party together in a regular and systematic way. From the end of February 1972, the Liaison Committee was a formal entity which met regularly and represented a clear-cut decision that the party would never again be a war with the unions.

The eighteen-strong committee had six representatives each from the PLP, the NEC and the TUC. The NEC contingent was the same as the informal 1971 group, with Barbara, Tony Benn and Ian Mikardo the lead players; Harold, Jim Callaghan and Douglas Houghton were the most important of the PLP contingent, and Vic Feather, Jack Jones and Hugh Scanlon led the TUC section. This committee, more than any other party committee, was to formulate the next Labour government's economic, industrial and social policies, including those for pensions, transport, housing and the NHS. Within six months the committee had issued a joint statement on future industrial-relations policies, which included repealing the Carr Bill and the creation of what became the Advisory, Conciliation and Arbitration Service (ACAS), an independent body.

There 'must be a social contract between the trade union movement and any Labour Government to work out together how to expand the economy and raise the real standard of life of the people', Barbara said in summer 1971.[81] Eighteen months later, the TUC–Labour Party Liaison Committee unveiled *Economic Policy and the Cost of Living*, a joint statement of aims and purposes which formed the basis for the social contract between the next Labour government and the unions.

It was launched by Harold and Vic Feather at a press conference. Its main provisos were for subsidies of food and fares, with free-travel experiments in some major conurbations; repeal of the Housing Finance Act, which had forced council rents up; nationalisation of land needed for housing; a large-scale redistribution of wealth and income through taxation; the phasing out of prescription charges; and immediately raising pensions to £10 a week for a single person, £16 for a married couple, to be updated annually in relation to average earnings.

The problem of inflation, which continued apace and was to bedevil the next Labour government, could, the document said, be considered only within the context of a coherent economic and social strategy. And therein was the rub for Barbara. It might be, as she now accepted, that consent had to be mobilised in the fight against inflation, but no consent was forthcoming from the unions for any incomes policy whatsoever, not even voluntary. That was not to her liking. There was 'not an expansionist economist who does not accept that prices and incomes policy is an essential part of the jigsaw puzzle of demand management', she had written,[82] and she had not changed her mind. But she was forced to accept that, for the moment, they had got as much out of the unions as they were going to get.

The party's leftward shift corresponded with a leftward shift in the country. Dissent from below, whether from the shopfloor or from liberation movements – women's, gay, black and others – grew apace. Most young people had never had any illusions about mainstream party politics. Politics to the people who came of age in the early 1970s was about consciousness-raising and direct political action, change from below, the people demanding their rights and fighting to get them, not about relying on moribund political parties.

Top-down government would not do any more. The class system and the power structure it produced and sustained had to be undone. Decision-making had to be collective, democratic, even in the Labour Party – especially in the Labour Party – so that past mistakes were not repeated. From now on there had to be government by consent, Barbara realised, not just with the unions but with the party as a whole. She became, with Tony Benn, a leading proponent of power-sharing.

Within the NEC, they were the main enthusiasts for Participation '72, a huge survey of party opinion that went out to every constituency party. The idea was for members to rank various areas of concerns such as unemployment, education and agriculture (twenty-four in all) into priorities for the party's programme: Nye Bevan's language of priorities spoken, according to Transport House, by some 10,000 ordinary members.

The exercise, which seems harmless enough, was highly controversial. The idea that a political party should actually ask its members what they wanted was 'moonshine', according to *The Times*, a 'confession of political bankruptcy ... [a] bogus and highly disposable public relations exercise'.[83] The establishment press naturally disliked pandering to the masses. It was Tony Benn, more than Barbara, who came under fire as panderer-in-chief. He had dashed up to Glasgow to show solidarity with the embryonic workers' republic of the Upper Clyde Shipbuilders;* they were occupying the Clyde Bank Yard, which was threatened with closure. In 1971, it was his turn to be party chairman. 'Chairman Benn', he was called, 'Big Benn'. His name soon 'became a four-letter word',[84] shorthand for the hard left.

Benn had committed the cardinal English sin of becoming radical in middle age (he was 46). A man who had drifted indolently leftward now hit the shore running. More, he was born and bred a member of the establishment, the son of a peer, the spiritual descendant of Cripps, a made-for-the-tabloids hate figure, a toff who'd gone red. The party's new Red Squire had some of his predecessor's qualities, his teetotalism and frugality, his capital-P Puritan aura, spiced with good looks, a whizkid naivety, a splash of wild-eyed danger: the heretic incarnate.

In his time in government Tony had discovered the enormity of the unaccountable power wielded by bankers and industrialists, and the relative impotence of government in the face of such economic might. And then a simple truth had come for him, a truth stretching over centuries, from the Diggers and the Levellers† in the 1640s to the 1970s liberation movements, perhaps especially the women's liberation movement. Real power comes from below; real change comes from the bottom up. 'The moment in time when history changes is when people stand up and say – and mean – "We won't accept it any more"', he wrote in April 1972, twenty-two years after he entered politics.[85]

---

* The 'First Step towards the Scottish Workers' Republic', pronounced the Trotskyist paper *Red Mole*.

† The Diggers advocated and set up communistic farming communities on common and waste land. The Levellers called for all but the very poorest to be enfranchised, and for the abolition of the monarch and the House of Lords.

Converts are not cautious. At last they know the truth and they want everyone else to know it, too. There was none more passionate than Tony Benn in full oratorical flight. His reckless fluency, his burning passion, could harness and mobilise. He was here, there and everywhere, embracing causes and fans: he made himself into 'a one-man Popular Front', Barbara sarcastically remarked.

Tony was fifteen years younger than Barbara and he was after the mantle of leader of the left – her mantle, as she saw it, Michael Foot's mantle, as others saw it now. Barbara had known him since, as Anthony Wedgwood Benn, he entered parliament in 1950, aged 25, the baby of the House, representing Cripps's old seat in Bristol, and she still called him Wedgie. He began his career in the centre of the party; centre right on some issues, centre left on others. He was not a joiner. The Bevanites pursued him during the 1950s and the Tribunites wooed him ever after, but he did not join the latter until 1981. He was a Bennite, a bit of a one-man band with a halo of acolytes.

From the beginning, they formed a comradeship of sorts. Barbara had supported his bid to rid himself of his peerage,* co-sponsoring (with Roy Jenkins, Michael Foot and a handful of Tory and Liberal MPs) a Bill which would enable him to renounce his title. She considered him 'a good and generous colleague'[86] for his financial and moral support over one of her libel actions. They were at one over colonial affairs; Benn was a co-founder and treasurer of the Movement for Colonial Freedom and a co-founder of the H-Bomb National Committee (a multilateralist, rather than a unilateralist, however). But there was not much in the way of human sympathy between them. The chemistry was not right. They were too competitive, jockeying for place on the NEC, gleefully reporting each other's political ups and downs.

The tension was partly generational. Barbara suspected Tony of continually trying to pull the left-wing rug out from under her.

---

*On his father's death he inherited the title of Viscount Stansgate, which meant automatic expulsion from the Commons. He fought for and won the right to renounce his peerage.

Later, when they were back in government, she rounded on him: 'You with your open government, with your facile speeches, getting all the publicity ... trying to be holier than thou and more left wing than me.' Benn was taken aback. 'Barbara's hatred really came out', he noted.[87] She objected to his posturing; she more than suspected that his highly publicised journey along the road to Damascus from centre to far left, from pro-Market apostate to anti-Market apostle, was motivated more by ambition than by conviction. She objected to his 'political pretentiousness', his annexation of causes, his about-turns. 'His ambition grows by the hour', she thought, watching him back-slapping at the 1974 conference;[88] a lust for the leadership dominated his existence and she thought it would do for him.

By 1971, Tony's 'political star was rising as mine was on the wane', Barbara wrote,[89] and it was true. Never again would she top the NEC poll and from 1972 she never again appeared in the top three slots. In April that year, Roy Jenkins resigned as deputy leader (ostensibly because he objected to the shadow cabinet's endorsement of Benn's idea for a referendum on Europe), and Barbara was re-elected to the shadow cabinet, beating Eric Heffer by 111 votes to 89. Benn, who voted for Heffer, noted that, despite the fact that she was vigorous and active, 'she really has no future'.[90]

Perhaps it was a popular surmise. Barbara was thrown out of the shadow cabinet again at the next PLP election, humiliatingly dropping to third place among the runners-up. She was hurt in a deeply personal way, doubly so because of all the fence-mending and bridge-building she had done. She refused Harold's offer to continue to shadow Health and Social Services and went on to the back benches. But Tony Benn was wrong. Barbara still had a future.

Chapter Eleven

ELEPHANTS AND CASTLE

In the lead-up to the March 1974 general election, Dick came to visit Barbara at the House. He was breathless from climbing the steps; he looked terrible. He told her he had stomach cancer. There was nothing to be done; he had between three months and three years to live. Dick, who had loved good food and wine, scarcely touched his dinner and only sipped his wine. He couldn't concentrate, not even on gossip, the other of his great passions. He wasn't in pain, just 'endless discomfort', he said. He had no energy now, and spent most of his time at his country house.

'My heart ached for him', Barbara wrote. 'My poor, darling Dick.'[1] Over the years, despite violent disagreements, they had indeed 'hunted like two animals of incongruous shapes and doubtful loyalty who were nonetheless inseparable'. Barbara had a love–hate relationship with Dick, and he with her, more love than hate for both of them. He was her bully, indiscreet, mercurial, ruthlessly honest, selfish. Even when she was out of her mind with anger at him, she knew 'political life would be terribly drab without him'. She was his only real friend in Cabinet, his prissy 'Girl Guider', the courageous, vital woman he jaw-droppingly admired; they were an 'amazing pair', he thought.[2] Unexpected.

A month after the election he was dead. 'Dick has died and a great abrasive, tonic force has gone out of my political life', Barbara wrote. 'I shall miss him terribly'.[3] They had been constantly in and out of each other's houses and lives, eaten more meals together and plotted more plots than the average married couple. There was little the one did not know about the other. But her diary obituary is short, just two sentences; her loss is in her 'political life'. It seems hard, unfeeling.

Barbara, though, did not let her private feelings leak out in public (and that diary was written as a public record). As she told Tony Benn, 'anyone who made their diaries too personal would be doing terrible damage to themselves'; indeed she thought Dick had 'emerged as a lesser person through his diaries than he was to those who knew him'.[4] For her taste, his posthumous record was too personal, too emotional, although it was really neither. Her dislike of written emotion was atavistic, visceral, superstitious. She believed that disclosure tempts the gods. When Dick's son, Patrick, killed himself just under a year after his father's death, she was possessed by a 'haunting feeling that this is some grim retribution for publication of the *Memoirs*'.*[5]

To Barbara, emotionally exposing yourself left you open to more than ridicule. She had 'cringed' when Ted poured out his humiliation to *The Times* after losing his alderman's seat; all her 'instinctive reticence' switched on at full voltage. Her autobiography is drained of sorrow. Bill Mellor's death and its devastating aftermath take one paragraph; her beloved father's death not even that. That her sister Marjorie died is mentioned in passing, with her age given incorrectly as 54, the age Barbara would have been at her next birthday in 1964; Marjorie was a week shy of her 57th birthday.

By the time Barbara wrote her story, everyone in her immediate family was dead; including Ted. Her account of his death is mostly about the unorthodox funeral; and her mother's death, one month later to the day, does not get a mention, nor does her brother's. Yet Barbara, often in inverse proportion, was not afraid to show her feelings. She could be, and often was, an openly emotional woman.

---

*The first volume of his cabinet diaries, published in 1975.

She had a reputation at her ministries for being lachrymose, which some people, such as Aubrey Jones of the Prices and Incomes Board and Marie Patterson of the TUC, thought merely switching on the waterworks, one of her many techniques for getting her way. She was even known to weep at press conferences, as she did after the collapse of *In Place of Strife*. *The Times*'s David Wood felt she 'did sometimes cheat on the strict rules of sex equality', and on that occasion, 'as she intended, my heart went out to her. I thought, and probably wrote, what rotters that male cabinet were.'[6] Weeping was a high-risk strategy. A tendency to hysteria and lack of emotional continence were probably items one and two on the 'Why women can't be trusted with power' list that men kept in their breast pockets. But Barbara, who played by her own rules, was not averse to high-risk strategies.

And there is no doubt that her feelings were often entirely genuine. She 'can be very emotional and sometimes when things go wrong she is nearly in tears', Alan Marre* told Dick (who wanted to know how they compared as ministers), 'but the civil servants don't mind that, they feel with her'.[7] In extremis, there could be much for them to feel. When those she loved died, she crumpled, fell apart, wept inconsolably; the ferocity of her anguish, shockingly raw and close to the bone, was utterly disconcerting.

Barbara would be 64 in October 1974 and she decided that this, her ninth election, would be her last. Just as Marjorie's daughter, Sonya, had been at her first election in July 1945, so Sonya's son, Mark, came with her on what she thought would be her last campaign trail in February. Things did not bode well for the Tories. The election was held during an official state of emergency, the third since Ted Heath had come to power. Far from retail prices being cut 'at a stroke', as he had promised, they had risen by 20 per cent the previous year, the fastest rise since 1947. The last monthly trade deficit was £383 million, over ten times the sum that had contributed to Labour's defeat in 1970. To support their pay claim,

---

* A senior civil servant, who worked with Barbara at DEP and Dick at DHSS.

the miners had been operating an overtime ban since November, and the subsequent shortage of coal, plus the reduction of oil supplies due to the 70 per cent price rise in the aftermath of the Arab–Israeli Yom Kippur War the previous October, meant that the country was on a three-day week to conserve power. At midnight on 9 February, every pit came out on strike.

Heath went to the country three weeks later to get an answer to the question: Who runs Britain, the government or the unions? Answer came there none: a hung parliament was returned by 79 per cent of the eligible voters.

Labour had four more seats than the Conservatives (who received more votes), but there were fourteen Liberals and twenty-three others, leaving Labour short of an overall majority. Heath tried and failed to form a coalition government with the Liberals. Harold issued a statement saying he was prepared to form a minority government, which he did on 5 March, the first time that had happened since the MacDonald government of 1929–31. Labour took power on the brink of the worst economic crisis for the West in over two decades, precipitated by the increase in the price of oil.

Labour had fought the election with *Let Us Work Together: Labour's Way out of the Crisis*, the most left-wing manifesto since *Let Us Face the Future* thirty years earlier; it was based on proposals which had come out of the TUC–Labour Liaison Committee, and much of it had been outlined in *Economic Policy and the Cost of Living*. Pensions would increase by 25 per cent and would also increase annually in proportion to average national earnings; new child benefit for all children, payable to the mother, would be introduced. There would be new help for the disabled, including a disability benefit. Price controls on key services and commodities would be enforced; the Housing Finance Act would be repealed. There would be nationalisation of industries vital to the national interest, such as North Sea oil. Land needed for houses, schools and hospitals would also be nationalised. The Industrial Relations Act would be repealed and ACAS set up. The NHS would be expanded, prescription charges abolished and private practice phased out from NHS hospitals. Through taxation, there would be a redistribution of income and wealth. This was the 'social contract' with the unions in which the unions agreed to cooperate with the government and hold their pay claims to reasonable levels.

The *raison d'être* of the new Labour government (on paper) was as the Liaison Committee had decreed: to 'bring about a fundamental and irreversible shift in the balance of power and wealth in favour of working people and their families'.[8] This was to be achieved both through economic and industrial policy and through the social services. Barbara, who, as expected, was appointed secretary of state for health and social security, was to be responsible for implementing the social services side, which consisted of six of the twelve firm commitments in the manifesto. She was to be one of the chief guardians and executors of the social contract.

Michael Foot, at Jack Jones's suggestion, had entered government for the first time, becoming secretary of state for employment. The three other left-wing members of the cabinet were Tony Benn, secretary of state for industry, Peter Shore, president of the Board of Trade, and Eric Varley, secretary of state for energy. With Benn, as he notes, they were the 'four powerful Secretaries of State on the Left … we are a formidable team'.[9] For whatever reasons, Barbara was left out of his left-wing menage. Nevertheless, it was Barbara, Michael, Peter Shore and Tony, who, with their spouses, formed the Husbands and Wives dinning club for left-wing ministers and friends (so called to disguise the political nature of the project from the civil servants and to allay Harold's fear of cabals). The dinners were usually every Tuesday, often in a private room at a restaurant such as Locket's, which relayed the division bell.

Roy Jenkins was once again appointed home secretary, Denis Healey became chancellor of the exchequer, and Jim Callaghan foreign secretary; 'a job I would have liked myself', Barbara said, adding that not even Harold, the first prime minister to have two women in his cabinet, first with Barbara and Judith Hart, then with Barbara and Shirley Williams, could stretch to the idea of a woman foreign secretary.[10]

The new and rising female star, Shirley Williams, entered cabinet to run the newly created Department of Prices and Consumer

Protection. Shirley, twenty years younger than Barbara, could not have been more different, in either style or content. Whereas Barbara was beautifully groomed, buffed and polished, Shirley was shambolic, hair tousled, clothes which looked as though they had been picked up randomly from odd corners of her house. She actually received letters of complaint about her appearance, informing her primly that she was letting the party down.

Barbara and Shirley were disinterested colleagues. They certainly didn't dislike each other and could chat quite amiably, but there was no real connection. Politically they were at variance. Barbara, anti-Common Market Bevanite left, Shirley pro-Market Gaitskellite centrist. Shirley was as chaotic as Barbara was organised, always and notoriously late. She had a wispy, distracted air and no one would have ever called her hard or tough with her soft, sexy, cracked voice and bemused demeanour. She came over as natural, as if she just said whatever popped into her head. Which is not to say she came over as dim, merely as unthreatening. She was disarmingly charming and she didn't provoke the extreme reactions that Barbara did. She had little capacity to annoy people.

At first Barbara was confused by her ambivalence at being back in office. She was reasonably confident that this would be a proper Labour government (I am the guardian of the manifesto, Harold kept telling her) but she was ambivalent about being one of its ministers. She felt intellectually on top of her game, but the frisson power had once given her had evaporated. The excitement of office eluded her: there was, she said, no stardust left. The thought of the rounds of red boxes and meetings and long, impossible cabinets and sleepless nights was depressing.

She would have been furious if she had not got a job, and was sublimely optimistic that she could do this one, but she was detached in a way she did not recognise in herself, even slightly bored, world-weary perhaps, like Harold. He had neither the physical or psychological energy of four years earlier. 'Wading through shit had taken its toll', Ben Pimlott remarked.[11] And Barbara had waded through more and deeper shit.

Even Number 10 was not what it had been. Ted Heath had had

the decorators in, and the results were not to Barbara's liking; it had been tarted up, all gold and white and silver (the colours of a suburban 1970s disco), with sideboards and ornamental bowls. The yachtsman displayed nice middle-class tastelessness, Barbara thought.

Her place at the cabinet table reflected her new relative lack of status. As first secretary she had sat in the centre, directly opposite the prime minister; now she was far from the centre, right down at the end; she was important to the manifesto but not important in government terms. 'Not to worry: I'll be back. I'm no has-been', Barbara declared in her diary,[12] ambition momentarily smothering ennui.

Harold's first pronouncement to his new cabinet was another change: they would call each other by their first names and not with the arch formality of their titles which had previously prevailed. What remained 'unchanged from the old days', as an irked Tony Benn said, was Barbara's cabinet tactics. At their first proper cabinet, 'she wanted her entire legislative programme spelled out in the Queen's Speech'. He thought 'politically greedy ... the only way of describing her'. He scribbled a note to Bob Mellish, who had been brought back as chief whip, suggesting she should 'deliver the Queen's Speech herself'.

She had begun as she meant to go on. A few months later they were discussing pensions, 'or rather Barbara spoke for twenty-five minutes', followed by a reply to a couple of questions from Healey which took a further forty minutes. Benn amused himself by shoving notes across the table to Mellish. 'Perhaps she will have to stop for lack of food', read one. 'It looks as if only the Dissolution of Parliament will stop her.'[13] Harold, of course, would not.

The team Barbara put together at DHSS was made up of David Owen, initially as parliamentary secretary for health, later promoted to minister of state for health; Brian O'Malley as minister of state for social security; Alf Morris as the first parliamentary secretary for the disabled and Jack Ashley as her PPS (this was seen as rather daring, because Ashley was deaf). This time there was to be an additional position created, on Harold's agreement, that of political adviser. This was something both Tony Benn and Barbara had been agitating for. As Barbara had told a gathering of civil servants in 1973, she was determined not to go back into office without 'political support' in the department, a 'political cabinet ... a politician in the private office',[14] not just specialist advisers, but a 'political adviser' who could read through the papers and give her a political take, and for this she picked Jack Straw.

The future home secretary was considerably further to the left in his youth than subsequently. (He once came up with a maximum incomes policy plan for Barbara which would have instituted a 100 per cent tax on pay increases above a to-be-defined level of income.) A former left-wing leader of the National Union of Students, he was a qualified barrister and had been elected to Islington Council where he had met and become friends with Ted, who brought him to Barbara's attention. Both Castles liked him enormously and Barbara found him of 'invaluable help' around the office.

Barbara had a great deal of admiration for David Owen (pre-Social Democrats), too. His moodiness sometimes exasperated her, and his preening, hair-tossing awareness of his good looks left her rolling her eyes, but on balance she felt he made an enormous contribution to the department. The admiration was mutual. Barbara was a 'wonderful boss', Owen said; 'some people only saw one side of her, doctrinaire, dogmatic which is very much not the case.'

He himself, from the vantage-point of the centre right, shared this one-sided view until he worked for her. 'It was a very happy period, a terrifically exciting period. Barbara welded us into a team', involving everyone in all aspects of the unwieldy ministry (nicknamed the Department of Stealth and Total Obscurity) through the weekly sandwich lunch, at which Owen was as involved in the social-security side of the discussions as O'Malley was in the health side.[15] Owen was pleasantly surprised at how opened-minded Barbara was, how willing she was to admit she had been wrong. When she went under protest to listen to a talk on the playgroup movement, which she had pooh-poohed as a lot of 'middle-class ladies with hats', she came back converted and was pleased to say so. Things like that impressed him.

Jack Ashley was equally impressed. He wanted Barbara to set up an Institute of Hearing Research, but she was far from convinced of the necessity for it. The Medical Research Council was opposed and her civil servants unenthusiastic. But she let Ashley put his case. 'She was reflective, weighing the pros and cons', Ashley said; then 'she said quietly but firmly that an institute should be set up'. As usual, once Barbara had reached a decision it was final; 'she brooked no opposition from civil servants or the Medical Research Council' after that, Ashley said. He, like Owen, found her surprisingly 'thoughtful' and 'sensitive' in meetings. 'If agreement could not be reached, she instinctively knew when to overrule and when to give way gracefully.'[16]

Barbara never shied away from dissent not even when it emanated from her own staff and semi-publicly. 'We did disagree, and on a number of occasions', remembered Edmund Dell, her minister of state at DEP and paymaster-general in 1974. 'She would then arrange – this was very admirable – she would arrange for me to go along to whatever committee it was – even if she herself was present – for me to go along and explain my contrary point of view, which was quite a thing for a cabinet minister to do.'[17]

Civil servants, too, were allowed their head. 'We had this permanent secretary, Sir Philip Rogers, who thought her policy on pay-beds* was absolute madness', said David Owen. 'He felt he had to let Barbara know and he insisted on telling her, which could have been very embarrassing. He formally presented the case against what we doing, an absolutely no-holds-barred demolition. She listened, she asked questions, then she summed up and she said, "Well, you've exercised your right to put your view, but we are going to go ahead and I have absolutely no doubt you'll carry this policy out" – which he did.'[18]

---

*To phase out private beds and private practice generally from NHS hospitals.

Barbara had brought one of her closest friends into the department: Brian O'Malley, twenty years her junior, with whom she had
formed an intense friendship, as he had with her. 'Brian loved
Barbara; I don't mean sexually – he just loved her', Gerald Kaufman
said.[19] And she just loved him. He had been the leader of a jazz band
and was the local secretary of the Musicians' Union in Rotherham,
whose MP he had been since 1963. Dick, for whom Brian had
worked at the DHSS, found him a 'strange young man'. He was tall,
gawky, with a 'small head and bespectacled brown eyes',[20] highly
intelligent and full of ideas; he had gone straight onto the fast track,
becoming an assistant government whip in 1964, deputy chief
whip in 1967 and then under-secretary of state at the DHSS.

Brian was on the left of the party and had become a member of
the Tribune Group in the early 1970s. Barbara and he had got to
know each other well during that period when they worked together
on an NEC committee revamping Dick's pension scheme, which had
been scuppered by the 1970 election. 'They had this odd way of
handling each other', David Owen said.[21] She was different with
Brian. It was one of those things. Something clicked. Barbara trusted
Brian implicitly. They meshed, slotted into place; they knew each
other instantly, were free with each other, able to talk about everything, not needing to talk about anything. Their intimacy made Ted
uneasy sometimes. It was exclusive; he was cut out from what
Barbara described as her and Brian's 'deep sense of political matey-
ness'.[22] They luxuriated in their politics. They were conspiratorial,
like giggly schoolgirls, planning their joint futures. A couple of years
at DHSS, Barbara thought, and then she'd go on to something bigger,
the first Lady President of the Council, perhaps (as Harold had offered
all those years ago), with Brian as her chief whip.

Barbara could always imagine a future. It was one of her great
strengths. There's life in the old girl yet, as she liked to tell Harold.
Life in the young girl, as he inevitably replied. Her capacity for hard
work and her mental stamina were undiminished, but physically
she felt the strain more. Once she was back in office she couldn't
sleep properly and she *felt* her exhaustion. Barbara, a chain-smoker,
was plagued by colds and coughs and flus that never quite disap-

peared. But nevertheless she plugged away. This two-headed hydra was the biggest ministry she had run; seventeen- and eighteen-hour days were once again the norm. Jack Ashley often found her in her room after midnight, 'beavering away at her desk on which were piled three or four red boxes'. Mostly she did not let her exhaustion show. She would be up all hours and the next day 'would still be the bright and energetic dynamo, driving the Department relentlessly'.[23]

Her obsession with her appearance was undiminished. She opened her wardrobe and she had nothing to wear; her tights were laddered, her clothes in tatters; she was forever dashing out to buy something because everything she had was ten years old. She tried to get to Xavier's once a week to have her hair done, eating her lunch under the dryer and reading briefs. In her perfect world she would have had a seamstress and hairdresser travel with her, as the Queen did (as she suspected Thatcher did*). In her perfect world she would have had a wife. But at least she had her government driver, a woman driver, who could pop out for tights or lipstick, who could nip down to the shops for bacon and eggs, one of the perks she had most missed in opposition.

Within ten days of taking office, Barbara was before the House announcing the promised increase in pensions and benefits, followed by an announcement that there would be free contraception for all who wanted it, regardless of marital status – 'Barbara's Free Love', hooted the tabloids. The country's prelates descended. The Roman Catholic archbishop of Westminster, Cardinal Heenan, seemed to be of the opinion that she had invented birth control. The letters columns in *The Times* were full of impassioned opposition. It was a rushed decision. It encouraged immorality. It promoted promiscuity. It should be limited to the married. Barbara wrote a long letter in response, refuting each of the 'mistaken statements', an act then unprecedented for a cabinet minister. Harold forbade her to put her name to it; a backbencher, John Cronin, signed it instead.

---

* In February 1975, Margaret Thatcher became the first woman to lead a major British political party, ousting Ted Heath from the Tory leadership.

In contrast to her immediate and glittering press conferences following her appointments to Transport and Employment, it took Barbara nearly three weeks to get around to meeting the press. She had not been in the mood for it. But her announcement of the biggest pension increase ever, coupled with a first-time commitment to link pensions with average earnings, meant that it should not be put off any longer. She was marvellous; she had not lost her performing abilities. But she had lost some of her love of performance.

It was in part that she accepted that she was on her last Westminster lap (although how long that lap would be and whether she would switch lanes she had not yet determined: a couple of years at DHSS then retirement 'or a bigger bid'? she mused). But there was less to play for. She was more relaxed, more detached. She did not worry so much about needing reams of written material to speak from to the House. Office, as usual, became her. 'You look ten years younger', she was constantly told. Barbara's 'vitamin of power' was doing its work. 'Success in politics does as much for a woman's looks as falling in love', she thought. And of course she was falling in love again – 'with success and power'.[24] By June the ennui was lifting, subsumed by the seductions of office.

By June 1974, Ted, too, had a new life in the offing. Harold, as he had promised four years earlier, had made him a peer of the realm, the Baron Castle of Islington. Ted had at last achieved his reward for a lifetime's unstinting service to the Labour Party, and his elevation was greeted enthusiastically. 'Ted Castle has shared in ... [Barbara's] remarkable career without sharing the limelight and it is a pleasure to his friends and colleagues to see him beginning a Westminster career at last', *The Times* exulted.[25]

Ted was immensely popular in his local party, too; despite his wife's cabinet status he had always been willing to canvass door to door, paint posters or do any work asked of him. Few begrudged him his reward, although most of his colleagues were opposed to the Lords; as indeed were both Castles. A second chamber of unelected legislators, whether hereditary or appointed, was not democratic, never mind socialist. But, as has frequently been observed, the Labour left dislikes peerages intensely but tends to accept them when offered.

Ted's decision to take the ermine and forget the nature of the beast was pragmatic. He'd become an alderman for Islington, which was nice but hardly consuming or gratifying. A gregarious man, he was often lonely as well as unfulfilled. He wanted something significant to do, and speaking for the government would be that. If Barbara had any misgivings, she had to swallow them. She had to be happy for Ted. He had, at last, a chance to be part of the parliament he had tried so many times to enter. She need not worry about him any more; his loneliness, his sense of failure, would be washed away.

In an age when the personal was always political, Barbara anticipated criticism that she was selling out her principles. She hated the Lords, but she loved one individual lord and it was 'a poor socialism that leaves no room for the illogicalities of love', she wrote,[26] airing her unease. Her main concern was that she should not have to adopt her husband's title and become Lady Castle. She gave the job of making sure she would not to the ever-resourceful Jack Straw, and Barbara, like Beatrice Webb before her, was allowed to keep her commoner's moniker.

Barbara's two big policy concerns were getting a pension bill onto the statute books and phasing out private practice from NHS hospitals. But her appointment coincided with both rising unionism within the NHS and growing militancy among its low-paid and long-suffering workers, who hitherto had been reluctant to wield the strike weapon. The first-ever series of nurses' stoppages began two months after she entered office; then the radiographers struck, followed by the hospital engineers and the lab technicians and finally, and most significantly, the junior doctors. By July she was complaining that the industrial disputes were sucking up all her time.

Nevertheless, she produced a far-reaching White Paper on pensions within seven months of taking office, which in turn formed the basis of the Social Security Pensions Act 1975. She had thrown out Tory pensions proposals, which 'would have meant means-tested supplements for millions of pensioners well into the next century',[27] and brought in a two-tier plan: a flat-rate basic pension, which was to be increased annually in line with earnings (or prices if higher), and a second State Earnings-Related Pension (Serps) which could be contracted out of by those who had at least an equally good occupational pension.

Only half the population had an occupational pension and the flat-rate pension had never been enough to live on. The thinking behind Serps (based on Dick's pension plan) was to provide a decent pension for all. Serps was calculated on the twenty best earning years and, with the flat-rate pension, would provide a person on average earnings an income of about half their working wage. The Act came into force in 1978 and Serps was set to become fully operational in 1998.

The most significant innovation of the Castle scheme was that the benefits provided for, and the contributions paid by, men and women would for the first time be equal (which worked in women's favour, as they retired five years earlier and generally lived longer). For the first time, too, there would be a widower pension, paid to a man over 65 or unable to work whose wife had died, and the lower married women's contribution rate would be phased out.

Both the CBI and the TUC supported the scheme and both organisations took an 'it depends' view of contracting out of Serps, with, not surprisingly, the TUC philosophically favouring state provision and the CBI philosophically favouring private provision. But, as the CBI all too correctly noted, 'while all political parties have supported the provisions of the 1975 Act, no Government can bind its successors'.[28] So it was to be.

Brian O'Malley had done all the detailed work on the proposals, which Barbara generously acknowledged (although she didn't let him take too much of the credit, making sure she went down to the floor of the House and onto the standing committee, and that it was she who addressed conferences organised by august bodies like *Financial Times*). She was impressed that Brian did not seem to resent the fact that it would be known as the Castle Plan. She held him aloft as living proof that, contrary to popular perception, men could indeed work for women without resenting it. The Castle

Plan's reception was mixed. The *Daily Mail* (like the *Telegraph* and the *Express*, one of her enemies) accused her of straightforward vote-catching gimmickry a month ahead of what was widely assumed would be an October election. It was, its editorial declared, 'one of the most cynical efforts to dazzle the electorate for years'.[29] Other papers were more temperate, seeing it for what it was, a provision for security in old age.

After seven months of limping along with a minority government Harold ended what he called the Short Parliament and called the election for 10 October. Barbara felt on top of her form, which delighted her as this really would be her last election, she told herself. Ten elections and not one lost. That was a good number. A good innings. She hated, she said, people who clung on, keeping the young out. This was really it: her last hurrah. She was returned with her highest majority ever.

Labour did not do so well. It got forty-two seats more than the Tories, but the Liberals took thirteen and other parties a total of twenty-six, leaving Labour with an overall majority of only three.

The issue of the Common Market had not gone away; it had only been renegotiated. As promised in the manifesto, Labour, in the personages of Jim Callaghan, as foreign secretary, and Fred Peart, as agriculture secretary, had been renegotiating the Tory terms of entry, chipping away round the edges of what was, after all, a done deal. In March 1975, the new terms were decreed by Harold to be acceptable and were duly submitted to the cabinet. The cabinet split, sixteen in favour and seven against. The anti-Marketeers, Barbara, Michael Foot, Tony Benn, Peter Shore, John Silkin, Eric Varley and Willie Ross, unsurprisingly rejected the terms.

The terms renegotiated, the decision whether to stay in Europe or withdraw would be, as promised, put to the people in the first-ever British referendum in June. Both sides of the cabinet had made it plain that they would not accept collective responsibility over this issue. Shirley Williams and Roy Jenkins had precipitously stated that they would resign if the government opted to recommend withdrawal. The anti-Marketeers expected the same freedom of speech, and Harold was forced to allow them to dissent openly and campaign for a No vote; an agreement to differ, he called it. They could speak anywhere but at the despatch box. That way he wouldn't split the government and there was little danger in the tactic. A small-c conservative electorate might possibly have voted not to go in, but it was unlikely to vote to withdraw.

Barbara came up with the notion of a Cabinet Ministers Against the Market group, a concerted effort by the cabinet anti-Marketeers, who would be ready with an 'authoritative alternative' to the pro-Market majority as soon as the announcement was made. She had the idea of turning them into a sort of *Tribune* Brains Trust as in the old Bevanite days, touring the county presenting an altern-ative programme for Britain.

Indeed, the dissenting ministers, the 'DMS', as they called them-selves (Judith Hart's nomenclature), lost no time. They issued a statement within hours of leaving the cabinet meeting in which the majority had agreed to recommend a yes vote. It said, 'We believe it is in the true interest of our people to regain the essential rights which permanent membership of the Common Market would deny us; the right of democratic self-government through our own elected Parliament; the right to determine for ourselves how we impose taxes and fix food prices; the right to pursue policies designed to ensure full employment; and the right to seek co-operation with other nations in a world-wide framework.'[30] It was an unprecedented act. They invited their fellow MPs to campaign for withdrawal and their fellow citizens to join them in voting no.

The opening salvo was a press conference for lobby correspond-ents; Harold sent a message to Barbara, asking her not to attend it, but she ignored him. This was followed by a meeting with anti-Market Labour backbenchers which culminated in a hundred members of the parliamentary party signing a declaration urging MPs to campaign for a No vote. The DMS drafted a motion for the NEC, declaring the renegotiated terms far short of what was needed and calling for the party to recommend withdrawal. Ian Mikardo released the document to the press.

Harold, as Barbara noted in her diary, went berserk. Organising an anti-government crusade was not what he had meant by dissent. It was Barbara he went for, in full outraged-husband mode. She was at home for a change, watching the 10 o'clock news when the phone rang. She had never heard him so angry. He screamed down the phone at her that he had been made an utter fool of, accusing her of disloyalty, telling her that no one but he himself would have brought her back into government. She screamed right back, telling him that she was the best minister he'd got and if he wanted her out he could have her resignation. He told her she could have his. Before he slammed down the phone, he issued her with a summons to his room in the House. She wasn't going to go. It was raining and she was marooned in Islington without a car. But then she thought better of it. He was, after all, the prime minister.

That was what Harold had banked on, that Barbara would support his leadership in public, no matter what. She had done so in the past, many times, even on Europe as recently as September 1973, changing her vote on the NEC when Harold had said that if the NEC voted (as the TUC had) for withdrawal, he would resign and they would have a leadership crisis ahead of a general election. He had always been able to count on Barbara's inextricable and often inexplicable loyalty. When it came to it, he had expected his totally loyal little minister to put him first and not to attend the lobby conference, not to be party to the NEC motion, not to speak out in public, perhaps, certainly not to rock the boat so violently.

Barbara found Harold skulking in the gloom of his room with Michael Foot (who had also been summoned) and Jim Callaghan (head in hands). She helped herself to a drink and Harold noted aloud that he had been very insulting to her and apologised. She went over and kissed him on the forehead. She apologised for upsetting him (and she had upset him, she could see that) but told him that she could not back off. Then, bizarrely, Jim Callaghan asked for a kiss, too; he needed it, he said. Barbara obliged. Harold seemed most upset that the statements and the press conference had all been pre-arranged by the DMS (instigated by Barbara, which he didn't know). If he knew that 'I really would be finished!' she thought, alarmed.[31]

The vote on accepting the renegotiated terms was put to the House on 9 April. Only 138 Labour MPS voted with the government; 145 voted against and 32 abstained. The new terms were accepted only with the assistance of the Conservatives, giving the government a majority of 226. The DMS took their show on the road to play to crowds as big as two thousand. The turnout throughout the country was impressive, 'a more revivalist atmosphere that the movement has known for years', Barbara thought.[32] She did a highly publicised shopping trip to Brussels, taking her greatniece Rachel with her to compare the price of her Marks & Spencer outfit in the Brussels store. In turn, Roy Jenkins sent a woman to Norway, which had decided in a referendum not to enter the EEC, and she came back with an even more expensive shopping basket.

The special Labour Party conference on the EEC was held a couple of weeks later. The NEC motion recommending (rather than calling upon) the party to campaign for a No vote was accepted by a two-to-one majority. Barbara was on the platform, sandwiched between Harold and Mik. Harold was in a foul mood, and she wondered whether it was because he was nervous (what kind of speech could he make to keep the party together?) or because of his still-smouldering anger at what he saw as Barbara's Betrayal. The previous evening she had addressed a Tribune meeting, the first time she'd been asked to do so at a party conference, for which honour she was serenely happy. She was no longer *persona non grata* with the left. The fracture was at last healed.

Barbara took part in a televised Oxford Union debate a few days before the referendum. The feelings of inadequacy that Oxford had engendered in her as an apparently noisily self-confident under-graduate forty-five years previously came back and winded her. At the station, assured undergraduates, politely self-important, were there to greet Barbara and Peter Shore. A cloud of fear and panic settled over her. The Union was aggressively pro-Market and the debating chamber was packed, without even a standing place left. The pro-Market Jeremy Thorpe, leader of the Liberal Party, and Ted Heath were heartily cheered, while Barbara and Peter Shore were greeted with boos, catcalls and jeers.

In his speech Thorpe rhetorically asked whether the dissenting ministers would resign if there was a Yes vote or stay on 'like five maggots in the European apple'; he interrupted Barbara's speech to ask her personally for an answer. 'If Britain votes to stay in the Common Market,' Barbara replied, with more chutzpah than was perhaps necessary, 'my country will need me more than ever.' Heath glowered, the undergraduates jeered, there 'were howls of derision', and Thorpe did a little dance.[33] The motion that This House would say Yes to Europe was carried by 493 votes to 92. Not since 1933, when the Union voted Yes to the motion not to fight for King and country, had a union debate garnered so much coverage.

Barbara had not made a good speech and she knew it, although afterwards she defiantly told the undergraduate magazine *Cherwell* that the Union had voted for Europe 'because it seems to them [an] assurance of the top people's jobs ... And mark my words, they'll get fat jobs in Europe, these boys.'[34]

The turnout for the first referendum in British history was not high at 64 per cent. Slightly more than 67 per cent voted to stay in; close to 33 per cent voted for withdrawal. It was 'an election that the Labour Party lost and the Labour government won', as one anti-Marketeer put it.[35] Harold had convinced Labour voters to support the Market against the wishes of the Labour Party in the country, in parliament and on the NEC. It was all over.

The Labour boycott of the European parliament was ended by the parliamentary party two weeks later. Ted, who had campaigned with Barbara for many years against the Common Market, was offered a position as one of the first appointed Labour delegates to the European parliament. Barbara was pleased, she said. This was what she had been praying for: Ted's success, his fulfilment. He was soon converted to the idea of a directly elected European parliament, which Barbara and the Labour Party were then opposed to, but she shrugged it off. It was his turn, she kept repeating, as if she really couldn't object to where he took it: her success had become a debt owed to Ted.

After the referendum there were reprisals against some of the DMs. Harold neutralised Big Benn, moving him from Industry to the less politically important Ministry of Power, a move Barbara thought tactically brilliant, from Harold's point of view, as it made Tony less of a threat to his leadership and less of a nuisance polit-ically. Judith Hart was to be removed from ODM (no longer in the cabinet, but with cabinet status), a job she loved, to Transport, also now not in the cabinet, a job she did not want. Barbara, Michael Foot and Tony Benn went to see Harold to fight for Judith, who they felt was being gratuitously singled out.

'Barbara was great', Tony Benn said afterwards. She had already gone home but she came back. 'I do admire her for that, it was nearing midnight and she had got dressed again after a heavy day, jumped in a taxi and come all the way to the House to save Judith. She fought her corner and even said she would accept being replaced by Judith at the DHSS.'[36] Barbara, Michael and Tony all threatened to resign if Judith was not put in the cabinet at Transport. After all, Harold had given Reg Prentice ODM and put that back in the cabinet because Roy Jenkins demanded it on the pain of *his* resignation. In the event, the only person to go was Hart, who resigned, rather petulantly, from the government the next day, before Harold had come back to Barbara and the others; it was a fit of pique that left Barbara with pursed lips.

Almost immediately upon entering office, Barbara had set up a working party under David Owen to look into new contracts for consultants working in the NHS, and to examine the issue of private practice. The two issues were connected. About 60 per cent of consultants had, by their own choice, part-time service contracts with the NHS to enable them to fit in their private practice. Barbara wanted to manoeuvre them into accepting a contract for full-time service to the NHS, by making it significantly financially disadvantageous to do otherwise. During one Husbands and Wives dinner, she 'talked about nothing but the need to bribe consultants to accept whole-time service in the Health Service', Tony Benn wrote in his diary.[37] Within six months she had offered the consultants a new contract; a 'take it or leave it' offer, the BMA sniffed, 'a thinly disguised attempt to induce all NHS consultants to become whole-time and to abandon private practice'.[38]

The consultants rejected the contract and began a work-to-rule, wherein 'all those services and facilities which consultants normally provide by goodwill beyond the extent of their NHS contracts' were now suspended.[39] This went on for five months until April 1975, when Barbara 'clarified misunderstandings' during an all-night negotiating session which became legendary at the DHSS. 'The dawn was breaking and we were all absolutely goggle-eyed', David Owen recalled. 'We were saying, "Oh Barbara, come on, we've got to finish now. Let's come back to this again tomorrow."' But Barbara was on a roll. Her negotiation technique rested on the belief that whoever has the extra ten minutes of energy wins. 'She said, "No, now's the time, now's the moment, this is it – an 'and' here, a comma there – we've got them against the ropes." '[40]

It was getting on for 6 a.m. and Barbara went down to the doctors and told them it was clear that they could not agree, which sent them into a panic. Within half an hour they had thrown in the towel. 'We're all absolutely aching to go, and where's Barbara Castle? Making herself up!' said David Owen. 'We're all dishevelled, and she bounces into the room absolutely looking like a million dollars – her sheer indefatigableness was amazing.'[41] The less indefatigable Jack Straw drove her home, slapping himself on the face to keep awake.

Having succeed in holding onto the differential for whole-time work in the consultants' contract, Barbara (in politics, guts is all, still and always) decided that this was the moment to go on the offensive over phasing out the almost five thousand pay-beds – about 10 per cent of all beds – from NHS hospitals. The existence of this two-tier system caused great resentment, not only among patients, who objected to queue-jumping through payment, but among hospital staff, who received none of the extra lucre but were expected to cater to the private patients' special requests. In some hospitals, most famously Charing Cross Hospital in London, the lowest-paid of the NHS workers, kitchen porters, orderlies etc, members of the National Union of Public Employees, led by Esther Brookstone, the tabloids' 'battling granny', began an emblematic struggle to get the private wing of the hospital – built, of course, with NHS money – opened up to all.

Added to the class resentment was race. Many private patients were foreign – 'rich Arabs' was the generalised description – their wallets stuffed full of hoarded petrodollars,* and they were pleased to pay £180 a week for their board and lodging and have their meals served and their floors cleaned by people earning less than a tenth of that. Brookstone, who declared that the very sight of Daimlers and Rolls-Royces caused her offence, set a deadline for the ward to be open to everyone. If not, she threatened, all services – food, laundry, porters, everything – would be withdrawn.

The BMA called on Barbara to condemn the action unequivocally. She would not. She made a statement sympathising with the aims, if not the actions, at Charing Cross and emphasised that it was party policy to phase out private practice from NHS hospitals. The BMA pronounced itself 'shocked and dismayed that the Secretary of State reacted so ineffectually . . . In fact, the BMA suspected' that this union action was 'not unwelcome to Mrs Castle'.[42]

Its suspicions were correct. Ending private practice in NHS hospitals was a passion for Barbara. She intended to undo the deal Nye Bevan had made with the doctors when he had, in his own words, 'stuffed their mouths with gold' by allowing them to continue private practice within the NHS as a bribe to work for it at all. Barbara told delegates to the 1973 and 1975 party conferences that 'We shall complete Nye Bevan's work by eliminating private practice from our National Health Service' and that she was 'proud of the fact that it has fallen to me to complete the work that Aneurin Bevan began'.[43]

The NHS was socialism incarnate, the 'unique expression of the unity of human society,' Barbara said, 'from each according to his ability when he is well and can afford to pay through taxes; to each according to his medical needs when he cannot pay because he is sick.' It was the 'brightest jewel in our socialist crown, a living

*Unrecycled oil money; the unspent billions sent the world into recession.

expression of our common humanity'. Yet in the middle of this lurked the 'canker of commercialism' that allowed queue-jumping.[44]

In her Nye Bevan memorial lecture she pointed out that the 'compromise which allowed pay beds to operate within the comfort-able cocoon of NHS hospitals, buttressed by all the specialist services these hospitals could provide in an emergency, enabled doctors to evade the test of just how much people are prepared to pay for private medical care when they have to pay for all of it'.[45] Separation would test private practice's ability to be self-supporting.

Barbara always made a point of saying that she had no intention of abolishing private medicine (which conference voted to do in 1975). The doctors didn't believe her. She was politically and instinctively opposed to private medicine, and they knew it: after she left office, she told the 1978 conference that 'Profiteering out of sickness is an immoral monstrosity.'[46] But she reluctantly accepted that in a free society it could not be outlawed, just corralled. She intended to regulate it so that it didn't grow like Topsy. Her aim was to ensure that, after pay-beds were phased out, private health care in Britain should not exceed 'that which obtained within and outside the NHS in March 1974'.[47]

She would control the fees, the standards, the location and the size of private facilities, and regulate advertising. She intended to keep private medicine on the periphery, of minority interest. She did not intend it to become a rival to the NHS which would lure away all the doctors and nurses trained at public expense. She did not intend to allow a two-tier health system to develop.

Politically, the BMA, Tory (and male) almost to a man, were disposed to dislike Barbara. They 'seemed to resent' her 'sex, let alone her politics'.[48] Most of the senior doctors she was dealing with had been doctors before the NHS was established in 1948 and seemed, or pretended, to believe that the deal they had struck with Nye was to last in perpetuity.

David Owen (himself a doctor but one who had never practised privately) thought Barbara had an 'archetypical lefty view of doctors as all on the make, all interested in money'.[49] If she did it was bolstered by her dealings with the obdurate souls at the BMA who tenaciously clung to every vestige of privilege. Divorcing private practice from the NHS was, the BMA claimed, 'perhaps the greatest threat to the independence of the medical profession since the controversy associated with the NHS 30 years ago'.[50] Which is to say since its establishment, decried by some doctors at the time as the first step on the bumpy road to fascism. They did not intend to be on the wrong end of this new controversy.

It was almost a rerun of *In Place of Strife*: Barbara versus entrenched powerful vested interests with friends in high places, in this case predominantly Harold Lever, the chancellor of the Duchy of Lancaster. Tony Benn thought it would not be long before Lever was put in charge of the pay-bed issue and Barbara was 'edged out, moved or made a peer'. Lever was in 'continual touch with the Royal College of Physicians and he tells them everything that is going on'.[51]

In August 1975 Barbara produced her paper, *The Separation of Private Practice from NHS Hospitals: A Consultative Document*, which was treated by the BMA like a declaration of war. Lawyers were hired, battle-plans drawn up, threats issued. In November the government's commitment to legislate on pay-beds in the forth-coming session was spelt out in the Queen's Speech. All eyes turned on Barbara. The consultants' response was immediate: they would join the junior doctors and do no work for the NHS except in emer-gencies.

The junior doctors were working to rule in protest over their pay claim. It had been mangled by the new maximum £6-a-week pay-increase deal, which had come into effect in July, leaving a third of them effectively worse off than before. For them, 'the suspicion remained that Barbara Castle had deliberately postponed the date of implementation for the contract in order that its pricing would be caught within the paycode',[52] which wasn't true. It was Michael Foot, Barbara's fiercest critic over prices and incomes, when she was employment secretary, who, she was amused to note, had become a fierce guardian of the pay code, 'more rigid than Jim Callaghan in his Chancellor days'.[53] He wouldn't budge for the doctors or anyone else. And the TUC would not have looked kindly on the juniors busting through a pay code they themselves had approved as part of the social contract.

The public were confronted with the 'sight of white-coated doctors brandishing banners and walking off the job at 5 o'clock' and the even less edifying spectacle of 'small boys and girls unable to gain admission to ... Gt Ormond Street ... old people wrapped in aluminium foil for warmth ... police guarding army ambulances on emergency civilian duties'.[54] And the message from the doctors was Blame Barbara Castle, which the press increasingly did.

The press attacks on her became a daily occurrence, which at least made her a heroine with Labour backbenchers once again. She could bask in the warmth of their trust. The press could hound her, the Tories censure her, but her people trusted her. Ian Wrigglesworth, Roy Jenkins's PPS, collected 170 signatures for an early day motion supporting Barbara in her war over private practice.

'Barbara-baiting is a national sport', she said. It was much worse than the way Nye had been treated. She understandably took it personally, and the attacks were very personal. Although she was only a couple of years older than Jim Callaghan and younger-looking than the emaciated Michael Foot, her age became a deadly weapon. She was 'ageing' whereas they were 'veterans'. She was an old woman, with all that that implied; a crone, a witch; wasn't it time she retired? She bitterly regretted putting her birth date in *Who's Who*. No one would have guessed she would be 65 next birthday. It seemed to her as if there was an orchestrated campaign to oust her. 'Why do the press hate me so?' she wondered.[55]

Once they had loved her, their glamour-girl in the red dress. Now they hated her and her ideas. The 'scarlet bogey' had awoken, forgetful and sleepy. She had forgotten that what she was pleased to call the Tory press would take only so much socialism. To the press, with the exception of the *Guardian* and *Sunday Times*, Barbara's attempts to kick private practice out of public hospitals was all of a piece with nationalisation and industrial democracy and the move to make schools comprehensive. It was a level playing-field too far. It was class warfare, the papers said.

Her 'political arteries have hardened', wrote the *Mail*; and 'while her own arrogance and intransigence sustain her during these last days in her self-built psychological bunker, outside there is full-scale medical devastation. The kindest thing to do would be for Harold Wilson to release her. She must go.'[56] 'Intransigence' was their favourite word. She could have backed down, of course. She could have given in to what she saw as the consultants' blackmail, she could have arrived at a fudge, kicked the issue down the road by giving it to a royal commission, which is what the consultants wanted. She could have been less intransigent.

But it happened to be a principle in which she, rightly or wrongly, believed. Yes, she was glad that she was the left's Joan of Arc once again (and the right's shrill harridan); yes, she thought the pay-beds issue politically important for the party; and yes she loved the fight, taking it to the brink, no less than she always had. But there was something else, something that underpinned her life: 'if one has a conviction that a certain course is right, the only thing to do is to stick to it, whatever the risks', she said over and over again.[57]

It was the simple, clear message of her ILP youth: 'The revolutionary ... is the man who presents an idea to his fellow human beings which he believes to be right, in a tone of voice that will make them listen, and stands by it in a minority or majority'; and from this she had never wavered. Removing pay-beds from the NHS was right and necessary, both ideologically and morally, and she was willing to stand by it, in a minority if necessary. It was what her father would have done. It was what Bill Mellor would have done. Nothing shifted them from what 'they believed to be right, no matter how inconvenient or dangerous it was to them personally', she said.[58] Little shifted Barbara, either.

Harold, the pragmatic premier, operated by different rules. This fight was not worth it. He 'wasn't prepared to go along with Barbara'. He'd been to the precipice with her once, and he was not prepared to return. 'He wasn't going to do *In Place of Strife* again', Joe Haines said.[59] It was not Harold Lever who took over pay-beds, but Arnold Goodman, a lawyer who gave advice to Labour politicians and had been used by Harold for various missions, but who did not take the Labour whip in the Lords. Most recently he had represented the doctors, advising them how to fight the pay-bed legislation, but he withdrew his services when they came out on strike. Goodman's sympathies lay where his legal advice had recently been given, a fact that Harold knew when he summoned him to cobble together a deal.

Goodman, a man both wide and tall, thick of eyebrows and baggy of chins, was licensed by Harold to settle the pay-beds dispute over Barbara's head if needs must. In his 'often traumatic' meetings with the BMA, Goodman found that most of the doctors 'had developed a positively insensate hatred' for Barbara and that the 'very mention of her name aroused fury'. The situation, he said, was 'thoroughly bedevilled by her own total intransigence in the matter, including antagonising the moderate elements in the DHSS'.[60]

In Goodman's account, when he suggested to the consultants that they had to resume discussions with the secretary of state, the 'howl of dissent that came from the entire room staggered' him. We will never 'meet that woman', they told him. Never. They would, of course, meet Harold. Harold was in Rome attending the European Summit. Goodman phoned him and he agreed (readily, according to Goodman), even though this would inevitably undermine Barbara's negotiations. 'But who will tell Barbara?' a nervous Harold asked Goodman. 'Will you?' Goodman refused. He did 'not get danger money', he replied.[61] Did not the prime minister have aides and secretaries to do his dirty work?

Functionaries at Number 10 duly told functionaries at the DHSS what was afoot. It was left to Norman Warner, Barbara's private secretary, to break the news. Not only had Harold agreed to this meeting but the invitations to the doctors had gone out with nary a word to her; and not only that but the press had been informed. It was worse than an insult. The prime minister was publicly proclaiming that he was sidelining his secretary of state, that he agreed with the press criticism. He was, in effect, removing her from her post as the *Telegraph*, *Daily Mail* and others had demanded.

Barbara went to see Goodman 'in one of the intensest furies' she had ever felt.[62] She went for him, no holds barred. She was the custodian of this policy, a manifesto commitment, she was the one answerable to the party, to parliament. He had gone over her head to Harold without consulting her. She had never, she said, been so insulted in all her life. She was outraged, deeply wounded, furious, a condition Goodman later acknowledged was more than justified. The 'good lady let fly', said he, but treating her thus was 'an intolerable affront'.[63]

Barbara sent a minute over to Number 10 telling Harold she wanted to speak to him before he met the consultants the following day. The meeting with the doctors was scheduled for 11.30 a.m. and his office promised to be in touch about a time for a meeting. Having heard nothing, Barbara now almost insensate with anger, arrived at Number 10 at 11.15, whereupon there ensued one of Barbara and Harold's meltdown rows. He wasn't to be told he couldn't negotiate or that he should leave it to her, he thundered. She accused him of playing into the hands of the critics who claimed it was her personality that was to blame. Did he seriously think that Attlee would have usurped Bevan in such a cavalier fashion? demanded Barbara. Of course not!

Goodman arrived for the meeting with the BMA, to which Barbara had still not been invited. She was not going to be left out. They were not going to make a fool of her like this; she marched after Harold into the cabinet room. What was he going to do? Throw her out? Tell her she couldn't stay? She was angrier than ever, beyond caring, but determined not to back down. She sat beside a tired and irritable Harold, annoyed at his alternating unctuousness with the doctors and rambling discourses.

As the meeting progressed, Harold, who had started out by saying they were not negotiating this morning, just listening, began to give away the store. He agreed, or seemed to agree, with Goodman's compromise, which gave the consultants what they wanted, including the retention of most pay-beds and a market-driven increase in private practice. Barbara seethed. Something 'very near hate is beginning to smoulder in me', she wrote.[64] Harold had trapped her.

How was she going to get out? Or, rather, what was she going to get out of it? What kind of policy could be salvaged? Harold had sold her out. Barbara knew she was going to have to make a compromise of her own.

Something had gone wrong with Barbara and Harold's relationship, something had been eroded. In the immediate aftermath of *In Place of Strife*, they had clung to each other, kept each other afloat. Against his better judgement, Harold had let her do what she needed to do. He had distanced himself somewhat from electoral defeat, going off to write his elliptical apologia,* getting one of his few good reviews from the publicly loyal Barbara. He had refused her a chance at the deputy leadership, of course, but it was Harold, much more than Barbara, who had moved away from their previous intimacy.

Then Europe had come between them, first in 1971 and more significantly in 1975. But they had drifted apart in some fundamental way that was beyond political disagreement. 'By 1974 he seemed a little frightened of her; even bored by her increasing shrillness', observed Bernard Donoughue, Harold's senior policy adviser.[65] Leaving aside the touching portrait of the henpecked prime minister, there was something to what he said. Harold didn't quite trust her any more, perhaps. Perhaps, once the after-shocks had ceased, he blamed her for the failure of *In Place of Strife*.

Barbara, who had of course lost the most over *Strife*, missed their old conspiratorial closeness. Harold still let her have much of her way in cabinet, but it was pro forma. He rarely praised her or thanked her. She felt he no longer appreciated her. When he did she was ecstatic. 'We are almost back on the "little Minister" terms', she noted when Harold told her what a good job she had done with the pension scheme. 'Perhaps I am beginning to come out of my eclipse.'[66] But she was not. There was worse to come.

* *The Labour Government, 1964-1970: A Personal Record* (London: Weidenfeld & Nicolson, 1971).

*

At the beginning of 1976, Barbara told friends and confidantes that she intended to retire from the government in the autumn, after the pay-beds legislation was through. What she called the 'steady drip of denigration' which went on in the right-wing press day in, day out, had taken its toll. And not only on the right. The 'Left' (meaning the hard left) on the NEC also sought to denigrate her: she, of course, took the blame for the sell-out over pay-beds.

On the evening of 4 March, Barbara went to see Harold and told him what she had in mind. And he told her what he had in mind, speaking to her, he said, as an old, loyal friend: he, too, was planing to resign. On the one hand, he said, he'd had enough; on the other, when he took office he had told the Queen the date when he would go, so no one could say he was pushed. Barbara did not want anyone to say she had been pushed, either. She pressed him to ensure that the pay-beds legislation, even in its current, neutered form, would go through this session. It would, he assured her, it would. Harold refused to tell his old, loyal friend the date he had given the Queen for his departure, but intimated that it lay six or so months into the future. Barbara was glad she had done the right thing and spoken to him. She was sure he would do the right thing, too, and facilitate her graceful exit.

Twelve days later, less than a week after his sixtieth birthday, Harold announced to a stunned cabinet that he was giving up office. Such was the shock that no one spoke for what seemed like close to a minute. Barbara felt close to tears, although she was not altogether certain why. Always keeping a-hold of Nurse, for fear of finding something worse? That might have crossed her mind. Jim Callaghan spoke second, to fill the silence with a cracked-voice thank you to Harold for all he had done; Jim was certain to throw his hat into the ring. Michael, Barbara told Shirley Williams as they sat writing a tribute to Harold for the press, Michael should stand as the compromise candidate. She grabbed him at the end of cabinet and told him he must stand, but Michael had already decided that he would.

Later, as the shock wore off, Barbara wondered what Harold was up to. Suspicions and annoyance began to multiply. His precipitous action seemed gratuitous, even frivolous. He had ducked out in mid-term, throwing the party into turmoil, and he 'certainly hadn't bothered a whit'[67] about how his premature departure would affect her retirement. That she had taken him into her confidence, to give him full due warning, to have done the right thing and not resigned on *him*, had meant nothing. He had resigned on her, his old, loyal political friend. Moreover, he had told Jim of his plans and, even worse, had told him the job was his for the taking.

Barbara wandered around trying to drum up support for a 'Stop Jim' movement. She knew she was for it if Callaghan walked through the doors of Number 10. Her only hope lay in Michael winning the leadership contest. 'Wedgie, we all agree the future is yours,' she told Tony Benn, who was thinking of standing,[68] but the present was not. The left had to be united behind Michael. Brian O'Malley threw himself into Michael's campaign, as did Neil Kinnock; the 'lively youngsters', Barbara called them. There was hope yet.

And then suddenly there wasn't. Brian collapsed in the House and was rushed to hospital. He had had a brain haemorrhage. As they put him in the ambulance, he told Barbara that he had already voted. It was the sort of thing she would have told him in the circumstances: they lived for their politics. The following day Brian underwent brain surgery. 'Worrying about him, the heart has gone out of me', she wrote.[69] He never regained consciousness. Nine days later he was dead.

Five contenders entered the contest for the Labour leadership, Michael Foot, Jim Callaghan, Tony Benn, Roy Jenkins and Denis Healey. Michael came top of the first ballot, but only six votes ahead of Jim. Jenkins and Benn dropped out of the second ballot; Healey who had done least well, with only thirty votes in the first round, did not. This time Jim got eight votes more than Michael. Denis Healey, who had gained only another eight votes in all, dropped out, and on 5 April a third ballot was held.

Jim Callaghan won by 176 votes to Michael's 139. Barbara, who had been trying to delude herself that she was indifferent to her fate, suddenly realised how desperately she wanted to stay in office. If she hadn't realised it before, Michael had. Accepting that he would be defeated, and knowing the profound antipathy Jim felt for Barbara, Michael had already been to see him and asked him not to fire Barbara. But Harold had betrayed Barbara's confidence. He had told Jim that she planned to retire. (How had that come up? Had Jim told Harold he was going to fire her?) Michael promised Barbara he would go back and tell Jim she wanted to go with dignity, after the pay-beds legislation was through. They agreed that she was surely owed that much.

Right up to the last moment, Barbara could not really believe that Jim would sack her, even when he cancelled his first cabinet and called her to Number 10. She did not deserve it. Even he would be above that, surely? But he was not. Firing Barbara was one of his first acts as prime minister. On 8 April 1976, at about 10.45 a.m., five days before she was supposed to introduce the Health Service Bill* to the House, Jim Callaghan snuffed out Barbara Castle's political life.

Thirty-one years they had been in the House together; ten years in government, the Darby and Joan of mutual loathing, always inches away from each other's throats. She tried to negotiate a little more time to finish the pay-beds business; she tried to cajole, to sweet-talk, to point out the error of his ways; she tried whatever she could to postpone the inevitable. He offered her the Lords. You can 'stuff it', she told him.[70] She was not going to let him off so lightly.

Michael Foot went back to Jim to plead her case. This is the one thing I cannot give you, Jim told him. It was final, inevitable, inexorable. It was an Old Testament 'I divorce you'. He was not open to negotiation or special pleading or compassion; he would not wait for her to go on her own terms: he was too enchanted by the glow of his vindictiveness. 'I had to end Barbara's career', Jim remarked to Tony Benn a few weeks later;[71] it was a deus ex machina; he could not help himself.

* The pay-beds legislation.

Chapter Twelve

FOOTFALLS ECHO

Brian O'Malley's funeral was held in his home town of Rotherham. The Westminster funeral party went up by train. Barbara, crammed into the carriage with Margaret Jackson,* David Owen, Jack Straw, Michael Meacher and Stan Orme, sobbed almost uncontrollably for most of the journey. They followed the coffin to the church, both Barbara and Margaret Jackson, coatless, freezing in the April winds. As soon as she stopped being a minister, Barbara had lost her car; she had also lost her place in the front pew of the church where cabinet ministers and local dignitaries were seated. She sat behind them, crippled with grief.

Outside the church, the party huddled together, waiting for transport. The crowd spotted Barbara, surrounded her, mobbed her as if she were a pop star, women mostly, calling her name, calling her 'love', trying to grab her hands, to touch her. 'It was a terrible thing what that Callaghan did, love', they said.[1] Such adulation in the midst of so much grief; her heart fractured, she was filled with an all-pervasive sense of loss: Brian, her ministerial career, her life, drained away like dishwater.

Being fired absolutely devastated Barbara, crushed her, even though on one level she had known it would come. One of the lowest

_____

* Now Margaret Beckett.

points of her life was walking into the House afterwards, for the first time as a former cabinet minister, stripped of office. Everybody's eyes were upon her as she made her way to the back benches. She felt naked, humiliated, mortified. The habit of authority died hard, she found. She couldn't believe that she wouldn't be conducting her negotiations with the Treasury or the doctors. She just couldn't believe it.

That Jim should discard her 'like so much old junk', as she said,[2] was utterly unforgivable. Despite their exhaustive contempt for each other, they were still members of the same party, the same movement. She had given fifty years of her life to the party and he had treated it as if it were *nothing*. He had had the brass neck to say that he wanted to give his government a younger profile, he, who was 64 and had taken over from a younger man. She had thought Michael would save her. She thought he should have; he was her oldest comrade and one of her oldest friends. She had known him for over forty years, longer than she had known Ted. They had been young together; he had known her as a precocious, idealistic 25-year-old; he had known Bill Mellor; he had loved her. He should have fought harder, he should have threatened to resign and done so if necessary. She would have done that for him; she would have done that for any of her close comrades. She and Michael and Tony Benn had threatened to do that for Judith Hart. But neither Tony nor, more importantly, Michael, whom Jim needed to hold the left, had done that for her. She felt totally alone. Ted was away in Brussels. She broke the news over the phone. She wished more than anything that he was with her.

The press reaction to Barbara's expulsion was more or less predictable. She was out of favour. It was one thing to take on special-interest groups like the publicans and the motorists over the breathalyser, it seemed, because she had *won*. Now it was bemoaned that she had battled with the unions but failed to get her legislation through, then battled with the doctors to similar end. 'Those who disliked Mrs Castle say that she cannot imaginatively comprehend the identity or integrity of an opposing view, and thus produces the temper to subdue the weak and the tears to cajole the strong. The bridge to true compromise, they say, is lacking', wrote *Guardian* columnist Terry Coleman.[3]

There was much written about her tears and temper tantrums, which, as the *Tribune*, perhaps alone, pointed out, were tactics by no means 'confined to the fair sex as Lord George-Brown would testify'. The *Tribune* was sympathetic, and so was the *Sunday Mirror*, which called in its editorial for a word of thanks to Barbara. She had, it declared, 'aroused more venom than any other British woman politician, past or present'. She was, it might have added, the only British woman politician to have been important enough to arouse such venom. More venom yet would be aroused, the *Tribune* predicted. She was now 'without the straitjacket of collective compromise'. The writer gleefully hoped she would give them hell; cracking his morning egg he felt 'safe in the knowledge that she will do just that'.[4]

He did not have long to wait. Barbara was not going to curl up and die. She had intended not to run for the NEC again in 1976, but now changed her mind. She was not going to lose that power base. On the day Callaghan sacked her she had vowed to herself that she would 'go to the backbenches and fight this reactionary new Prime Minister',[5] and go she would: onto the NEC, onto the committees, into the newspapers.

She would fight to the death to protect her legacies, the phasing out of pay-beds, NHS reorganisation and child benefits. She had insisted and insisted, against opposition from the whips, that she be put on the standing committee for the Health Services Bill to make sure David Ennals, her successor at DHSS, gave nothing more away on pay-beds. And onto the standing committee she went. She took a line-by-line approach, as they say. Nothing was going to get past her.

When Ennals announced that the introduction of Barbara's Child Benefits Bill was to be postponed indefinitely, she began a sustained, relentless campaign to force the government to enact it, beginning with an emergency NEC motion that the NEC 'deeply regrets the decision of the Government to postpone the introduction of the child benefit scheme'.[6]

Under the existing system, tax relief and family endowment, for the second and subsequent children, went to the – predominately male – breadwinner through his pay packet. The new system, with child benefit paid for every child and paid directly to the mother, was a manifesto commitment which it had fallen to Barbara to enact. She had published her Bill in April 1975, and the reforms were supposed to come onstream in 1977.

In the *New Statesman* and the *Tribune*, she wrote articles decrying the government's perfidy. There wasn't a Liaison Committee meeting where she did not criticise Callaghan, who had never liked this transfer from father's wallet to mother's purse. As chairman of the NEC's Social Policy subcommittee she was in a strong position to make a colossal nuisance of herself and she did, not just over child benefits but over everything else as well, trying to set the DHSS's agenda from this powerful back room. It took her two years to get the government to reinstate her Child Benefits Bill, which she eventually achieved by instigating a threatened backbench revolt during the 1978 budget debate.

Barbara was accused by her enemies in the party of not being a good loser, of being an embittered critic of Mr Callaghan and all his works, of making personal political capital out of her personal political tragedy. She certainly – and unsurprisingly – wanted to damage the prime minister for what he had done to her. But she also disagreed with the direction the government was taking. At the 1976 party conference, Jim announced that the old social democratic shibboleth that you could spend your way out of recession was no longer an option. From now on public expenditure was going to be cut, cut and cut again.

The arguments over those cuts that she would have had in cabinet were now conducted in the more open arenas of the NEC, the PLP, the Liaison Committee, Conference and the *Tribune*. She said nothing that she would not have said in cabinet and she opposed everything that she would have opposed in cabinet. It was embarrassing for Jim Callaghan and it made his life difficult. 'I hope what I say won't be taken as a criticism' was often an opening statement by Barbara to Jim in committees, and, as Tony Benn remarked, this 'meant that that was exactly what it was'.[7]

The announcement in July by Denis Healey of further cuts in public expenditure was 'old-style Tory deflation', she wrote on the front page of the *Tribune*, 'an advance obeisance to the demands of the International Monetary Fund'.[8] There was no more public-expenditure fat to trim, she told the PLP, in what was in Tony Benn's view a 'marvellous speech'. She called for import controls and temporary mobilisation of overseas assets and a complete change of policy. This time she came under attack from the harder left. Eric Heffer greeted the speech by sarcastically welcoming her 'conversion to Party policy'; some of us had thought all this 'before they were reshuffled out of Government', he said.[9]

At the 1977 conference, Barbara, as chairman of the NEC's Finance and Economic Affairs subcommittee, made the major speech in the economic debate, which Jim Callaghan, interestingly, thought 'helpful'. Perhaps he did not listen carefully, or was merely thankful that she mentioned that the government had had to struggle through what 'must have seemed to be insurmountable obstacles', which is to say the ongoing financial crisis, which was not of its making (although some might argue it made it worse) and which, as Barbara put it, had driven 'us into the arms of the IMF'.[10]

The bulk of Barbara's 'helpful' speech was a critique-cum-attack on how the government had lost its way over the past year, operating 'conventional deflationary policies' forced on them by the IMF, which could not 'stimulate economic activity, increase our standard of life or create jobs'. Reserves had trebled since the IMF loan was negotiated, so it was time, she said, to 'thumb our noses at the IMF'.[11] On the NEC Barbara continually called for the IMF to be defied or ignored. Her clashes with Jim were frequent and fierce. The prime minister, she declared, was running a government practising near-monetarism.

In the end it was not Barbara who brought Jim Callaghan down; he did it all by himself. He made two tactical errors. He imposed a 5 per cent maximum wage increase, in the face of TUC and party opposition, only to see it immediately ignored by Ford, which gave its workers 15 per cent. (The government's attempt to impose sanctions on the company was defeated in the House.) And he took

Michael Foot's advice and did not call the election for the autumn of 1978.

By the end of the year, Britain was living through the famous 'Winter of Discontent', with strikes followed by more strikes: dustmen, local authority workers, hospital porters, ambulance drivers, street cleaners, school caretakers, and even, in Liverpool, gravediggers. A million local government workers stopped work in January, the biggest one-day stoppage since the 1926 general strike. Television coverage homed in on each unburied body and each pile of rubbish.

The recorder of disorder, television itself, was affected on and off by striking technicians, until the BBC awarded them a 15 per cent pay rise so that the public would not be deprived of the Queen's speech and *The Sound of Music* on Christmas Day. Civil servants walked out, paralysing government. Water went unpurified. Lorry drivers, operating an overtime ban, failed to deliver petrol. Pickets flew here and there. The weather was foul, freezing, with constant blizzards, the worst winter in decades. Wildcat strikes on the railways left commuters shivering on platforms. There were physical fights between bowler-hatted gents and train drivers. There was violence on the picket lines.

'The country seemed to be caught in the grip of a militant trade union psychology, with everything politicised and proletarianised', the political observer Peter Jenkins wrote.[12] Class warfare and solidarity took new and peculiar turns, with children at one school, where the dinner ladies were out, being told by their headmaster that they would have to go home at lunchtime because a packed lunch 'could be regarded as a form of strike-breaking'. Yet, while it seemed that three-quarters of the nation was out on strike, three-quarters of the nation was telling pollsters that excessive union power was the most important problem facing the country.

The prime minister, meanwhile, flew out of the blizzards to a conference in sun-drenched Guadeloupe, where he was photographed in a dazzling short-sleeved shirt, leaning against a palm tree. It did little for his popularity. When he returned, looking tanned and relaxed, he told reporters at Heathrow, in his usual avuncular tones, that the country had not descended into chaos. 'Crisis? What Crisis?' was the *Daily Mail*'s shorthand front-page headline version of his statement. That headline stuck to Jim like flypaper. It defined his leadership, or, rather, what was perceived as his lack of leadership.

On 3 May 1979, Barbara watched as Margaret Thatcher became Britain's first woman prime minister, ironically with a mandate to curb trade-union power. As he relinquished Number 10, Jim Callaghan was heard to remark that 'for a woman to occupy that office is a tremendous moment in the country's history'.[13] Give the girl a chance! the *Daily Express* had cried, the chance that had eluded Barbara. Barbara herself did as she had planned: she resigned her Blackburn seat, which she had held for thirty-four years (her successor was her former political adviser, Jack Straw), and left the Commons, its longest-serving woman member.

A couple of years earlier, Jim, perhaps to shut Barbara up, had once again offered her a peerage. This time she didn't tell him to stuff it. She told him something much more irritating: that she would think about it. She asked him to hang on while she decided what she wanted to do, which absolutely infuriated him. By summer 1978, she had made her decision. She announced that she would stand in the first direct elections to the European parliament, which were due to take place in June 1979. Barbara the virulent anti-Marketeer, who had almost consistently voted No to Europe in cabinet, in the referendum, in the House, on the NEC and in the PLP, who had been a member of all those anti-Market committees, who had toured the country as a dissenting minister and voted against direct elections to the European parliament was going to stand, albeit as an anti-Market candidate, for that very parliament.

Cries of derision were loud in the land, and Barbara set about trying to explain her apparent turnround. 'Politics is not just about policies: it is about fighting for them in every available forum and at every opportunity', she wrote in the *Tribune*. Europe was now the battleground nearest to Barbara's hand; and she did not, she said, intend to vacate any political place to a Tory. 'Wherever there is a political platform, you should occupy it', she told the *Sunday Telegraph* later. What had people expected after the anti-Marketeers lost the referendum? 'That I should return to my tent and sulk? That has never been my way.'[14]

As friend and foe have observed, the centre is always where Barbara is; and it is not enough to be there alone: she has to try and drag everyone along with her. 'We'd better have some of the right people there fighting for Britain', she announced on the BBC.[15] And to the Tribune Group she 'made an unpopular speech saying that socialists must fight in the Common Market'. In the *Tribune* itself, she argued that the direct elections she had once vehemently opposed had been brought into being by a coalition of pro-EEC Tory and Labour MPs, and that the question was whether to 'allow this coalition to dominate' the parliament, 'or whether we are going to go in and fight against the drift towards federalist policies'.[16]

Barbara always understood that the purpose of the European project was federalisation. 'The EMS [European Monetary System], by linking the European currencies together, would force all its members to coordinate their economic and fiscal policies', she wrote in 1978. 'Having done that, it would be a short step for them to accept a common currency and common economic policies',[17] all of which came to pass within twenty years, and all of which she had foreseen many years before she wrote that article. Common economic policies would mean capitalist economic policies. And so, Barbara concluded, non-federalist socialists should be in the European parliament, fighting any such moves.

The European election followed a month after the general election and was, for the most part, as flat as stale beer. The party activists were uninterested or overtly hostile. Likewise the public. One of the more memorable events of the campaign was the run-in Barbara had with the gargantuan Liberal MP, Cyril Smith, who said that she, soon to be 69, was too old and past it, to which she retorted that he was too fat and had never made it.

The electorate stayed away in droves; a mere 32 per cent bothered to vote, lower even than an average local-government election. Even for Barbara – the biggest name in the election – the turnout was, at 31.7 per cent, slightly below the national average. But she became the MEP for Greater Manchester North, one of seventeen Labour MEPs out of the eighty-one-strong United Kingdom contingent, and the only British MEP to have been a cabinet minister.

In effect, Barbara replaced Ted in Europe. As a peer he couldn't run for office, and in any case he was not physically up to it. His heart problems had not gone away and his health continued to deteriorate. 'Ted Castle is dying, I'm afraid', Tony Benn noted in 1977; 'he looks terribly ill.'[18] And he was; he had had a series of heart operations and had become increasingly short of breath.

Her election coincided with their thirty-fifth wedding anniversary, their last together. Ted died five months later, on Boxing Day 1979, 'a great shattering blow', to Barbara, the thing she had so feared and dreaded. 'She was really profoundly shaken', said the Castles' old friend Geoffrey Goodman. He was shocked at the violence of her grief. 'Nobody takes that kind of death in their stride, but she really sort of cracked up. She was dependent on him and perhaps she didn't realise just how dependent.'[19]

Almost everyone who came into contact with Barbara was surprised by both the depth of her pain and her inability to conceal it. 'Her life was Ted,' said Stan Orme; 'it was a severe blow when he died. She worshipped him: "my Ted", "Ted said this", "Ted went there", "Ted did that" – we got that all the time. Nobody came up to Ted.' She was, as Paul Rose said, 'totally devoted to Ted and was absolutely shattered when he died'.[20]

Sometimes she could pull out the old wisecracking Barbara, telling Henry Plumb, chairman of the European parliament's Agriculture Committee, that the 'the old bugger' always said she would go before him 'and now the old bugger's left me alone'. She was, Plumb observed, 'very upset. She obviously missed him terribly, but – typical of her – she didn't say, "Well, that's me finished." '[21] She threw herself into her work.

'It was almost as though she'd just shut herself off, working her way out of it. She just worked and worked and worked – just buried herself in agricultural prices', recalled fellow MEP Richard Balfe.[22] As she told friends, it was how she got through. She seldom came up for air and when she did she was filled with Ted's absence, with a terrible loneliness; her companion, her confidant, who was ferociously loyal, her greatest fan of thirty-six years, had gone. There wasn't a thing she didn't miss. One month later to the day, Barbara's mother, Annie, died, aged 96, compounding her sense of desolation.

Five months after Ted's death Barbara dispensed with her usual circumspection about written emotion. In a guest column for *The Times*, she tried to explain how she felt. 'How does one come to terms with such a loss?' she wrote. 'Does one keep him alive by endlessly remembering – and nearly destroy oneself? Or move on briskly to new fields of pragmatic common sense and suppress one of life's significant experiences? Or just go numb and wait for death? I fluctuate between the three.'[23]

Or rather, as she went on to explain, she had done so until she read Dennis Potter's account of his chronic illness and how he used it in his work. It was a revelation. It showed her a way forward. It suddenly occurred to her that, as he 'had used his pain to extend himself, I could use mine ... I saw that my husband would live through what I continued to be and do. I must not embalm him in memory ... somehow I now believe I can use his loss without diminishing it or him. I can thrust through it and with it to new discovery, all the richer because the roots of my being have gone so deep into what we shared.'[24]

Her critics read this as Barbara taking her boundless ego out for a run, using even Ted's death in furtherance of herself. And it is toe-curling. She was right to be wary of indulging in this kind of writing. It isn't natural to her; it sounds unauthentic. But the piece reads more like a clumsy statement of intent ('You might as well live') than an exercise in egomania. Barbara was trying to say that she had found a way of going on alone.

When they were first elected to the European parliament together, like everyone else Henry Plumb, a Conservative MEP and former president of the farmers union, 'believed that Barbara went to Europe with one thing in mind: to kill Parliament and to argue against our membership of Europe'. He reacted warily when he saw her in the Agriculture Committee, which he chaired, 'sitting in the front row with Edith Cresson', the French representative.[25] The Agriculture Committee was a natural for Barbara. It was the most important committee in the EEC, responsible for agriculture subsidies through the Common Agriculture Policy (CAP) which was two-thirds of the Community's budget, and, as Barbara observed, in Europe as elsewhere 'Power lies where the money is'. She wanted to take on the CAP and its notorious food mountains of butter and beef, its lakes of wine and milk.[26]

'Barbara really was the bane of my life', Plumb said. A stickler for procedure, and intolerant of anything she considered sloppy, she would hold up committee meetings if she didn't have 'all the papers relating to the various items on the agenda – in English'. But it wasn't obstructionism, as Plumb soon discovered; Barbara asked the questions nobody else had seen were there, 'questions that should be asked'. He developed a 'sort of love–hate relationship with her. She was difficult, but there was no room for complacency in any meeting at which she was present. The adrenalin would start flowing because you would know you had to be on the ball.' Barbara used her familiar technique of 'going on and on and being a bit boring about it'[27] and it often worked, as it had in cabinet. She got results, and even when she didn't it wasn't for lack of trying.

As the only well-known national figure in the British Labour Group's first elected intake, Barbara 'created something of a stir as the first serious significant Labour person to appear'.[28] The difference in stature between Barbara and her colleagues – a large number of 'lightweights and deadbeats', in the *Tribune*'s phrase – caused problems. She 'assumed she was going to lead' the group, which indeed she did. Some members felt she had been foisted on them by Transport House. 'There was a vote to elect her, but there was no real contest', Richard Balfe said.[29]

The choice of the 'obsessively anti-European'[30] Barbara to lead the group alarmed the right, who 'expected the worst' and thought she would 'play a destructive role' as an anti-European. In fact, 'she played a very positive role and was a very good influence on the very raw and inexperienced Labour Group', former Labour MP Dick Leonard said. Being the Labour leader, Barbara was also a vice-chair of the bureau of the Socialist Group – the largest political grouping in the parliament – and within it 'she tried to cooperate so the Labour Group wasn't a permanent awkward squad. Under Barbara's leadership they were awkward but not as awkward as they might well have been.'[31]

In 1979, Barbara, in her last speech to party conference as an NEC constituency member, had railed against the absurdities of the CAP and pledged that, as Britain would not be able to 'get out for the next few years', she would show her socialist European colleagues that the British Labour Group wasn't merely nationalistic or anti-European. She would, she said, get the other socialists onside to fight for a socialist Europe. 'Let us say this to this country and to our comrades in the wider Europe: the Community must go Socialist or we will come out', she concluded,[32] to rapturous applause.

What she soon found out from her European colleagues was that not only were they pro-EEC (some because they knew nothing else), but they wanted the British socialists to stay in and fight with them for social legislation and reform of policies like the CAP. Their arguments, plus an awareness that the British public were even less likely to vote for withdrawal now, convinced Barbara that leaving the EEC was no longer an option.

She tried (and failed) to get the NEC to agree that it should be the Labour Group which decided what to recommend over withdrawal, and she 'strongly opposed the decision to debate the [NEC] motion for withdrawal' at the 1981 Conference. Conference, as she knew it would, voted to leave the Community – without even holding another referendum. To her annoyance, she was held in suspicion over her change of heart. She was accused of going native, of becoming too fond of life at the top tables of Europe. She was fed up, she said, of the party treating MEPs as 'pariahs who had sold out to the gravy train'.[33]

Barbara's change of position irked some members of the Labour Group, too, especially those who disliked her for what they saw as her elitism and snobbery. It had been one thing to lead a ministerial team of (mostly) bright young things, to allow criticism and debate, to be inclusive and to generate enthusiasm. It was quite another to lead a team she had not chosen and could not change, a good handful of whom she would have regarded as her intellectual, social and experiential inferiors. She had not the patience nor the ability nor the desire to get them on board.

The beginning of the end with the Labour Group came when Barbara wrote an article for the *New Statesman* ahead of the 1982 Labour Party conference, arguing once again against party policy for withdrawal. In it she referred to herself as an anti-Marketeer and agreed that 'the Treaty of Rome, if rigorously applied, would make it impossible for a Labour government to carry out its alternative economic strategy'. Her complaint was about tactics: 'Instead of arguing that we know we couldn't carry out socialist policies within the Community, let us announce that we are going ahead with our own polices and make the European authorities react to us. If they then rule us out of court, the responsibility for the breach will be theirs, not ours.'[34]

Richard Balfe and Alf Lomas, Barbara's deputy at the Labour Group, whom, he complained, 'she never consulted', wrote a letter to the *New Statesman* calling for her resignation: they 'were dismayed at the attack on Labour Party policy and on the Party itself'.[35] It took three more years for Lomas to oust her from the leadership. He was hard left, which was not to the taste of most of the group, including Balfe; but Balfe became Lomas's backroom boy in order to get rid of Barbara, who characteristically asked for one more year. Thirty-two Labour MPs had been returned in the 1984 European election, and two-thirds of them were implacably anti-Market. Barbara was ousted by Lomas the following year, in an open show of hands, eighteen votes to fourteen.

Whatever misgivings some Labour Group members had about Barbara's high-handed leadership style, there was universal admiration for her work, especially her ability to get on top of the complex agriculture policy, which few people understood, and to explain it in simple terms. She still had remarkable rserves of energy. As an MEP, she led a peripatetic life, shuttling between Strasbourg, Brussels and London each week, and flying off to various European capitals for meetings of the Socialist Group. She still kept her Islington flat, but in Europe she lived in hotels and, she sometimes thought, in airport lounges.

But she held up well. She refused to use her age as an excuse for not doing something and rarely complained about being tired. She got up between 6 and 6.30 every morning, and if she had a speech to make she arrived at the office by 7 a.m. to read all the papers beforehand. When she got up to speak, 'everybody listened', Plumb said, 'because she always had something to say. It was always pertinent. You might not agree with her but nevertheless it was on the ball.'[36]

Shortly after Barbara lost the leadership of the Labour Group, Gerald Kaufman saw her at a wreath-laying ceremony at the Holocaust memorial in Stuttgart, commemorating the fortieth anniversary of the end of the war. The official pan-European groups, including the Socialist Group, represented by its president, Rudi Arndt, had wreaths to lay; Kaufman was laying a wreath for the Labour Party; and Barbara, who 'had not been allocated to lay a wreath for anyone' was a spectator. Jesse Jackson was laying a wreath and as he did so 'Barbara stepped forward and took hold of the side of it and laid it down with him'. There was uproar. The sheer cheek, the gall, the nerve of the woman! It was 'absolutely wonderful', Kaufman marvelled:[37] at 75 'she still cared enough' to go through such machinations.

Barbara was temperamentally unsuited to being a European parliamentarian. The non-adversarial system; the lack of cut and thrust; the proportional representation system, which engendered backstairs horse-trading between the various groups; the lack of immediacy due to the plethora of languages; reading statements into the record rather than debating: it was exactly what she thought a parliament should not be. She wanted to be back in real politics, and in 1988 she announced that she would not be standing for re-election to the European parliament the following year.

Real politics meant British politics, which she had never really left. During her time in Europe she spent most weekends at Hell Corner Farm, and she was fully conversant with what was going on. Her pronouncements from Strasbourg were covered fulsomely in the papers and the first volume of her ministerial diaries* were published in January 1980, mostly to critical acclaim.

Her diaries are considered by most of her contemporaries to be honest and accurate most of the time. She did not 'make up false facts' in Roy Jenkins's phrase. To political commentator Hugo Young they were a 'matchless chronicle of the years she held office',[38] and Michael Foot told his nephew, the journalist Paul Foot, that if he wanted to understand the pressures of government, and how politicians 'get swept off into the stratosphere and lose all their youth and their exuberance and the reasons they came to polit-ics in the first place', he could do worse than read Barbara's account of governance, which Michael considered the best of all the cabinet diaries.[39]

The diaries were serialised by the *Sunday Times*, with an advertising campaign that asked, 'Is it polite to read a lady's diaries?' Maybe, but Barbara thought it most impolite to review a lady's diaries quite as irreverently as Michael Foot did. Like most diarists setting down their personal account for history, Barbara was naturally partisan and tried to present herself and all her works in the best light. 'Barbara frequently appeared as the best Minister at Harold Wilson's disposal,' Michael wrote, 'sometimes as Joan of Arc facing (and confounding) her inquisitors, sometimes almost as a new Queen Elizabeth at Tilbury, rousing the troops and her countrymen as no one else could do.'[40]

That sort of thing was to be expected from Michael, who, when he picked up a pen, was no respecter of persons. But Barbara was not amused; so little so that when the second volume of her diaries†

---

* Covering the years 1974–76.
† The volume covering the years 1964–70.

came out in 1984 she asked him, with that 'waspish note of warning in her voice' which he knew all too well, not to review it. He did, of course. He had great fun: his opening line said she had asked him not to write the review. As he had previously pointed out, 'Great diarists must have some sense of their own insignificance, and Barbara's best friend never claimed she had that.'[41]

Barbara's skirmishes with Jim Callaghan had continued apace while she was in Europe. In June 1980, speaking on BBC television, she said that 'as next Labour leader she wanted Mr Benn, as the most ardent believer in our alternative radical and challenging strategy', which had to be 'carried out by somebody who believes in it, not messed about with and watered down'.[42]

The alternative strategy would, it was hoped, prove to be an al-ternative to further international borrowing. Its highlights were import controls, compulsory planning agreements for companies, reflation and reversing cuts in public expenditure, all of which, when Benn, strongly backed by Barbara, had proposed them during the last months of the Callaghan government, had been decried by the prime minister as 'an attack on the Government's economic policies'.[43]

Tony and Jim had just had a well-publicised spat. Jim had made a speech telling the unions they had to agree an incomes policy with Labour if the party was to have any chance of forming a government again. Tony, in an overt leadership grab, in effect warned the unions that under Jim's leadership they 'could be shackled again' by an incomes policy. Then, as *The Times* said, 'Mrs Castle weighed in'. Her call for Tony to replace Jim as leader – an 'excellent alternative' – caused a sensation, as she must have known it would. It is unlikely to have been motivated by an unqual-ified enthusiasm for 'Wedgie', whom she never completely trusted (nor completely agreed with: she still wanted to 'plan wages'). He was by now hard left to her soft left, a political Puritan enveloped, she said, in an 'aura of witch-burnings'.[44] He was more a flag of convenience for her to sail under. Promoting him had the added advantage of being a well-aimed kick below Jim's belt while he was out cold on the floor.

Jim did resign as leader the following autumn, three months ahead of the special conference at Wembley which was to ratify an electoral college system whereby the whole party and the unions would elect the Labour leader. Tony Benn, knowing he would not be elected by the PLP, did not stand. Barbara called for Michael to be installed as a temporary leader until after Wembley. In the event, the PLP elected the party leader for the last time. There were four contenders, three loosely from the left, John Silkin, Peter Shore (both knocked out in the first ballot) and Michael Foot, and one from the right, Denis Healey.

Barbara's public 'backing' of Michael concentrated on his defects. He was in danger of repeating Harold's mistake of 'making a shibboleth of party unity – something to be pursued as an end in itself', she wrote. ('The language of party unity was the religion of Harold Wilson', she had once quipped.) She was openly critical of his role in the Callaghan government: 'He was one of the stoutest defenders of its deflationary and defensive policies.' Worse, perhaps, was that he had been at the heart of the deal-making with the Liberals and then the Ulster Unionists until 'it seemed as though the decent instinct of people who want to do something had degenerated into a determination to survive at any cost'.[45] But, she concluded, he was tolerant and civilised and cultivated and a Foot government would be tilted to the left, so, well, all right.

As she often remarked, the Michael Foot she had backed when Harold resigned in 1976 was a different person to the Michael Foot of 1980, and in her autobiography, published thirteen years later, in 1993, Barbara noted that had she had a vote, which as an MEP then she did not, she would have been 'very torn' between Michael and Denis Healey, who was widely expected to win. What she saw as Michael's slavish support for 'Jim Callaghan's rigidities', his adherence to Jim and his policies 'almost to the point of idolatry',[46] had profoundly alienated her, personally as well as politically. Nevertheless, much to the 'simultaneous astonishment' of Foot and Neil Kinnock (who helped run the campaign), 'Denis was beaten – nobody expected that'.[47] Michael Foot became leader of the Labour Party.

*

Barbara was aware that Michael was no match for Margaret Thatcher. He came over as a kindly, bumbling, absent-minded don from another age, with his walking stick, swept-back white hair, owlish black-framed glasses and crumpled, mismatched clothes. Moreover, by the time of the 1983 election he was rising 70. 'Do you seriously want this old man to run Britain?' the *Sun* asked. In contrast, Thatcher had been transformed from the fifty-something Tory Lady frump she had been in 1979 into Eighties Wonder Woman, cloaked in power-dressing suits, her hairdo sculpted, her teeth capped and her voice lowered in pitch. She was Gloriana Imperatrix, the once and future Boadicea, swathed in a chiffon scarf, the Falklands victory laid at her feet. She was going to take the country by tank.

The prime minister, unlike her male counterparts who seemed to age overnight, actually grew younger in office, as if she had swallowed a megadose of Barbara's vitamin of power. Barbara was both appalled and fascinated. She had seen Thatcher coming. Her male Labour colleagues had laughed. How was that prim missy, a rather shrill *woman* going to lead a major British party? When Thatcher had snatched the Tory leadership in February 1975, Barbara could not help 'feeling a thrill', despite herself; and a frisson of anger against her own conservative, male-dominated colleagues, who couldn't even bring themselves to envisage a woman leader. Harold had enjoyed going up against Thatcher. It revived his flagging interest. 'Nothing like a bit of sex challenge for bringing the best out in a man', Barbara noted, watching him joust with her.[48] Thatcher in the early days was often not up to it, but when she was Barbara often watched her, 'one woman willing another on',[49] the woman with whom she herself would have clashed if things had turned out differently.

Thatcher, the British nationalist, was the first Americanised prime minister, the product of the image consultant and the advertising agency. Like the American president she was a televisual experience, a series of iconic photo opportunities, everything controlled, scripted, sound-bitten and spun; the Max Headroom of Downing Street. Like her chum Ronald Reagan she had a firm grasp of the folksy tale, which she could retell in a 'greed is good' parable for the age. No one could touch her, because she was what was wanted.

Despite all the evidence to the contrary, Barbara still believed that you could persuade people to want what was good for them, what was good for society as a whole and that that was the same thing. Barbara, the old William Morris socialist, still 'dreaming of a society in which revolutionary change is achieved by love and tolerance and in which collectivism and the pursuit of aesthetic satisfaction are synonymous',[50] was once again confronted with the fact that brittle one-dimensional individualistic materialism has, like cheap music, a brash seductive potency which often proves irresistible.

Labour fought the 1983 election with 'the longest suicide note in history', in Gerald Kaufman's famous phrase, a 'manifesto of pure Bennery', in Barbara's: unilateral disarmament, more public ownership and withdrawal from the EEC, all things Barbara had once passionately believed in. She had long since changed her mind over withdrawal from the EEC, but her objection to the call for more public ownership was based on pragmatic grounds more than principle: she thought it would help lose the election.

On the issue of unilateral disarmament, Barbara trod a taut, fine line. She was commissioned by *The Times* to be one of its election diary columnists, and she defended the party's stance by shifting the argument. 'A majority of people probably now agree that the installation of cruise missiles and the acquisition of Trident would put us in greater peril', she argued, because it would encourage an enemy to adopt a kill-or-be-killed policy. She therefore called for 'Britain's abandonment of *unnecessary* [my italics] nuclear weapons'. She did not argue that Britain should unilaterally stand down its nuclear capability, nor that the Labour Party was arguing for it. 'Labour's contribution to *multilateral* [my italics] disarmament is not to trade weapon for weapon, but to create a new atmosphere and to proceed from there step by step towards the creation of a non-nuclear weapons world', she wrote.[51] But the party was, of course, arguing for 'the removal of all existing nuclear bases and weapons' from British soil, as it plainly stated in the manifesto,[52] and nothing Barbara said could change that.

Whether she had already changed her mind on unilateralism as a morally correct policy is unclear. She knew it lost the party votes: 'Most working-class people had a simple reflex action on defence: as long as they've got the bomb, we must have it', she wrote in her autobiography (echoing Nye Bevan). Certainly by 1987 she was convinced that, with Gorbachev in the Kremlin and the Cold War thawing, Labour could and should advocate multilateral disarmament or face further electoral defeat.

Defeat in 1983 was spectacular. The Social Democratic Party, formed two years earlier, joined the Liberals to form the Alliance, which picked up 26 per cent of the vote. Labour got only 28 per cent, its worst result since 1918. The peculiarities of the system meant that the Alliance had only 23 seats, and Labour 209. But the Tories had a majority over Labour of 187 seats. It was an utter, demoralising rout.

Michael resigned as leader and four hats went into the ring. Roy Hattersley was the right-wing candidate, Peter Shore, Eric Heffer and Neil Kinnock the left-wing candidates. In the first election for party leader under the new electoral college, Neil Kinnock garnered an amazing 71 per cent of the vote, to Hattersley's 19 per cent, Heffer's 6 per cent and Shore's 3 per cent. He became, at 41, the youngest-ever leader of the Labour Party, a record broken (by a few months) nine years later by the newly elected member for Sedgefield, Tony Blair.

Kinnock inherited a party in utter disarray: split, demoralised, unelectable. 'Unity is the price of victory', he told them in his first speech as leader, not cosmetic unity, but one of principle and purpose, 'unity here and now and from henceforth'.[53] His huge popular mandate meant that he could get things done. He went after the Militant Tendency, a Trotskyist group which had taken over some inner-city constituency Labour parties, and had control of Liverpool Council.

He also reorganised the party's structure and began the process of modernisation. In October 1985, he created the post of campaigns and communications director, which was filled by Peter Mandelson. A few months into the job, Mandelson met Philip Gould, an advertising executive, who explained to him the modern communications and marketing strategies that the Tories had been using since 1979, and of which Labour was woefully ignorant. Out of this meeting was born the idea for a communications agency to 'focus and structure outside communications expertise and assist-ance'. From the moment it was set up, the agency's 'direct input to Labour's entire strategic outlook, as well as its purely presentational style, was continuous'.[54] This was the beginning of what became New Labour. Power had passed to the top floor.

Barbara was glad to see the back of 'inefficient organization and out-of-date attitudes',[55] and even approved of Mandelson's visual pyrotechnics: gone from the conference platform were the rickety trellis tables covered in red cloth, on which she had always laddered her tights; in came the Starship *Enterprise* set. The red rose, which Neil Kinnock had first used in the 1984 European elections, albeit clutched in a socialist realist fist,* soon replaced the red flag.

She was glad to see the back of Michael's leadership, too. 'Never has an honourable man been more miscast' was her verdict on his stewardship.[56] She got on well with Neil, who was funny and earthy, and when left to his own devices a good, rousing orator. He also had the necessary steel to lead the party. A person would cross him only once.

It was decided that Neil should be sold as a presidential figure for the 1987 election: President Kinnock versus President Thatcher. Barbara, always up for campaigning appearances, took part in the 'Chariots of Fire' party election broadcast, directed by the man who had waved his Oscar and announced to Hollywood that the British were coming. 'Kinnock', as the broadcast was called, proved the opposite was true: the Americans were here. Neil and his wife, Glenys, walked hand in hand over a sunlit upland while Neil did a

---

*The symbol of the Socialist International.

mellifluous voiceover. Aunt Sadie, Uncle Bill, Barbara Castle, Jim Callaghan and others provided the eulogies amid the soft-focus, strong-jawed cameos and the seagulls. This was fighting Saatchi & Saatchi with British Hollywood and it got immense coverage, boosting Neil's ratings by 19 points, but, as was pointed out to Mandelson when he claimed it was the best party election broadcast ever made, it did not bring Labour victory: the Tories won the election with a 102-seat majority.

Something untoward had happened to Neil, Barbara thought. Whereas Thatcher's marketing makeover had made her seem more powerful, more of a presence, Neil had vanished behind his new 'colour me beautiful' clothes and his sanitized, dull but responsible prime-minister-in-waiting rhetoric. What had happened to the inspiring, passionate left-wing orator? She believed that you should fight fire with fire, that Labour should present radical Labour pol-icies as a real alternative to Thatcher's radical Tory policies, and that Neil should do so with all his natural gusto, verve and eloquence. It was what he called her 'David Hare thesis'.*

Barbara wasn't the only one to wonder about his 'changed leadership personality [which] appeared to have drained the sap from his speaking style'. David Blunkett urged him to speak from the gut more and 're-discover that former fire'; as did others, but usually only once or twice.[57] Not so Barbara. Restoring to Neil his rightful fire and brimstone became her project.

She sent him 'long letters' lamenting 'that here is this gift of oratory and instinctive radicalism that was diluted and then subdued altogether under the shroud of respectability'. Sometimes she appeared in his room at the House and told him 'how to run the Labour Party'. She wanted him to be himself and lead the troops into attack. He told her that he 'didn't have any bloody troops – that was the problem. The party was all over the place. There wasn't a daily crisis, there was an hourly crisis, and it wasn't

---

* Hare had written a play which featured a Labour Party leader sapped of his natural radical socialist instincts by his minders.

necessarily helped by someone coming in and saying, "If you'd only be yourself".[58]

But Barbara persisted; it made no difference what he said in response, Kinnock said. 'Since I was a bloody fool to have succumbed to this starchiness and caution and respectability in the first place, I could be expected, as a bloody fool, to defend it!' Eventually Neil, despite his 'huge affection for her', exploded and they had a violent row. He told her that she'd 'run a lot of things but she had never led a political party that was about a hundred feet below the surface'. He told her to 'let those who know how to dig dig!' Barbara 'just crackled right back' at him, he said.[59] It didn't affect their relationship. She could dish it out but she could take it too.

She happily went back on the campaign trail with him in 1992. She was the one who provided the fire and the brimstone. She shrieked about socialism, electrifying audiences with her millennial prophecies, even at the notorious Sheffield rally of din, hoopla, razzmatazz and glitz at which the Kinnocks arrived by helicopter and Neil shook his fist in premature triumph and the BBC's John Cole breathlessly told the gob-smacked viewing public that it was 'the most astonishing political meeting' he had seen since the John F. Kennedy Democratic Party convention in 1960.

Backstage there was always some poor fool who offered Barbara a cup of tea afterwards. 'A cup of tea be buggered – where's the gin?' Barbara would demand, puffing on her cigarette. 'I would always love her for that, even if I couldn't love her for anything else,' Neil Kinnock said, 'and there are lots and lots of things to love her for.'[60]

In June 1990, Barbara finally accepted that peerage, becoming the Baroness Castle of Blackburn. 'Ideologically I hate the House of Lords', she had recorded in her diary when Ted became a peer.[61] And indeed she did. She was ambivalent when the Labour government was drawing up plans for reform in the late 1960s; perhaps it would be better, she thought, if they simply abolished it. She was, in Dick Crossman's opinon, a 'fanatical socialist who has always been opposed to second chambers',[62] especially second chambers where

335

membership was by birthright or patronage. She had strongly backed Tony Benn when he tried to get the abolition of the Lords included in the 1979 election manifesto. The NEC–cabinet manifesto group voted 11 to 4 in support of abolition, but Jim Callaghan refused to include it and instead inserted a sentence that stated the House of Lords was 'indefensible' without saying what was to be done.

Barbara's ascension to the indefensible happened in July. She was introduced by her sponsors, Lord Wedderburn, and Baroness Serota. The latter had worked with Dick at the DHSS and was somewhat surprised to have been chosen, because she did not know Barbara well. Barbara refused to wear the tricorne hat because it would mess up her hair. She refused to kneel and, of course, she affirmed, instead of taking the oath. When asked to explain why she had entered the Lords, she told the *Sunday Telegraph* that she wanted 'to be there in order to plan its destruction', adding: 'You have to permeate the centre and manipulate from the inside. You have to understand your enemy.'[63] And if you're Barbara you have to have something to do, something to fight for or against; you cannot just sit back and smell the roses.

Barbara's maiden speech to the Lords in November 1990 was vintage Castle. It was everything it should not have been: political, partisan, controversial and twice as long as the allocated ten minutes. She lambasted the 'prime minister's Boadicea chariot-type nationalism ... [and] her nineteenth-century values'. She attacked everything about Thatcher and Thatcher's Britain. It was a month after Barbara's eightieth birthday and she proved that she could still have them rolling in the aisles.

As she told that year's party conference, the 'truth is that everybody loves a survivor, and, after all, survival is something not to be despised in politics'.[64] Lady Castle, the Queen Mother of the Labour Movement, the Red Queen, the party's only elder states-*woman* knew whereof she spoke. Everybody does love a survivor, especially one who survives with such style and verve: Barbara, the immaculately turned out blast from the past, still able to address an audience with wit and passion, watched, with a sly smile, as the press came back to lay garlands at her feet. They had fallen in love with her all over again, and she was going to make the most of it.

In the last week of May 1995, Harold Wilson died, aged 79; he'd been suffering from Alzheimer's disease. The funeral was held on the Isles of Scilly, where the Wilsons had had a house for forty years. At Mary Wilson's request the official Westminster mourners were kept to an absolute minimum. All the living leaders of the Labour Party were invited: Jim Callaghan, who like Barbara had gone to the Lords, Margaret Beckett, who had been pro-tem leader after John Smith's death, and Tony Blair, who had become leader the previous year, all attended. Michael Foot was not well enough for the journey and Neil Kinnock, now a member of the European Commission, couldn't get away. Gerald Kaufman, the senior Labour backbencher (and a member of Wilson's kitchen cabinet) attended, as did the party's general secretary, Tom Sawyer. The other member of the official delegation was Barbara, Harold's little minister, dressed in bright orange for her cheeky chappie. The former Marcia Williams, now Lady Falkender (Harold had sent her to the Lords at the same time as Ted), came not as part of the Westminster delegation but as a friend.

Because the tiny Norman church of St Mary's, in whose church-yard Wilson was to be buried, could seat only sixty-four, the service was held at a large Victorian church half a mile away. The Westminster contingent had lunch before being bused to the service. When the bus stopped outside the church, Barbara made her distinguished colleagues wait while she adjusted her clothes, arranged her collar just so, poked her hair into place and checked her make-up. It was a hot June day, and after the service the mourners, gawked at by the tourists, had to walk the half-mile up the hill to St Mary's, with the exception of the octogenarians, Lady Castle and Lord Callaghan, who were installed in a limous-ine (imported for the occasion), side by side once more for the uphill journey.

At Harold's memorial service at Westminster Abbey the following

July, in the congregation were the Prince of Wales, John Major* and most of his cabinet, almost the entire shadow front bench and many of the survivors of the Labour governments of 1964-70 and 1974-79, including Roy Jenkins, Denis Healey, Jim Callaghan and Barbara. Tony Blair read from Aelred of Rievaulx, a twelfth-century monk at the Yorkshire abbey from which Harold (who had also gone to the Lords) had taken his title. 'The spiritual friendship that exists between people of integrity springs out of their common attitude to life, their shared moral outlook and the kind of activities they engage in', recited Blair,[65] who had never met Harold.

Until he became party leader in 1994, he and Barbara had not met, either; he had been elected to parliament in 1983, while she was in Europe. From the outset she found him something of an enigma, not the first party leader to be the product of a comfortable Tory household, but the first who had not been active or apparently even interested in politics as a young teenager or at Oxford (he had stood in his private school's mock elections when he was 12, as the Tory candidate, but without evident enthusiasm).

Blair came to politics through a conversion to Christianity and was famously influenced by the Australian vicar Peter Thomson, whom he met at university. Thomson introduced Blair to the ideas of John Macmurray, a Scottish philosopher whose theories have dripped down into what Americans call 'communitarianism'. Loosely, communitarians believe that Western societies have become so obsessed with individual rights that people have lost sight of their responsibilities and obligations to one another, a view with which Blair agrees. What he feels about the more draconian aspects of communitarianism, such as making divorce almost impossible for couples with children, is known only to his close friends.

Blair with his lightly boiled Christianity and communitarian phrasebook was lampooned by *Private Eye* as the Vicar of St Albion's, weaving platitudes in the air and controlling his flock with a Religious Correctness smiley face. The press dubbed him 'Tony

* In November 1990, Margaret Thatcher's colleagues concluded that the Iron Lady had become irretrievably rusty. She was ousted and replaced by the seemingly mild-mannered John Major.

Blur' for his elliptical and often contradictory messages; or 'Bambi' for his caught-in-the-headlights expression. He was the Gaitskellite's Gaitskellite. Roy Jenkins was a great fan (although he later became concerned by what he perceived as Blair's lack of a first-class mind).

Under Blair's leadership socialism was not redefined, revised or modernised; it was banned, the very word wiped from Labour lips. Labour now became New Labour, a name suggested to, and rejected by, John Smith, who had replaced Neil Kinnock when he resigned after the 1992 defeat. Barbara had been sorry to see Neil go. She thought he would have made a good prime minister, although, as she put it, 'I would have been on his tail to detach him from his own right wing.'[66]

John Smith, a Christian socialist, had been undetachably right-wing, but in a traditional Labour Party sense. Under Smith, New Labour policies continued to develop, but too slowly for Gordon Brown, his shadow chancellor, and Tony Blair, his shadow home secretary. Their perception was that Labour had lost the 1992 election precisely because it *was* Labour. Ergo the modernisers – the 'Famous Five' of Blair, Brown (who had also entered parliament in 1983), Mandelson (an MP since 1992), and two unelected individuals, Philip Gould and Alastair Campbell (a journalist and subsequently Blair's press secretary) – decided that what was needed was to create a new party from within, one that accepted the social effects of Thatcherism and played to the upwardly mobile, socially aspiring, individualistic middle-class (and would-be middle-class) voters.

The making of the new model party had begun with Neil Kinnock but what it became was not necessarily what he intended. As Smith's shadow chancellor, Brown made much of the running. He wasted little time in announcing that a Labour government would no longer tax for taxing's sake, that is, as a redistributive tool: 'we will only tax if it increases opportunity for individuals or for the community as a whole', he announced after the 1992 defeat. Moreover, Labour would cut taxes when it was prudent (a favourite word) to do so. Brown's tax statement had the advantage of meaning exactly what he said it meant, whatever that might be at the time. Like so much of New Labour rhetoric, it had no intrinsic meaning.

From the outset Barbara was uneasy with, and suspicious of, New Labour thinking. She told BBC TV's *On the Record* that Brown's statement 'begged every question under the sun ... It's absurd for Labour to be fighting on negatives like "We won't tax, and we won't even spend, unless it will lead to opportunity".'[67] She could see which way they were facing, and just before the 1997 election wrote in the *Tribune*'s sixtieth birthday supplement: 'What Labour badly needs is a coherent economic and social philosophy. The two are inextricably intertwined. *Tribune* must tell our movement that if we make ourselves the prisoners of Tory economic policy we shall not be able to achieve our social aims.'[68]

But by the time of John Smith's unexpected death from a heart attack in 1994, Labour new and old had been out of office for fifteen years and had lost four consecutive elections. When the party voted for Blair they voted for the person most likely to take them to victory, not necessarily for the one they felt most comfortable with. Tony Blair was 'Bill Clinton with his flies done up', as one rueful Tory minister remarked,[69] and like Bill Clinton, whose 1992 victory strongly influenced Gould and therefore Labour Party electioneering strategy, Blair was perceived as having the right, election-winning stuff.

Like Clinton's new Democratic Party, New Labour would no longer be the party of the poor and the left and the organised working classes (whose numbers did not add up to victory); it would be the party of a populist middle-class centre (whose numbers did). Britain was, the modernisers decided, now a two-thirds, one-third nation, in which two-thirds of the population could afford to buy their own home. Home-owners, in this ana-lysis, were not going to vote for a party they perceived as one that levelled down and championed only the dispossessed.

In the leadership contest between John Prescott, Margaret Beckett and Tony Blair – 'the lion, the witch and the wardrobe', as comedian Rory Bremner dubbed them (with the lion and the witch standing for both the leadership and the deputy leadership) –

340

Barbara voted for John Prescott. He had strongly and vociferously opposed what he called this 'Clintonisation' of Labour. It was that old matter of the heart and soul of the party, he said, and Barbara agreed. But she, as much as anyone, wanted a Labour victory and once Blair was elected leader (with Prescott beating Beckett for the deputy leadership) she was willing to do what she could to help.

Reluctantly she reversed a position she had held all her life: the importance, symbolic or otherwise, of retaining Clause 4 of the party's constitution, something she had always regarded as 'the guiding principle of socialism' because it acknowledged that wealth was created not by individuals but by working people as a whole.[70] She believed, she wrote in her autobiography, that it would be wrong for the party to drop it as if it were part of a 'disreputable past'.

She still believed that. 'It is always dangerous for a political movement to repudiate its past', she wrote in the *Tribune*, shortly before the party's 1995 special conference on the clause. But Blair had threatened to resign if the vote to remove Clause 4 went against him, because, he said, it would show that the party was not interested in changing. Barbara reluctantly got behind him. 'Like it or not, Tony Blair has made this issue a test of loyalty', her article went on. 'I am loyal to him and want to see him Prime Minister. His defeat on Saturday would seriously dent his credibility. More importantly, I have been heartened by the inclusion in the rewrite of his commitment to a community in which power, wealth and opportunity are in the hands of the many and not the few. These are powerful words. If we adopt them we must spell out how we hope to achieve it ... You will win on Saturday, Tony, but we will hold you to your words.'[71]

The words were many. The rewrite of Clause 4 was six times as long as the original, and had more in common with a corporate mission statement than with a political philosophy. Within two years, Barbara was dismissing it as a rhetorical generalisation.

In July 1996, New Labour issued a policy document, *New Life, New Britain*, which began the process of reversing the party's long commitment to restoring the link, scrapped by the Tories in 1980, between the basic state pension and average earnings. Pensions would remain linked to inflation as they had under the Tories; anything else was deemed too expensive. Barbara's Serps, from which the Tories had tried to extract as many people as possible, would not be revived and promoted. Instead, company and stake-holder pensions would be the norm.'At the last minute, we are being asked to turn upside down the whole of our traditional policy,' Barbara said,'which is a state insurance scheme, a contributory one, a compulsory one.That is the betrayal of the welfare state.'[72]

With Professor Peter Townsend she wrote a booklet, *We Can Afford the Welfare State*, to counteract Labour's claims. Her main demands were for no means-testing, which would inevitably become more widespread as the state pension lost more and more of its value, a restoration of the earnings link to pensions, and the re-establishment of Serps for all who wanted it.As for the claim by Harriet Harman (shadow minister for social security) that Barbara's plan was not affordable, it drew Barbara's contempt:'Frankly, this is just illiterate. State schemes are self-financing because they are contributory and earnings-related contributions rise as earnings rise.'[73]

Barbara announced that she intended to take this argument to the pre-election 1996 party conference and get it put to the vote. It was the moment of terror for the New Labour machine as the almost blind, frail, and soon to be 86-year-old headed towards Blackpool like an unpredictable hurricane. Gordon Brown was despatched to try and talk her out of it over a gin and bitter lemon or two. Harriet Harman tried tea. Barbara puffed on her cigarettes and rejected their compromise, which was to set up a pension commission. 'Can one propose oneself for a place on it?' Barbara asked.[74] Oh yes, they chorused. But a commission, to have any meaning, had to start on a level playing field, she pointed out.The decision not to consider the state option couldn't be taken in advance.'I'll remit if you remit', she told them.

They would not. And there was a good possibility of being defeated and they knew it. Harriet Harman sent out letters to the unions, the constituency parties and pressure groups saying

Barbara's plan would commit the next Labour government to spending an additional £69 billion by 2030 – slightly more than £2 billion a year – and should be rejected. Gordon Brown and John Prescott retired to the back rooms with the union leaders. Barbara went on *Breakfast with Frost* and *Newsnight* and gave countless radio interviews. 'I'm not a wrecker. Never have been, never will be,' she told *Newsnight*, 'but I have a conscience and I couldn't die happy without putting up a fight for something which my whole history, seventy years of public life, tells me that a civilised society must have.'[75]

Seventy years since she had joined the Labour Party, through the Independent Labour Party, before anyone she was dealing with was born. She had fought these conference battles for decades. She could still hold the audience better than any of them. She wanted to inspire people, 'carry them with me along the road of euphoric faith', as she put it;[76] that was what she had always loved about speaking. And she did. It wasn't just her great age they cheered, it was her passion, the clarity of her vision that politics was about more than management: it was about meaning.

The Times had a nice cartoon: Tony Blair at the lectern reading from a document entitled 'New Labour: In Place of Strife', and Barbara walking onto the stage carrying a document entitled 'Old Labour: In Place of Stage Management'. Stage management won. Deals had been done, most significantly with Jack Jones in his role as pensioners' leader. Barbara was defeated by a majority of three to two. But she would not give up; she would be back the next year and the next, while she had breath in her body, as she said.

She gave evidence to the party's Pension Review Body on behalf of her campaign group, Security in Retirement for Everyone (Sire), calling for a restoration of the earnings link, and of course for Serps; 'the choice between a secure pay-as-you-go scheme, leading to a guaranteed pension, and the lottery of playing the market'. But, in the words of Frank Field, the future minister for social security and welfare reform (charged with thinking the unthinkable, until he himself was thought unthinkable and booted out), 'we have closed our mind to the state option'. She could say what she liked, spout her 'dangerous nonsense', Field said, but it would get her nowhere. She threatened to walk out, calling the review a sham. 'I shall not indefinitely go on lending myself to this farce', she said. 'The review body clearly has no real say in policy making'[77] – and indeed it did not.

On 1 May 1997, eighteen years, almost to the day, after Jim Callaghan had left Number 10, Labour was returned spectacularly to office, with 419 MPs, a record, as was the 179 seat majority. Or rather New Labour, with its repudiation of much of what the Labour Party had stood for in its 97-year history, took power. The sheer relief among the majority of voters that Tory economic mismanagement – which had seen £20 billion drain away from the reserves during the debacle over the European exchange-rate mechanism, record numbers of business bankruptcies, house repossessions, mass unemployment, wrecked lives, boom, bust, recession, raging inflation and interest rates of 15 per cent (with nary an apology) – was at an end. So, it was hoped, was the chronic underfunding of the NHS and the schools.

In London, the outpouring of enthusiasm on the streets around Whitehall and Buckingham Palace was genuine, spontaneous and painfully optimistic. But the New Labour image machine had left nothing to chance. In Downing Street itself, nicely dressed children were lined up with Union Jacks to wave at the Blairs as they entered Number 10, just as they might for the Queen, a curiously old imperial British sight; 'traditional values in a modern setting', no doubt.

It was a scene (Act I, Scene 1: The children greet their New Leader) which illustrated what would undermine Tony Blair's government. The medium is the message and Blair's medium was advertising and marketing. His product, the New Labour brand, as the Famous Five called it, was a triumph of image over substance, as Barbara pointed out, and as the electorate soon came to believe. 'The New Labour brand has been badly contaminated', Philip Gould wrote in one of his famously leaked memos. He portrayed Peter Mandelson as plaintively holding his head in his hands and bemoaning: something had gone seriously wrong – but what?*

The medium is the message. The party as a product, branded goods, was what had gone wrong: the refusal to treat the electorate as grown-up, capable of understanding issues, the tendency to pour gobbledygook over it, to smother it with the language of the advertising agency and the management consultancy: 'renewal' and 'values' and 'stakeholder' and 'partnership with the people' and 'traditional values in a modern setting', the language of vacuity and concealment at the heart of government. No one in New Labour seemed able to talk straight. A fact was never simply a fact. The same millions going to this department or that were announced and re-announced four, five, six times, and never seemed to reach a destination until no one believed any monies were going anywhere, ever.

What were New Labour's values? wondered Barbara aloud. Certainly not the values she had espoused when she'd co-written Labour's colonial policy, which had pledged the next Labour government to spend 1 per cent of GNP in overseas aid,† a level that 'may mean some delay in increasing our own standards of good living, but the poorer areas must have priority'. Nor the values of Barbara's DHSS: 'Our government will give overriding priority to the old, the sick, the poor and the disabled', she had said;[78] and meant. She had got more money for the old, the sick, the poor and the disabled, and this during a time of economic crisis.

Gordon Brown used stealth to redistribute wealth to a certain extent, but the government, shaped by focus groups, and what it called Middle England, and the tabloid editorial, was afraid of offending its New Electorate. It would never ask it to do anything difficult, such as give priority to those less fortunate than itself. One sneer from the *Mail* or the *Sun* and it ran for cover, even on small

*The memos were leaked to the *Sun* and *The Times*, July 2000.
† It fell short, but not for lack of Barbara's trying.

promises, on fox hunting, for instance. It searched for the 'third way'; it sought to reconcile the unreconcilable – foxes mangled by dogs in only some counties, perhaps – and pleased no one.

Compromise and a big tent are good things, of course, but sometimes a refusal to compromise has its advantages. If Barbara had been allowed to get the doctors to accept either full-time service in the NHS or full-time private practice, the intractable problem of waiting lists, which did so much harm to New Labour in its first three years, would have been a lesser one. Doctors with long NHS waiting lists are the ones with the most extensive private practice. They have a financial incentive to keep their NHS waiting lists long, because patients who can afford it will pay them to operate privately.

In politics, guts is all, as Barbara says over and over again. It may not be all, but it is of consequence. As she told the *New Statesman*, 'this lot' would not have introduced the NHS. 'It would have been too expensive for them and they would have worried about the opposition of the doctors and some in the media.'[79]

Barbara is no Luddite: 'Methodology must change as the world changes,' she readily acknowledged, 'but that is secondary to preserving the philosophy which inspires our aims.' She could and did change her mind throughout her political life, when the facts, and sometimes pragmatism, demanded. But to her what could and should change are the methods of socialism, not the essence, not the *principles*. While it was true that only 'a blinkered bigot would fail to realise that the dramatic developments of modern technology has made many of our earlier economic ideas out of date', she wrote,[80] the fundamentals of socialism still applied.

In that respect Barbara was, as she told a *Tribune* rally in 1996, an 'unreconstructed Bevanite'. The economic structure might have changed but the eternal human values remained the same. There were certain things we should do as a society for each other: help our poor out of poverty, educate our children, tend to our sick and provide for our old. 'Hang on to the simplicities, comrades', she told rallies back in the 1992 election campaign. Don't forget who you are, what kind of society you want.

Late in the game, three years after entering office, the Blair government began to spend, to do what it had been elected to do, to fund the hospitals and the schools and try and sort out the transport chaos; but about pensions it did nothing in the long or short term except to continue to mumble about private provision and the minimum income guarantee, the means-tested guaranteed minimum income of £75 a week. The pensioners, as Barbara pointed out, had been promised in the manifesto a fair share in the nation's prosperity. Instead, a Britain richer than it ever had been had given them an increase of precisely 75p a week, the lowest since annual uprating began. A single pensioner in twenty-first-century Britain received £67.50 a week; a married couple, £107.90. Many of the ten million pensioners had to apply for the means-tested income-support supplement if they wished to bring themselves up to the guaranteed minimum income, which itself was £20 below the weekly poverty line of £95. If the earnings link had not been broken in 1980, the pension for a single person would have been £97.45.

Barbara in the year 2000, the year of her ninetieth birthday: the pensioners' champion, always ready to get up on a platform in Trafalgar Square and address the pensioners' rally, always ready to do what she could. It is getting less of course. She doesn't always get seamlessly through her speeches any more, which from habit and necessity are delivered without notes. She loses her way sometimes, forgets what she was saying. And she could not do what many wanted her to do and head a national convention of pensioners to bring about a new 'grey power' organisation of the type existent in America, where few politicians would dare undermine the decent state pension accrued by most people during their working lives. Barbara admitted that her health would not allow her to do this.

She still lives alone at Hell Corner Farm. She still has her independence. She is far from incapable, but she is old. As frail as a cobweb, her face a riot of lines, she can no longer walk very far, although she usually takes the dogs out every morning. She cannot see very well with her still extraordinarily vivid china-blue eyes, not well enough to read more than the headlines. She relies on the television and radio for information, but she still writes articles and reviews, typing them out on her forty-year-old Olivetti. Joanie, her secretary-friend, as she calls her, comes in a few times a week and Barbara sometimes hires one of the local ladies to read her government Bills and proposals, such as the Welfare Reform Bill; Barbara drafted amendments to it for the Lords' campaign against it. She still goes to the Lords, getting a friend to drive her to London, and she still speaks in debates and attends rallies. Politics still suffuses her life as it always has done.

From her bedroom window she can just about make out the shape of a branch of an apple tree in her orchard, perhaps the tree Harold had sat under when he came to the Castles' twenty-fifth wedding anniversary all those years ago, when she was the first lady of the land, the first woman prime-minister-in-waiting. The deckchair had collapsed beneath Harold as he sat down and he only just missed being snapped by a photographer who had been chased from his hiding-place in the bushes. The prime minister flat on his back in his first secretary's orchard: it would have been some photo. Dick had been there, and Michael – her old Bevanite colleagues, their trousers rolled. Only Michael was still alive now, three years younger than Barbara but often frailer; their bodies might be failing, but their minds are intact, their memories live and vivid. They phone each other regularly and get together for dinner and gossip and arguments.

Barbara accompanied Michael when he received his award as a freeman of Camden in July 1999. 'She deserves this freedom more than I do', he said and then made a crack about what a 'hell of a problem' it had been trying to teach her to drive.[81] Barbara smiled at the camera. Michael looked at her. Over sixty years ago she had begun her mainstream political career on St Pancras Borough Council, which was now part of Camden. Over sixty years ago Barbara and Michael had agitated on these streets, convinced that they were going to change the world, and walk hand in hand into that socialist dawn.

Fundamentally, Barbara never wandered far from the ideals of her youth, even though they led her into some odd byways, such as her deep reluctance to let go of the idea that the early Soviet Union was the hope of world, as her strange and continual dissembling about her youthful writings from Russia suggested; as did her romantic championing of Lenin. 'Things might have been different in Russia and for the rest of us' if Lenin had lived, she told the *New Statesman*. And in her autobiography she said, 'I firmly believe that, if Lenin had not died in 1924, the Russian Revolution would have taken a different turn';[82] well, yes, but a turn not necessarily for the better, given his life as an 'enthusiastic state-terrorist'[83] and propagator of the one-party state. This was perhaps no more than a curiosity, a fidelity to a first love, which had grown strong in the 1930s soil of slump and slum and mass poverty and unemployment, and fascism, when, as she said, the enemy was capitalism itself.

But even when, as in the case of *In Place of Strife*, Barbara appeared to have made a complete volte-face, she had, in fact, reached back to the ILP and the Bevanite view of the unions' role in a socialist society. It was a huge political mistake, of course, a blunderbuss, career-destroying, heroic failure. She should have remembered the words of Ernie Bevin when he attacked the ILP at its 1927 conference for entering 'into the realm of what was legitimate trade union business' and warning them, as Hugh Scanlon and Jack Jones warned the Labour government forty odd years later, not to 'cut across Trade Union functions in dealing with your own programme'.[84]

Barbara said that, as a matter of self-preservation, if she had to introduce her White Paper again she would not do it, but she still maintained that it was in essence right. Even Hugh Scanlon eventually half agreed. 'When you look at *In Place of Strife* and compare it with what Margaret Thatcher subsequently did, you realise that Barbara's bill was not as vicious as we thought', he said. 'In hindsight it becomes more and more obvious that the debilitating exercise of unofficial strikes was something that sooner or later had to be tackled.'[85] But he still thought the unions were right to resist parliamentary control. Jim Callaghan, too, had his regrets. He felt that he had been wrong in the way he opposed *Strife*. He told one of his senior civil servants that in undermining Barbara he had let his country down. Roy Jenkins told another senior civil servant that he 'did not behave well over *In Place of Strife*' and that 'he regrets that now'.[86]

There is not much house-room for regret in Barbara's life. She could always imagine a future, even one she would not be in; she still wanted to influence what it was. But she did regret that she never became prime minister and there was, as Tony Benn noted, a 'burning sense of personal injustice' which in part motivated her. 'You say I am not fair,' she told him once, 'but nobody has ever been fair to me.'[87] As if to illustrate her point, the *New Statesman* carried out a poll asking members of the PLP who would have been (or would be) the most successful leader of the Labour Party. Gordon Brown came top. Barbara, despite her comeback as the 'veteran leftwinger' (no longer the old woman) 'one of Labour's most distinguished elder statesmen', as the *Daily Mail* (sic!) called her, came nowhere at all: the *Statesman* had put not a single woman on its list. 'Apologies are due particularly to Barbara Castle, who would surely have scored highly', it sheepishly noted.[88]

Apologies, once more, to the scarlet termagant, the best woman leader the party never had, a fundamentally romantic socialist, who could have built a hard-headed cabinet, a government which could have been about economic management and social fairness and vision and excitement. Barbara was, by most accounts, one of the best – and to some, *the* best – minister in the Wilson governments, an inspiring departmental head who commanded incredible loyalty from her staff, someone who could get things done, did not pass the buck or shrink from hard choices. Many of her cabinet colleagues found her difficult and annoying. She had, as has been said, an in-finite capacity to annoy, but she would have been less annoying as prime minister. She was not very good at being an equal among equals, but she was extremely good at being a leader. A country led by Barbara Castle would have known where it was going; whether it would have got there is another matter.

To Barbara, core values were just that. At heart she had an inner conviction that was utterly consistent: as it had been in 1959, so it was in 2000. 'The morality of a society is not created in a vacuum it springs from the way it organises its economic life and distributes its rewards,' she told the 1959 party conference, 'economic and social morality go hand in hand.'[89] Forty years on, her message was unchanged, which was why she argued against means-testing. Not only was it more expensive to administer what was fast becoming a means-tested state pension for the poor, but it was degrading for the recipients and socially divisive. Whereas universal benefits, which are clawed back from the well-off through taxation, are socially cohesive.

To the New Labour hierarchy this was all claptrap, of course, a piece of clotted nonsense, as Hugh Dalton would no doubt have said. She was a nuisance, even a dangerous nuisance; the media, starved of dissent and personalities in New Labour ranks, could not get enough of her. She was a colourful focus for dissension. In February 2000, at the celebration bash for Labour's centenary, Tony Blair gave the scarlet bogey redux a barbed nod. He said that today's New Labour Party had got over a hundred women elected to parliament in 1997, whereas, he added (incorrectly) 'in 1945 there were less than ten.* One was Barbara Castle. She is here today. Her passion and courage has been an example not just to women in the Labour Movement but to all of us. But throughout our history, radicalism has too often been followed by long periods of Conservative rule.'[90]

Yet without a vision the party perishes: boredom is, as Barbara so often said, the enemy of democracy. But her criticism went beyond that. The 'problem which still haunts British politics', she wrote, was 'how to marry Socialist ideals with our increasingly materialistic world'.[91] It was a problem that had haunted her for decades because to Barbara Castle politics is, and has always been, about what kind of country we want to be; it's about how we become a truly moral and happy society; it's about who we are as a people.

---

*Twenty-one Labour women MPS were elected in 1945; there were twenty-four women MPS in all.

POSTSCRIPT

When Barbara died on 3 May 2002 she did so not only as the darling of Labour Party Conferences, pensioners and the left, but also as 'one of the dominating political figures of the twentieth century', as Tony Blair, the then prime minister, put it; 'the people's politician', he might have added, if she hadn't spent the last years of her life attacking him and 'his Achilles heel... [of] self-love' – when she wasn't eviscerating much of his New Labour project – especially the refusal to restore the link between pensions and earnings, which she had introduced.

The link was part of her legacy, and Barbara was nothing if not ferocious in protecting that, but there were also principles at stake: security in old age should be a matter for the state, not the capricious roulette wheel known as the stock exchange, and means-testing undermined the welfare state. For good or ill, principles always underwrote Barbara's policies: 'In politics, guts is all,' she famously said, though, as with *In Place of Strife*, she found that sometimes in politics, politics is all.

Nevertheless, guts in politics, as elsewhere, are not negligible; legislation that Barbara got enacted, often in the teeth of seething opposition, changed people's lives for the better, and not only the bread-and-butter issues of pensions, universal child benefit and equal pay for women, but also the seatbelts she mandated to be fitted in cars, the 70-mph speed limit and the breathalyser which saved, and which continues to save, hundreds upon thousands of lives, and for which she was vilified at the time: 'You're only a woman, what do you know about it?' as a BBC interviewer, who objected to her 'spoiling my fun', said, echoing prevailing sentiment.

Her record is quite an achievement for a minister of either sex, notwithstanding that legislation can be undone (pensions) or undermined (universal child benefit) by the next government or the one after that, or not yet quite attained (equal pay) forty years after enactment. Few ministers achieve as much.

In the past couple of years she has had a train named after her, her head put on the most expensive stamp of the Royal Mail's 'Women of Distinction' series, and been played by Miranda Richardson in the film *Made in Dagenham*, in which the fictional Barbara Castle says, 'I'm what's known as a fiery redhead...' Red of hair and deed: her first question to Parliament on 11 October 1945 was addressed to Nye Bevan, the Health Minister, asking him, 'pending the establishment of an adequate number of nursery schools', to retain the free war-time nurseries for 'all mothers who go out to work'. Her last parliamentary speech was to the Lords on 18 December 2001 on the pension legislation that 'worries a number of us who do not believe that this country wants to live in the means-testing ethic'. From the cradle to the grave, like Labour's 1945 manifesto, Barbara Castle was a socialist, and proud of it. That, too, is her legacy.

Lisa Martineau
November, 2010

NOTES

Abbreviations

TBD: *Tony Benn's Diaries*

BCD: *Barbara Castle's Diaries*

RCD: *Richard Crossman's Diaries*

BWD: *Beatrice Webb's Diaries*

LPACR: *Labour Party Annual Conference Report*

Part I: Forward to Socialism

Chapter 1   Mine for Life

1 Kenneth Harris, *Kenneth Harris Talking To* (Weidenfeld & Nicolson, 1971), p. 20.
2 Olive Shapley, quoted in Wilfred De'ath, *Barbara Castle: A Portrait from Life* (Clifton Books, 1970), p. 114.
3 *Sentimental Journey*, BBC Radio 4, 18 October 1998.
4 Robert Skidelsky, *Oswald Mosley* (Macmillan, 1975), p. 169.
5 Barbara Castle, *Fighting All the Way* (Macmillan, 1993), p. 29.
6 *Observer*, 28 September 1969.
7 Mary Clark, quoted in De'ath, *Barbara Castle*, pp. 103, 101.
8 *Observer*, 28 September 1969.
9 Mary Clark, quoted in De'ath, *Barbara Castle*, p. 97.
10 Castle, *Fighting*, p. 17.
11 *Guardian*, 25 September 1999.

12 *Sentimental Journey*.

13 Ibid.

14 Ibid.

15 Vic Feather, quoted in De'ath, *Barbara Castle*, p. 26.

16 Gilbert Murray, preface to *The Iron Age*, by Frank Betts, p. 5.

17 Castle, *Fighting*, p. 5.

18 William Morris, *The Water of the Wondrous Isles* (Prior, 1979), p. 93.

19 Fiona MacCarthy, *William Morris: A Life for Our Time* (Faber and Faber, 1994), p. 636.

20 Morris, *The Water*, p. 253.

21 *Observer*, 5 October 1969.

22 *The Texture of Welfare: A Survey of Social Service in Bradford*, p. 20.

23 Ibid, p. 100.

24 Eric Silver, *Victor Feather,* TUC (Victor Gollancz, 1973), p. 48.

25 Ibid.

26 *The Times*, 19 June 1993.

27 *Lancashire Evening Post*, 28 July 1969.

28 *The Times*, 19 June 1993.

29 *The Texture of Welfare*, p. 85.

30 *Socialist Review*, vol. 26 (1925), no. 144.

31 *Sentimental Journey*.

32 *The Bradfordian*, March 1926, p. 19.

33 Ibid, November 1922, p. 17.

34 Ibid, March 1929, pp. 12–13.

35 *Observer*, 28 September 1969.

36 *Sentimental Journey*.

37 Olive Shapley, *Broadcasting a Life: The Autobiography of Olive Shapley* (Scarlet Press, 1996), pp. 23–4.

38 Ibid.

39 Ibid, p. 26.

40 *Liverpool Echo*, 13 December 1967.

41 Penny Griffin, ed., *St Hugh's: One Hundred Years of Women's Education in Oxford* (Macmillan, 1986), p. 122.

42 De'ath, *Barbara Castle*, p. 98.

43 Vera Brittain, *The Women at Oxford: A Fragment of History* (George G. Harrap, 1960), p. 167.

44 Griffin, *St Hugh's*, p. 144.

45 Christopher Hollis, *Oxford in the Twenties: Recollections of Five Friends* (Heinemann, 1976), p. 115.

46 David Walter, *The Oxford Union: Playground of Power* (Macdonald, 1984), p. 15.

47 Ibid, p. 162.

48 *Observer*, 16 November 1958.

49 Hollis, *Oxford in the Twenties*, p. 115.

50 Walter, *The Oxford Union*, p. 162.

51 Shapley, *Broadcasting a Life*, p. 26.

52 Ibid, p. 27.

53 *Evening Standard*, 13 December 1967.

54 De'ath, *Barbara Castle*, p. 98.

55 Brian Harrison, ed., *The History of the University of Oxford*, vol. 3 (Oxford: Clarendon Press, 1994), p. 399.

56 Ibid.

57 Walter, *The Oxford Union*, p. 74.

58 Patricia Hollis, *Jennie Lee: A Life* (Oxford University Press, 1997), p. 73.

59 *Manchester Guardian*, 9 June 1942.

60 Joyce M. Bellamy and John Saville, eds, *Dictionary of Labour Biography*, vol. 4 (Macmillan, 1977), p. 124.

61 Margaret Postgate, *Growing Up into Revolution* (Longmans, Green & Co, 1949), p. 66.

62 Ibid.

63 Nicholas Davenport, *Memoirs of a City Radical* (Weidenfeld & Nicolson, 1974), p. 61.

64 Henry Pelling, *A Short History of the Labour Party*, 3rd edn (Macmillan, 1968), p. 69.

65 Beatrice Webb, *The Diary of Beatrice Webb*; vol. 4: *1924–1943*, ed. Norman and Jeanne MacKenzie (Virago/London School of Economics and Political Science, 1985), 23 August 1931, p. 253.

66 Henry Pelling, *America and the British Left: From Bright to Bevan* (Adam and Charles Black, 1956), p. 132.

67 Anthony Greenwood papers, c 6276, folio 84, Bodleian Library.

68 BWD, 11 November 1937, p. 397.

69 Castle, *Fighting*, p. 57.

70 Ronald Blythe, *The Age of Illusion: England in the Twenties and Thirties* (Hamish Hamilton, 1963), p. 156.

71 Ibid.

72 Silver, *Victor Feather*, p. 52.

73 *Bradford Pioneer*, 9 October 1931.

74 Ibid, 16 October 1931.

75 Castle, *Fighting*, p. 58.

Chapter 2   Agitate, Agitate, Agitate

1 Elizabeth Thomas, ed., *Tribune 21: An Anthology of Literary Contributions to 'The Tribune' during Twenty-one Years* (MacGibbon

& Kee, 1958), p. 5.

2 Michael Foot, *Aneurin Bevan*, vol. 1: *1897-1945* (Paladin, 1975), p. 246.

3 *Liverpool Echo*, 12 December 1967.

4 *New Statesman*, 1 October 1971.

5 Ronald Mellor, interview with the author.

6 Patricia Hollis, *Jennie Lee: A Life* (Oxford University Press, 1997), p. 76.

7 Olive Shapley, *Broadcasting a Life: The Autobiography of Olive Shapley* (Scarlet Press, 1996), p. 25.

8 Paul Foot, interview with the author.

9 Gerald Kaufman, interview with the author.

10 Melanie Phillips, *The Divided House:Women at Westminster* (Sidgwick & Jackson, 1980), p. 99.

11 *Tribune*, 12 March 1937.

12 John Thomas Murphy, *New Horizons: An Autobiography* (John Lane, 1941), p. 308.

13 Mervyn Jones, *Michael Foot* (Victor Gollancz, 1994), p. 45.

14 *Hampstead and Highgate Gazette*, 7 December 1984.

15 Jones, *Michael Foot*, p. 45.

16 *Hampstead and Highgate Gazette*, 7 December 1984.

17 LPACR 1932.

18 G. D. H. Cole, letter to Clement Attlee, Stafford Cripps, and others, 19 September 1932, Cole Archives, Nuffield College, Oxford.

19 Teddy Radace, letter to Zip members, 8 October 1932, Cole Archives.

20 Ernest Bevin, letter to G. D. H. Cole, 24 September 1932, Cole Archives.

21 *New Statesman & Nation*, 21 April 1951.

22 Hugh Dalton, *The Fateful Years: Memoirs 1931-1945* (Frederick Muller, 1957), p. 24.

23 BWD, 9 July 1939, p. 436.

24 Murphy, *New Horizons*, p. 312.

25 M. Foot, *Aneurin Bevan*, vol. 1, p. 157.

26 Dalton, *The Fateful Years*, p. 130.

27 Ben Pimlott, *Labour and the Left in the 1930s* (Cambridge University Press, 1977), p. 30.

28 Ronald Mellor, interview.

29 *British Weekly*, 5 October 1933.

30 M. Foot, *Aneurin Bevan*, vol. 1, p. 158.

31 Pimlott, *Labour and the Left*, p. 53.

32 LPACR 1933.

33 M. Foot, *Aneurin Bevan*, vol. 1, p. 158.

34 Ibid, p. 157.

35 *Socialist Leaguer*, August–September 1934.

36 Dalton, *The Fateful Years*, p. 53.

37 Castle, *Fighting*, p. 73.

38 Storm Jameson, *Journey from the North: The Autobiography of Storm Jameson* (Collins/Harvill Press, 1969), vol. 1, p. 322.

39 Pimlott, *Labour and the Left*, p. 55.

40 William Mellor, letter to Stafford Cripps, 11 September 1935, from Cripps papers held by Professor Peter Clarke, St John's College, Cambridge, to whom I am grateful for access.

41 Castle, *Fighting*, p. 76.

42 Leah Manning, *A Life for Education: An Autobiography* (Victor Gollancz, 1970), p. 107.

43 Charles Mowat, *Britain Between the Wars, 1918–1940* (Methuen, 1955), p. 578.

44 M. Foot, *Aneurin Bevan*, vol. 1, p. 161.

45 Ronald Blythe, *The Age of Illusion: England in the Twenties and Thirties* (Hamish Hamilton, 1963), p. 160.

46 Patricia Hollis, *Jennie Lee: A Life* (Oxford University Press, 1997), p. 85.

47 M. Foot, *Aneurin Bevan*, vol. 1, p. 163–4.

48 Barbara Ayrton Gould, who had worked on a report on the distressed areas, LPACR 1936.

49 M. Foot, *Aneurin Bevan*, vol. 1, p. 198.

50 *Socialist Leaguer*, October–November 1934.

51 LPACR 1934.

52 *Socialist Leaguer*, October–November 1934.

53 LPACR 1935.

54 *Socialist Leaguer*, June–July 1934.

55 *The Left Book Club*, BBC Radio 3, 26 March 1994.

56 M. Foot, *Aneurin Bevan*, vol. 1, p. 200.

57 Kingsley Martin, *Editor: A Second Volume of Autobiography, 1931–45* (Hutchinson, 1968) p. 57.

58 Harold Nicolson, *Diaries and Letters, 1930–1939*, ed. Nigel Nicolson (Collins, 1966), 6 June 1938, p. 346.

59 Ibid, 6 June 1938, p. 345.

60 Ibid, 18 May 1938, p. 342.

61 Angus Calder, *The People's War: Britain 1939–45* (Jonathan Cape, 1969), p. 23.

62 *Chips: The Diaries of Sir Henry Channon*, ed. Robert Rhodes James (Weidenfeld & Nicolson, 1967), p. 35.

63 Ibid, 22 November 1936, p. 84.

64 Ibid, 27 September 1935, p. 42.

65 Ibid, 21 November 1938, p. 178.

66 Castle, *Fighting*, p. 77.

67 M. Foot, *Aneurin Bevan*, vol. 1, p. 245.

68 Fenner Brockway, *Inside the Left: Thirty Years of Platform, Press, Prison and Parliament* (George Allen & Unwin, 1942), p. 266.

69 Ibid, p. 269.

70 Eric Silver, *Victor Feather,* TUC (Victor Gollancz, 1973), p. 66.

Chapter 3 Hope and History

1 *Daily Mirror*, 1 January 1937.

2 Stafford Cripps, letter to William Mellor, 2 January 1937, Ronald Mellor private collection.

3 Joyce M. Bellamy and John Saville, eds, *Dictionary of Labour Biography*, vol. 4 (Macmillan, 1977), p. 124.

4 Elizabeth Thomas, ed., *Tribune 21: An Anthology of Literary Contributions to 'The Tribune' during Twenty-one Years* (MacGibbon & Kee, 1958), p. 5.

5 Mervyn Jones, *Michael Foot* (Victor Gollancz, 1994), p. 60.

6 Michael Foot, *Aneurin Bevan* (Paladin, 1975), vol. 1, p. 246.

7 De'ath, *Barbara Castle*, p. 12.

8 Richard Clements, interview with the author.

9 Hollis, *Jennie Lee*, p. 214.

10 M. Foot, *Aneurin Bevan*, p. 249.

11 *News Chronicle*, 17 May 1937.

12 Hugh Dalton, *The Fateful Years: Memoirs 1931-1945* (Frederick Muller, 1957), p. 129.

13 Charles Mowat, *Britain Between the Wars, 1918-1940* (Methuen, 1955), p. 548.

14 Henry Pelling, *A Short History of the Labour Party*, 3rd edn (Macmillan, 1968), p. 83.

15 *Tribune*, 23 July 1937.

16 Ibid, 8 October 1937.

17 Hugh Thomas, *The Spanish Civil War* (Eyre & Spottiswoode, 1961), p. 363.

18 Thomas, *Tribune* 21, p. 7.

19 Hollis, *Jennie Lee*, p. 176.

20 BWD, 6 December 1937, pp. 397-8.

21 *Tribune*, 8 October 1937.

22 Quotes from Barbara's *Tribune* series are from issues published in the seven weeks from 15 October 1937 to 26 November 1937.

23 Sidney and Beatrice Webb, *Soviet Communism: A New Civilisation* (Victor Gollancz, 1937), p. 1205.

24 BWD, editors' introduction to Part III, p. 269.

25 M. Jones, *Michael Foot*, p. 55.

26 Elizabeth Vallance and Elizabeth Davies, *Women of Europe: Women MEPs and Equality Policy* (Cambridge University Press, 1986), p. 70.

27 Minutes of the Contracts and Stores Committee meeting, 14 March 1939, Camden Local Studies and Archives Centre, Holborn, London.

28 *The Government's Evacuation Scheme*, April 1939, Camden Archives.

29 ARP Committee Minutes, 8 October 1938, Camden Archives.

30 *Daily Mail*, 27 May 1938.

31 Fenner Brockway, *Inside the Left: Thirty Years of Platform, Press, Prison and Parliament* (George Allen & Unwin, 1942), p. 265.

32 M. Jones, *Michael Foot*, p. 61; M. Foot, *Aneurin Bevan*, p. 280.

33 M. Jones, *Michael Foot*, p. 66.

34 *Chips: The Diaries of Sir Henry Channon*, ed. Robert Rhodes James (Weidenfeld & Nicolson, 1967), 17 May 1939, p. 199.

35 Winston Churchill, *The Second World War*, vol. 1: *The Gathering Storm* (Cassell, 1949), p. 328.

36 BWD, 23 August 1939, p. 438.

37 Castle, *Fighting*, p. 88.

38 Philip Ziegler, *London at War 1939-45* (Sinclair-Stevenson, 1995), p. 42.

39 Ibid, p. 51.

40 Library Committee Minutes, 1 February 1940, Camden Archives.

41 Castle, *Fighting*, p. 110.

42 *The Red Queen*, BBC TV, 21 September 1995.

43 *Daily Herald*, 9 June 1942.

44 *The Times*, 28 January 1995.

45 De'ath, *Barbara Castle*, p. 35.

46 Hollis, *Jennie Lee*, p. 152.

47 Ibid, p. 204.

Part II: Let Us Face the Future

Chapter 4   Barbara's Castle

1 J. B. Priestley, quoted in Angust Calder, *The People's War, Britain 1939-45* (Jonathan Cape, 1969), p. 163.

2 LPACR 1943, p. 130.

3 LPACR 1944, p. 115.
4 LPACR 1943, p. 140.
5 Wilfred De'ath, *Barbara Castle* (Clifton Books, 1970), p. 55.
6 Ibid, p. 14.
7 Richard Clements, Joe Haines, Neil Kinnock and Dick Leonard, interviews with the author.
8 *Liverpool Echo*, 12 December 1967.
9 De'ath, *Barbara Castle*, p. 58.
10 Ibid, p. 14.
11 Kinnock, interview.
12 *Picture Post*, 23 June 1945.
13 *Let Us Face the Future: The Labour Party Manifesto*, April 1945.
14 LPACR 1945, p. 98.
15 Pamela Brookes, *Women at Westminster: An Account of Women in the British Parliament, 1918-1966* (Peter Davies, 1967), p. 153.
16 *Class Rule*, BBC2, 26 November 1991.
17 *Sentimental Journey*, BBC Radio 4, 18 October 1998.
18 Michael Foot, *Aneurin Bevan* (Paladin, 1975), vol. 2: *1945-1960*, p. 15.
19 Hugh Dalton, *The Fateful Years: Memoirs 1931-1945* (Frederick Muller, 1957), pp. 481-2.
20 *Daily Telegraph*, 10 August 1945.
21 Leah Manning, *A Life for Education: An Autobiography* (Victor Gollancz, 1970), p. 202.
22 *News Chronicle*, 8 September 1945.
23 Jean Mann, *Woman in Parliament* (Odhams Press, 1962), p. 11.
24 Daily Herald, 10 March 1961.
25 Manning, *A Life for Education*, p. 165.
26 Mann, *Woman in Parliament*, p. 11.
27 Ibid, p. 17.
28 Manning, *A Life for Education*, pp. 202-3.
29 Bernard Ingham, interview with the author.
30 Mann, *Woman in Parliament*, p. 11; Patricia *Hollis, Jennie Lee, A Life* (Oxford University Press, 1997), p. 121.
31 *Liverpool Echo*, 12 December 1967.
32 De'ath, *Barbara Castle*, p. 61.
33 Ibid.
34 Ben Pimlott, *Hugh Dalton* (Jonathan Cape, 1985), p. 424.
35 Manning, *A Life for Education*, p. 203.
36 Pimlott, *Hugh Dalton*, p. 443.
37 Hugh Dalton, *High Tide and After: Memoirs, 1945-1960* (Frederick Muller, 1962), p. 306.

38 Hugh Dalton, *Fateful Years*, p. 433.

39 Ben Pimlott, *Harold Wilson* (HarperCollins, 1993), p. 92.

40 *Chips: The Diaries of Sir Henry Channon*, ed. Robert Rhodes James (Weidenfeld & Nicolson, 1967), 20 August 1945, p. 412.

41 *Tribune,* 30 August 1946.

42 Alan Watkins, *Brief Lives* (Hamish Hamilton, 1982), p. 37.

43 Pimlott, *Harold Wilson*, p. 337.

44 Roy Jenkins, *Roy Jenkins' Gallery of 20th-Century Portraits* (David & Charles, 1988), p. 61.

45 RCD, 9 March 1969, p. 404.

46 Gerald Kaufman, interview with the author.

47 RCD, 11 September 1968, p. 185.

48 RCD, 13 November 1951, p. 36.

49 Paul Foot, interview with the author.

50 Kinnock, interview.

51 Geoffrey Goodman, interview with the author.

52 Stan Orme, interview with the author.

53 'The Prime Minister talks to The Observer', *Observer*, April 1979.

54 Kenneth Morgan, *Callaghan: A Life* (Oxford University Press, 1997), p. 76.

55 *Labour in Number Ten*, BBC Radio 4, 17 October 1994.

56 Alan Sked and Chris Cook, *Post-War Britain: A Political History* (Penguin, 1979), p. 27.

57 'The Prime Minister talks to The Observer'.

58 David E. Martin and David Rubenstein, eds, *Ideology and the Labour Movement: Essays Presented to John Saville* (Croom Helm, 1979), p. 243.

59 *Slice of Life*, BBC2, 22 November 1995.

60 Herbert Matthews and Nancy Matthews, *The Britain We Saw* (Victor Gollancz, 1950), p. 127.

61 Ibid, p. 122.

62 M. Foot, *Aneurin Bevan*, vol. 2, p. 33.

63 Philip Ziegler, *Wilson: The Authorised Life of Lord Wilson of Rievaulx* (Weidenfeld & Nicolson, 1993), p. 55.

64 Pimlott, *Harold Wilson*, p. 175.

65 Goodman, interview.

66 Pimlott, *Harold Wilson*, p. 106.

67 Goodman, interview.

68 De'ath, *Barbara Castle*, p. 89.

69 Jad Adams, *Tony Benn* (Macmillan, 1992), p. 139.

70 *Daily Herald*, 10 March 1961.

71 De'ath, *Barbara Castle*, pp. 104–5.

72 RCD, 13 April 1969, p. 417.
73 Clements interview.
74 Pimlott, *Harold Wilson*, p. 175.
75 Kaufman, interview.
76 *Tribune*, 26 November 1948.
77 LPACR 1949, p. 162.
78 Ibid, p. 161.
79 Martin and Rubenstein, *Ideology*, p. 227.
80 David Owen, interview with the author.
81 M. Foot, *Aneurin Bevan*, vol. 2, p. 23.
82 Manning, *A Life for Education*, p. 203.
83 *Picture Post*, 27 July 1946.
84 Keep Left minutes, 14 June 1950, Jo Richardson Papers, The Museum of Labour History, Manchester.
85 Henry Pelling, *A Short History of the Labour Party*, 3rd edn (Macmillan, 1968), p 105.
86 Hollis, *Jennie Lee*, p. 162.
87 Robert Edwards, *Goodbye Fleet Street* (Jonathan Cape, 1988), p. 35.

Chapter 5   The Troubles

1 Ian Mikardo, *Back-Bencher* (Weidenfeld & Nicolson, 1988), p. 151.
2 Peggy Duff, *Left, Left, Left: A Personal Account of Six Protest Campaigns 1945-65* (Allison & Busby, 1971), pp. 43-5.
3 Patricia Hollis, *Jennie Lee: A Life* (Oxford University Press, 1997), p. 175.
4 David Coates, *The Labour Party and the Struggle for Socialism* (Cambridge University Press, 1975), p. 76.
5 Stan Orme, interview with the author.
6 Geoffrey Goodman, interview with the author.
7 Mark Jenkins, *Bevanism: Labour's High Tide* (Spokesman, 1979), p. 170.
8 Orme, interview.
9 Goodman, interview.
10 Duff, *Left, Left Left*, p. 47.
11 Leslie Hunter, *The Road to Brighton Pier* (Arthur Barker, 1959), p. 55.
12 Hugh Dalton, *The Political Diary of Hugh Dalton*, ed. Ben Pimlott (Jonathan Cape/London School of Economics and Political Science, 1986), 20 June 1951, p. 546.
13 Ibid, 30 October 1951, p. 566; 4 October 1951, p. 558.
14 Hunter, *Road to Brighton Pier*, p. 56.

15 Jean Mann, *Woman in Parliament* (Odhams Press, 1962), p. 192.

16 Hunter, *Road to Brighton Pier*, p. 57.

17 *New Statesman and Nation*, 4 October 1952.

18 Henry Pelling, *A Short History of the Labour Party*, 3rd edn (Macmillan, 1968), p. 105.

19 RCD, 4 February 1953, p. 198; RCD, 2 October 1952, p. 153; Dalton, *Political Diary*, 13 November 1952, p. 602.

20 *New Statesman*, 9 July 1960.

21 *The Diary of Hugh Gaitskell 1945-1956*, ed. Philip M. Williams (Jonathan Cape, 1983), 21 March 1952, pp. 312-3.

22 RCD, 11 March 1952, p. 94.

23 *New Socialist*, March–April 1982.

24 Melanie Phillips, *The Divided House: Women at Westminster* (Sidgwick & Jackson, 1980), p. 28.

25 *The Wilson Years*, BBC Radio 3, 3 October 1990.

26 David Owen, interview with the author.

27 Douglas Jay, *Change and Fortune: A Political Record* (Hutchinson, 1980), p. 223.

28 M. Jenkins, *Bevanism*, p. 171.

29 LPACR 1952, p. 78.

30 *New Statesman and Nation*, 4 October 1952.

31 LPACR 1952, p. 79.

32 Eric Shaw, *Discipline and Discord in the Labour Party: The Politics of Managerial Control in the Labour Party 1951-87* (Manchester University Press, 1988), p. 33.

33 Dalton, *Political Diary*, 1 October 1952, p. 599.

34 *New Statesman and Nation*, 4 October 1952.

35 *New Statesman and Nation*, 11 October 1952.

36 Marcia Williams, *Inside No. 10*, p. 309.

37 Speech Gaitskell made at Stalybridge, 5 October 1952.

38 Peter Kellner and Christopher Hitchens, *Callaghan: The Road to Number Ten* (Cassell, 1976), p. 32.

Chapter 6   Scarlet Bogey

1 RCD, 4 December 1951, p. 47.

2 CIA, letter to the author, 29 May 1998.

3 *New York Times*, 21 November 1951.

4 Ibid.

5 *Sunday Times*, 22 May 1955.

6 RCD, 23 February 1955, p. 389.

7 Dick Clements, interview with the author.

8 *Sunday Times*, 22 May 1955.

9 *The Post*, 10 May 1952; *Sunday Dispatch*, 29 November 1958; Gerald Kaufman, interview with the author.

10 *The Times*, 7 November 1961.

11 Fenner Brockway, *Towards Tomorrow: The Autobiography of Fenner Brockway* (Hart-Davis MacGibbon, 1977), p. 208.

12 *Manchester Guardian*, 23 November 1959; *The Guardian*, 5 July 1960; *Sunday Dispatch*, 29 November 1958.

13 *Sunday Dispatch*, ibid; Tam Dalyell, letter to the author.

14 Castle, *Fighting*, p. 252; Barbara Castle, letter to Tony Greenwood, 18 December 1959, Greenwood papers.

15 Kenneth Morgan, *Callaghan: A Life* (Oxford University Press, 1997), p. 140.

16 *Daily Express*, 21 January 1958.

17 David Goldsworthy, *Colonial Issues in British Politics, 1945-1961: From 'Colonial Development' to 'Wind of Change'* (Oxford: Clarendon Press, 1971), p. 335; Labour Party, *Labour's Colonial Policy: The Plural Society*, July 1956; *Sunday Times*, 22 July 1956.

18 Labour Party, *Economic Aid*, May 1957.

19 *Tribune*, 28 November 1952.

20 *New Statesman*, 29 June 1962.

21 *Sunday Express*, 14 December 1958.

22 RCD, 26 September 1952, p. 141, 15 December 1952, p. 190.

23 Castle, *Fighting*, p. 192.

24 Ian Mikardo, *Back-Bencher* (Weidenfeld & Nicolson, 1988), p. 1.

25 Profile, BBC Radio, 8 October 1980.

26 De'ath, *Barbara Castle*, p. 41.

27 *Guardian*, 25 September 1999; De'ath, ibid.

28 Hugh Dalton, *The Political Diary of Hugh Dalton*, ed. Ben Pimlott (Jonathan Cape/London School of Economics and Political Science, 1986), 13 November 1952, p. 602.

29 RCD, 4 February 1953, p. 198; *Daily Herald*, 10 March 1961.

30 *Daily Herald*, ibid.

31 Patricia Hollis, *Jennie Lee: A Life* (Oxford University Press, 1997), p. 190.

32 RCD, 15 March 1955, p. 400.

33 RCD, 23 September 1955, p. 441.

34 Leslie Hunter, *The Road to Brighton Pier* (Arthur Barker, 1959), pp. 135, 138-9.

35 Hugh Gaitskell, *The Diary of Hugh Gaitskell 1945-1956*, ed. Philip M. Williams (Jonathan Cape, 1983), p. 347.

36 *The Times*, 9 December 1960.

37 Michael Foot, *Aneurin Bevan*, vol. 2: *1945-1960*, p. 568.

38 Ibid, pp. 572–4.
39 Ibid; RCD, 4 October 1957, p. 620.
40 Christopher Driver, *The Disarmers: A Study in Protest* (Hodder & Stoughton, 1964), p. 37.
41 *Liverpool Echo*, 11 December 1967.
42 Pat Arrowsmith, telephone conversation with the author.
43 Richard Taylor, *Against the Bomb: The British Peace Movement 1958–1965* (Oxford: Clarendon Press, 1988), p. 284.
44 Ibid, p. 285.
45 LPACR 1957, p. 196.
46 Stephen Xydis, *Cyprus: Conflict and Conciliation 1954–1958* (Columbus, 1967), p. 249.
47 TBD, 23 September 1958, p. 287.
48 *Daily Telegraph*, 22 September 1958.
49 *Daily Sketch*, 23 September 1958.
50 Morgan, *Callaghan*, p. 140; Kellner and Hitchens, *Callaghan*, p. 36; TBD, 23 May 1958, p. 279.
51 TBD, 23 September 1958, p. 287.
52 *Daily Telegraph*, 24 September 1958.
53 Goldsworthy, *Colonial Issues*, p. 357.
54 Interview with fellow MP.
55 *The Observer*, 16 November 1958; Hugh Dalton, *The Fateful Years: Memoirs 1931–1945* (Frederick Muller, 1957), p. 141.
56 Gaitskell, *Diary*, p. 313.
57 RCD, 9 October 1959, p. 786.
58 Ibid, 9 December 1959, p. 802.
59 All quotes from Barbara's speech are from the LPACR 1959, pp. 84–6.
60 M. Foot, *Aneurin Bevan*, vol. 2, pp. 636–7.
61 TBD, 28 November 1959, p. 320.
62 RCD, 9 December 1959, p. 803.
63 John Campbell, *Roy Jenkins: A Biography* (Weidenfeld & Nicolson, 1983), p. 231; Anthony Crosland, *The Conservative Enemy: A Programme of Radical Reform for the 1960s* (Jonathan Cape, 1962), p. 129.
64 J. K. Galbraith, *The Affluent Society* (Boston, MA: Houghton Mifflin, 1958), p. 1.
65 Neil Kinnock, interview with the author.
66 *Sunday Dispatch*, 29 November 1958.
67 Brian Brivati, *Hugh Gaitskell* (Richard Cohen, 1996), p. 348.
68 *New Statesman*, 9 July 1960.
69 TBD, 6 July 1969, p. 333.
70 RCD, 13 October 1960, p. 881.

71 Ibid; Clements, interview.

72 RCD, 13 October 1960; *The Observer*, 16 November 1958.

73 Michael Bentley and John Stevenson, eds, *High and Low Politics in Modern Britain* (Oxford: Clarendon Press, 1983), p. 307.

74 Ben Pimlott, *Harold Wilson* (HarperCollins, 1993), pp. 255–6.

75 Wigg, Lord, *George Wigg* (Michael Joseph, 1972), p. 269; C. Irving, Ron Hall and Jeremy Wallington, *Scandal '63: A Study of the Profumo Affair* (Heinemann, 1963), p. 220.

76 Irving, Hall and Wallinton, *Scandal '63*, p. 101.

77 TBD, 30 September 1963, p. 66; 2 December 1963, p. 80; 3 December 1963, p. 81.

78 *Tribune*, 5 November 1976.

Part III: The Most Powerful Woman in Britain

Chapter 7 His Little Minister

1 Ben Pimlott, *Harold Wilson* (HarperCollins, 1993), p. 327.

2 Philip Ziegler, *Wilson: The Authorised Life of Lord Wilson of Rievaulx* (Weidenfeld & Nicolson, 1993), p. 175; *Sunday Mirror*, 2 December 1964.

3 Christopher Tugendhat and Bert Oram, interviews with the author.

4 *Platform 1*, BBC TV, 3 June 1980.

5 Tugendhat, interview.

6 Gerald Kaufman, interview with the author.

7 *Daily Telegraph*, 23 October 1964.

8 Roy Jenkins, *Roy Jenkins' Gallery of 20th-Century Portraits and Oxford Papers* (David & Charles, 1988) p. 62.

9 Bernard Ingham, interview with the author.

10 *Sunday Mirror*, 2 December 1964.

11 Austin Mitchell and David Wiener, *Last Time: Labour's Lessons from the Sixties* (Bellew, 1997), p. 87.

12 Clive Ponting, *Breach of Promise: Labour in Power 1964–70* (Hamish Hamilton, 1989), p. 216.

13 Harold Wilson, cabinet memorandum, 16 December 1964, State Papers, Public Record Office (PRO), Kew.

14 Pimlott, *Harold Wilson*, p. 328.

15 Barbara's use of womanly wiles and her flirtatiousness were commented on by almost all interviewees. Margaret Stewart, *Frank Cousins: A Study* (Hutchinson, 1968), p. 133; Geoffrey Goodman, interview with the author.

16 Roy Jenkins, *Gallery*, p. 60.

17 Edmund Dell, interview with the author.
18 Patrick Gordon Walker, *The Cabinet* (Jonathan Cape, 1970), p. 108; Susan Crosland, *Tony Crosland* (Jonathan Cape, 1982), p. 290.
19 BCD, 25 February 1965, p. 16.
20 Roy Jenkins, *A Life at the Centre* (Pan/Macmillan, 1992), p. 224.
21 Dell, interview.
22 Ibid; BCD, 30 November 1965, p. 35; Geoffrey Goodman, interview with the author.
23 Joe Haines, interview with the author.
24 Pimlott, *Harold Wilson*, p. 345.
25 TBD, 1 June 1967, p. 502.
26 Oram, interview.
27 *Sunday Times*, 10 June 1973.
28 *New Statesman*, 7 January 1966.
29 *Sunday Times*, 10 June 1973.
30 Ibid.
31 RCD 22 October 1964, pp. 21, 26.
32 *Labour in Number 10*, BBC Radio, 17 October 1994; *Sunday Times*, 10 June 1973.
33 TBD, 19 February 1965, p. 223.
34 R. Jenkins, *Gallery*, p. 60.
35 John Burgh, interview with the author; his view was strongly echoed by other civil servants.
36 Burgh and Richard Bird, interviews with the author.
37 Owen and Bird, interviews.
38 *New Statesman*, 7 January 1966; Dell, interview.
39 Paul Foot and Neil Kinnock, interviews with the author.
40 LPACR 1963, p. 223.
41 Cabinet Conclusions (CAB), 24 November 1964.
42 A. Darnborough, *Labour's Record on Southern Africa*, Anti-Apartheid Movement pamphlet, June 1967, p. 1.
43 Tam Dalyell, letter to the author; Dalyell, *Dick Crossman: A Portrait* (Weidenfeld & Nicolson, 1989), p. 4.
44 Tony Greenwood, letters to Richard Fletcher, 12 August 1965, 16 May 1966, Greenwood papers.
45 Pimlott, *Harold Wilson*, p. 350.
46 Ibid and p. 351.
47 Ponting, *Breach of Promise*, p. 50.
48 CAB, 11 December 1964.
49 Ponting, *Breach of Promise*, p. 50.
50 CAB, 11 December 1964.
51 *The Wilson Years*, BBC Radio 3, 10 October 1990.

52 BCD, (Papermac, 1990), 28 November 1966, p. 192.
53 CAB, 4 November 1965.
54 RCD, 14 November 1965, p. 378; BCD, 9 November 1965, p. 66, 25 November 1965, p. 70; Pimlott, *Harold Wilson*, p. 337.
55 Christopher Tugendhat, interview with the author.
56 Paul Foot, *The Politics of Harold Wilson* (Penguin, 1968), p. 293.
57 *New Statesman*, 7 January 1966.
58 Sun, 11 March 1968; De'ath, *Barbara Castle*, p. 110; Castle, *Fighting*, p. 357; *Shropshire Star*, 6 September 1966.
59 Christopher Booker, *The Neophiliacs: A Study of the Revolution in English Life in the Fifties and Sixties* (Collins, 1969), p. 168.
60 CAB, 1 February 1965.
61 *Playing the Race Card*, BBC TV 1999
62 RCD, 20 July 1965, p. 282.
63 CAB, 9 July 1965; CAB, 5 August 1965.
64 BCD, 20 July 1965, p. 26.
65 *Overseas Development: The Work of the New Ministry*, August 1965, Cmnd 2736, p. 6.
66 *New Statesman*, 7 January 1966.
67 Arthur Bottomley, *Commonwealth, Comrades and Friends* (Somaiya, 1985), p. 162.
68 RCD, 22 December 1965, p. 419.
69 Edward Short, *Whip to Wilson* (Macdonald, 1989), p. 204.

Chapter 8 Socialism in One Ministry

1 *The Guardian*, 7 January 1966.
2 *Shropshire Star*, 6 September 1966; *London Evening News*, 24 February 1966.
3 Correspondence with the author.
4 Geoffrey Goodman, interview with the author.
5 TBD, 9 November 1964, p. 180.
6 Jad Adams, *Tony Benn* (Macmillan, 1992), p. 139.
7 Conversation with the author.
8 Neil Kinnock, interview with the author.
9 Ian Mikardo, *Back-Bencher* (Weidenfeld & Nicolson, 1988), p. 177.
10 BCD, 29 November 1966, p. 192; 2–4 December 1965, p. 74; 29 July 1966, p. 155; 29 November 1966, p. 192.
11 De'ath, *Barbara Castle: A Portrait from Life* (Clifton Books, 1970), p. 103.
12 Bernard Ingham, interview with the author.
13 BCD, 14 February 1968, p. 373.

14 *Sunday Times*, 10 June 1973.
15 TBD, 26 January 1966, p. 380, quoting the Warden of Nuffield College on the civil service view.
16 Interview with the author.
17 Ibid.
18 Richard Bird, interview with the author.
19 TBD, 15 June 1966, p. 431.
20 Mikardo, *Back-Bencher*, p. 189.
21 Bird, interview.
22 Ibid.
23 Paul Rose, interview with the author.
24 Ibid.
25 BCD, (Papermac, 1990), 28 April 1966, p. 62.
26 *The Times*, 21 November 1967.
27 TBD, 28 January 1966, p. 380.
28 BCD, 26 September 1967, p. 299; confidential interview with the author.
29 Harold Wilson, *The Labour Government 1964-1970: A Personal Record* (Weidenfeld & Nicolson, 1971), p. 211.
30 William Plowden, *The Motor Car and Politics 1896-1970* (Bodley Head, 1971), p. 376.
31 Ibid, p. 385.
32 Rose and Joe Ashton, interviews with the author.
33 CAB, 7 July 1966.
34 CAB, 9 November 1967.
35 BCD, Barbara's postscript to 1965, p. 84.
36 *Transport Policy*, July 1966, Cmnd 3057, p. 1.
37 Plowden, *Motor Car*, p. 356.
38 Ibid, p. 402; *Evening Standard*, 8 December 1967; *Daily Telegraph*, 23 December 1965.
39 BCD, 22 April 1966, p. 117.
40 *Transport Policy*, p. 3.
41 *New Statesman*, 23 February 1968; *The Times*, 22 June 1967.
42 RCD, 7 July 1966, p. 564, 16 November 1967, p. 556; *Journal of Transport, Economics and Policy*, vol. 2 (1968), no. 2, p. 136.
43 *Journal of Transport*, p. 136; *New Statesman*, 23 February 1968.
44 RCD, 7 March 1967, p. 267.
45 *The Times*, 21 November 1967.
46 *Playing the Race Card*, BBC 1999.
47 Interview with the author.
48 James Callaghan, *Time and Chance* (Collins, 1987), p. 42.
49 LPACR 1966, p. 143.

50 *Journal of Transport*, p. 137.

51 *Sunday Mirror*, 1 October 1967.

52 David Butler and Michael Pinto-Duschinsky, *The British General Election of 1970* (Macmillan, 1971), p. 27.

53 *Tribune*, 12 April 1968.

54 BCD, 4 March 1968, p. 388.

55 The Wilson Years, BBC Radio 3, 10 October 1990.

56 Introduction to Hugh Scanlon, *The Way Forward for Workers' Control*, Institute for Workers' Control pamphlet no. 1, 1968.

57 Pimlot, *Harold Wilson*, p. 429.

58 Ibid p. 481.

59 CAB, 12 January 1968.

60 Pimlott, *Harold Wilson*, p. 488.

61 Robert Taylor, *The Trade Union Question in British Politics: Government and Unions since 1945* (Oxford: Basil Blackwell, 1993), p. 148.

62 R. Jenkins, *Life At The Centre*, p. 249; RCD, 2 April 1968, p. 756.

63 Edmund Dell, *The Chancellors: A History of the Chancellors of the Exchequer, 1945–1990* (HarperCollins, 1996), p. 361.

64 Edmund Dell, interview with the author.

65 Dell, *The Chancellors*, p. 361.

66 Pimlott, *Harold Wilson*, p. 480.

67 BCD, 2 April 1968, p. 418.

68 RCD, 16 April 1968, p. 784.

69 Ibid; *The Guardian*, 6 April 1968.

70 Peter Jenkins, *The Battle of Downing Street* (Charles Knight, 1970) p. 5.

71 Wilson, *The Labour Government 1964–1970*, p. 521.

72 RCD, 3 April 1968, p. 761; BCD, 4 April 1968, p. 421.

Chapter 9 The Game's Afoot

1 *The Guardian*, 6 and 8 April 1968.

2 RCD, 29 March 1968, p. 747.

3 Leah Manning, *A Life for Education: An Autobiography* (Victor Gollancz, 1970), p. 203.

4 *Daily Telegraph*, 10 April 1968; *New Statesman*, 12 April 1968.

5 RCD, 16 April 1968, p. 784.

6 BCD, 18 June 1968, p. 464.

7 Ben Pimlott, *Harold Wilson* (HarperCollins, 1993), p. 337.

8 *The Economist*, 15 June 1968.

9 Pimlott, *Harold Wilson*, p. 530; Peter Jenkins, *The Battle of Downing Street* (Charles Knight, 1970), p. 81.

10 BCD, 12 May 1968, p. 441.

11 James Callaghan, *Time and Chance* (Collins, 1987), p. 272.

12 Denis Barnes and Eileen Reid, *Governments and Trade Unions: The British Experience, 1964-79* (Heinemann Educational, 1980), p. 106.

13 BCD, 22 June 1968, p. 466.

14 Cecil King, *The Cecil King Diary, 1965-1970* (Jonathan Cape, 1972), 2 July 1968, p. 201.

15 Bernard Ingham, interview with the author.

16 Eric Silver, *Victor Feather, TUC* (Victor Gollancz, 1973), p. 136.

17 Ingham, interview.

18 Kenneth Morgan, *Callaghan: A Life* (Oxford University Press, 1997), p. 338.

19 *Evening Standard*, 15 December 1967.

20 BCD, 9 April 1968, p. 427.

21 Leo Panitch, *Social Democracy and Industrial Militancy: The Labour Party, the Trade Unions and Incomes Policy 1945-1947* (Cambridge University Press, 1976), p. 155.

22 *The Guardian*, 22 April 1968.

23 Panitch, *Social Democracy*, p. 123.

24 Jack Jones, *Union Man: The Autobiography of Jack Jones* (Collins, 1986), p. 193.

25 Stan Orme, interview with the author.

26 Jack Jones, *Union Man*, p. 194.

27 Moss Evans, interview with the author.

28 Ingham, interview.

29 Nicholas Davenport, *Memoirs of a City Radical* (Weidenfeld & Nicolson, 1974), p. 221.

30 Marie Patterson, interview with the author.

31 Joe Haines, interview with the author.

32 P. Jenkins, *Battle of Downing Street*, p. 9; *The Red Queen*, BBC TV, 21 September 1995.

33 Gerald Dorfman, *Government versus Trade Unionism in British Politics since 1968* (Macmillan 1979), pp. 17-18.

34 Ibid, p. 18.

35 Eric Heffer, *The Class Struggle in Parliament: A Socialist View of Industrial Relations* (Victor Gollancz, 1973), p. 100; Orme, interview.

36 BCD, 5 November 1968, p. 544.

37 RCD, 24 June 1969, p. 534.

38 Pimlott, *Harold Wilson*, p. 528.

39 Barbara Castle, Richard Crossman *et al.*, 'Keeping Left', *New Statesman*, January 1950, p. 39.

40 *New Statesman*, 9 July 1960.

41 Barbara Castle, *Are Controls Necessary?*, London Co-op pamphlet, January 1947.

42 Interview with the author.

43 TBD, 16 November 1968, p. 123.

44 Interview with the author.

45 Pimlott, *Harold Wilson*, p. 529.

46 *In Place of Strife: A Policy for Industrial Relations*, January 1969, Cmnd 3888, p. 5.

47 Keith Middlemas, *Power, Competition and the State*, vol. 2: *Threats to the Post-war Settlement: Britain 1961-74* (Macmillan, 1990), p. 235.

48 David McKie and Chris Cook, eds, *The Decade of Disillusion: British Politics in the Sixties* (Macmillan, 1972), p. 57.

49 *The Brothers*, 12 January 1993, BBC Radio.

50 RCD, 31 December 1968, p. 299.

51 *The Times*, 18 January 1969.

52 Edmund Dell, interview with the author.

53 RCD, 11 January 1969, pp. 303-4; *Profile*, BBC Radio 8 October 1980.

54 P. Jenkins, *The Battle of Downing Street*, p. 37.

55 Silver, *Victor Feather*, p. 134; Dorfman, *Government versus Trade Unionism*, p. 19.

56 P. Jenkins, *The Battle of Downing Street*, p. 9.

57 Geoffrey Goodman, interview with the author.

58 RCD, 1 January 1969, p. 303.

59 TBD, 3 January 1969, p. 140.

60 Pimlott, *Harold Wilson*, p. 532.

61 RCD, 3 January 1969, p. 305.

62 Peter Kellner and Christopher Hitchens, *Callaghan: The Road to Number Ten* (Cassell, 1976), p. 96; P. Jenkins, *The Battle of Downing Street*, p. 82.

63 CAB, 3 January 1969.

64 CAB, 14 January 1969.

65 Davenport, *Memoirs*, p. 221.

66 Tribune Group minutes, 20 January 1969.

67 Dorfman, *Government versus Trade Unionism*, p. 17.

68 Castle, Crossman *et al.*, 'Keeping Left', p. 40.

69 *Industrial Relations and Trade Union Law: Comments on Ministerial Proposals by the* TUC *General Council*, January 1969, pp. 26-7.

70 Kellner and Hitchens, *Callaghan*, p. 96.

71 Jack Jones, *Union Man*, p. 203.

72 Panitch, *Social Democracy*, p. 178.

73 *Tribune*, 18 April 1969.

74 M. Jones, *Michael Foot* (Victor Gollancz, 1994), p. 317.

75 Interview with the author.

76 D. Houghton, 'The Labour Back-Benchers', *Political Quarterly*, vol. 40 (1969), no. 4, p. 461.

77 BCD, (Papermac, 1990), 26 March 1969, p. 315.

78 Callaghan, *Time and Chance*, p. 274.

79 CAB 3, April 1969, confidential annex.

80 Ibid.

81 Mervyn Jones, *Michael Foot*, p. 317.

82 Kaufman, interview.

83 BCD, 29 April 1969, p. 641.

84 Pimlott, *Harold Wilson*, p. 534.

85 RCD, 29 April 1969, p. 465, Pimlott, ibid.

86 Harold Wilson, *The Labour Government*, p. 643.

87 RCD, 1 May 1969, p. 470.

88 Susan Crosland, *Tony Crosland* (Jonathan Cape, 1982), p. 203.

89 CAB, confidential annex, 8 May 1969.

90 Ibid.

91 Houghton, 'Labour Backbenchers', p. 461; Harold Wilson, *The Labour Government*, p. 644.

92 RCD, 9 May 1969, p. 483.

93 TBD, 9 May 1969, p. 168.

94 BCD, 9 May 1969, p. 649.

95 Dorfman, *Government versus Trade Unionism*, p. 27.

96 Panitch, *Social Democracy*, p. 197.

97 Jack Jones, *Union Man*, p. 206.

98 RCD, 23 May–6 June 1969, p. 503.

99 Ibid, p. 504.

100 R Jenkins, *Life at the Centre*, p. 273

101 *The Brothers*, part 2, BBC Radio; Jack Jones, *Union Man*, p. 207.

102 Jack Jones, *Union Man*, p. 204.

103 Silver, *Victor Feather*, p. 142.

104 RCD 23 May–6 June 1969, p. 505.

105 BCD, Barbara's note to text, p. 664.

106 Roy Jenkins, *Life at the Centre*, p. 274.

107 P. Jenkins, *The Battle of Downing Street*, p. 154.

108 BCD, (Papermac, 1990) 17 June 1969, p. 342.

109 Harold Wilson, *The Labour Government*, p. 657.

110 Roy Jenkins, *Life at the Centre*, p. 274; BCD, 17 June 1969 (Papermac, 1990), p. 343.

111 Jenkins, ibid.

112 Edmund Dell, *The Chancellors*, p. 364.

113 TBD, 17 June 1969, p. 186.
114 RCD, 17 June 1969, p. 523.
115 Pimlott, *Harold Wilson*, p. 541.
116 Haines, interview.
117 *The Brothers* part 2, BBC Radio.
118 Silver, *Victor Feather*, p. 140.
119 Harold Wilson, *The Labour Government*, p. 661.
120 BCD (Papermac, 1990), 18 June 1969, p. 347.
121 Goodman, interview.
122 Hugh Scanlon, interview with the author.
123 Scanlon, interview.

Part IV: The Future's Not What It Was

Chapter 10 Power Resides Elsewhere

1 Hugh Scanlon, interview with the author.
2 Interview with the author; BCD, 4 March 1970, p. 768.
3 BCD, 19 June 1969, p. 679.
4 Ibid.
5 BCD, (Papermac, 1990), 24 June 1969, p. 348; Ben Pimlott, *Harold Wilson* (HarperCollins, 1993), p. 544.
6 RCD, 3 July 1969, pp. 548-9.
7 TBD, 25 June 1969, p. 188.
8 RCD, 12 October 1969, p. 678.
9 TBD, 3 September 1969, p. 200; Susan Crosland, *Anthony Crosland* (Jonathan Cape, 1982), p. 204.
10 CAB, 25 September 1969.
11 Ibid, attachment statement to the lobby.
12 TBD, 15 January 1970, p. 226; 9 March 1970, p. 250.
13 RCD, 15 January 1970, p. 781.
14 CAB, 9 October 1969.
15 CAB, 4 September 1969.
16 CAB, memorandum, 28 August 1969; CAB, 4 September 1969; BCD, 4 September 1969, p. 705.
17 CAB, memorandum, 22 September 1969.
18 National Conference of Labour Women, 1969.
19 CAB, memo, 23 September 1969.
20 BCD, 4 March 1970, p. 768.
21 Note dated April, 1970. Crosland Papers, British Library of Political and Economic Science, LSE, London. The handwriting was unknown to the archivists.

22 *New Statesman*, 25 September 1970; CAB, 9 October 1969; CAB, memo, 23 September 1969.

23 LPACR 1969, p. 195.

24 CAB, 23 October 1969.

25 Tribune Group minutes, 11 December 1969.

26 Robin Oakley and Peter Rose, *The Political Year: 1970* (Pitman Publishing, 1970), pp. 27-30.

27 BCD, 12 May 1970, p. 798.

28 CAB, 23 October 1969.

29 D. Webster, *The Labour Party and the New Left*, Fabian Society tract 477, 1981.

30 'The Prime Minister [James Callaghan] talks to The Observer', *The Observer*, April 1979.

31 RCD, 31 December 1969, p. 767.

32 Pimlott, *Harold Wilson*, p. 570; Joe Haines, interview with the author.

33 TBD, 23 June 1970, p. 298.

34 Marcia Falkender, *Downing Street in Perspective* (Weidenfeld & Nicolson, 1983), p. 34.

35 R. Jenkins, *Life at the Centre*, p. 310; Falkender, ibid.

36 *New Statesman*, 5 February 1971.

37 Haines, interview.

38 *New Statesman*, 17 July 1970.

39 Tribune Group Minutes, 8 November 1970.

40 LPACR 1970, p. 119.

41 LPACR 1970, p. 126.

42 *New Statesman*, 16 October 1970.

43 Eric Heffer, *The Class Struggle in Parliament: A Socialist View of Industrial Relations* (Victor Gollancz, 1973), p. 97.

44 Paul Rose, interview with the author.

45 Robin Oakley and Peter Rose, *The Political Year: 1971* (Pitman Publishing, 1971), pp. 73, 77.

46 Ibid, pp. 71, 73.

47 Neil Kinnock, interview with the author.

48 Heffer, *The Class Struggle*, p. 204.

49 Interview with the author.

50 Roy Jenkins, *Roy Jenkins' Gallery of 20th-Century Portraits and Oxford Papers* (David & Charles, 1988), p. 61; Jenkins, *A Life at the Centre* (Pan/Macmillan, 1992), p. 322.

51 S. A. Walkland and Michael Ryle, eds, *The Commons in the Seventies* (Martin Robertson, 1977), p. 83.

52 I. Burton and G. Drewry, 'Public Legislation: A Survey of the Session 1970/71', *Parliamentary Affairs*, vol. 25 (1972), no. 2, p. 133; Oakley

and Rose, *The Political Year: 1971*, p. 85.

53 Burton and Drewry, ibid.

54 Walkland and Ryle, *The Commons*, p. 84.

55 Burton and Drewry, 'Public Legislation 1970/71', p. 131.

56 Ibid; TBD, 28 January 1971, p. 328.

57 Heffer, *The Class Struggle*, p. 231.

58 TBD, 28 January 1971, p. 328; Paul Rose, interview.

59 *The Red Queen*, BBC TV, 21 September 1995; BCD, 24–8 December 1969, p. 743.

60 Haines, interview.

61 BCD, (Papermac, 1990) 17 April 1970, p. 399.

62 L. J. Robins, *The Reluctant Party: Labour and the EEC 1961–75* (G. W. and A. Hesketh, 1979), p. 21.

63 R. Jenkins, *Life at the Centre*, p. 320.

64 TBD, 17 July 1971, p. 356.

65 Philip Whitehead, *The Writing on the Wall: Britain in the Seventies* (Michael Joseph, 1985), p. 67.

66 R. Jenkins, *Life at the Centre*, p. 303.

67 TBD, 19 July 1971, p. 358.

68 TBD, 30 May 1971, p. 345.

69 Pimlott, *Harold Wilson*, p. 587.

70 Uwe Kitzinger, *Diplomacy and Persuasion: How Britain Joined the Common Market* (Thames and Hudson, 1973), pp. 311, 309.

71 *The Times*, 24 July 1971.

72 Tribune Group Minutes, 22 November 1971.

73 Kitzinger, *Diplomacy*, p. 336.

74 TBD, 28 October 1971, p. 382.

75 R. Jenkins, *Life at the Centre*, p. 330.

76 RCD, 29 May 1970, p. 931.

77 *It's Your Line*, BBC Radio.

78 D. Webster, *The Labour Party*, p. 23; Whitehead, *The Writing on the Wall*, p. 117.

79 *New Statesman*, 25 September 1970.

80 Harry Nicholas, general secretary of the Labour Party, letter to Vic Feather, 30 November 1971, attachment to NEC minutes.

81 *The Times*, 24 July 1971.

82 *New Statesman*, 25 September 1970.

83 *The Times*, 3 January 1972.

84 Michael Hatfield, *The House the Left Built: Inside Labour Policy-Making 1970–1975* (Victor Gollancz, 1978), p. 68.

85 TBD, 28 April 1972, p. 427.

86 Jad Adams, *Tony Benn* (Macmillan, 1992), p. 198.

87 TBD, 11 June 1974, pp. 172-3.
88 BCD, 27 November 1974, p. 239.
89 Castle, *Fighting*, p. 445.
90 TBD, 3 May 1972, p. 428.

Chapter 11   Elephants and Castle

1 BCD, 21 January 1974, p. 25.
2 BCD, 10 January 1969, p. 587; RCD, 24 June 1969, p. 534.
3 BCD, 5 April 1974, p. 73.
4 TBD, 21 January 1976, p. 502, 16 June 1975, p. 402.
5 BCD, 18 February 1975, p. 312.
6 Elizabeth Vallance *When in the House: A Study of Women Members of Parliament* (Athlone, 1979), p. 77.
7 RCD, 11 July 1969, p. 564.
8 Let Us Work Together, manifesto 1974.
9 TBD, 5 March 1974, p. 115.
10 Castle, *Fighting*, p. 454.
11 Ben Pimlott, *Harold Wilson*, p. 617.
12 BCD, (Papermac, 1990), 7 March 1974, p. 431.
13 TBD, 7 March 1974, p. 116, 29 July 1974, p. 208.
14 *Sunday Times*, 10 June 1973.
15 David Owen, interview with the author.
16 Jack Ashley, *Acts of Defiance* (Reinhardt/Viking, 1992), pp. 346-7.
17 Edmund Dell, interview with the author.
18 Owen, interview.
19 Gerald Kaufman, interview with the author.
20 RCD, 19 November 1966, p. 132, 13 October 1969, p. 684.
21 Owen, interview.
22 BCD, 3 April 1975, p. 329.
23 Ashley, *Acts of Defiance*, p. 233.
24 BCD, 11 October 1975, p. 518.
25 *The Times*, 24 May 1974.
26 BCD, 26 June 1974, p. 122.
27 David McKie, Chris Cook, and Melanie Phillips, *The Guardian/Quartet Election Guide* (Quartet Books, 1978), p. 102.
28 Confederation of British Industry (CBI), *Social Security Pensions Act, 1975: Guidance for Employers*, July 1976, p. 5.
29 *Daily Mail*, 12 September 1974.
30 Michael Hatfield, *The House the Left Built: Inside Labour Policy-Making 1970-1975* (Victor Gollancz, 1978), p. 246.
31 BCD, 19 March 1975, p. 580.
32 BCD, 11 April 1975, p. 361.

33 David Walter, *The Oxford Union: Playground of Power* (Macdonald, 1984), p. 193.

34 Ibid, p. 192.

35 David Butler and Dennis Kavanagh, *The British General Election of 1979* (Macmillan, 1980), p. 22.

36 TBD, 10 June 1975, pp. 396-7.

37 TBD, 23 April 1974, p. 141.

38 Elston Grey-Turner and F. M. Sutherland, *History of the British Medical Association*, vol. 2: *1932-1981* (British Medical Association, 1982), p. 143.

39 Ibid.

40 Owen, interview.

41 Ibid.

42 Grey-Turner and Sutherland, *British Medical Association*, p. 143.

43 LPACR 1973, p. 248; LPACR 1975, p. 243.

44 LPACR 1978, p. 199; LPACR 1975, p. 243.

45 Barbara Castle, *The NHS Revisited*, Fabian Society tract 440, 1975, p. 11.

46 LPACR 1978, p. 199.

47 *The Separation of Private Practice from NHS Hospitals*, August 1975, A Consultative Document.

48 D Widgery, *Health in Danger: The Crisis of the National Health Service* (Macmillan, 1979), p. 100.

49 Owen, interview.

50 Grey-Turner and Sutherland, *British Medical Association*, p. 143.

51 TBD, 27 October 1975, p. 450.

52 Harvey Gordon and Steve Iliffe, *Pickets in White: The Junior Doctors' Dispute of 1975* (MPU Publications, 1977), p. 52.

53 BCD, 24 April 1974, p. 88.

54 Gordon and Iliffe, *Pickets in White*, p. 7; S. Herd, *Industrial Relations in the National Health Service*, p. 1.

55 BCD, 5 March 1975, p. 331, 20 June 1975, p. 4.

56 *Daily Mail*, 1 December 1975.

57 BCD, 18 April 1975, p. 369.

58 Clifford Allen, Chairman of the ILP, *Socialist Review*, vol. 26 (1925), no. 144; *Liverpool Echo*, 12 December 1967.

59 Joe Haines, interview with the author.

60 Arnold Goodman, *Tell Them I'm On My Way* (Chapmans, 1993), p. 233.

61 Ibid, pp. 236-7.

62 BCD, 2 December 1975, p. 573.

63 Goodman, *Tell Them*, p. 233.

64 BCD, 4 December 1975, p. 00.

65 Bernard Donoughue, *Prime Minister: The Conduct of Policy under Harold Wilson and James Callaghan* (Jonathan Cape, 1987), p. 50.

66 BCD, 12 September 1974, p. 177.

67 BCD, 16 March 1976, p. 690.

68 TBD, 16 March 1976, p. 536.

69 BCD, 24 March 1976, p. 702.

70 *Sunday Times*, 3 May 1987.

71 TBD, 29 April 1976, p. 561.

Chapter 12   Footfalls Echo

1 Interview with the author.

2 BCD, 11 April 1976, p. 730.

3 *The Guardian*, 15 April 1976.

4 *Tribune*, 16 April 1976; *Sunday Mirror*, 11 April 1976.

5 BCD, 8 April 1976, p. 729.

6 NEC minutes, 26 May 1976.

7 TBD, 23 May 1977, p. 148.

8 *Tribune*, 30 July 1976.

9 TBD, 14 July 1976, p. 594.

10 LPACR 1977, p. 180.

11 LPACR 1977, pp. 180–181.

12 Peter Jenkins, *Mrs Thatcher's Revolution: The Ending of the Socialist Era* (Jonathan Cape, 1987), p. 27.

13 David Butler and Dennis Kavanagh, *The British General Election of 1979* (Macmillan, 1980), p. 336.

14 *Tribune*, 18 May 1979, p. 17; *Sunday Telegraph*, 16 June 1993.

15 *Platform 1*, BBC TV, 3 June 1980.

16 TBD, 3 October 1979, p. 546; *Tribune*, 29 September 1978.

17 *Tribune*, 29 September 1978.

18 TBD, 3 October 1977, p. 224.

19 Geoffrey Goodman, interview with the author.

20 Stan Orme and Paul Rose, interviews with the author.

21 Sir Henry Plumb, interview with the author.

22 Richard Balfe, interview with the author.

23 *The Times*, 29 May 1980.

24 Ibid.

25 Plumb, interview.

26 Elizabeth Vallance and Elizabeth Davies, *Women of Europe: Women MEPs and Equality Policy* (Cambridge University Press, 1986), p. 70.

27 Plumb, interview.

28 Christopher Tugendhat, interview with the author.

29 Balfe, interview.

30 Kenneth Morgan, *Callaghan: A Life* (Oxford University Press, 1997), p. 709.

31 Dick Leonard, interview with the author.

32 LPACR 1979, p. 332.

33 *The Times*, 3 October 1980.

34 *New Statesman*, 17 September 1982.

35 Alf Lomas, interview with the author; *New Statesman*, 24 September 1982.

36 Plumb, interview.

37 Gerald Kaufman, interview with the author.

38 Hugo Young, *The Iron Lady: A Biography of Margaret Thatcher* (New York: Noonday Press, 1990), p. 122.

39 Paul Foot, interview with the author.

40 Michael Foot, *Loyalists and Loners* (Collins, 1986), p. 47.

41 *Hampstead & Highgate Gazette*, 7 December 1984; Michael Foot, ibid.

42 *The Times*, 4 June 1980.

43 TBD, 1 October 1978, p. 354.

44 Castle, *Fighting*, p. 529.

45 *Sunday Times*, 16 November 1980.

46 Castle, *Fighting*, pp. 527, 528, 508.

47 Neil Kinnock, interview with the author.

48 BCD (Papermac, 1990), 11 February 1975, p. 562.

49 Young, *The Iron Lady*, p. 122.

50 Castle, *Fighting*, p. 529.

51 *The Times*, 30 May 1983.

52 *New Hope for Britain: Labour's Manifesto 1983*, p. 36.

53 Colin Hughes and Patrick Wintour, *Labour Rebuilt: The New Model Party* (Fourth Estate, 1990), p. 7.

54 Hughes and Wintour, *Labour Rebuilt*, p. 49, 151.

55 Castle, *Fighting*, p. 575.

56 Ibid, p. 535.

57 Hughes and Wintour, *Labour Rebuilt*, pp. 25-6.

58 Kinnock, interview.

59 Ibid.

60 Ibid.

61 BCD, (Papermac, 1990) 26 June 1974, p. 471.

62 RCD, 11 September 1968, p. 185.

63 *Sunday Telegraph*, 13 June 1993.

64 LPACR 1990, p. 330.

65 *The Times*, 13 July 1995.

66 Castle, *Fighting*, p. 595.

67 *On the Record*, BBC TV, 26 September 1993.

68 *Tribune* sixtieth anniversary supplement, 1997.

69 Jon Sopel, *Tony Blair, The Moderniser* (Michael Joseph, 1995), p. 143.

70 Castle, *Fighting*, p. 26.

71 *Tribune*, 28 April 1995.

72 *The Times*, 30 September 1996.

73 *Tribune*, 27 September 1996.

74 *Tribune*, 4 October 1996.

75 *Newsnight*, BBC TV, 27 September 1996.

76 BCD, 22 November 1974, p. 235.

77 *Financial Times*, 12 February 1996.

78 Labour Party, *Economic Aid*, May 1957; *The Times*, 19 April 1974.

79 *New Statesman*, 28 February 2000.

80 *Daily Mail*, 18 February 2000.

81 *Hampstead & Highgate Gazette*, 9 July 1999.

82 *New Statesman*, 18 February 2000; Castle, *Fighting*, p. 26.

83 Robert Service, *Lenin: A Political Life*, vol. 3: *The Iron Ring* (Macmillan, 1995), p. xiv.

84 LPACR 1927.

85 Hugh Scanlon, interview with the author.

86 Interview with the author.

87 TBD, 3 July 1975, p. 413.

88 *Daily Mail*, 29 September 1998; *New Statesman*, 18 February 2000.

89 LPACR 1959, p. 84.

90 Press Association, 27 February 2000.

91 *Daily Mail*, 18 February 2000.

Bibliography

ARCHIVES

Bodleian Library, Oxford: Oxford Labour Club documents; Anthony Greenwood papers; Geoffrey de Freitas papers; note: Harold Wilson papers closed for cataloguing

British Library, St Pancras and Colindale, London: National Sound Archive, tapes of television and radio programmes, recordings of Barbara Castle speeches, etc; Humanities and Science reading rooms, books, journals, Labour Party Annual Conference Reports, White Papers etc; Newspaper Library, various newspapers and magazines

British Library of Political and Economic Science, London School of Economics and Political Science: Alastair Hetherington papers; Tony Crosland papers; Hugh Dalton papers; Fabian Society papers

Camden Local Studies and Archives Centre, London: St Pancras Borough Council Records

National Museum of Labour History, Manchester: Michael Foot papers; Keep Left minutes; Bevanite ('The Group') minutes; Tribune Group minutes; NEC minutes; British Labour Group minutes

Nuffield College, Oxford: G. D. H. Cole papers; Stafford Cripps papers

St John's College, Cambridge: Socialist League documents; Stafford Cripps papers, temporarily held by Professor Peter Clarke

Refugee Studies Programme, Oxford: Tristram Betts papers

TUC Library, London: TUC-Labour Party Liaison Committee documents; TUC annual reports; TUC policy documents

Labour Party

Labour Party Annual Conference Reports, 1927–99
The London Labour Party Annual Reports, 1936–45
National Conference of Labour Women, various

General Election manifestos, 1945–79

European Assembly elections manifesto, January 1979

Labour's Colonial Policy: The Plural Society, July 1956; *Economic Aid*, May 1957; *Smaller Territories*, June 1957

Labour and the Common Market: report of special conference, Central Hall, Westminster, July 1971

Labour and the Common Market: Report of special conference, Sobell Sports Centre, April 1975

TUC-Labour Party Liaison Committee: *Economic Policy and the Cost of Living*, February 1973; *The Next Three Years and the Problem of Priorities*, July 1976; *Into the Eighties: An Agreement*, 1978

Official Papers

Overseas Development: The Work of the New Ministry, August 1965, Cmnd 2736

Transport Policy, July 1966, Cmnd 3057

Road Safety - A Fresh Approach, July 1967, Cmnd 3338

British Waterways: Recreation and Amenity, September 1967, Cmnd 3401

The Transport of Freight, November 1967, Cmnd 3470

Railway Policy, November 1967, Cmnd 3439

Public Transport and Traffic, December 1967, Cmnd 3481

In Place of Strife: A Policy for Industrial Relations, January 1969, Cmnd 3888

Productivity, Prices and Incomes Policy after 1969, December 1969, Cmnd 4327

The Separation of Private Practice from NHS *Hospitals*, August 1975, A Consultative Document.

State Papers, Public Record Office, Kew

Cabinet Conclusions, CAB 128, 1964–9

Cabinet Memoranda, CAB 129, 1964–9

Journals, Miscellaneous Pamphlets, Reports

Bevan, Aneurin, Castle, Barbara, Crossman, Richard, Driberg, Tom, Mikardo, Ian and Wilson, Harold, *It Need Not Happen: The Alternative to German Rearmament*, Tribune pamphlet, 1954

The Bradfordian (Bradford Grammar School magazine), November 1922–March 1929

British Road Federation, *Basic Road Statistics* (various)

Burton, I., and Drewry, G., 'Public Legislation: A Survey of the Session 1968/69', *Parliamentary Affairs*, vol. 23 (1970), no 2

—— 'Public Legislation: A Survey of the Session 1969/70', *Parliamentary Affairs*, vol. 23 (1970), no. 4

—— 'Public Legislation: A Survey of the Session 1970/71', *Parliamentary Affairs*, vol. 25 (1972), no. 2

—— 'Public Legislation: A Survey of the Session 1971/72', *Parliamentary Affairs*, vol. 26 (1973), no. 2

Castle, Barbara, *Are Controls Necessary?*, London Co-op pamphlet, January 1947

—— *Back to the Dole*, Tribune pamphlet, 1952

—— *The* NHS *Revisited*, Fabian Society tract 440, 1975

Castle, Barbara, Crossman, Richard, *et al.*, 'Keeping Left', *New Statesman*, January 1950

Castle, B., Flynn, P., Lynes, T., and Townsend, P., *Pensions as a Right for All: A Response to the Green Papers*, May 1999

Coates, K., and Topham, T., *The Law versus the Unions*, Institute for Workers' Control, pamphlet no. 15, 1969

Common Market Safeguards Campaign, various pamphlets

Confederation of British Industry, *Social Security Pensions Act 1975: Guidance for Employers*, July 1976

Crossman, Richard, Foot, Michael, and Mikardo, Ian, 'Keep Left', *New Statesman*, May 1947

Darnborough, A., *Labour's Record on Southern Africa*, Anti-Apartheid Movement, June 1967

Faith, N., *Road Safety*, *Economist* brief no. 9, 1968

Gittings, John, and Gott, Richard, *The End of the Alliance: Labour's Defence Policy and CND*, Cambridge University CND, January 1965

Herd, S., *Industrial Relations in the National Health Service*, 1980

Houghton, D., 'The Labour Back-Benchers', *Political Quarterly*, vol. 40 (1969), no. 4

Industrial Relations and Trade Union Law: Comments on Ministerial Proposals by the TUC *General Council*, January 1969

McCarthy, W., 'The Nature of Britain's Strike Problem', *British Journal of Industrial Relations*, vol. 8 (1970), no. 2

Metropolitan Pensions Association Limited, *The Castle Scheme and its Effect on the Design of Occupational Pension Schemes*, 1975

Munby, D. L., 'Mrs Castle's Transport Policy', *Journal of Transport, Economics and Policy*, vol. 2 (1968), no. 2

National Association of Pension Funds, *Social Security Pensions Act 1975*, 1976

Occupational Pension Schemes: A TUC *Guide*, February 1976

Pimlott, Ben, 'The Socialist League: Intellectuals and the Labour Left in the 1930s', *Journal of Contemporary History*, vol. 6 (1971), no 3

'The Prime Minister talks to The Observer', *Observer*, April 1979

Reports on the Trades Union Congress, *Guardian*, 1965–70

St Pancras Borough Council, *Official Pocket Almanack and Diary*, 1938–45

Scanlon, Hugh, *The Way Forward for Workers' Control*, Institute for Workers' Control pamphlet no. 1, 1968

Sherman, Alfred, *Everybody's Business: The Economic Consequences of Mrs Barbara Castle*, Aims of Industry

Socialist Review, 1926–29

Taylor, R., *Labour and the Social Contract*, Fabian Society tract 458, 1978

The Texture of Welfare: A Survey of Social Service in Bradford, 1923

Town and County Councillor, March 1936–February 1938

Trades Union Congress, *Industrial Relations Programme for Action*, May 1969

——*Social Security Act 1975: Trade Unions and Contracting Out*

Webster, D., *The Labour Party and the New Left*, Fabian Society tract 477, 1981

Williams, Shirley, 'Women in Politics', The Fawcett Lecture, University of London, 1979–80

Woodcock, George, *The Trade Union Movement and the Government*, 29 April 1968

Books

Adams, Jad, *Tony Benn* (Macmillan, 1992)

Ashley, Jack, *Acts of Defiance* (Reinhardt/Viking, 1992)

Ashley, M. P., and Saunders, C. T., *Red Oxford: A History of the Growth of Socialism in the University of Oxford* (Oxford: Oxford University Labour Club, 1933)

Barnes, Denis, and Reid, Eileen, *Governments and Trade Unions: The British Experience, 1964–79* (Heinemann Educational, 1980)

Barnes, Susan, *Behind the Image* (Jonathan Cape, 1974)

Barnett, Joel, *Inside the Treasury* (André Deutsch, 1982)

Bassett, Reginald, *Nineteen Thirty-one: Political Crisis* (Macmillan, 1958)

Bellamy, Joyce M., and Saville, John, eds, *Dictionary of Labour Biography*, vol. 4 (Macmillan, 1977)

Benn, Tony, *Years of Hope: Diaries and Letters, 1940–1962* (Arrow, 1995)

——*Out of the Wilderness: Diaries 1963–67* (Arrow, 1988)

——*Office Without Power: Diaries 1968–72* (Arrow, 1989)

——*Against the Tide: Diaries 1973–76* (Arrow, 1990)

——*Conflicts of Interest: Diaries, 1977–80* (Arrow, 1991)

——*End of an Era: Diaries, 1980–90* (Hutchinson, 1992)

Bentley, Michael, and Stevenson, John, eds, *High and Low Politics in Modern Britain* (Oxford: Clarendon Press, 1983)

Berrington, Hugh, *Backbench Opinion in the House of Commons, 1945-55* (Oxford: Pergamon, 1973)

Berrington, Hugh, with Finer, S. E., and Bartholomew, D. J., *Backbench Opinion in the House of Commons, 1955-59* (Oxford: Pergamon, 1961)

Betts [Castle], Barbara, 'War Pensions', in William Robson, ed., *Social Security*, (George Allen & Unwin, 1943)

Blundell, Sir Michael, *So Rough a Wind: The Kenya Memoirs of Sir Michael Blundell* (Weidenfeld & Nicholson, 1964)

Blythe, Ronald, *The Age of Illusion: England in the Twenties and Thirties* (Hamish Hamilton, 1963)

Booker, Christopher, *The Neophiliacs: A Study of the Revolution in English Life in the Fifties and Sixties* (Collins, 1969)

Bosanquet, Nick, and Townsend, Peter, eds, *Labour and Equality: A Fabian Study of Labour in Power, 1974-79* (Heinemann Educational, 1980)

Bottomley, Arthur, *Commonwealth, Comrades and Friends* (Somaiya, 1985)

Branson, Noreen, and Heinemann, Margot, *Britain in the Nineteen-thirties* (Weidenfeld & Nicolson, 1971)

Briggs, Asa, and Saville, John, eds, *Essays in Labour History*, vol. 3: *1918-1939* (Macmillan, 1977)

Brittain, Vera, *The Women at Oxford: A Fragment of History* (George G. Harrap, 1960)

Brivati, Brian, *Hugh Gaitskell* (Richard Cohen, 1996)

Brockway, Fenner, *Inside the Left: Thirty Years of Platform, Press, Prison and Parliament* (George Allen & Unwin, 1942)

—— *Towards Tomorrow: The Autobiography of Fenner Brockway* (Hart-Davis MacGibbon, 1977)

Brookes, Pamela, *Women at Westminster: An Account of Women in the British Parliament, 1918-1966* (Peter Davies, 1967)

Buchanan, Colin, *Traffic in Towns*, abridged edition of the Buchanan Report (Penguin/HMSO, 1964)

Bullock, Alan, *The Life and Times of Ernest Bevin* (Heinemann, 1960)

Butler, David, *British General Elections since 1945* (Oxford: Basil Blackwell, 1989)

—— *The British General Election of 1951* (Macmillan, 1952)

—— *The British General Election of 1955* (Macmillan, 1955)

Butler, David, and Kavanagh, Dennis, *The British General Election of February 1974* (Macmillan, 1974)

—— *The British General Election of October 1974* (Macmillan, 1975)

—— *The British General Election of 1979* (Macmillan, 1980)

—— *The British General Election of 1987* (Macmillan, 1988)

—— *The British General Election of 1983* (Macmillan, 1984)

—— *The British General Election of 1992* (Macmillan, 1992)

Butler, David, and King, Anthony, *The British General Election of 1964* (Macmillan, 1965)

—— *The British General Election of 1966* (Macmillan, 1966)

Butler, David, and Kitzinger, Uwe, *The 1975 Referendum* (Macmillan, 1996)

Butler, David, and Pinto-Duschinsky, Michael, *The British General Election of 1970* (Macmillan, 1971)

Butler, David, and Rose, Charles, *The British General Election of 1959* (Macmillan, 1960)

Butler, David, and Sloman, Anne, *British Political Facts, 1900-1975* (Macmillan, 1975)

Byrne, Paul, *The Campaign for Nuclear Disarmament* (Croom Helm, 1988)

Calder, Angus, *The People's War, Britain 1939-45* (Jonathan Cape, 1969)

Callaghan, James, *Time and Chance* (Collins, 1987)

Calvocoressi, Peter, *The British Experience 1945-75* (Bodley Head, 1978)

Campbell, John, *Roy Jenkins: A Biography* (Weidenfeld & Nicolson, 1983)

Carmichael, Joel, *Stalin's Masterpiece: The Show Trials and Purges of the Thirties, the Consolidation of the Bolshevik Dictatorship* (Weidenfeld & Nicolson, 1976)

Castle, Barbara, *The Castle Diaries*; vol. 1: *1974-76*; vol. 2: *1964-70* (Weidenfeld & Nicolson, 1980, 1984)

—— *The Castle Diaries 1964-76* (Papermac, 1990)

—— *Fighting All the Way* (Macmillan, 1993)

Channon, Sir Henry, *Chips: The Diaries of Sir Henry Channon*, ed. Robert Rhodes James (Weidenfeld & Nicolson, 1967)

Churchill, Sir Winston, *The Second World War*, vol. 1: *The Gathering Storm* (Cassell, 1949)

Coates, David, *The Labour Party and the Struggle for Socialism* (Cambridge University Press, 1975)

—— *Labour in Power? A Study of the Labour Government 1974-1979* (Longman, 1980)

Cockburn, Claud, *The Devil's Decade* (Sidgwick & Jackson, 1973)

Cockburn, John Henry, *The Years of the Week* (Penguin, 1971)

Conquest, Robert, *The Great Terror: Stalin's Purges of the Thirties* (Macmillan, 1968)

Cooke, Colin, *The Life of Richard Stafford Cripps* (Hodder & Stoughton, 1957)

Craig, Frederick W. S., *British General Election Manifestos 1900-1974* (Macmillan, 1975)

Crosland, Anthony, *The Future of Socialism* (Jonathan Cape, 1956)

—— *The Conservative Enemy: A Programme of Radical Reform for the 1960s* (Jonathan Cape, 1962)

Crosland, Susan, *Tony Crosland* (Jonathan Cape, 1982)

Crossman, Richard, *The Diaries of a Cabinet Minister*, ed. Janet Morgan; vol. 1: *Minister of Housing 1964-66*; vol. 2: *Lord President of the Council and Leader of the House of Commons 1966-68*; vol. 3: *Secretary of State for*

Social Services 1968-70 (Hamish Hamilton/Jonathan Cape, 1975, 1976, 1977)

—— *The Backbench Diaries of Richard Crossman*, ed. Janet Morgan (Hamish Hamilton/Jonathan Cape, 1981)

Dalton, Hugh, *The Fateful Years: Memoirs 1931-1945* (Frederick Muller, 1957)

—— *High Tide and After: Memoirs, 1945-1960* (Frederick Muller, 1962)

—— *The Political Diary of Hugh Dalton*, ed. Ben Pimlott (Jonathan Cape/ London School of Economics and Political Science, 1986)

Dalyell, Tam, *Dick Crossman: A Portrait* (Weidenfeld & Nicolson, 1989)

Davenport, Nicholas, *Memoirs of a City Radical* (Weidenfeld & Nicolson, 1974)

De'ath, Wilfred, *Barbara Castle: A Portrait from Life* (Clifton Books, 1970)

Dell, Edmund, *A Hard Pounding: Politics and Economic Crisis, 1974-1976* (Oxford University Press, 1991)

—— *The Chancellors: A History of the Chancellors of the Exchequer, 1945-1990* (HarperCollins, 1996)

Donoughue, Bernard, *Prime Minister: The Conduct of Policy under Harold Wilson and James Callaghan* (Jonathan Cape, 1987)

Dorfman, Gerald, *Government versus Trade Unionism in British Politics since 1968* (Macmillan 1979)

Douie, Vera, *Daughters of Britain: An Account of the Work of British Women during the Second World War* (privately printed by the author, 1949)

Driver, Christopher, *The Disarmers: A Study in Protest* (Hodder & Stoughton, 1964)

Duff, Peggy, *Left, Left, Left: A Personal Account of Six Protest Campaigns, 1945-65* (Allison & Busby, 1971)

Edwards, Robert, *Goodbye Fleet Street* (Jonathan Cape, 1988)

Epstein, Leon, *Britain: Uneasy Ally. On the Reactions of British Public Opinion to Post-war American Foreign Policy* (University of Chicago Press, 1954)

Falkender [Williams], Marcia, *Downing Street in Perspective* (Weidenfeld & Nicolson, 1983)

Feather, Victor, *The Essence of Trade Unionism* (Bodley Head, 1971)

Fenn, L Anderson *et al.*, *Problems of the Socialist Transition* (Victor Gollancz, 1934)

Fletcher, Joseph Smith, *Pontefract* (SPCK, 1920)

Foot, Michael, *Aneurin Bevan*; vol. 1: *1897-1945*; vol. 2: *1945-1960* (Paladin, 1975)

—— *Loyalists and Loners* (Collins, 1986)

Foot, Paul, *The Politics of Harold Wilson* (Penguin, 1968)

Foote, Geoffrey, *The Labour Party's Political Thought: A History* (Macmillan, 1997)

Fyrth, Jim, ed., *Britain, Fascism and the Popular Front* (Lawrence & Wishart, 1985)

Gaitskell, Hugh, *The Diary of Hugh Gaitskell 1945-1956*, ed. Philip M. Williams (Jonathan Cape, 1983)

Galbraith, J. K., *The Affluent Society* (Boston, MA: Houghton Mifflin, 1958)

Garrett, John, *Managing the Civil Service* (Heinemann, 1980)

George-Brown, Lord, *In My Way: The Political Memoirs of Lord George-Brown* (Victor Gollancz, 1971)

Goldie, Grace Wyndham, *Facing the Nation: Television and Politics, 1936-1976* (Bodley Head, 1977)

Goldsworthy, David, *Colonial Issues in British Politics, 1945-1961: From 'Colonial Development' to 'Wind of Change'* (Oxford: Clarendon Press, 1971)

Goodman, Arnold, *Tell Them I'm On My Way* (Chapmans, 1993)

Goodman, Geoffrey, *The Awkward Warrior: Frank Cousins: His Life and Times* (Davis-Poynter, 1979)

—— ed., *The State of the Nation: The Political Legacy of Aneurin Bevan* (Victor Gollancz, 1997)

Gordon Walker, Patrick, *The Cabinet* (Jonathan Cape, 1970)

—— *Political Diaries 1932-1971*, ed. Robert Pearce (Historians' Press, 1991)

Gordon, Harvey, and Iliffe, Steve, *Pickets in White: The Junior Doctors' Dispute of 1975* (MPU Publications, 1977)

Gormley, Joe, *Battered Cherub: The Autobiography of Joe Gormley* (Hamish Hamilton, 1982)

Graves, Robert, and Hodge, Alan, *The Long Week-end: A Social History of Great Britain 1918-1939* (Faber and Faber, 1940)

Grey-Turner, Elston, and Sutherland, F. M., *History of the British Medical Association*, vol. 2: *1932-1981* (British Medical Association, 1982)

Griffin, Penny, ed., *St Hugh's: One Hundred Years of Women's Education in Oxford* (Macmillan, 1986)

Gupta, Partha Sarathi, *Imperialism and the British Labour Movement, 1914-1964* (Macmillan, 1975)

Haines, Joe, *The Politics of Power* (Jonathan Cape, 1977)

Harrington, William, and Young, Peter, *The 1945 Revolution* (Davis-Poynter, 1978)

Harris, Kenneth, *Kenneth Harris Talking To* (Weidenfeld & Nicolson, 1971)

Harris, Robert, *The Making of Neil Kinnock* (Faber and Faber, 1984)

Harrison Brian, ed., *The History of the University of Oxford*, vol. 3 (Oxford: Clarendon Press, 1994)

Haseler, Stephen, *The Gaitskellites. Revisionism in the British Labour Party* (Macmillan, 1969)

Hatfield, Michael, *The House the Left Built: Inside Labour Policy-Making 1970-1975* (Victor Gollancz, 1978)

Healey, Denis, *The Time of My Life* (Michael Joseph, 1989)

Heffer, Eric, *The Class Struggle in Parliament: A Socialist View of Industrial*

Relations (Victor Gollancz, 1973)

Hill, Douglas, ed., *Tribune 40: The First Forty Years of a Socialist Newspaper* (Quartet Books, 1977)

Hoggart, Simon, and Leigh, David, *Michael Foot: A Portrait* (Hodder & Stoughton, 1981)

Hollis, Christopher, *Oxford in the Twenties: Recollections of Five Friends* (Heinemann, 1976)

Hollis, Patricia, *Jennie Lee: A Life* (Oxford University Press, 1997)

Holmes, Martin, *The Labour Government 1974–79: Political Aims and Economic Reality* (Macmillan, 1985)

Howard, Anthony, *Crossman: The Pursuit of Power* (Jonathan Cape, 1990)

Howe, Stephen, *Anticolonialism in British Politics: The Left and the End of Empire, 1918–1964* (Oxford: Clarendon Press, 1993)

Hughes, Colin, and Wintour, Patrick, *Labour Rebuilt: The New Model Party* (Fourth Estate, 1990)

Hunter, Leslie, *The Road to Brighton Pier* (Arthur Barker, 1959)

Irving, C., Hall, Ron, and Wallington, Jeremy, *Scandal '63: A Study of the Profumo Affair* (Heinemann, 1963)

Jackson, Robert, *Rebels and Whips* (Macmillan, 1968)

James, David, *Bradford* (Ryburn, 1990)

Jameson, Storm, *Journey from the North: The Autobiography of Storm Jameson* (Collins/Harvill Press, 1969)

Jay, Douglas, *Change and Fortune: A Political Record* (Hutchinson, 1980)

Jeffreys, Kevin, *The Labour Party since 1945* (Macmillan, 1993)

Jenkins, Mark, *Bevanism: Labour's High Tide* (Spokesman, 1979)

Jenkins, Peter, *The Battle of Downing Street* (Charles Knight, 1970)

—— *Mrs Thatcher's Revolution: The Ending of the Socialist Era* (Jonathan Cape, 1987)

Jenkins, Robert, *Tony Benn: A Political Biography* (Writers and Readers Publishing Cooperative, 1980)

Jenkins, Roy, *Roy Jenkins' Gallery of 20th-Century Portraits and Oxford Papers* (David & Charles, 1988)

—— *A Life at the Centre* (Pan/Macmillan, 1992)

Jones, Aubrey, *Britain's Economy: The Roots of Stagnation* (Cambridge University Press, 1985)

Jones, Bill, *The Russia Complex: The British Labour Party and the Soviet Union* (Manchester University Press, 1977)

Jones, Jack, *Union Man: The Autobiography of Jack Jones* (Collins, 1986)

Jones, Mervyn, *Michael Foot* (Victor Gollancz, 1994)

Jones, Thomas, *A Diary with Letters, 1931–1950* (Oxford University Press, 1954)

Jones, Tudor, *Remaking the Labour Party: From Gaitskell to Blair* (Routledge, 1996)

Jupp, James, *The Radical Left in Britain, 1931–1941* (Frank Cass, 1982)

POLITICS AND POWER

Kavanagh, Dennis, ed., *The Politics of the Labour Party* (Allen & Unwin, 1982)

Kellner, Peter, and Hitchens, Christopher, *Callaghan: The Road to Number Ten* (Cassell, 1976)

King, Anthony, ed., *Why Is Britain Becoming Harder to Govern?* (BBC, 1976)

King, Cecil, *The Cecil King Diary, 1965-1970* (Jonathan Cape, 1972)

Kitzinger, Uwe, *The Second Try: Labour and the EEC* (Oxford: Pergamon, 1968)

—— *Diplomacy and Persuasion: How Britain Joined the Common Market* (Thames and Hudson, 1973)

Kogan, David, and Kogan, Maurice, *The Battle for the Labour Party* (Kogan Page, 1982)

Leigh, David, *The Wilson Plot: The Intelligence Services and the Discrediting of a Prime Minister* (Heinemann, 1988)

McCallum, Ronald, and Readman, Alison, *The British General Election of 1945* (Oxford University Press, 1947)

MacCarthy, Fiona, *William Morris: A Life for Our Time* (Faber and Faber, 1994)

McCarthy, Mary, *Generation in Revolt* (William Heinemann, 1953)

McKie, David, and Cook, Chris, eds, *The Decade of Disillusion: British Politics in the Sixties* (Macmillan, 1972)

—— *The Guardian/Quartet Election Guide* (Quartet Books, 1974)

McKie, David, Cook, Chris, and Phillips, Melanie, *The Guardian/Quartet Election Guide* (Quartet Books, 1978)

Madge, Charles, and Harrison, Tom, eds, *Britain By Mass Observation* (Penguin, 1939)

—— eds, *War Begins at Home, By Mass Observation* (Chatto & Windus, 1940)

Maillaud, Pierre, *The English Way* (Oxford University Press, 1945)

Mann, Jean, *Woman in Parliament* (Odhams Press, 1962)

Manning, Leah, *A Life for Education: An Autobiography* (Victor Gollancz, 1970)

Martin, David E., and Rubenstein, David, eds, *Ideology and the Labour Movement: Essays Presented to John Saville* (Croom Helm, 1979)

Martin, Kingsley, *Harold Laski, 1893-1950* (Victor Gollancz, 1953)

—— *Editor: A Second Volume of Autobiography, 1931-45* (Hutchinson, 1968)

Matthews, Herbert, and Matthews, Nancy, *The Britain We Saw* (Victor Gollancz, 1950)

Mellor, William, *Direct Action* (Leonard Parsons, 1920)

Middlemas, Keith, *Power, Competition and the State*; vol. 1: *Britain in Search of Balance 1950-61* (Macmillan, 1986); vol. 2: *Threats to the Postwar Settlement: Britain 1961-74* (Macmillan, 1990)

Mikardo, Ian, *Back-Bencher* (Weidenfeld & Nicolson, 1988)

Miliband, Ralph, *Parliamentary Socialism: A Study in the Politics of Labour* (George Allen & Unwin, 1961)

Minkin, Lewis, *The Labour Party Conference: A Study in the Politics of Intra-party Democracy* (Manchester University Press, 1980)

Mitchell, Austin, *Election '45: Reflections on the Revolution in Britain* (Fabian Society, 1995)

Mitchell, Austin, and Wienir, David, *Last Time: Labour's Lessons from the Sixties* (Bellew, 1997)

Moonman, Eric, *Reluctant Partnership: A Critical Study of the Relationship between Government and Industry* (Victor Gollancz, 1971)

Morgan, Kenneth, *Callaghan: A Life* (Oxford University Press, 1997)

Morris, William, *The Water of the Wondrous Isles* (Prior, 1979)

—— *Collected Works*, ed. Mary Morris (Routledge/Thoemmes Press, 1992)

—— *Selected Poems*, ed. Peter Faulkner (Carcanet, 1992)

Mowat, Charles, *Britain Between the Wars, 1918-1940* (Methuen, 1955)

Murphy, John Thomas, *New Horizons: An Autobiography* (John Lane, 1941)

Nairn, Tom, *The Left Against Europe?* (Penguin, 1973)

Nicolson, Harold, *Diaries and Letters 1930-1939*, ed. Nigel Nicolson (Collins, 1966)

Norton, Philip, ed., *Dissension in the House of Commons. Intra-party Dissent in the House of Commons Division Lobbies 1945-1974* (Macmillan, 1975)

—— *Dissension in the House of Commons 1974-1979* (Oxford: Clarendon Press, 1980)

Oakley, Robin, and Rose, Peter, *The Political Year: 1970* (Pitman Publishing, 1970)

—— *The Political Year: 1971* (Pitman Publishing, 1971)

Panitch, Leo, *Social Democracy and Industrial Militancy: The Labour Party, the Trade Unions and Incomes Policy 1945-1947* (Cambridge University Press, 1976)

Pelling, Henry, *America and the British Left: From Bright to Bevan* (Adam & Charles Black, 1956)

—— *A Short History of the Labour Party*, 3rd edn (Macmillan, 1968)

Philllips, Melanie, *The Divided House: Women at Westminster* (Sidgwick & Jackson, 1980)

Pimlott, Ben, *Labour and the Left in the 1930s* (Cambridge University Press, 1977)

—— *Hugh Dalton* (Jonathan Cape, 1985)

—— *Harold Wilson* (HarperCollins, 1993)

Plowden, William, *The Motor Car and Politics 1896-1970* (Bodley Head, 1971)

Ponting, Clive, *Breach of Promise: Labour in Power 1964-70* (Hamish Hamilton, 1989)

Postgate [Cole], Margaret, *Growing Up into Revolution* (Longmans, Green, 1949)

Priestly, John Boynton, *Out of the People* (Collins/Heinemann, 1941)

Rentoul, John, *Tony Blair* (Little, Brown, 1995)

Richards, Peter Godfrey, *Honourable Members: A Study of the British Backbencher* (Faber and Faber, 1959)

Robertson, Alex J., *The Bleak Midwinter, 1947* (Manchester University Press, 1987)

Robins, L. J., *The Reluctant Party: Labour and the EEC 1961-75* (G.W. and A. Hesketh, 1979)

Rose, Paul, *Backbencher's Dilemma* (Frederick Muller, 1981)

Ross, Alan, *The Forties: A Period Piece* (Weidenfeld & Nicolson, 1950)

Rush, Michael, *The Cabinet and Policy Formation* (Longman, 1984)

Schneer, Jonathan, *Labour's Conscience: The Labour Left 1945-51* (Unwin Hyman, 1988)

Sethi, Amarjit Singh, and Dimmock, Stuart J., eds, *Industrial Relations and Health Services* (Croom Helm, 1982)

Seyd, Patrick, *The Rise and Fall of the Labour Left* (Macmillan Education, 1987)

Service, Robert, *Lenin: A Political Life*; vol. 1: *The Strengths of Contradiction*; vol. 2: *Worlds in Collision*; vol. 3: *The Iron Ring* (Macmillan, 1985, 1991, 1995)

Shapley, Olive, *Broadcasting a Life: The Autobiography of Olive Shapley* (Scarlet Press, 1996)

Shaw, Eric, *Discipline and Discord in the Labour Party: The Politics of Managerial Control in the Labour Party 1951-87* (Manchester University Press, 1988)

Shore, Peter, *Leading the Left* (Weidenfeld & Nicolson, 1993)

Short, Edward, *Whip to Wilson* (Macdonald, 1989)

Silver, Eric, *Victor Feather,* TUC (Victor Gollancz, 1973)

Sked, Alan, and Cook, Chris, *Post-War Britain: A Political History* (Penguin, 1979)

Skidelsky, Robert, *Oswald Mosley* (Macmillan, 1975)

Sopel, Jon, *Tony Blair, The Moderniser* (Michael Joseph 1995)

Stewart, Margaret, *Frank Cousins: A Study* (Hutchinson, 1968)

—— *Protest or Power? A Study of the Labour Party* (Allen & Unwin, 1974)

Symons, Julian, *The Thirties: A Dream Revolved* (Cresset Press, 1960)

Taylor, Richard, *Against the Bomb: The British Peace Movement 1958-1965* (Oxford: Clarendon Press, 1988)

Taylor, Richard, and Pritchard, Colin, *The Protest Makers: The British Nuclear Disarmament Movement of 1958-1965 Twenty Years On* (Oxford: Pergamon, 1980)

Taylor, Robert, *The Fifth Estate: Britains Unions in the Seventies* (Routledge & Kegan Paul, 1978)

—— *The Trade Union Question in British Politics: Government and Unions since 1945* (Oxford: Basil Blackwell, 1993)

Theakston, Kevin, *The Labour Party and Whitehall* (Routledge, 1992)

Thomas, Elizabeth, ed., *Tribune 21: An Anthology of Literary Contributions to 'The Tribune' during Twenty-one Years* (MacGibbon & Kee, 1958)

Thomas, Hugh, *The Spanish Civil War* (Eyre & Spottiswoode, 1961)

The Times Guide to the House of Commons (election years)

Vallance, Elizabeth, *Women in the House. A Study of Women Members of Parliament* (Athlone, 1979)

Vallance, Elizabeth, and Davies, Elizabeth, *Women of Europe: Women MEPs and Equality Policy* (Cambridge University Press, 1986)

Van Reil, Richard, ed., *Pontefract in Old Photographs* (A. Sutton, 1993)

Walkland, S.A., and Ryle, Michael, eds, *The Commons in the Seventies* (Martin Robertson, 1977)

Walter, David, *The Oxford Union: Playground of Power* (Macdonald, 1984)

Watkins, Alan, *Brief Lives* (Hamish Hamilton, 1982)

Watkins, Ernest, *The Cautious Revolution: On the Work of the Labour Government 1945-51* (Secker & Warburg, 1951)

Webb, Beatrice, *Diaries 1924-1932*, ed. Margaret Cole (Longmans, Green, 1956)

—— *The Diary of Beatrice Webb*; vol. 4: *1924-1943*, ed. Norman and Jeanne MacKenzie (Virago/London School of Economics and Political Science, 1985)

Webb, Sydney and Beatrice, *Soviet Communism: A New Civilisation* (Victor Gollancz, 1937)

Whitehead, Phillip, *The Writing on the Wall: Britain in the Seventies* (Michael Joseph, 1985)

Whiteley, Paul, *The Labour Party in Crises* (Methuen, 1983)

Widgery, David, *The Left in Britain 1956-1968* (Penguin, 1976)

—— *Health in Danger: The Crisis of the National Health Service* (Macmillan, 1979)

Wigg, Lord, *George Wigg* (Michael Joseph, 1972)

Wilkinson, Ellen, *The Town that was Murdered. The Life-story of Jarrow* (Victor Gollancz, 1939)

Williams, Marcia, *Inside Number 10* (Weidenfeld & Nicolson, 1972)

Williams, Philip M., *Hugh Gaitskell* (Oxford University Press, 1982)

Wilson, Harold, *The Labour Government 1964-1970: A Personal Record* (Weidenfeld & Nicolson, 1971)

—— *Final Term: The Labour Government 1974-1976* (Weidenfeld & Nicolson/Michael Joseph, 1979)

—— *Memoirs: The Making of a Prime Minister, 1916-1964* (Weidenfeld & Nicolson/Michael Joseph 1986)

Wood, Daniel, and Wood, Alan, *The Times Guide to the European Parliament*

(Times Books, 1979)

Xydis, Stephen, *Cyprus: Conflict and Conciliation 1954-1958* (Columbus, 1967)

Young, Hugo, *The Iron Lady: A Biography of Margaret Thatcher* (New York: Noonday Press, 1990)

Ziegler, Philip, *Wilson: The Authorised Life of Lord Wilson of Rievaulx* (Weidenfeld & Nicolson, 1993)

——*London at War 1939-45* (Sinclair-Stevenson, 1995)

Index